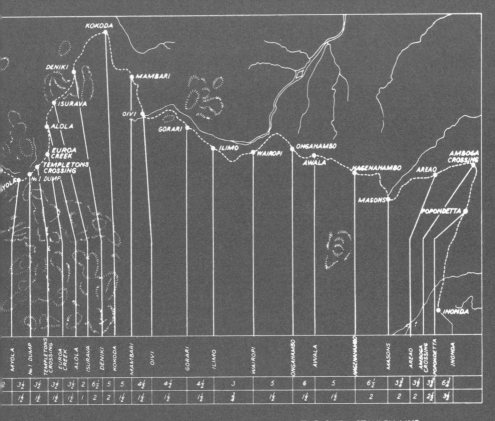

THE OWEN STANLEY LINE

UNITING
A NATION

UNITING A NATION

THE POSTAL AND TELECOMMUNICATION SERVICES OF PAPUA NEW GUINEA

JAMES SINCLAIR

MELBOURNE
OXFORD UNIVERSITY PRESS

OXFORD UNIVERSITY PRESS
Oxford London Glasgow New York Toronto
Delhi Bombay Calcutta Madras Karachi
Kuala Lumpur Singapore Hong Kong Tokyo
Nairobi Dar es Salaam Cape Town
Melbourne Auckland
and associates in
Beirut Berlin Ibadan Mexico City Nicosia
OXFORD is a trademark of Oxford University Press

© James Sinclair 1984
First published in 1984

National Library of Australia
Cataloguing-in-Publication data:

Sinclair, James, 1928–.
Uniting a nation

Bibliography
ISBN 0 19 554437 4
ISBN 0 19 554436 6 (pbk)

1. Postal service — Papua New Guinea — History.
2. Telecommunication — Papua New Guinea — History. I. Title.

383'1.49953

Designed by Guy Mirabella
Typeset by Abb-type, Melbourne
Printed by Kings Time, Hong Kong
Published by Oxford University Press, 7 Bowen Crescent, Melbourne

CONTENTS

PREFACE

In April 1980, I was invited by the then Secretary, Department of Public Utilities, Mr Israel Edoni, to write a history of the postal and telecommunication services of Papua New Guinea, with emphasis on the part that these services have played in the development of the nation. Mr Edoni asked me to trace the story from the beginning of the colonial era in the late nineteenth century to 1 July 1980, the twenty-fifth anniversary of the formation of the Department of Posts and Telegraphs.

I was given a completely free hand and have not been subjected to any constraints by the Department. This is in no sense a technical work, or a philatelic study, neither of which I am qualified to write. It is a broad account which will, it is hoped, appeal to those who have an interest in the history of Papua New Guinea, that fascinating country that has for more than a hundred years been a magnet to the youth of Australia.

There is little about individual Papua New Guineans in the first part of this book; during the major part of the colonial era few whites were much concerned about the indigenous inhabitants of the country they lived in, and unfortunately little material relevant to the work of Papua New Guineans during the period was recorded.

I have not considered myself bound by the narrow definitions of the words 'post' and 'telegraph' in the writing of this book. (In any case, the word 'telecommunications' has largely replaced 'telegraph' in popular usage.) I have ranged quite widely, taking as my theme the motto of the Postal and Telecommunication Services: 'Development Through Communication'. I have delved into the early shipping history of PNG, for until the widespread use of aircraft that began in the 1930s and flowered after the Second World War, ships carried most of the nation's mails. Originally by maritime custom and later ordained by law, ships' masters in PNG — as in most other maritime countries in the world — were required to obtain a mail clearance before quitting port. (They still are.)

Early aviation history is similarly relevant to this study. PNG is a country of great mountains and mighty rivers, and it is only in recent times that road communications have become important: even today there is no highway across the country. Some account is given of the development of roads. I have also included some material — brief summaries of the work of the different administrators, for example — that while not postal or telecommunication history seems necessary for a balanced account. The Second World War was a landmark event in PNG history, and some attempt to outline its course and effects appears to me essential. I have given space to such matters as the use of radio by exploratory expeditions, and to aspects of the work of the *kiaps* (patrol officers), for as this book will show, they act as agents in the field for posts and telegraphs to the present day.

I have not attempted the almost impossible task of converting the value of the currencies used at different periods in PNG history to kina and toea, the present national currency. Because of inflation, direct conversions would be meaningless. Pounds (£), shillings and pence were in use in PNG until 14 February 1966, when

Australian decimal currency was adopted. The standard decimal unit, the dollar ($) was then valued at half the old pound, or ten shillings. On 19 April 1975, kina and toea were introduced in PNG, the value of one kina then being set at one Australian dollar. Since then, the kina has been revalued upward against foreign currencies, including the dollar. Other non-metric measurements have been used if they were current at that period.

I have received a great deal of assistance in the writing of this book. I am particularly indebted to Wally McPherson, Ted Brown, Bill Carter and Bill Peckover, each of whom read the manuscript and made many valuable comments and corrections as well as making available papers and photographs. It should be said that I am alone responsible for what appears in the following pages.

Other assistance of various kinds was given by many individuals. I am particularly grateful to the people who are listed below, in random order: Israel Edoni, Dale Kamara, Patrick Tomausi, Smael Manikot, Bob Magin, Carien McGuin, Tom Pearson, Phil Casanovas, Ron Johnston, Alan Kilby, Gordon Austin, Les Canute, Geoff Hutton, Hookey Morley, Doug Rowell, Alex Nonwo, Stephen Harrison (New Guinea Collection Librarian, University of Papua New Guinea Library), Bob Miller, Mac Rich, Ivan Champion, Claude Champion, Ted Bishton, Ian Fisher, Bert Weston, George Schultz, J.W. Walker, Ian Skinner, George Andersen, Philip Geeves, G. Swain (Assistant Editor, *Electronics Australia*), D.E. Macdonald (Editor, *AWA Technical Review*), E.L. Douglas (Chief Archivist, National Archives and Public Records Service of Papua New Guinea), Keith Armistead, I.W. Jordan, Geoff Perkins, Maurie Dobbin (Laurie Systems Engineers Pty. Ltd.), John Vivers, Keith Mattingley and John Solomon.

This book was commenced in April, 1980, and completed in September, ·1981.

James Sinclair

INTRODUCTION

Man has lived in New Guinea for perhaps 40 000 years. Certainly, when the legions of Rome began their conquest of the ancient world, tribes of nomadic hunters and gatherers had long been established on New Guinea's shores. But theirs was a closed world. Civilizations rose from the dust, flourished and declined; the men of New Guinea knew nothing of them. Nations grew in Asia and Europe bound by ties of language, religion and custom, united in their dislike and distrust of their neighbours, their growth spurred by technological advances of immense importance. Man learned to work in metal, to make tools, wheeled vehicles, roads, and vessels stout enough to blunder, wind-blown, across unknown oceans finding new paths of conquest. Then came the Industrial Revolution; and the harnessing of the power of steam, the greatest leap forward of all until electricity was mastered. The printing press had freed the human mind; the need to exchange written communications was one of the most powerful of the urges that drove man along his dim-lit road into an uncertain future. In New Guinea the people hunted, gathered and began to grow crops, unknown and unknowing, isolated by a quirk of history from the influences that shaped the world outside.

Isolation was a factor common also to the human societies within New Guinea. An implacable terrain, a geography of formidable dimensions, spawned a multitude of mutually-hostile tribal groups, small in scale, with distinct languages and cultural forms, in a population that was minute by world standards. There was some communication between these groups; their isolation was not absolute. They never evolved a written language, but oratory was of absorbing interest to them. They made wide use of the human voice, sending loud yodelling cries across the valleys and ranges; they exchanged message sticks and signals with smoke and fire; in other communities, the blare of the conch shell or the rattle of the garamut drum served. Most significant of all the techniques of communication evolved by the people of New Guinea was the extraordinarily complex web of trade routes and relationships that linked, however tenuously, groups far apart in location and understanding. These were methods well suited to societies suspended in time, but by the mid-nineteenth century the world outside was about to engulf New Guinea. Traditional methods of communication, while never entirely to vanish, would soon be inadequate. The most effective communication technique of that outside world was then the postal system, which had taken centuries to evolve.

The Egyptians had a postal system two thousand years before the birth of Christ. The ancient Chinese and Persians employed relays of mounted messengers to maintain contact with the outposts of their empires, a method later developed by the Romans into the most highly organized system of communication of the ancient world, the *cursus publicus*, not to be equalled for speed and efficiency in Europe until the nineteenth century. Relay systems, but using foot messengers, were in use in the pre-Columbian civilizations in America.

The growth of international commerce in the Middle Ages saw the evolution of postal systems in Europe that were the true ancestors of the state-run postal monopolies of today. Of particular consequence was the British system. As a result of the work of the great reformer Rowland Hill, the British system became the model for the world. The introduction of adhesive stamps in 1840 with the 'penny post' brought the post to most people for the first time.

The incredible development of railways in Europe, the United States and India in this period and the later proliferation of world steamship routes all had a profound effect upon international mail services and led to the creation of the Universal Postal Union in 1874. This would eventually claim as members almost all the world's nations. The basic treaty of the Union, the Universal Postal Convention, regulated the exchange of international mails and has been carefully tended and modified as circumstances warranted, up to the present day.

As was usual in British colonies, the basic elements of the British postal system were adopted as the pattern for Australia. A post office was established in Sydney in 1809, and others were opened as New South Wales was settled. Mail routes were laid down, postage rates fixed, and in 1828 a Postmaster General appointed. As the other Australian colonies grew, so did their postal systems. Uniform rates of postage were agreed on by the colonies in 1849, and when NSW made the use of adhesive postage stamps compulsory in 1852, the others soon followed. A regular, heavily-subsidized mail steamship service with England began in 1856, and in 1891 the Australian colonies joined the Universal Postal Union.

Efficient though the international postal system undoubtedly was at the beginning of the nineteenth century, geographically isolated countries like Australia still experienced long delays in communication with other parts of the world. As recently as 1882, the average sailing time of the Royal Mail steamers between Brisbane (capital of Queensland, the Australian colony which had most to do with New Guinea during its early years) and London, via Brindisi, was fifty days thirteen hours. In a world still experiencing the giant advances in technology of the Industrial Revolution, such delays were unacceptable. The position was soon to change.

In 1791, the Frenchman, Claude Chappe, patented a two-arm semaphore system of signalling which he called a 'telegraph', a term which was to be retained and applied to the amazing developments in long-distance communication based on electricity that were to follow. Many attempts had been made to transmit messages by electrical means, but man had not yet learned to control this marvellous form of energy. The great pioneers were at work: Volta, Oersted, Ampère, Gauss, Cooke, Henry, Davy, Faraday, Thomson, Maxwell, Ohm and many others, men who gave their very names to modern electrical practice. Out of the cumulative work of the pioneers there emerged the electric telegraph. In England, Cooke and Wheatstone introduced electric telegraphy in 1837 as an adjunct to visual signals on railways — indeed, the development of the electric telegraph world-wide was to be closely linked with the progress of the railway — and in the same year the American Samuel Morse, patented his revolutionary system of telegraphy, employing the electromagnet and what soon became famous as the Morse Code. His work quickly attracted government support and Morse built his first telegraph line between Baltimore and Washington, a distance of thirty-seven miles. This opened for public use in May 1844. By 1851, more than fifty companies were operating telegraph lines in the United States alone. In 1865, the International Telegraph (Telecommunication) Union was formed, and in the following year the first successful submarine cable was laid across the Atlantic and a new area of international communication began. [In 1851 the first successful submarine cable was laid in the open sea from Dover to Calais]. There were by this time about half a million miles of land telegraph lines in America, England, Europe, Asia, India and Africa, connected by more than 25 000 miles of submarine cables, and the world network continued to expand with extraordinary rapidity.

Until the invention of the first successful telephone by Bell in 1876, the telegraph was the principal conveyor of rapid news throughout the world. It is difficult to imagine today that, until 1876, electricity as a part of daily life was for practical purposes unknown except for the telegraph. Electric light, electric motors and dynamos, trams and trolley cars, electric domestic appliances, storage batteries, wireless and wireless telephone and of course, television, were unknown.

The electric telegraph was a boon of immeasurable value to remote countries like Australia, and it was quickly embraced. The epic of Australian communications history was the construction of the first telegraphic system to span the continent from coast to coast — the great Overland Telegraph Line, stretching for over 1800 miles from Port Augusta in South Australia to Port Darwin in the Northern Territory, and constructed at a cost of six lives, half a million pounds and enormous human effort. Completed in 1872, the Overland Telegraph connected with a submarine cable laid the year before between Port Darwin and Banjuwangi in Java, and thence with the chain of networks fast linking the nations of the world.

Internal telegraph services within Australia had meanwhile been steadily growing. Only ten years after Morse began the era of commercial telegraph services in 1844, a telegraph line was in existence between Melbourne and the port of Williamstown, and by 1861, the cities of Melbourne, Sydney, Adelaide, Launceston and Brisbane were linked.

In August 1872, a fabulous gold discovery was made on one of the great rivers of North Queensland, the Palmer, and this focused the attention of Australia — and other parts of the world — on the almost unexplored Cape York Peninsula, the nothern thrust of the Australian continent, which ends in a scattering of islands close to New Guinea's shores. (At the time, West Irian was also part of what was called New Guinea.) Men poured in their thousands into the sodden green wilderness of the Palmer, and died in untold numbers, victims of disease, ignorance and the spears of the Palmer Aboriginals. A township, crude and basic and called Palmerville, grew on the field. This was in the interior and clearly a coastal supply port was essential. So Cooktown was born, a town whose population exploded from zero to 30 000 within three years, a rough, tough town with a main street two miles long containing ninety-four hotels. So important were the Palmer and Cooktown to the Queensland economy that the telegraph line was extended there.

In 1882, the Queensland government decided to take the line on to Thursday Island, via Cape York. Interest in the far north of the colony was increasing. As far back as 1863, a small settlement had been established for the Queensland Government at Somerset, on Cape York Peninsula, but in 1877 the administrative headquarters of the Torres Strait region was transferred to Thursday Island, soon to achieve the peak of its development as a pearling and trading centre. It was a colourful, cosmopolitan settlement, home port to a fleet of small craft: schooners, ketches, cutters, luggers. The blackbirders supplying labour from the Islands to the fast-growing sugar plantations of the north used Thursday Island as a base of operations.

The extension of the telegraph line to the north proved to be a difficult business. All work had to stop during the long wet season, and hostile Aboriginals took their toll, but by the end of 1886, a telegraph station had been opened at Coen and a submarine cable laid from Paterson on the mainland to Thursday Island. The telegraph was linked to Paterson in 1887, although it was not finally extended to Cape York itself until 1893.

In the mid-1870s the question of New Guinea began to arouse a good deal of popular interest in the Australian colonies. The bare existence of New Guinea had been known to Europeans since the sixteenth century (and to Asians long before that), and the Dutch laid claim to the island west of 141 degrees as early as 1828. In 1846 Lieutenant Yule, RN, of HMS *Bramble* took possession in the name of the Queen of that territory not claimed by the Dutch, but his action was not officially recognized. Another British naval officer, Captain John Moresby, discovered the superb harbour of Port Moresby in 1873 in HMS *Basilisk* and he, too, raised the Union Jack and claimed the whole of Eastern New Guinea. But yet again, Britain, preoccupied in other parts of the Pacific, refused to act. In 1875, the New South Wales and Queensland governments asked Britain to annex New Guinea, to no avail.

During 1871, the London Missionary Society established a base station at Somerset and in 1874 sent Revd W.G. Lawes to the recently-discovered harbour of Port Moresby to open a station there — the forward bastion of Christianity in heathen New Guinea. Lawes and his family were the only permanent white settlers in southern New Guinea, but they were soon joined by a handful of others. In 1878, one of these settlers, a Scottish trader and naturalist called Andrew Goldie discovered gold in the Laloki River, behind Port Moresby. In the absence of any local authority, Goldie reported the find to the Government Agency at Thursday Island. There was a rush of miners to the Laloki, many of them Queenslanders, and to protect their interests one W.B. Ingham was set to Port Moresby as Queensland Government Agent. Ingham's official authority in Port Moresby was exceedingly dubious, but, not deterred, he proceeded to register land titles, hold court and report on New Guinea affairs to the Colonial Secretary in Brisbane.

By this time, New Guinea was a lively issue in Australia, and particularly in Queensland. Germany was steadily and unmistakeably expanding her trading activies into the Bismarck Archipelago, and by 1883 had established a string of stations there. To the increasingly nervous Australian colonies, German intentions were obvious: Germany meant to seize New Guinea! They implored Britain to act immediately and forestall the Germans; the Premier of Queensland, Sir Thomas McIlwraith, promised that his government would bear the costs. But Britain was not convinced of German intentions and McIlwraith, by now thoroughly alarmed, took matters into his own hands. He ordered the Government Agent at Thursday Island, H.M. Chester, to proceed to Port Moresby and take formal possession of south-eastern New Guinea. The British Government angrily refused to sanction this impudence, but the other Australian colonies were united in their support of Queensland and, grumbling, Britain was forced to act. Provided the colonies would share the cost of administration, a Protectorate would be established.

When informed of the British intention, Germany protested. She had vital interests in northern New Guinea, and to preserve harmony, Britain agreed to confine her declaration to the south coast and contiguous islands. A naval squadron duly proceeded to Port Moresby, where on 6 November 1884, the Protectorate was proclaimed by Commodore J.E. Erskine of HMS *Nelson*. Unknown to the British, and to the intense fury of the Australian colonies, Germany was even then swiftly and silently annexing the northern coast of the mainland, New Britain and New Ireland. It was a close-run thing.

The partition of New Guinea was thus complete. Having been prodded into action, the British government now acted briskly, and in the same month appointed as Her Majesty's Special Commissioner for New Guinea — a retired general with considerable experience of Australia: Sir Peter Scratchley.

1
GUDPELA TAIM BIPO — FROM THE BEGINNING OF SETTLEMENT TO THE SECOND WORLD WAR

THE PROTECTORATE

Sir Peter Scratchley arrived at Port Moresby, in state, on 28 August 1885, on the chartered steamer *Governor Blackall,* a fine ship of 487 tons gross register, specially fitted out at considerable expense for New Guinea service, cooled by an elaborate engine-driven exhaust fan and complete with a fresh water condensation plant and the latest machine for the manufacture of ice. No administrator in New Guinea would ever again claim the services of so splendid a vessel, but Sir Peter was not fated to enjoy her for long. Three months later he died on board, a victim of the malaria fever which would take the lives of many more, less exalted Europeans in the years to come.

Brief though his New Guinea service was, Scratchley is important to this story. His was a daunting task. No form of government had been decided on for the new Protectorate. Scratchley had the powers of a Deputy Commissioner under the Western Pacific Orders-in-Council, but in fact his hands were largely tied. His status and authority were not clearly defined. He could not make laws or levy taxes and he had no means of enforcing his decisions. British New Guinea was almost entirely unknown and unexplored, apart from brief stretches of the coastline. There was but a scant handful of settlers, principally missionaries and their families, and traders; there were no government establishments. The resources available to him for the administration of the Protectorate were the paltry £15 000 guaranteed by the Australian colonies, and the provision and maintenance of a steamer by the British government. His staff limitations were even more severe.

Scratchley did his best. Reaching Australia in January 1885, he was obliged to delay his departure for New Guinea while he negotiated with the Australian Premiers for the financial contributions and arranged the charter for the *Governor Blackall.* He quickly decided to make Port Moresby the centre of administration in British New Guinea, although Hall Sound, Suau and Samarai (then known by the name Dinner Island) were considered. Port Moresby was the only place where there was permanent settlement, the harbour was without peer and — of particular significance — it was within easy sailing distance of Cooktown, where there was a telegraph station and post office, and Thursday Island, soon to be linked by submarine cable to the mainland.

In Brisbane prior to sailing for New Guinea, Scratchley made the best arrangements he could in the matter of communications. There were no regular mail services to British New Guinea. The pioneer Islands shipping and trading firm, Burns, Philp & Co., was already sending occasional vessels from Cooktown to several trading stations and ports in British New Guinea, including Port Moresby and Samarai, and their little schooner *Elsea* had for some time been making voyages between Thursday Island and Moresby. A small steamer, the *Herbert*, made at least two advertised voyages to Port Moresby in 1885. The London Missionary Society steamer *Ellangowan*, of 36 tons, made frequent visits to Thursday Island and Cooktown, and traders and blackbirders, some with most dubious reputations, roamed New Guinea waters in small sailing craft with bland-sounding names such as *Ada, Daisy, Lizzie, Emily* and *Sybil*. Warships of the Royal Navy frequented New Guinea waters, often on the business of the High Commissioner for the Western Pacific at Fiji. The British ships *Dart, Harrier, Diamond, Raven* and *Swinger* were often seen in Port Moresby and particularly in Samarai, a favoured anchorage; although fast vanishing, this was still the era of gunboat justice in the Pacific. All of these ships from time to time carried mails, but on a completely random basis. It would prove to be difficult to administer the Protectorate with such unreliable communications.

On his way north in the *Governor Blackall*, Scratchley stopped at Brisbane and came to an arrangement with the Queensland Department of Post and Telegraphs. The department agreed to regard British New Guinea in the same light as an isolated station in Queensland. All mails, official and private, to and from British New Guinea would carry Queensland stamps, in accordance with the rates shown in the Queensland Postal Guide. The government of British New Guinea would be at liberty to impose an extra charge for private mails; if no such charge were levied, the department would pay 'the usual rate' of one penny for each letter, to masters of vessels on receipt of mails from Cooktown, this arrangement to continue so long as Queensland stamps were used (and they remained in use until 1901). The Postmaster at Cooktown would sell Queensland stamps to British New Guinea as required, and would dispatch mails 'by every vessel'. For the time being, Scratchley's official address would be 'care of Postmaster, Cooktown', and the premier of Queensland agreed to receive any telegrams that might arrive for the Special Commissioner from Lord Derby, the Colonial Secretary, in London.

Despite the informal nature of mail transmission between Queensland and British New Guinea at this time, a considerable volume of correspondence — surprising in view of the tiny European population in the Protectorate — was carried on. Official records show that from September to December 1885, 674 letters were dispatched to British New Guinea from the Cooktown Post Office, and 463 received. Significantly, 1792 newspapers were sent during this period; the pioneers were hungry for news of the outside world.

While in Brisbane, Scratchley had appointed Anthony Musgrave, nephew of the Governor of Queensland, as an Assistant Deputy Commissioner, and had sent him ahead to Port Moresby. The British Government had already appointed H.H. Romilly as Deputy Commissioner. Immediately after his arrival in Port Moresby, Scratchley placed Musgrave in charge of local administration — for he intended to spend at least twelve months cruising the coastline of the Protectorate — and appointed Frank Lawes, son of the London Missionary Society missionary, W.G. Lawes, to the office of Post Master, Harbour Master, Collector of Customs and Chief Clerk, a goodly load of responsibility. For many years thereafter, officers serving in the administration would be forced to shoulder multiple duties; funds were never sufficient for the employment of many specialists.

It is clear that the formal postal service began prior to Lawes' official appointment. The Queensland Department of Posts and Telegraphs had supplied a canceller for use at Port Moresby consisting of the Letters 'N.G.' in an oval of eight bars, two each at top and bottom, and four at the sides, and there is in existence a franking with a circular date stamp on the envelope clear of the Queensland stamps, reading 'Port Moresby New Guinea August 26 1885'. On this date Scratchley was on board the *Governor Blackall* at Cooktown, planning to sail for Port Moresby the following morning. The most likely explanation is that the canceller with a stock of Queensland stamps was sent to Port Moresby ahead of Scratchley, immediately following the completion of postal arrangements.

In the brief span of life left to him, Scratchley established Port Moresby as the seat of government and drew up a plan for an administration and land policy. He made several inspections, visited Samarai and investigated a number of reported killings of white seamen in clashes with tribesmen. He appointed two brothers, George and Robert Hunter, as Inspectors of Timber Licences and *Bêche-de-mer* Fisheries. He fell ill late in November 1885, and died at sea on the *Governor Blackall* between Cooktown and Townsville on 2 December.

Deputy Commissioner Romilly assumed temporary control of the administration of British New Guinea, but in February 1886, John Douglas, Queensland Government Resident at Thursday Island, was appointed Special Commissioner. He was an able and energetic man, an ex-Premier of Queensland but he was constrained by the same factors that had shackled Scratchley. Much of his time was spent away from the Protectorate, in Brisbane, Sydney and Melbourne, trying to place the precarious finances of British New Guinea on a sound footing. Although the Australian colonies had agreed to jointly contribute £15 000 towards the cost of administering British New Guinea, by 1887 the three eastern ones were carrying the full load. Plainly, Douglas was no more able than was Scratchley to expand the administration of British New Guinea. Under his direction surveyor W.R. Cuthbertson prepared a design for a township at Port Moresby, which now became officially termed Granville, after the then Foreign Secretary, Lord Granville. (Official currency of the name was short-lived; by the end of 1888 the original name was again in general use.) Douglas ordered the construction of government buildings at West Granville, among them a customs house and post office, which was at first used also as a church, a public reading room and a store. Such were the measures forced upon an administration with practically no money. This building was completed in 1887.

Soon after his appointment, Douglas concluded an agreement with Burns, Philp & Co. which gave British New Guinea its first scheduled mail steamer service. The agreement was to run for three years from 1 July 1886, and called for a monthly voyage between Thursday Island and Port Moresby, and 'if required by the development of trade' along the south-east coast. For the sum of £50 a month, the company agreed to 'carry the public mails and dispatches for the Honorable John Douglas' at no further charge. The company placed the 80-ton steamer *Victory* on the run, and for eighteen months kept to the terms of the contract.

On her initial voyage the little steamer sailed to Port Moresby, via Yorke, Darnley, Murray and Yule Islands. The Roman Catholic missionaries of the Sacred Heart had begun work on Yule Island in 1885 and now, under the direction of the ascetic Vicar Apostolic, Louis André Navarre, were engaged in establishing their base preparatory to extending their faith to the wild tribes of the unexplored interior of the mainland. The Sacred Heart missionaries maintained tenuous contact with their headquarters at Thursday Island by lugger. From Port Moresby, the *Victory* sailed to Hula — where considerable business was done in *bêche-de-mer* — and through Hood Bay, Cloudy Bay and the China Straits to Samarai.

Samarai was fast becoming the headquarters of a colourful lot of seafarers. W.D. Pitcairn, who visited the island in 1887, described it in a book, *Two Years among the Savages of New Guinea* published in 1891 as 'a small but picturesque island . . . situated in China Straits, which is the loveliest and most romantic-looking harbour I have ever seen'.

The London Missionary Society had placed a Rarotongan teacher there years before, and when Douglas sent H.O. Forbes in June 1886 as Acting Deputy Commissioner, the Mission was happy to rent its dilapidated quarters to him, and to retire to the nearby island of Kwato, which was still free of the corrupting influence of seamen. Despite its remoteness, life at Samarai was not devoid of pleasure. Pitcairn tells of a notable dinner served on Christmas Day 1887:

BILL OF FARE

Soup	—	Real Turtle
Fish	—	Kingfish
Joints	—	Roast Lamb and Peas (Kid)
		Roast Pork
		Cold Corned Beef
Entrées	—	Omelette, Fruit Pie
Vegetables	—	Yams, Taro, Spinach
		Cheese
Dessert	—	Bananas, Pineapples, Mangots, Pawpaws, Coconuts, Oranges, etc.
Wine and Spirits	—	Lager Beer, Whisky, Sherry, Port

We had quite a respectable gathering, consisting of captains, mates, traders, fishermen and divers — 15 in all . . . Captain Runcie of the SS *Gympie*, an old *habitué* of New Guinea, took the chair . . .

1 W.D. Pitcairn, *Two Years Among the Savages of New Guinea*, Ward and Downey, London.

From Samarai, the *Victory* steamed to Teste Island, where two men, Kissack and Thompson were carrying on a large business in copra trading. They had another prosperous copra station in Milne Bay which was run by a Maltese.

It is apparent that white settlement along the coast of British New Guinea was gradually increasing, heightening the need for reliable postal communications. But Burns Philp found it impossible to make the mail service pay, and in January 1888 informed Douglas that they would be terminating the contract in July. Douglas thereupon called for fresh tenders; none was received, and he arranged with Burns Philp — the owners of the topsail schooner, *Lucy and Adelaide* — to make six monthly voyages from Cooktown to Samarai and Port Moresby and back to Cooktown, at a subsidy of £80 per trip. The schooner made the voyage in approximately thirteen days, but this was merely a short-term measure.

The first formal mail transport arrangements between the Protectorate and German New Guinea were made at this time. Administration of the German colony was then in the hands of the Neu Guinea Kompagnie, whose headquarters were at Finschhafen. There was no direct link between Europe and German New Guinea, but the P. and O. ships of the mail service between London and Brisbane called at Cooktown, the closest port to German New Guinea with postal and telegraph facilities. The Neu Guinea Kompagnie therefore acquired three small steamers and began a regular monthly service between Finschhafen and Cooktown, connecting with the P. and O. vessels. Douglas now asked the Kompagnie to have their steamers call in at Samarai, in return for a subsidy payment. The agreement was in force only from 1 March to 31 August 1888, and the subsidy payment totalled £150.

Given the severe limitations of his authority, Douglas' achievements were considerable. For administrative purposes, he divided British New Guinea into three Divisions — the Western, from the Dutch New Guinea boundary to Aird River; the Central, from the Aird to Toulon Island; and the Eastern, from Toulon to Rossel Island. There was no government station in the Western Division, and Douglas had to rely on whatever supervision Hugh Milman, Resident at Thursday Island, could provide during infrequent visits to this huge territory. He had the services of only a handful of officers: Musgrave, Romilly, Lawes — who took over from Forbes at Samarai in April, 1887; the Hunter brothers (he appointed George as Government Agent, Rigo, which became the third permanent government establishment); and E.G. Edelfeldt, the Burns Philp agent at Motu Motu, who was paid a small salary to double as Government Agent there. Douglas continually urged the necessity for an armed police force, for without police tribal fighting and conflict with white settlers could not be checked. He urged, too, the provision of a suitable government vessel, essential for the efficient administration of the Protectorate. He was very conscious of the need for water transport in a territory with as long a coastline as British New Guinea. On the death of Sir Peter Scratchley, Douglas had quickly terminated the expensive charter of the *Governor Blackall* and in May 1887, he purchased a 73-foot schooner, *Hygeia*, for £1 100, for the service of the Protectorate. A cutter, *Maino*, was also acquired for £300 and another, *Juanita*, for £150.

Small sailing vessels of this unpretentious kind have an honoured place in the history of New Guinea. Operated by the government, by the missions, by companies, plantations, traders and individuals they were frequently the only link with the outside for lonely people in remote places. They were maids-of-all-work. They took government officers on patrols and inspections, fetched plantation supplies, carried produce and transported the sick. They often hit reefs, and, over the years, many were lost. But life would have been difficult, indeed impossible, without them. And wherever they went, they carried mails.

For all his ability, Douglas could not possibly administer British New Guinea with efficiency under the terms of the Protectorate. It was simply a device whereby Britain was able to extend the existing machinery of the Western Pacific High Commission, with the minimum of fuss, to a territory which she had been reluctantly pushed into accepting. Douglas had even been told by the Colonial Office that his appointment as Special Commissioner was only a temporary measure.

It was not until 1886 that the question of the future status and administration of British New Guinea was seriously raised, by the Queensland Premier, Sir Samuel Griffith. After much discussion between Britain and the colonies, it was agreed that British New Guinea would be annexed, and for the first ten years, administered jointly by Britain, Queensland, New South Wales and Victoria. The three Colonies agreed to contribute £15 000 per annum over this period towards the cost of government; Britain would provide a steamer to the value of £18 500 and an annual grant of £3 600 to maintain her. As a matter of practicability, Queensland would act for the other two colonies; all official correspondence from British New Guinea would be routed through the Governor of Queensland, who would exercise a general supervision over the affairs of the new colony. It was a curious arrangement, but at least it served to break the Protectorate deadlock.

John Douglas thankfully laid down the burden of his office as Special Commissioner and returned to Thursday Island, where he was to die in 1904. The post of Administrator of British New Guinea was then offered to a seasoned colonial administrator, Dr William MacGregor.

On 4 September 1888, MacGregor arrived in Port Moresby, and immediately proclaimed British sovereignty. The Protectorate was no more; British New Guinea was now a Possession.

CHAPTER TWO

BRITISH NEW GUINEA

Sir William MacGregor (he was knighted in 1889) was a man of powerful character. Stubborn and opinionated, solitary in his habits and unusually able in diverse fields, he inspired the deep loyalty of his subordinates. One of his officers, C.A.W. Monckton — himself a dominating man — said of him 'once, and only once in my life, have I felt that a man was my master in every way, a person to be blindly obeyed and one who must be right and infallible, and that was when I met Sir William MacGregor'.

For ten years MacGregor virtually ruled British New Guinea. In that brief decade he stamped his pattern so firmly on the administration of the Possession that substantial elements of it endured for the next forty years.

For ten years, he was never free of financial worries. The funds available to him were never sufficient for all that he wanted to do. He had to weigh the spending of every pound, the employment of every officer, the purchase of every item. Indeed, he watched the spending of every penny. When Anthony Musgrave, who now occupied the important position of Government Secretary, was in Sydney on official business in September 1890, he kept MacGregor informed of his activities through the Thursday Island telegraph, until the day he received the terse message, 'Your wires too costly. Do not send any more'.

He was hampered by the need to conduct his official dealings with the Colonial Office in London through the Queensland government, an arrangement unique in British colonial annals, although in practice this gave him a freedom of action that was also unusual. Broadly speaking, the New South Wales and Victorian governments were quite happy to leave the supervision of British New Guinea affairs to Queensland, while the Queensland government was usually too preoccupied with its own affairs to worry much about what Sir William was doing. So leisurely were the mails that it took up to ten months before MacGregor received replies to his letters and reports from London; six months was considered normal. The result was that he made most of his decisions and took most of his actions without waiting for the receipt of formal approval or instruction. As was usual in British colonial practice, the Letters Patent of 8 June 1888, which established the Possession of British New Guinea, directed that the Administrator was to be advised and assisted by an Executive Council, with legislative powers being exercised by the Administrator and a Legislative Council, the Administrator to preside over both bodies. Soon after MacGregor took up his duties, he made the first appointments to both Councils: Anthony Musgrave; B.A. Hely, the acting Chief Judicial Officer (soon replaced by F.P. Winter, who remained CJO until his retirement in 1902), and F.E. Lawes. Such government officers were hardly likely to resist the will of a MacGregor!

Throughout his term of office, MacGregor tried to place the interests of the indigenous people first. He was not opposed to white settlement, for he accepted the current assumption that the colony had to become self-supporting as rapidly as possible, but he was very cautious in his encouragement of whites with limited capital. He lacked the funds to provide education and health services for the people, but he supported mission efforts in this direction as actively as possible. (During his term, the Anglican and Methodist churches entered the mission field in British New Guinea, agreeing to confine their work to defined districts). But the principal object of MacGregor's administration was exploration and the extension of law and order — a colossal task in so vast and little-known a territory.

He could afford only a skeleton staff. In the ten years of his control, a total of only 64 officers was employed by the government, never more than about 20 at the same time. The key officer was the Resident Magistrate, (who commonly held an extra-ordinary number of offices — C.A.W. Monckton once listed his as Gold Warden, Senior Officer of Armed Native Constabulary, Senior Postmaster, Senior Native Magistrate, Visiting Justice, Commissioner for Affidavits, High Bailiff, Agent for the Curator of Intestate Estates, Assistant Registrar for Births, Marriages and Deaths, Inspector under the Indigenous Timber Ordinance, Inspector under the Diseased Animals Ordinance, Acting Sheriff, Justice of the Peace for the Celebration of Marriages, Justice empowered to consent to the Marriage of Minors, Officer empowered to grant or revoke Permits under the Arms, Liquor and Opium Ordi-nance, and Receiver of Wrecks). The Resident Magistrate (RM) was in charge of a division, of which there were four by 1892; Central, with headquarters at Port Moresby; Eastern, headquarters Samarai; South-Eastern, headquarters Bwagaoia, and Western, headquarters Daru (originally Mabadauan). As circumstances dictated and funds permitted, government agents were employed at minor stations within the divisions.

The RM was responsible for the everyday tasks of administration within his division, for the maintenance of law and order and the extension of government influence. He was expected to be able to cope with all functions of government, with all problems. If he was fortunate, the RM would have one or two officers to assist him. He had, too, a detachment of the Armed Native Constabulary at his command, and government-appointed Village Constables in the settled districts. A simple code of law, the Native Regulations, helped him to maintain order in the villages. MacGregor had quickly realized the vital necessity of an armed force to assist in the task of government and in 1890 had formed the Armed Native Constabulary with a nucleus of two Fijians and twelve Solomon Islanders, a force which had grown to 110 by the time he left British New Guinea. By this time, too, more than 200 Village Constables had been appointed.

MacGregor himself did more exploration work than any of his RMs. He climbed Mount Victoria, twice crossed the mainland from Port Moresby to the north coast and ascended all major rivers, including the Fly. He clashed with tribesmen many times and broke the power of the feared Tugeri raiders from Dutch New Guinea. No RM, burdened with a multitude of duties, could match MacGregor's achievements in exploration and pacification.

One of the principal difficulties facing MacGregor was the random nature of com-munications in huge, sparsely-populated British New Guinea. His officers were scattered. The nearest telegraph station was at Thursday Island and the only post offices within the Possession were at Port Moresby and Samarai (opened in September 1888). British New Guinea was still being treated as a postal department of Queens-land during these years, and Queensland stamps continued to be used for overseas postage, no domestic postage being charged. Queensland's Postage Act however, was not in operation in British New Guinea. Musgrave, who was Local Auditor as well as Government Secretary, described the simple method of obtaining stamps then apply-ing, in his '*Report on the Public Accounts for the Financial Year ended on 30 June 1891*':

> The practice . . . has been to purchase (with a cheque entered 'to account' a certain quantity of stamps for the use of the government and convenience of the public. The moneys paid in by the latter are exchanged for stamps, while a current account is kept, besides, of official postage, until by degrees the local supply of stamps is exhausted. A fresh cheque or balance of cash in hand is then advanced for stamps.

Despite the increasing volume of mails being handled in British New Guinea (in the ten years to 30 June 1898, 194 169 letters, packets and newspapers were received and dispatched), no specialist appointment of Postmaster was made during MacGregor's administration. Thus, the Treasurer, David Ballantine, who had been appointed to this position in 1892, was the Chief Postmaster. He was also the Chief Collector of Customs, Member of the Legislative and Executive Councils, Registrar of Titles, Curator of Intestate Estates and Assistant Resident Magistrate for the Central Division, all at a salary of £350 per annum! In practice, the officer filling the position of Customs Officer and Deputy (later Assistant) Postmaster — a position created in 1898 — supervised post office operations. The Sub-Collector of Customs at Samarai was Postmaster at that centre, as was the Sub-Collector at Daru, although an official post office was not opened there until 1899.

In 1891, Queensland, along with the other Australian colonies, joined the Uni-versal Postal Union. To enable postal affairs in British New Guinea to be kept on the same footing, Ordinance No. 3 of 1892 was passed. This adopted as law the Queens-land Act to Consolidate and Amend the Law relating to Posts and Telegraphs. On 2 July 1892, an Order-in-Council was made under this new ordinance, directing that the Possession should also join the Union. At the same time, Postal Regulations along the same lines as those in force in Queensland were prepared and approved by the Administrator-in-Council.

MacGregor well knew the need for better communications in the achievement of administrative efficiency and the attraction of European settlement to British New Guinea. Essentially, this meant improved water transport. The subsidized mail service between Port Moresby, Samarai and Cooktown, arranged by Douglas, soon lapsed, and in April, 1892, MacGregor wrote to the then Governor of Queensland, Sir Henry Norman, enclosing his expenditure estimates for the next financial year. These included an item of £1 000 as a subsidy towards a mail service:

> This sum — all that can possibly be spared for this purpose — is so small that only a sailing ship could be expected for it. It is felt that the settlement of a useful class of planters in the Possession cannot be obtained unless there is regular communication established for several years between Queensland and this country. If even a two-monthly service could be secured for, say, three or four years to make a round trip from Cooktown to Samarai and along the coast westward to Mabadauan and thence Cooktown, or in the opposite direction to suit the tradewinds, this would be of great assistance to settlers, traders and others, until trade is sufficiently developed to support regular trading vessels.

The estimates were approved, and in mid-1892, MacGregor entered into an agreement with Burns Philp & Co. for a bi-monthly service at the rate of £150 per round trip. At about this time the schooner *Clara Ethel* began voyages between Thursday Island and Port Moresby, and another Burns Philp schooner, *Ivanhoe* made quarterly voyages from Cooktown to Samarai, and thence through the islands of the Louisiade Archipelago, where recent gold discoveries at Misima, Sudest Island and Woodlark Island had attracted a considerable population of European miners. Burns Philp used the *Myrtle*, a smart 167-ton brigantine, on the subsidized run, and the service was well received, but the contract ran out in 1897 and was not renewed for the remainder of MacGregor's term. However, the exchange of mails was still reasonably frequent, if irregular, for the volume of overseas shipping visiting British New Guinea continued to increase, and all ships carried mails.

Mail services *within* British New Guinea remained heavily dependent upon small craft, particularly those of the government. When MacGregor became Administrator (the title and status of the position were changed to Lieutenant-Governor in 1894) there were three of these, apart from a number of whaleboats: the cutters *Maino* and *Juanita*, and the 56-ton schooner *Hygeia*. Both cutters had European masters, despite their minute size (about ten tons) and the *Hygeia* had a European crew of nine. She was used by MacGregor pending the arrival of the steamer pledged by Britain. She was so slow a craft and so expensive to run — more than £1 800 per year — that he soon concluded she was a luxury he could well do without. He sold her and used the proceeds to purchase a handy ketch. But when the steamer supplied by the Imperial government, the *Merrie England*, went into service in May 1889, she proved to be an even greater burden.

A beautiful vessel, with lovely yacht-like lines, the *Merrie England* had been built in Scotland of teak and iron for service in the North Sea. She displaced 260 tons, was

147 feet long and had a draft of more than 13 feet. Despite heavy keel ballast, she rolled terribly. Her two engines, each of 50 horse-power, gave her a service speed of a little over eight knots, but she swallowed coal at the rate of four-and-a-half tons every twenty-four hours. She was stoutly built, but her design did not suit her for tropical service. She carried a large European crew: master, first and second officers, a petty officer, two engineers, six seamen, three firemen, one lamp trimmer, two stewards, two cooks, a cabin boy and a carpenter.

To the end of her life the *Merrie England* was the subject of heated controversy. So excessive was her draft that she was forever grounding on reef and shoal, at great cost in repairs. She was out of service three months in every twelve, undergoing maintenance and refits, and her annual upkeep was ruinous. Britain had agreed to pay £3 500 per year for three years for her upkeep only, but in fact she cost at least twice that sum to run. It was with great reluctance that the Imperial government finally agreed to continue to contribute to this, the balance being made up by the three Australian colonies. Total expenditure on the *Merrie England* during MacGregor's term of office was £76 000, compared with a total of £153 000 for all other administrative purposes combined, but he was never in doubt that the steamer was essential. By the end of his term, the Resident Magistrates in the four divisions each had a serviceable sailing craft at his disposal — the *Peuleue, Siai* and *Lokohu* had been built to the order of the government — and a spare vessel was stationed in Port Moresby. Each was manned entirely by Papuans, which cut down annual maintenance costs. The question of the continued service of the *Merrie England* was by this time again under serious doubt, and in his final Annual Report, for 1897-8, MacGregor wrote:

> The sailing vessels . . . represent the minimum of what is required for administrative purposes . . . they at the same time constitute the maximum of what can be maintained on the funds now at disposal. They are capable of keeping the Administration alive in each division without the steamer; but the latter is indispensable for anything approaching efficient administration. It would be quite impossible for the Administrator to visit, say, the north-east coast more than about once a year without the steamer, unless this were done to the complete neglect of other divisions. It would be impossible to deal promptly with any sudden emergency arising at a distance at any spot to be reached by sea. The Administration would lose greatly in force and power by the discontinuance of the steamer . . .

The *Merrie England* was retained, although she was always to be a handy target for people wanting to attack the government on grounds of economy. She made frequent trips to Thursday Island and Cooktown for mails. For many years she was the only vessel visiting all parts of the coastline. Her coming was eagerly awaited by government officers, missionaries, traders and planters, for she seldom failed to bring mails.

In the frantic world of today, surrounded by the marvels of electronics and space technology, it is difficult to appreciate how important letters and newspapers were to the pioneers of another, more leisurely era, and one must turn to contemporary accounts. In a little booklet published in 1930,[1] a gently-bred young South Australian girl, Minnie Billing, told of her life as a missionary sister at Dobu, the Methodist Mission headquarters station in the D'Entrecasteaux Group, from 1894 until her death in 1901:

> In the afternoon great shouting and excitement was heard among the natives and they announced a steamer was in sight . . . it was the *Merrie England* . . . she brought us a mail . . . a feast for a hungry soul contained in a brotherly letter . . . we got home and found a pile of letters awaiting us and we could not resist them. Mrs Bromilow had a laugh at us when she found our tea growing cold while we were deep in letters . . .

She records her disappointment when the mission vessels *Ellengowan* and *Albert McLaren* failed to bring mails. Dobu once went for eleven weeks without mails, and then she received so many letters that she read until her 'eyes ached'. On another occasion, a trader arrived late at night:

> We were already in bed when we heard an anchor. From the verandah we could see a cutter — voices rang out. 'Have you come from Samarai?' 'Yes!' 'Got a mail?' 'Yes.' 'How many bags?' 'One!'. We put our wrappers on and went across to Mr Bromilow's to help sort out the letters and papers.

The mails were sacred. Gradually, shipping services improved and regular scheduled runs began to most parts of British New Guinea. These carried the bulk of the mails, but it was standard practice for all ship's masters to call at the nearest post office for mails when setting out in small craft. Normally worldly traders thought nothing of sailing twenty miles out of their way to bring mails to a lonely mission station. The number of post offices increased as more government stations were opened. They were almost invariably operated by the Resident Magistrate or his staff. Daru, Tamata (Northern Division) and Kulumadau (Woodlark Island) Post Offices were opened in 1899. Some early offices — such as Sudest and Nivani in the Louisiades Archipelago — were short-lived, existing only to service mining communities that moved on to greener fields when the gold failed.

On the smaller one-man government stations, when the officer-in-charge was away on patrol or visits of inspection, the precious mails had perforce to await his return before they could be sorted and delivered, for no one dared open them. The Anglican missionary priest, Arthur Kent Chighall, records the frustration that resulted, in his book *An Outpost in Papua*:[2]

> The post office people at Samarai had made use of our schooner and had consigned two bulging mail bags to Wanigera, with a polite request that we would be so very good as to forward them at our earliest convenience to the RM at Tufi . . . it was a doleful experience last night, to see those two mail bags lying at my feet, and to know that one

---

1 *Sister Minnie's (Billing) Life and Work in Papua*, Epworth Printing and Publishing House, Sydney, 1930.

2 A.K. Chignall, *An Outpost in Papua*, Smith, Elder and Co., London 1915.

of them contained the long overdue allowance of letters for which we had been waiting since Christmas, and yet to remember that the ungainly awkward masses of paper and soiled canvas were as sacred and inviolable as if George the Fifth himself had melted the wax for the untidy black seals, and tied the ragged bits of string round their mouths and entrusted them to us with his own kingly hands!

Government officers employed many means to distribute the mails. 'Our letters come and go frequently, if irregularly, and by queer carriers and queerer craft', Chignall continued:

Sometimes it is a party of armed native constables travelling in a canoe, or in the government whaleboat ... or a mob of discharged prisoners being sent home in a wonderful double canoe that looks like a cross between the old twin Calais-Dover steamboat and a Chinese scow ... or we have sent our own whaleboat, with a South Sea Islander in charge, or chartered a canoe with its crew of five natives ... at irregular intervals the *Merrie England* calls in at Tufi, and soon thereafter police will be scattering in all directions on the King's business ... there is generally time for one of them to call in here as he passes, and leave our letters with the RM's compliments ...

When a strike by coal-miners in Australia threw the mail service into disarray, letters stopped and life hardly seemed worth living. Chighall wrote:

I wake in the morning to wonder, instantly, once again, what has become of that mail? It is only six o'clock, and there is nothing particular to get up for — what is the use of getting up when the mails have stopped coming — what's the use of anything?

The day-to-day administration of British New Guinea was greatly affected by the quality of the mail service. Only Rigo was within reasonable distance of Port Moresby, and by mid-1891, the Government Agent A.C. English had made good progress on a walking track to the capital. He received regular mails by postal messengers and built rest-houses along the track for their overnight accommodation. He was even able to send surplus food from his station gardens to Port Moresby. But the RM at Daru in the Western Division, B.A. Hely, received mails on average once every six weeks and sometimes waited for up to five months. He was engaged in building the station, recently transferred from Mabadauan, and his requisitions for materials from the main government store at Port Moresby took so long to be supplied that he made slight progress. When MacGregor criticized him, Hely said that because of his poor communications and lack of transport, the efficient working of his division was almost impossible. Hely had earlier been RM in charge of the Eastern Division, and he lamented that in the event of any serious native uprising there, 'I could do nothing and the whole prestige of the government would be destroyed' before assistance could arrive from Port Moresby.

When Sir William MacGregor left British New Guinea, the force and drive that had distinguished his administration slackened. The original agreement between Britain and the Australian colonies was for joint control for a period of ten years. Britain had no desire to extend the arrangement, and the colonies were by now tired of the continual drain on their finances that British New Guinea represented. Federation was soon to come and the administration of British New Guinea would then become an Australian Commonwealth responsibility. In the meantime, British New Guinea was something of an embarrassment to all concerned. The Chief Judicial Officer, Sir Francis Winter (he was knighted in 1900) acted as Administrator on MacGregor's departure, until the arrival of the new Lieutenant-Governor, Sir George Le Hunte, in March 1899.

Le Hunte well knew that his position was, to use his own words, that of a 'mere caretaker' until the cumbersome legal and constitutional formalities attending Federation and the transfer of control to Australia proceeded to finality. It was not an enviable position and was complicated by financial difficulties that sometimes brought the administration close to total breakdown. Neither Britain nor the colonies wanted to spend more money in British New Guinea during this long interregnum, which eventually lasted for seven years. The new Australian Commonwealth, when Federation came in 1901, was not anxious to assume immediate financial responsibility. Le Hunte was obliged to use the Accumulated Revenue Fund of some £20 000 — carefully husbanded by MacGregor — to make ends meet, but even so had to go cap-in-hand to the various governments when short-falls appeared imminent. He actually spent some two years of his term away from British New Guinea, in Australia and Europe, mainly after funds. It is hardly surprising that Le Hunte did little more than maintain the principal features of MacGregor's administration. Two new divisions were created — the Northern and North-Eastern — but Le Hunte spent most of his time while in the country in Port Moresby. The complexity of administration was increasing and it was no longer feasible for the Lieutenant-Governor to roam widely in the field.

It was during Le Hunte's term that the first British New Guinea postage stamps were introduced. On 1 March 1901, the administration of all postal and telecommunication services in Australia passed to the new Commonwealth government, and it became necessary for British New Guinea to make its own postal arrangements. Le Hunte broached the matter of postage stamps for British New Guinea with Lord Lamington, Governor of Queensland, in 1900, and on receipt of his consent to the proposal, arranged with Sir Horace Tozer, Agent-General for Queensland in London, for the printing of a total of 47 000 stamps of six denominations from one half-penny to one shilling, and 9 000 postcards. The design was based on a photograph of a *lakatoi* — the big trading canoe of the Motu peoples — taken by Le Hunte's private secretary, Captain F.R. Barton. The work was executed by the contractors for the printing of stamps for the Crown Agents for the colonies, Thomas De La Rue & Co. Ltd. The beautiful stamps that resulted were to become extraordinarily popular among the world's philatelists. They soon had to be reprinted, and in 1905 a 2/6d. denomination was added to the series. The Lakatoi design was destined to remain in use for thirty-two years, by any standards a remarkable run.

The Lakatoi stamps went on sale on 1 July 1901, replacing the Queensland stamps used to this time. The postage rate in British New Guinea remained at two pence per half ounce until penny postage was introduced in 1911, three years after it was adopted in Australia. A new item of revenue was added to the accounts of British New Guinea in 1901-2, showing receipts of £828.16.11d. from the sale of Lakatoi stamps and postcards.

Mail services to Australia during Le Hunte's administration fluctuated according to the state of the finances available. Burns Philp & Co. vessels continued to trade into British New Guinea and to carry mails, but without subsidy. In August 1902, James Burns offered to provide Le Hunte with a 200-ton, 9-knot steamer on charter for £4 000 per annum, to make two trips each month Cooktown-Port Moresby-Samarai, then to remain in British New Guinea for fourteen days before returning to Cooktown, but this proposal was not accepted. An amount of £1 200 allowed for a 'steam service to Australia' had to be struck out of the 1902-3 estimates because of a lack of funds, but the situation improved the following year and Burns Philp began the regular subsidized mail service that was to be maintained, almost unbroken, for over half a century. When funds permitted, small subsidies were paid to local shipowners for the carriage of mails within British New Guinea, usually no more than £100 per annum.

The vagaries of the mail service continued to plague those responsible for the administration of the Possession, including the Lieutenant-Governor. In 1900, two small steamers, the *Adelaide*, owned by Clunn and Sons, and the *President*, operated by Whitten Brothers, commenced voyages between Cooktown, Samarai, Woodlark Island, Cape Nelson and the Mambare, greatly improving communications in those isolated regions. Earlier that year Le Hunte had sent his draft estimates for 1900-1 to Brisbane, for approval and return. It was highly important that they be received before the end of the financial year. Late in May, Le Hunte left in the *Merrie England* on a tour of the South-Eastern Division. He was anchored at Kwato Mission when the *Adelaide* arrived at Samarai from Cooktown via Port Moresby. Le Hunte sent over the ship's boat for his mail, confidently expecting the return of his draft estimates. 'To my great disappointment', he later wrote, 'I was informed that, for some occult reason, the Port Moresby officials had taken my mail and kept it there. There was nothing for it but to return myself to Port Moresby . . . This will cause me some three weeks' loss of time at a period when I can ill spare it . . .' On the way back, they encountered the *President*, and sent off a boat to ask whether she had the vital mails, but there was only one letter, from Musgrave, telling Le Hunte that he was keeping them at Port! Thus did the uncertainties of the mails affect the administration of the Possession.

The most momentous event of Le Hunte's years was undoubtedly the murder of the London Missionary Society's James Chalmers, with his young companion Oliver Tomkins and nine Papuans, at Goaribari Island in April 1901. This event shocked the world and indirectly led to the suicide of an Administrator. Upon receipt of the news, Le Hunte led a punitive expedition to Goaribari Island and in the ensuing clash many islanders were shot dead, sacred *dubu* houses were burned to the ground and great war-canoes destroyed. It was a bloody revenge. The following year, Le Hunte went back to attempt to re-establish contact with the people, and he warned them that he would return to arrest those responsible for the slaying of the missionaries. But he never did return. He was appointed Governor of South Australia, and, on 11 June 1903, left British New Guinea. He was replaced by C.S. Robinson, who had recently succeeded Sir Francis Winter as Chief Judicial Officer.

There are few more tragic figures in New Guinea history than Christopher Stansfeld Robinson. Only thirty-four years old when he became Acting Administrator, he was a brilliant lawyer who seemed to be on the threshold of a distinguished career. Perhaps to demonstrate his mettle, he determined to arrest the killers of the missionaries. In March 1904, he went in the *Merrie England* to Goaribari Island with a number of officers and a powerful detachment of the Armed Native Constabulary. The affair ended in total disaster. On the arrival of the steamer, villagers came out in their canoes; an informer identified the man who had clubbed down Chalmers; he was seized with some of his fellows by the police; arrows flew, and rifles crashed. In seconds, the open canoes were being fired on as they retreated. Without doubt, Robinson lost all semblance of control over the situation — he even joined in the firing. At least eight islanders died.

Sensational accounts of this sad affair, wildly inaccurate and savagely critical of Robinson, filled Australian newspapers. To still the public outcry, the government removed Robinson from office and replaced him with Captain Barton, Le Hunte's erstwhile Private Secretary and lately Resident Magistrate, who was on leave in Australia. Returning to Port Moresby to take up the appointment, Barton brought written instructions to Robinson to proceed to Sydney to face a Royal Commission.

The disgrace was too much for Robinson to bear: he shot himself. Barton took up the reins of government, but he was a weak man, and his administration was to be clouded by division within the Public Service and such dissatisfaction with his policies that within three years he, too, would be facing a Royal Commission.

When Barton became Administrator, the European population of British New Guinea was almost 600. Many of these were goldminers. The principal exports were still *bêche-de-mer*, sandalwood, a little copra, pearlshell and gold, the last by far the most significant item. Total exports in 1902-3 were valued at £62 892 and gold accounted for £40 322. Much of it came from the new goldfields of the Northern Division; the Yodda, the Gira and the Mambare.

The miners were rough men and they came into frequent collision with the warlike tribesmen of the interior. The gold they won was tainted with the blood of uncounted numbers of warriors, and to protect life and property, the government established two small stations, Bogi and Papangi. Bloodshed continued; patrols from the new stations were often attacked. In 1903, during the one major expedition of his brief rule, C.S. Robinson and his party were forced to retaliate when they were attacked with spears. Robinson was so impressed by the endeavours of the miners that he agreed to have a track cleared from Buna Bay on the coast to the Yodda, and he allocated £1 000 for the job, the biggest single allocation yet made to open the interior.

In 1904, Bogi and Papangi were abandoned. A post office had been briefly established at Bogi late in 1901, located in Clunas and Clark's store there, and in June 1905, the RM of the Northern Division, the caustic C.A.W. Monckton, sent C.J. Marriott, ARM, to Bogi to bring back the post office books. (At the same time, the Kulumadau Post Office, Woodlark Island, located at Finn Brothers' store, was transferred to the new government station at Bonagai). 'He is very willing and keen on his work',

Monckton wrote of Marriott to the Government Secretary, 'but an awful ass and smells like a polecat at times — time will cure the one and soap and water the other.'

To replace Bogi and Papangi, a new, permanent station was built at Kokoda, on the Buna-Yodda track, which was completed in 1905. Kokoda was then the farthest government station inland in British New Guinea. It was beautiful, located as it was on a plateau at a height of 1 000 feet, overlooking the Yodda Valley and backed by the looming Owen Stanley Ranges. It was very difficult to supply. Buna was seventy miles away and the track, though roughly cleared, was hard. Loaded carriers took up to six days to make the journey. Letters from Port Moresby to the Northern Division were transported by sea, and often took two months to reach their destination.

On 10 December 1904, a party led by the Administrator, Captain Barton, left Port Moresby on an overland journey to Kokoda by way of the well-known Gap in the Owen Stanleys. At the same time, another patrol led by the ARM Kokoda, H.L. Griffin, left the station under instructions to meet Barton's party at the summit of the Gap on Christmas Day. The main object of the journey was, in Barton's words, 'to test the feasibility of establishing an overland mail service between Port Moresby and Kokoda'. So began the most remarkable mail route in New Guinea history, a route that was to remain in use until after the Second World War.

The service was inaugurated during the Administrator's expedition. Once each fortnight, two policemen would leave Port Moresby with the mail bags, assisted as required by village constables and carriers, and carry them through to Kokoda, where the mail was sorted. Kokoda police then walked on to Ioma (established in 1905 a few miles from Tamata, which it replaced), and to Buna, with the mail for those centres. The Port Moresby police would meanwhile return with the Kokoda mails. Additional constables were recruited from inland tribes of the Northern Division especially for this work. Mails reached Kokoda on average once in seven days, and Ioma and Buna once in ten days. It was a dramatic improvement over the old arrangements and was received by the miners with the greatest of enthusiasm. The Kokoda and Ioma post offices were officially established on 1 July 1905, the ARM being appointed Postmaster in each instance, in addition to his other duties.

In the first full year of operation (1906-7), 89 overland mails were received at Kokoda and 79 dispatched, and in his annual report the ARM, F.H. Naylor complained of the amount of time that his postal duties consumed. L.L. Bell, ARM Ioma, gave full details of the mails he handled and these are worth quoting as an illustration of the work involved in supervising the mails on a remote outstation:

Seventeen mails have been dispatched between 1 July 1906, and 30 June 1907, for Kokoda overland and via Buna Bay. The total number of letters being 128, packets 5, newspapers 30, and registered correspondence 1. For Samarai, via Buna Bay and Cape Nelson [the headquarters of the North-Eastern Division, later named Tufi] 22 mails were dispatched, the letters numbering 706, packets 17, newspapers 48 and registered correspondence 47. The mails received from Kokoda were 18, in which were 180 letters, 21 registered, 10 packets and 47 newspapers. From Samarai 25 mails were received, the letters being 971, registered 18, packets 102 and newspapers 1 152. The

Merrie England brought 2 mails from Samarai. Two were despatched by her. The remainder were carried by the contractor, Messrs Whitten Bros., Samarai.

The volume of mails continued to increase, and the complaints of the officers at Kokoda, Ioma and Buna became loud. A station had been built at Buna principally for the purpose of the receipt and dispatch of mails for the Yodda and Kokoda, and it became the headquarters station for the Northern Division. An official post office was opened there in October 1907.

A hint of the direction that communications were to take in British New Guinea went almost unnoticed by the public in 1905, when the Wireless Telegraphy Ordinance was passed. It was a measure suggested by the Imperial government, and conferred upon the administration the exclusive right to 'establish stations for Wireless Telegraphy'. The Administrator was still obliged to travel to Thursday Island in the *Merrie England* when he wished to transact official business by telegraph, and years were to pass before the situation improved. (In the same year the Australian government passed the Wireless Telegraphy Act, which gave the Postmaster-General similar exclusive powers).

In 1905, the Australian Parliament finally passed the Papua Act, which came into force in 1906. Joint control was now legally ended. The Act changed the name of British New Guinea to Papua, made financial provision for the cost of administration, and largely preserved the internal machinery of government that had existed since 1888. A Lieutenant-Governor, appointed by the Governor-General of Australia, would be responsible for the efficient administration of the Territory of Papua.

Barton ardently desired the position of Lieutenant-Governor, but his career was about to come to an abrupt end. The Public Service was seething with discontent and jealousy. Barton had quite failed to provide the strong leadership that had enabled Sir William MacGregor to mould his untrained, ill-assorted handful of officers into an effective, if uneven, service. (Anthony Musgrave, the Government Secretary, once wrote, primly, 'We have had in our small ranks individuals who are gentlemen but not good officers, officers who are not gentlemen and not a few who were neither gentlemen nor officers.') A deep division had opened in the Public Service between the supporters of Barton and those opposed. The anti-Barton faction was headed by Anthony Musgrave; David Ballantine, the Treasurer, supported Barton, as did C.A.W. Monckton and other senior officers. No service so tiny — about fifty strong — could survive such bitter turmoil. Finally, after a series of incidents, Barton himself asked for an official enquiry into his administration and certain allegations that had been made about his conduct of affairs. By doing this, he sealed his own fate.

On 22 August 1906, the Australian Prime Minister, Alfred Deakin, appointed a Royal Commission 'to inquire into and report upon the present condition, including the method of government, of the territory, and the best means for the improvement'. The Royal Commissioners spent three months touring Papua, taking evidence from a wide variety of people, before returning to Melbourne in December 1906. Their report was strongly critical of Barton, and recommended that he should not be retained as Administrator. The Commissioners charged Barton with a lack of administrative ability and found him wanting in a true sense of justice and fair play, although they acknowledged that he had tried to protect the rights of the indigenous people. The Chief Judicial Officer, J.H.P. Murray (who had been appointed on the death of Robinson), told the Commission that Barton was an amiable but weak man, easily manipulated. His evidence told heavily. The Public Service as a whole also came under severe criticism. The report recommended the immediate retirement of the Treasurer, Ballantine, and the RM of the South-Eastern Division, M.H. Moreton, and the retirement of Musgrave within twelve months. The position of Commandant of Armed Native Constabulary, occupied by W.C. Bruce, should, it continued, be abolished.

A number of general recommendations were also made. Papua should be developed by European enterprise and capital, employing the labour of the indigenous people and whatever land was needed for strong agricultural development. 'The hour has struck for the commencement of a vigorous forward policy so far as white settlement is concerned', wrote the Commissioners, portentously.

So Barton was out. He was permitted to retire after a year's leave, and left the country a bitterly disappointed man. Ballantine was replaced as Treasurer, Chief Postmaster *et al.* by H.W. Champion, who had joined the service in March 1902 as Government Storekeeper. Musgrave went, and his place was taken by one of the senior RMs, A.M. Campbell, and RMs C.A.W. Monckton and G.O. Manning resigned in protest over the treatment of Barton. W.C. Bruce, his position abolished, retired to private life, and became an implacably bitter enemy of the one senior officer who emerged from the Royal Commission with credit, J.H.P. Murray.

In March 1907, Murray was appointed Acting Administrator, and in November 1908, Lieutenant-Governor. He was to hold the position for almost thirty-three years, a term unprecedented in British colonial history. A legend was in the making.

CHAPTER THREE

PAPUA

When J.H.P. Murray went to British New Guinea he was almost forty-three years old, an age which sees most men well launched upon the careers they will follow throughout their lives. Few successfully change direction in mid-stream, but Murray did. He had achieved a certain standing in his profession of lawyer, but there was nothing in his background to suggest that he would attain far greater heights during the second half of his life as a colonial governor of world fame. He was a tall, aloof man of strong personality, with scholarly, even ascetic tastes; a graduate of Oxford, a fine amateur boxer in his youth and a soldier, but no student of colonial administration. Ambition led him to British New Guinea, not any burning desire to better the lot of the Papuan. Yet long before his death he was revered as the great protector of the Papuan people.

He was governor of Papua for so long that his name came to be a symbol of all that was finest in the administration of a subject people, and men spoke of a 'Murray tradition'. By the standards of the colonial world in the early part of the twentieth century, his administration was enlightened, but by the time of his death in 1940, Papua had become a colonial backwater, wedded to policies unchanged for decades.

During the early years, Murray had to cope with many problems. He inherited a Public Service still bleeding from the wounds of the Barton era, and these were slow to heal. His first concern was to build a service that would be loyal and efficient, but he had enemies within it, the most powerful being Staniforth Smith, a former Senator from Western Australia, who had come to Papua in 1907 as Director of Agriculture. Smith was a man of unbounded ambition and considerable ability, and he kept up his political contacts; he was on close terms with Atlee Hunt, the Secretary for External Affairs, the Commonwealth department responsible for Papua, and he was open in his quest for Murray's job. He never got it, but he got the next best position, that of

Administrator, and he gave Murray scant support. Murray had enemies with long memories, too, among the rest of the European population and for some fifteen years this faction assailed him and his policies at every turn. At first, Murray had high hopes of Papua becoming self-supporting within a few years, and he encouraged European enterprise, but as the years went by his hopes, one by one, were dashed. For the whole of his service his administration was to depend heavily upon annual grants from Australia which never exceeded £50 000 and for some dark years varied between £20 000 and £34 000, beggarly amounts which when added to always scanty local revenue barely sufficed to maintain a small, lean administration.

As his dreams of a prosperous Papua slowly faded — gold production slowed to a trickle, the *bêche-de-mer* and sandalwood trade died, copper mining failed, the Great Depression almost wiped out the plantation industry — Murray more and more turned to the Papuan people for solace, and to his policies for their advancement. The means that he employed were largely those established by MacGregor. He retained and extended the divisional system of administration and the hierarchy of Resident Magistrate and Assistant RM and added a third office, that of Patrol Officer, which replaced the earlier position of Government Agent. He retained and expanded the Armed Native Constabulary and the system of Village Constables, and experimented, not very successfully, with a new office of Village Councillor. He retained and developed the MacGregor code of simple laws, the Native Regulations. Most important-ly, he gradually built up a Public Service he could trust, around a core of field officers who, using Murray's policy of 'peaceful penetration', completed the broad exploration of Papua. Many were the sons of local families. By the standards of most colonial services, Murray's field officers, the 'outside men', were poorly trained, with no prescribed educational standards or academic qualifications. They learned on the job. Many 'outside men' came from the clerical ranks of the various departments — one of the best-known, Jack Hides, began his career as a cadet clerk in the Port Moresby Post Office — and Murray kept a jealous eye on their progress. He spent half of his time during the early years in the field, on foot, carrying out his judicial duties (he retained his position of Chief Judicial Officer) and inspecting the work of his officers. He could match and usually beat the walking feats of men half his age, and he was notoriously careless of his own comfort. Small wonder that his officers respected, even revered him.

In the beginning, Murray was just as circumscribed by communication diffi-culties as were his predecessors. Until 1913, the only contact with the outside world was by steamer. The first of the subsidized Burns Philp & Co. mail steamers was the *Moresby* (she was also the first of a grand line of small BP vessels with names beginning with the letter M and containing seven letters); she was followed by the *Mataram* and the *Matunga*. Under the agreement between Burns Philp and the Commonwealth government, two steamers were employed, leaving Sydney monthly for Papua via Brisbane and the Solomon Islands, and calling at Woodlark Island, Samarai and Port Moresby (every other trip at Hall Sound), thence to Cairns (later Cooktown). The vessels then returned to Sydney by the same route. By 1912, the route structure had changed. One steamer left Sydney every six weeks, calling at Brisbane, Cairns, Port Moresby, Samarai and Woodlark, then back by the same route. The other left

Thursday Island each month, calling at Daru, Port Moresby, south coast ports, Samarai, Woodlark Island and north-east coast ports, and returned, connecting at Thursday Island with BP vessels engaged on the Sydney-Singapore run. The flagship of the BP line was then the *Montoro*, a fine ship of 5 000 tons gross launched in 1911. When she made her maiden voyage to Port Moresby in March 1912, she was the largest vessel ever to have berthed there. She was normally employed on the Sydney-Singapore service, replacing the SS *Guthrie*.

As well as the Burns Philp steamers, ships of other, unsubsidized companies regularly visited Papuan ports, carrying overseas mails. The most important of these was Koninklitke Paketvaart Maatschappij, a long-established company usually referred to as KPM or 'the Dutch company', but more correctly as the Royal Dutch Packet Company. The Dutch company operated seventy-two ships, and employed the two steamers *Van Linschoten* and *Van Waerwijck* (inevitably, they were simply called the 'Dutch boats'), to provide monthly sailings from Melbourne to Sydney, Brisbane, Port Moresby, Thursday Island and Darwin to Java, connecting with no fewer than forty-two mail services operated by KPM to Singapore, Penang, and throughout the Dutch East Indies. Passengers from Port Moresby wishing to travel through to Europe via Java were offered reduced rates on what were described as the 'fast and luxurious mail steamers of the Nederland and Rotterdam Lloyd Steam Navigation Companies'. In 1913 the KPM steamers *Tasman* and *Van Houtman* came into service on the Port Moresby run — fast, modern vessels of 6 000 tons. (In this year, too, the latest addition to the BP fleet was launched, the 2 000 ton *Morinda*). Every nine weeks, ships of the Norddeutscher Lloyd company travelling between German New Guinea and Sydney called at Samarai.

Mail services within Papua gradually improved. The overland service between Port Moresby and Kokoda continued, and in 1910 the RM of the Mambare Division (the Northern Division had been divided into the two divisions of Mambare and Kumusi in 1908) noted in his annual report that 'as occasion demands' a police runner was sent from Ioma across the border to Morobe post, in German New Guinea, with mails. In 1914, Patrol Officer A. Liston Blyth made a journey from his station, Baniara, to Abau in the Central Division, one of a series of 'cross patrols' made at the direction of Murray to assist the process of 'peaceful penetration'. He reported that he had investigated the possibility of an overland mail runner service between the two stations; however no regular service eventuated. Whitten Bros. of Samarai sent their little steamer *Kiaora* at regular intervals along the south coast with mails; their small launch, *Bulldog*, serviced the mining community on the new Lakekamu goldfield, where a government station, Nepa, was opened in January 1910, complete with post office. The RM Nepa, A.P. Lyons, was amongst other things the postmaster. The Nepa mails were delivered by the *Bulldog* to Kukipi, on the coast. Mails were also sent to Kukipi from the government station at Kerema, headquarters of the Gulf Division, by carrier, and were picked up there by passing coastal vessels. The *Wakefield*, a small steamer owned by the BNG Development Co., made regular voyages to Papuan ports. Odd sailing craft operated by traders and planters continued to carry mails.

Probably the best coastal and island service was provided by Burns Philp & Co., by now the leading firm of merchants and shipowners in Papua. The company erected a fine new headquarters building in Port Moresby in 1912, dominated by a high tower, as a fitting monument to its success — 'the largest and most costly ever erected in Papua' in the words of a report in the *Papuan Times*, the newspaper which commenced publishing in January 1911. With the benefit of a government subsidy, Burns Philp sent its steamer *Mindoro* on voyages that included many out-of-the-way places, a service deeply appreciated on outstations. The RM Kumusi Division, A.E. Oelrichs, wrote in 1912:

> SS *Mindoro* has run with a regularity that is a credit to the captains in command. No one, unless he has lived in these outside places, can realize what a benefit it is to know that, on a given date between 11 and noon, the cry of 'Sail O!' will be heard, and on looking out to sea there is the faint outline of a vessel . . . at last there is the rattle of the anchor chains and then, so far as the residents are concerned, the sun, the whole world is at a standstill; they are deep in their correspondence, mostly bills perhaps and probably the handwriting is quite familiar by this time; but what does it matter — it is something from 'the outside' . . .

But alas for the *Mindoro*! In April 1913, she struck a reef in Cloudy Bay and was lost. The dangerous waters of Papua claimed many a small vessel — *Misima*, the replacement for *Mindoro*, was herself wrecked in early 1917. The Whitten Bros. steamer *Kiaora* was a total loss in June 1914; earlier, a violent storm had wiped out the fleet of small sailing craft based in Milne Bay. Such incidents were a commonplace in Papua. Mails were often lost.

The saddest loss was that of the brave old *Merrie England*. On the night of 24 October 1912, she struck a reef outside Port Moresby. She had been a direct link with the beginning of white settlement, but her passing was not universally mourned. The newspaper the *Papuan Times* was then controlled by the ex-Commandant of Armed Constabulary, W.C. Bruce, who never lost an opportunity to attack his enemy, J.H.P. Murray. A spiteful little paragraph appeared:

> The taxpayers of the Territory will be delighted to hear of the loss of this useless and expensive yacht which, of late years, has been used almost solely for the convenience of the Lieutenant-Governor and his friends, at enormous cost to the community . . .

Despite the choler of Bruce, the administration of Papua could not be efficiently conducted without a government vessel, and as an emergency measure, a steamer of 1 150 tons, the *Upolu*, was chartered for four months at a cost of almost £1 200. 'A gross injustice to a struggling Territory!' bellowed Bruce. She arrived in Port Moresby on 7 January 1913, with twenty-six bags of southern mail. In the meantime, work proceeded in Sydney on a handsome auxiliary ketch, 70 feet long and fitted with a 50 horse-power Standard engine, designed as an official vessel for the Lieutenant-Governor pending the building of a replacement for the *Merrie England*. This ketch, the *Elevala*, arrived in Port Moresby in January 1914. She soon became a familiar sight along the coastline of Papua, and during her long life carried thousands of bags of mail.

By this time, the era of communication by mails only, conveyed by vessels or by humans on foot, was coming to an end in Papua. Great technological advances were fast changing the face of the world and even remote Papua could not escape. It would be many years before the life of the Papuan villager — or, for that matter, the average white settler — was much affected by such things as telephones, wireless telegraphy and radio, but from small beginnings great things were to flow.

The telephone was the first of the new inventions to be introduced. It had been eagerly welcomed in that country of far distances, Australia. Only two years after Alexander Graham Bell first demonstrated his invention of the telephone in America in 1876, the first trunk telephone calls were made in Australia, and by 1880 telephone services were well established in Brisbane, Sydney and Melbourne. By the end of 1883, a telephone exchange had been opened in Townsville, North Queensland, with forty-two subscribers. Many of the early white settlers in British New Guinea were at least aware of the existence of the telephone, and of the demonstrations of wireless telegraphy being made at the turn of the century by the Italian genius, Guglielmo Marconi. By the early years of the twentieth century, demands for the introduction of this wonderful new technology to Papua were being made by companies and individuals. Murray was receptive: right up to the time of the stranding of the *Merrie England*, he was still obliged to make occasional visits to Thursday Island purely to make use of the telegraph facilities there. But funds were too limited to be wasted on luxuries, and initial pressure from the white community was slight.

The first recorded move to install a telephone link in Papua was made on Woodlark Island in 1907, when a line for 'telephonic communication' was cleared between Bonagi and Kulumadau, a distance of 1¼ miles, but it is not known whether a telephone was actually used. The government, however, was now planning to improve communications and other services, to encourage industrial and general development in Papua. The Administrator, Staniforth Smith, wrote in the 1909-10 *Annual Report* (Murray was on leave):

> Early in the coming year a government telephone service will be inaugurated, street lighting instituted and a government school for white children opened. It is hoped before many months elapse Port Moresby will be connected by wireless telegraphy with the Commonwealth and the rest of the civilized world and I trust that similar stations will be established without delay at Samarai and Woodlark Island . . .

Port Moresby in 1910 certainly needed more of what Staniforth Smith referred to as 'the ordinary concomitants of civilization'. It was a drab, dusty little town quite devoid of tropical character, with a permanent population of perhaps a hundred, swollen at times when parties of rowdy miners came in from their isolated camps to carouse at the single hotel, the Papua, owned by Tim Ryan, which was 'brilliantly lit with acetylene gas'. Tom McCrann was constructing what he proudly advertised as 'the Premier Hotel in Papua, with plunge and shower baths and the most modern appointments and conveniences'. There were as yet no banks — the Bank of New South Wales and the Union Bank opened branches in 1911 — and it was not until then that a butcher, baker and chemist opened their doors. The movies were still years away

— Tim Ryan opened the first, open-air picture show in January 1914. It screened films each Thursday at the not inconsiderable admission charge of three shillings. There was no other public entertainment apart from the frequent fights between inebriated customers on the vacant block known as the Slaughter Yard, next to the Papua Hotel. Government offices were humble, and scattered. The Post Office still shared facilities with the Treasury and Customs department. Mails were not delivered and it was not until March 1912 that the first fifty private post boxes were installed. The *Papuan Times* complained that they were so small that a shoe-horn was required to remove letters. In fact, the good old custom of 'knocking' the mail service was already well established. One of the first editorials in the *Papuan Times* was a long diatribe about delays in mail sorting and the delivery of telegrams from Thursday Island, which of course had to be sent to Port Moresby by steamer.

It was a dreary existence for the small band of housewives, who had much to contend with. There were some stores — Burns Philp & Co, C.R. Baldwin, Whitten Bros., the BNG Development Company — but stock was limited. Fresh foods were scarce and expensive. Drapery and clothing were best imported from Australia. One of the early advertisements in the newspaper, inserted by the firm of Finney Isles & Co., Drapers of Brisbane, suggested one way to obtain requirements 'quickly':

BRISBANE IS YOUR NEAREST CENTRE! If you study the time-tables of the Burns Philp and the Dutch Boats, you will see long gaps between sailings . . . send us a telegram via Thursday Island for your requirements . . . we can have your goods on SS *Matunga* leaving Brisbane on the 13th (she leaves Sydney on the 10th). To send your order to Sydney would mean a delay of nearly three weeks.

Clearly, Papua was ripe for better communications.

The telephone service became a reality in 1910. A small central magneto manual exchange of 100-line capacity was installed by the Public Works department at Port Moresby, and the principal government offices and business houses were connected. The initial cost was only £150. In the following year, a 'Telephone and Mechanical Engineer' was engaged at a salary of £202, with a Papuan attendant to look after the exchange who was paid £9 per annum. It was a very modest service, with some thirty subscribers, and it was slow to expand. Receipts for the 1910-11 financial year were only £32 and by 1913-14 had reached just £137. The charge per connection was five guineas a year.

Wireless telegraphy was slower in coming, and there were those who placed little faith in this new-fangled invention. In 1911, G.H. Nicholls, Headquarters Officer of the Armed Native Constabulary, reported that he was training a squad of signallers with the object of connecting certain inland stations with Port Moresby by heliograph. 'It should be possible . . . to connect Kokoda, Ioma, Buna and Kairuku . . . by establishing a transmitting station on Mount Stratchley', he wrote. 'When the signallers become proficient, a message can be transmitted to headquarters in a few minutes'. However, Nicholls soon afterwards resigned, and nothing came of his idea.

In Australia, official acceptance of wireless telegraphy was long delayed. Experimenters had been at work there since 1896, and in 1901 a greeting was successfully transmitted by wireless to King George V at sea off Port Phillip Heads in Victoria. But the government was suspicious of this radical new technology. In 1906, the Marconi Wireless Telegraph Company — formed by Guglielmo Marconi in England — was granted a temporary licence to erect stations at Queenscliff, Victoria and Devonport, Tasmania. Although these stations quickly demonstrated that long-distance wireless telegraphy was perfectly feasible, the government was still not impressed, and refused to buy them from the company.

Then came the breakthrough. In 1909, the government was forced by mounting public pressure to recognize the value of wireless telegraphy. The Federal Parliament passed a resolution calling for the establishment of 'Wireless Telegraphic Stations' around the coastline, and the installation of wireless equipment on merchant ships, to provide speedy notice of the appearance of hostile forces in Australian waters, and to protect the lives of seafarers and the safety of their ships.

Although the Marconi Company was the world leader in wireless telegraphy, it had powerful competitors. Probably the most formidable of these was the state-supported Telefunken group of Germany. To represent Telefunken in Australia, the Australasian Wireless Company was formed, and when the Postmaster-General's department called tenders for stations at Sydney and Perth, this company was successful, and installed Telefunken equipment.

In 1911, the Prime Minister, Andrew Fisher, appointed J.G. Balsillie to take charge of the development of wireless telegraphy in Australia. He was a brilliant engineer, and quickly developed his own superior system which he proposed should be used for the balance of the coastal stations. Fisher's government backed his proposals, while both the Marconi Company and Australasian Wireless protested vigorously. There was a protracted and expensive series of battles in the courts over alleged patent infringements, and in 1913, when the dust had settled, a new company was born destined to become a giant in the field: Amalgamated Wireless (Australasia) Limited (AWA), which took over the Australasian Wireless Company and the Australian business of Marconi.

Meanwhile, in February 1911, tenders had been called for the construction of two stations, at Port Moresby and Thursday Island, part of the national coastal network. The Port Moresby station was to be built at Konedobu, in front of the Police Barracks. The news was well received in Port Moresby — even the *Papuan Times* declared that the government deserved 'a pat on the back' — but it was overshadowed by public concern over the safety of the Administrator, Miles Staniforth Smith, and his party, who were somewhere in the wild, unknown country drained by the Purari River, and feared lost.

Staniforth Smith revelled in the power and prestige he enjoyed as Administrator of Papua whenever J.H.P. Murray was on leave, and this time he decided to undertake a major expedition and so make a name for himself as an explorer. It was no part of his duty as head of government to go off into the bush on such an escapade, but he went anyway, and took as his companions men scarcely less ignorant than he was of the perils and problems of this kind of work. The expedition was a disaster. Smith planned to complete the explorations of Donald Mackay, who had found coal near the Upper Purari in 1908; he would walk, he thought, to the farthest point inland reached by Mackay and then strike to the west through unexplored territory to the Strickland.

The party left Goaribari on 20 November 1910. They had a dreadful time. Through ignorance, stubbornness or a mixture of both, Smith had supplied his large party with foods such as soup powder, meat lozenges, concentrated meat and cocoa (which his carriers hated), and inadequate equipment. They were soon lost, at the mercy of the fearful terrain. Before the journey was over, eleven carriers were dead and the survivors of the expedition were on the verge of starvation. The planned date of their return passed, and Port Moresby waited in vain for some word. In Australia, the government and the public became alarmed; a disaster of unprecedented magnitude seemed imminent. Late in February 1911, three patrols under seasoned leaders set off along different routes to find the missing Administrator.

In Sydney, the radio pioneer and Catholic priest, Father Archibald Shaw, made final plans to come to the rescue. He had served in the missionary field in British New Guinea for five years and was a personal friend of Staniforth Smith. He was also a leading figure in Australian wireless telegraphy, holding an experimental licence for a station at Randwick, which later became Shaw's Wireless Works and the Marine Wireless Company; he also operated a small station on King Island. His Randwick station had just established an Australian record by transmitting messages over a distance of 2 100 miles, and he announced that he would employ his equipment, skills and staff to guide the search for the Administrator.

He sailed to Port Moresby in March on the *Mataram*, with five assistants and six small wireless sets, each with a range of approximately five hundred miles. Four thousand people were on the wharf to cheer him on his way. His plan was to set up base stations at Port Moresby and Thursday Island. Another set would be installed on the *Merrie England*, and two more used to equip ground expeditions, while the sixth would be used in Port Moresby on stand-by. At agreed times each day, the six stations would communicate with one another, exchange the latest information, and guide the searchers.

In Port Moresby, Father Shaw directed the installation of two wireless masts, one 120 feet high and the other 100 feet, on Paga Hill and then sailed to Thursday Island to erect masts there. By 22 March, the Port Moresby station was transmitting, but the Thursday Island station could not receive. Then came news from the west — Staniforth Smith and the survivors of his expedition had reached the coast! They arrived at Port Moresby on 29 March 1911.

No doubt Father Shaw was relieved that his friend was safe, but the excitement and drama of his bold enterprise had certainly evaporated. For some weeks, the two base stations continued, without success, trying to establish communication, then Father Shaw gave up the attempt and returned with his equipment and operators to Sydney. The editor of the *Papuan Times* wrote in the issue of 21 June 1911:

> Port Moresby will never become the important trading centre which it is destined to be until an efficient system of wireless telegraphy is established with Australia. Of course a cable service is really what is required but ... what we require immediately, however, and what there is not the slightest excuse by government to refuse, is wireless communication.

Tenders for the proposed government wireless stations at Port Moresby and Thursday Island closed on 14 April 1911, but a decision was slow in coming. There was argument over the choice of a site at Port Moresby. The postal authorities wanted a location convenient for the public, while the Australian Department of Defence was interested primarily in defence aspects. The question of possible patent infringements was also involved. The lowest tender was submitted by the Australasian Wireless Company, which planned to install Telefunken equipment, but the decision in a recent prosecution of the British Radio Telegraph and Telephone Company by Marconi had raised the possibility that the German company might also be in breach of Marconi patents. In Papua, the public outcry for wireless communications increased. In October, the Legislative Council passed a motion calling on the Commonwealth government to assist the Papuan government to provide 'wireless telegraphic stations' at Samarai and Woodlark Island once the Port Moresby station was completed.

Australia's decision to adopt the Balsillie system for its network of coastal stations cleared the way for work to begin. It was announced that construction of the Brisbane station would commence in May 1912, to be followed by those at Thursday Island and Port Moresby. On 14 May the *Matunga* arrived with the necessary equipment, and a team headed by Supervising Engineer D. MacDonald began to erect the wireless masts on the Konedobu site.

The progress of the work was watched with absorbed interest by the citizens of Port Moresby, white and black, for wireless was still akin to magic to the layman then. The *Papuan Times* kept its readers in other parts of Papua closely informed. It reported on 20 November 1912:

> Both masts are completed and ready to raise. They are 144 feet high set in a concrete bed 9 feet deep . . . the masts will be kept in position by three sets of iron wire-rope guys, the guys being secured to a heavy piece of jarrah timber buried 7 feet below the ground. The masts are built of a core of 5 planks bolted together. Covering nearly the whole area occupied by the wireless station is a grid of copper wire buried a foot beneath the surface known as 'the ground'. When complete the ground will contain 7 miles of wire. The masts are 360 feet apart . . . the aerial will consist of a stranded silicon bronze wire. The office will consist of two buildings, a power house and transmitting house, and will probably be the first buildings in Port Moresby to be lit by electricity.

Early in February 1913, the Port Moresby station began making test transmissions. The transmitter had an output of seven kilowatts, and these early experiments established the daytime range under average conditions as 300-500 miles, extended at night to between 1 500 and 2 000 miles. Sydney, Brisbane, Darwin, Timor and Java were within range under favourable conditions. The Dutch had already erected four stations in the Dutch East Indies, using the Telefunken system, but the Royal Dutch Packet Company had elected to install Marconi sets on several of its vessels, including the *Tasman* and the *Van Houtman*. Burns Philp had a similar type of set placed on its fine new *Montoro* to test the practicability of ship-borne wireless. During a voyage from Singapore to Sydney, the Port Moresby station contacted *Montoro* at Darwin, and maintained the contact over three days.

On 12 February 1913, Murray sent the first official wireless message from the new station to the Prime Minister, Andrew Fisher. It was declared open for public business on 26 February. Messages were charged at two pence per word between Port Moresby and Thursday Island, plus land and cable charges to the office of destination, which for most parts of Australia was one shilling for sixteen words. A telephone line was completed between the wireless station and the Post Office, for the convenience of the public. The editor of the *Papuan Times* was outraged by the press rate charged, thirteen shillings per one hundred words — in Australia the rate was seventeen shillings per thousand words. 'We have no vote and are therefore treated as rabbits or vermin!' he howled. Nevertheless, he proudly announced that arrangements had been completed for 'a regular supply of all the world's cables and news generally' to be sent to the paper. 'The advent of wireless telegraphy has galvanized Port Moresby into life' he wrote on 23 April. 'Instead of waiting weeks for news, it is now flashed over space in a very short time . . . Port Moresby now occupies a position that might well be envied by many a country town in the Commonwealth'.

So rapid was the pace of change in the world of wireless that only a week after the station was officially opened, the engineer C.E. Tapp arrived to install new equipment and take charge of operations. With him came the operators Jordan, Vause and Wilson, and the engineer, Jessop. Within ten days, these men, operating round the clock in six-hour shifts, transmitted and received by Morse Code 7 000 words. In a period of one week they contacted Hobart, Wellington, Adelaide, Fremantle, Melbourne and Macquarie Island, in the Antarctic. The 'awful isolation of Papua' as one observer called it, had been shattered, once and for all.

Late in April 1913, the Burns Philp mail steamer *Matunga* caught fire in wild weather eighty miles south of Port Moresby. The blaze started in the mail hold, and 115 bags were destroyed. The *Matunga* was now fitted with Marconi wireless — rapidly spreading throughout the fleets of the world — and when the news was received in Port Moresby, emergency arrangements were speedily made to cope with the situation should the master require help. The fire had been brought under control by the time the ship berthed.

By May 1914, the Australian coastal chain of nineteen wireless stations had been completed. Stations were now operating at Port Moresby, Thursday Island, Cooktown, Townsville, Rockhampton, Brisbane, Sydney, Melbourne, Flinders Island, Hobart, Mount Gambier, Adelaide, Esperance, Perth, Geraldton, Roebourne, Broome, Wyndham and Darwin; a stout, invisible shield for the nation upon which the defence authorities would soon heavily depend. The success of the Port Moresby station brought renewed demands for like facilities from the other main centres of white population in Papua, Samarai and Woodlark Island. They got wireless stations in 1915, but only because the security situation demanded them, for the nation was at war, and the Department of the Navy was made responsible for wireless telegraphy throughout Australia and her territories.

On 4 August 1914, England declared war on Germany, and the bloody holocaust of the First World War began. The coming of war meant nothing to the Papuan villager, but it caused much excitement among the European population. Papua was about as remote from Europe as it was possible to be, but next door was the colony of

German New Guinea! A German naval squadron which included two powerful cruisers, the *Gneisenau* and the *Scharnhorst*, was known to be prowling somewhere not far away in the Pacific, and at Port Moresby there was the Wireless Station, that marvel of technology so eagerly welcomed a year before, but now likely to be a magnet that would involve Papua in a war that had started on the other side of the world.

As the war-clouds were gathering, Murray learned by telegraph that his government would be responsible for the defence of Papua. On the face of it, this was a ludicrous proposal. There were no soldiers in the Territory nor military installations of any kind. The only armed force was the Native Constabulary, less than 300 strong, and stationed in small detachments in the several divisions, using obsolete single-shot .303 Martini-Enfield rifles. The total white population — men, women and children — numbered little more than 1 000, most of them widely scattered. When Murray drew the attention of the Australian authorities to the vulnerability of the Wireless Station, he was sternly told to 'take any steps' to protect it, and a few days later was ordered to defend it 'to the death', even in the face of enemy naval bombardment.

What happened during the next few days seems farcical at this comfortable distance in time, but it was no joking matter then. When war was declared, a special ordinance was rushed through the Legislative Council to allow the immediate formation of an armed European force to protect the Wireless Station and the town. Government officers between the ages of twenty and forty were conscripted. H.W. Champion, by this time Government Secretary, was appointed Censor. A permanent guard of Armed Constabulary was placed on the Wireless Station and all unauthorized access was forbidden. One Lance-Corporal, Isobara, could not see the point of all this frantic activity; he found it cold on guard-duty at night, so he left his post for shelter, and was instantly reduced to the ranks. Trenches were dug, breast-works of sandbags positioned and a barbed-wire fence erected. The staff of the Wireless Station assured Murray that it would not be necessary to blow it up should the German warships appear; it could be put out of action instantly by removing a vital part of the transmitter, and in any case if anyone attempted forced entry, they would feed current into the barbed-wire fence and electrocute them.

On 9 August, one of the European volunteers on lookout on Paga Hill pounded in on horseback to report two sinister-looking ships coming though Basilisk Passage. In his unpublished diary, Murray records what followed, with dry humour:

> I went to the wireless and told Smith . . . to fall in the police and serve out 50 rounds . . . sent word to alarm Port Moresby . . . all AC to the wireless; the police were placed in position in the trenches; Europeans arrived in ones and two.

Then the Customs men telephoned to report that the sinister ships where actually one perfectly innocent vessel from Borneo, with a cargo of oil. Europeans, however, kept arriving at the Wireless Station:

> Jack Russell turned up not in uniform (our uniform is khaki coat and trousers with red AC on shoulders) and I told him he could not fight. He was very near to tears . . . Trotter (formerly in gaol over birds-of-paradise) also no uniform . . . said he would

sooner be hanged as *franc tireur* than out of it altogether . . . alarm as to two steamers approaching about 12.30 . . . then came a report there was one steamer, then that it was the *Wakefield*, then that there was no steamer at all. This seemed to be correct, so I went back to lunch.

During this period of emergency, Murray never left the Wireless Station. He camped inside the barbed-wire fence in a small tent. A horse patrol of European volunteers had been organized, using sorry old nags that normally scavenged for their feed in the Waigani Swamp, to patrol the coast as far as Pari village to watch for the German cruisers. At daybreak on 11 August, one of the volunteers, Kenrick, raced in on a lathered old horse, highly excited, and reported the presence of a gunboat in the harbour. Murray wrote:

> Stood to arms and manned trenches, Kenrick to Simpson's [Simpson's Gap, on the high ridge between Konedobu and Ela Beach] to watch. He came back and said he saw men landing from boats on Ela Beach — he said they were Germans all right. Sent Kenrick to warn the residents of Konedobu . . . wireless men to stand by to disable installation. Sent Leonard [Leonard Murray had been appointed as his uncle's private secretary in 1909] to look for gunboat . . . he could not see it . . . in meantime, Kenrick had gone off, mounted, to Fairfax to 'warn the shipping' . . . whole thing fizzed out . . . Kenrick mad.

What Kenrick had seen was the prison sanitary gang returning to shore in two big double canoes with the night's collection of pans, which had been cleaned in the open sea! He was found two days later near the LMS mission station, trying to tear open coconuts with his teeth, and Murray thoughtfully sent a doctor to care for him.

Then, on 16 August, a long line of warships appeared in Basilisk Passage, gilded by the late afternoon sun. They were the ships of the Australian Naval and Military Expeditionary Force, on its way to Rabaul, capital of German New Guinea, its primary task being the capture of the powerful Wireless Station at Bitapaka.

CHAPTER FOUR

GERMAN NEW GUINEA

Although German New Guinea existed as a colony for only thirty years — from 1885 to 1914 — German commerce was important in the Pacific for twice that span of time. The colony itself was administered until 1899 by a private trading company rather than the Imperial German government. Pacific trade, however, was never very significant economically to Germany, and the New Guinea colony, so vast a distance away from the Fatherland, was for much of its life the neglected child of the Empire. Africa was more important to Chancellor Bismarck and his government, and it was only in the final years of German control that the New Guinea colony began to forge ahead as the Imperial government increased its financial support. British New Guinea was fortunate that its course was shaped by a man like MacGregor; the affairs of German New Guinea during the latter half of its life were in the hands of another man remarkable in his way: Albert Hahl.

German expansion in the Pacific began in 1857, when the Hamburg shipping firm of J.C. Godeffroy & Sohn began to trade in copra at Apia Bay, Samoa. They prospered, and extended their network of trading stations across the Pacific. They were certainly established in New Britain by 1872, and in the Duke of York Group by 1876. Then, in 1879, the firm went bankrupt, following a general fall in world commodity prices. The debts of Godeffroy & Sohn were taken over by the Deutsche Handels-und Plantagen-Gesellschaft der Sudseeinseln. This was too imposing a name for the English traders operating in the Pacific; they took to calling it the Long Handle Firm, or the DH and PG. By 1883, the Long Handle Firm had a string of trading stations in the Bismarck Archipelago. They were not the only German company in the region — Eduard and Franz Hernsheim were by then established on Matupi Island in the Gazelle Peninsula — but they were the largest.

In 1884, the German involvement in New Guinea escalated dramatically with the formation of the Neu Guinea Kompagnie (New Guinea Company) by a number of powerful Berlin financiers headed by Adolph von Hansemann, president of the private bank, Disconto-Gesellschraft. They harboured many romantic misconceptions about faraway New Guinea, which they thought to be a latter-day Eden, ripe for the production by sturdy German settlers of crops such as tobacco, cotton, cacao and coffee, in rich abundance. They planned to secure large land concessions to supply the needs of the settlers. It was a rosy dream, which harsh reality would soon dispel. News of the formation of the Company caused renewed alarm in the Australian colonies, already deeply apprehensive of German intentions in New Guinea. Bismarck had earlier rejected an appeal by von Hansemann for government support for a similar scheme of colonization, but the climate in the Pacific was changing. Bismarck now supported a more active German colonial policy, based on the principle that the flag must follow trade. There was a sufficient German commercial presence in New Guinea to justify protection by the Fatherland. When Britain announced that she was about to accede to Australian demands, Bismarck protested; Britain gave way to the extent that she agreed to annex only the southern part of New Guinea, where there were no German interests.

Meanwhile, in July 1884, Dr Otto Finsch and Captain C. Dallman had arrived in Sydney, with a commission from the New Guinea Company to look for suitable sites for settlement in New Guinea. They purchased a small steamer of 114 tons, which they christened *Samoa*, refitted her, and on 26 September arrived at Mioko, a trading station in the Duke of Yorks. Using Mioko as a base, they made five voyages to Kaiser Wilhelmsland; on one of these voyages Finsch discovered the site now known as Finschhafen, where the New Guinea Company was to establish its first settlement. Bismarck had earlier agreed to extend the protection of Germany to all areas occupied by Finsch, and in November, even as Commodore Erskine was proclaiming the Protectorate of British New Guinea in Port Moresby, Finsch was raising the German flag at several points on the mainland, New Britain and surrounding islands. Bismarck sent four warships to New Guinea to support Finsch's action.

The German move came as a painful surprise to the trusting British, who had assumed that further negotiation would take place before Germany acted. Faced by a *fait accompli*, there was little that could be done. In 1885, the border between German and British New Guinea was formally defined. (German New Guinea was subsequently extended by the addition of Buka and Bougainville in the Solomons, and the Marianne, Marshall and Caroline Islands, which became known as the 'Island Territory').

On 17 May 1885, an Imperial Charter granted to the New Guinea Company sovereign powers over German New Guinea, extended in December 1886 to include Buka and Bougainville.

For the next fourteen years the Company ruled German New Guinea, pouring a vast amount of money into the colony in an ultimately vain endeavour to realize its dream. For in spite of all the expenditure of money and human effort, its administration was a failure. The Company headquarters was established at Finschhafen, but malaria fever took so terrible a toll of its officials that in 1892 it moved to Stephansort (Bogadjim). This proved to be no healthier, and in 1897 Friedrich Wilhelmshafen (Madang) was selected. But Company officials continued to die — almost twenty per cent of them ultimately perished — and the expected influx of settlers from Germany did not eventuate. When the Company finally admitted failure and handed over administration to the Imperial government there were still less than a hundred Europeans in Kaiser Wilhelmsland. Labour difficulties, clashes — usually bloody — with the people, sickness, shipping losses, bad management and the unforgiving nature of the land all combined to defeat the efforts of the Company to produce cacao, cotton, coffee and tobacco.

The greatest difficulty faced was the establishment of efficient communications. Headquarters in Berlin were on the other side of the world and a regular shipping link was an urgent need. To an even greater extent than in British New Guinea, which had the support of the Australian colonies, the officers in German New Guinea were dependent upon the mails. During the first twenty-seven months of settlement, the New Guinea Company spent three million marks, of which forty-five per cent went on its vessels, a measure of the importance it attached to the shipping service.

As mentioned in Chapter 1, the Company put three steamers onto a run from its headquarters at Finschhafen to Cooktown in North Queensland, the closest post and telegraph office. The first was the little *Samoa*, soon joined by two other steamers constructed to order in Danzig, the *Papua* (170 tons) and the *Ottilie* (171 tons). The *Papua* sank near Cooktown on her first voyage in December 1885, and she was replaced by the 366-ton *Ysabel*, built in the Blohm and Voss shipyard in Hamburg. Three large barque-rigged sailing ships were also purchased, the *Florence Danvers* (492 tons), the *Esmeralda* (788 tons) and the *Norma* (645 tons), which were sent to Sydney and sometimes Europe, for freight as required.

The operations of the steamers were scheduled so that one connected with the P. and O. mail steamer at Cooktown each month. Under the most favourable conditions, it took forty-five days for a letter to reach Finschhafen from Berlin; the best time for the transport of freight was sixty-six days. The early annual reports of the Company contain bitter complaints about the treatment afforded German cargo in transit by the British authorities; it was convinced that its goods were subjected to deliberate delays. In 1889, the Company decided to abandon Cooktown. It entered into an agreement with the Dutch shipping line Stoomvaart Maatschappij Nederland, whose vessels sailed every fortnight from Amsterdam to Soerabaya in the East Indies. Every six weeks, a New Guinea Company steamer connected with one of the Dutch vessels to set down and pick up mails and freight. The *Samoa* was now in poor repair, so she was sold in Sydney and the proceeds used to purchase a 60-ton schooner, the *Senta*, which was used within the colony. The Company soon found it difficult to maintain the Soerabaya service with only two small, slow steamers. The Hamburg-based Kingsin Line was planning to begin a monthly service to Soerabaya in 1891, and they offered to extend the route to German New Guinea provided freight was guaranteed and the government granted a subsidy giving a reasonable rate of interest on capital outlay. The Company was spending some 200 000 marks each year to maintain the shipping line (it employed eight captains, eight mates, six engineers, twenty-four sailors and many Malay stokers and seamen), and this oppressive burden threatened the economic stability of the colony. Nevertheless, the Imperial government refused the subsidy request, despite the precedent offered by the Dutch government, which was paying a subsidy to the Maatschappij Nederland company to enable it to extend its route to Amboina to connect with ships serving Dutch New Guinea. Then the *Ottilie* was lost. The sole surviving steamer, *Ysabel*, was now fully employed on a mail and freight service within German New Guinea, so the Company was obliged to turn to charter vessels.

At this time, the great German shipping company Norddeutscher Lloyd (NDL) was operating its East Asia Line on a direct four-weekly service to Singapore. A connection with this port was highly attractive to the New Guinea Company. It was proving very difficult to obtain New Guinean labourers for the Company plantations, and it was endeavouring to recruit Chinese coolies, much easier to obtain in Singapore than in Soerabaya. An agreement was reached with Norddeutscher Lloyd. All Company traffic from Europe would be transferred to the East Asia Line, and its steamer *Schwalbe* was chartered to make a voyage every eight weeks between Singapore and German New Guinea and return. The service began on 15 April 1891, and was very successful, reducing by forty per cent the time taken for mails and passengers to reach New Guinea. It was, however, tremendously costly, the total annual expenditure on shipping amounting to 441 000 marks. (The Company deficit on the shipping account to 31 March 1891 totalled 1.9 million marks). The turning-point came in 1893, when Norddeutscher Lloyd was granted a subsidy by the Imperial government to maintain the Singapore service without cost to the New Guinea Company. The steamer *Lubeck* was employed initially on the run. She ran to Finschhafen, Simbang (where the Neuendettelsau Lutheran Mission Society had established its headquarters), Herbertshöhe (Kokopo) and Friedrich Wilhelmshafen, providing a regular, reliable mail service to these major centres. She was replaced by the larger *Stettin* the following year.

Prior to 1888, there was no formal postal service in German New Guinea, although arrangements were made in 1887 by the German Post Office for agencies to be opened the following year. Mails were carried in Company vessels. German New Guinea entered the Universal Postal Union on 1 January 1888, and postage rates were reduced to those approved by the Union. In this year, German Post Office agencies were opened at Finschhafen (15 February), Konstantinhafen (15 May), Hatzfeldthafen (1 April) and Kerewara (4 April); all these were stations of the Company. It staffed the post offices, which were responsible for accounting purposes to the General Post Office in Bremen in Germany, which also gave training in postal administration to a number of new appointees. The issue of the first German New Guinea stamp co-incided with the opening of the Finschhafen Post Office; it was a red parcels stamp with a denomination of two marks, carrying the emblem of the Company. It was soon replaced by the two-mark German Empire stamp.

Five other post offices were opened in German New Guinea during the admin-istration of the New Guinea Company: Stephansort (1889), Herbertshöhe (1890), Friedrich Wilhelmshafen (1892), Matupi (1894) and Berlinhafen (1898).

This period saw the final acceptance by the Company of the inevitable. In 1889, the Imperial government had agreed to handle the administration of German New Guinea at the expense of the Company, to enable it to concentrate on commercial development. Results were cautiously encouraging, and four years later the Company took back the responsibility for administration, but with no more success than formerly. In 1896, Adolph von Hansemann began negotiations with the Imperial government for the surrender of the Charter, and in 1898 agreement was reached, to take effect on 1 April 1899. In return for the sum of four million marks and the right to add 50 000 hectares of land to that already held, the Company surrendered its rights of sovereignty. The New Guinea Company continued to operate, but as a purely commercial enterprise. It paid its first dividend to its patient shareholders in the 1912-13 financial year, twenty-seven years after its formation. It remained the largest concern in German New Guinea, followed by the Hamburg company founded by the planter H.R. Whalen, which took over the extensive interests of Emma Kolbe ('Queen Emma'), and the Hernsheim Company.

The rule of the New Guinea Company had from the first been unashamedly motivated by commercial considerations. The interests of the indigenous population came a bad second. New Guinea was a potential source of riches, to be exploited by the white man. Imperial rule was marked in the beginning by basic indifference; Berlin had been obliged to assume the responsibility for administration to save the New Guinea Company from collapse, but this colony on the other side of the world had quite failed to measure up to expectations. Here was no Eden, but rather a fever-ridden, harsh and violent land that soaked up money like a sponge, for little return. It merited only cursory attention from Berlin.

The first Imperial governor of German New Guinea was Rudolph von Bennigsen. One of his first actions was to transfer the capital of the colony to Herbertshöhe. His administration was marked by a series of punitive expeditions of stark ruthlessness against tribes involved in attacks against German settlers. He opened a new station on New Ireland in 1900, Kawieng (Kavieng), and placed in charge an extraordinary individual who was to remain there until his death in 1913: Franz Bulominski. Under the spur of his fierce will, tribal fighting was quickly brought under control and the energies of the people were channelled into the construction of the North Coast Road that was one of the major achievements of the German era.

It was in 1900 that the German Colonial 'Yacht' series of stamps was introduced in New Guinea, as in other German colonies; these remained in use until September 1914. A post office was established at Kawieng in January 1904.

Von Bennigsen resigned in 1901, and his place was taken by Dr Albert Hahl, the outstanding figure in German New Guinea colonial history. Hahl was well qualified for the position. He had served as Imperial Judge at Herbertshöhe from 1896-8, and had been nominally in charge of the Bismarck Archipelago and the Solomons. The actual degree of control that had been established in this area was in fact slight, and attacks upon Europeans, with accompanying bloody retaliation by German native police, were constant. Hahl firmly supported official policy: the native people had to be protected but also pacified and led to industrious habits, not for their own good but for the sake of commercial development. The people's labour was needed on German plantations. Whatever force required to be used to achieve this aim must be used, unhesitatingly. It was a harsh policy, but Hahl interpreted it as liberally as the circumstances of the time and place allowed. He learnt Kuanua, the language of the Tolai people of the Gazelle Peninsula, and studied their customs. It was among the

Tolai that he first introduced the *luluai* system that was roughly equivalent to the village constable system of British New Guinea and Papua.

Hahl returned to Germany at the end of 1898, and was made Acting Governor on the resignation of von Bennigsen. He was confirmed in the position in 1903, and retained it until June 1914. He worked tirelessly to extend government control. The *luluai* system was introduced into the villages as rapidly as possible, and to assist them *Tultuls* were appointed, usually younger men who had served in the police force and who knew something of the wider world outside the tribal environment. Medical services to the indigenous people were improved by the appointment of Medical *Tultuls*, who were given a rather skimpy training and sent back home to help their people. Hahl introduced a head tax, to force able-bodied New Guineans to work on the plantations, and increased the size of the native police force. He encouraged the people to produce copra for sale. Under the rule of the New Guinea Company, massive alienation of tribal lands had occurred, particularly on the Gazelle; under Hahl, the sole right to acquire land was vested in the government. Land alienation continued, but some regard was now paid to the customary rights of the people. During Hahl's administration, the Christian missions greatly increased their influence, and a number of important scientific expeditions of exploration were conducted into the interior.

Prior to 1908, Hahl's plans for the development of German New Guinea were severely hampered by the reluctance of the Imperial government to provide more than a bare minimum of financial assistance. He could afford only a small Public Service — less than sixty — but many of his officers were professionals, with tertiary qualifications. Hahl was anxious to establish new government stations, but this was difficult with restricted funds and staff, and only four were opened in the period: Namatanai (1904), Kieta (1905), Eitape (1906 — now Aitape, this station was built near the settlement of Berlinhafen) and Simpsonhafen (1906).

After 1908, things improved. The white population almost doubled between 1908 and 1914, to almost a thousand. The market for copra strengthened, and the value of exports rose from approximately 1.7 million marks to more than 8 million. Internal revenue jumped from less than 400 000 marks to more than 2 million, and the subsidy from the Imperial government was doubled. The Public Service, too, almost doubled in strength. Hahl was able to open new stations at Morobe in 1909 and Manus in 1911. A station was established at Angoram on the lower reaches of the Sepik River in 1913, and a temporary station at Lae (or Burgberg, as it was officially known), near the Markham River mouth.

The increasing prosperity of German New Guinea owed much to improved communications. At the time of the takeover by the Imperial government there had been five postal agencies in operation; Friedrich Wilhelmshafen, Stephansort, Berlinhafen, Herbertshöhe, and Matupi. The first four were conducted by New Guinea Company employees and the Matupi Agency by Hernsheim and Co. The four original offices were no longer in existence. Finschhafen was temporarily closed in 1892, and did not reopen as a post office until July 1904, although it was re-established as a government station in 1902. Konstantinhafen and Hatzfeldthafen were permanently closed in 1891, and Kerewara was abandoned in 1890.

Mail services to the post offices had improved. As well as the eight-weekly sailings of the NDL mail steamer, *Stettin*, to Singapore, the Burns Philp & Co. vessel *Moresby* made a voyage every six weeks to German New Guinea. Mails were frequently carried by German warships and by foreign steamers. In 1900, NDL replaced the direct Singapore service to New Guinea with two others, one from Singapore to New Guinea, thence to Sydney and back to Singapore; the other from Hong Kong to Saipan, Ponape, New Guinea, Sydney and return. These operated once every six weeks. Burns Philp also put a second ship on its service from Sydney.

In 1903, NDL placed two modern twin-screw steamers, each of 3 300-ton capacity, on the Singapore run. Harbour facilities at Herbertshöhe were inadequate for vessels of this size, and the company decided to build wharves and cargo storage sheds at nearby Simpsonhafen, the finest harbour in German New Guinea, which was to become the principal port for the colony. At the same time, the government began to prepare to shift the administrative headquarters from Herbertshöhe to Simpsonhafen: this move was completed in October 1909, and the settlement was renamed Rabaul. In 1906-7 a motor boat ran three times per week between Herbertshöhe and Simpson-hafen, with mails.

NDL dropped the Singapore run in 1905, and replaced it with a service between Sydney, Hong Kong, Yokohama (and later Manila), Herbertshöhe and Friedrich Wilhelmshafen. Burns Philp stopped calling at Herbertshöhe on its Sydney–Singapore run, but the *Moresby* continued her voyages from Australia and return. This year saw the completion of a significant agreement between NDL and the principal merchant shipowners in German New Guinea, whereby NDL provided a regular service within the colony, relieving the merchant companies of the trouble and expense of maintaining their own vessels. (The New Guinea Company continued to operate its small steamer, *Siar*).

This arrangement completely transformed the commercial life of German New Guinea. Two NDL steamers were withdrawn from the east coast of Asia and placed on the New Guinea coastal run; they were the *Langeoog* and the larger *Sumatra*, of 407 tons. Faced with this formidable opposition from the subsidized NDL steamers, Burns Philp gave up the fight and ceased running to German New Guinea.

By 1910, shipping services to and within the colony were stabilized at the level maintained until the First World War. NDL ships of their Austral-Japan Line provided a mail service every four weeks between German New Guinea and Europe via Sydney and Hong Kong, and their *Manila* made a similar voyage via Singapore once every eight weeks. Every sixteen weeks, the Jaluit Line steamer *Germania* ran between Europe and the colony via Sydney, and between the colony and the Island Territory. The *Langeoog* was replaced by the *Roland*, and that vessel by the *Meklong*, which, with the *Sumatra*, maintained an excellent internal mail service, supplemented by private vessels as they were available, and by German ships-of-war stationed in New Guinea waters, which carried mails as a matter of course.

By this time, the various German administrative stations all had serviceable vessels, and these, too, carried mails. An official yacht for Governor Hahl, the *Seestern*, had been provided in 1904, but she was lost at sea in June 1909, and her crew of six whites, fifteen Chinese and eighteen New Guineans all perished. Her replacement, the *Komet*, went into service in August 1911. Hahl used these ships for his official inspections in the same way as the *Merrie England* was employed in Papua, and, like her, they regularly carried mails.

On the eve of war, only Rabaul was classed as a post office by the Germans. There were eleven postal agencies and one sub-office at Maron, the main atoll in the Hermit Group of islands, opened in 1911. Stephansort had been closed in July 1914, and Matupi in January, 1906[1] but the three other agencies of Finschhafen, Friedrich Wihelmshafen and Herbertshöhe were still in use. The other postal agencies were Eitape, the former Berlinhafen; Buka, opened in July 1913; Deulon, open for only nine months in 1914; Kawieng 1904; Kieta (April 1907); Manus (December 1912); Morobe (January 1913) and Namatanai (September 1911). The Rabaul Post Office was under the control of a professional Postsekretar (Postmaster) who was also Director of Post and Telegraph Services; Herbertshöhe and Friedrich Wilhelmshafen, too, were conducted by professional postal staff, while the others were run by government officers, mission personnel and merchants. The sub-office at Maron sold postage stamps and accepted and delivered ordinary and registered letters only, while the others provided a full service, also handling declared-value letters, money orders and newspapers and parcels, including those dispatched cash-on-delivery.

The Germans were quick to recognize the value of the new invention of the telephone, and in 1907 the towns of Herbertshöhe and Rabaul were connected by a telephone line. A small local exchange was installed in each centre; the initial ten lines and eleven extensions at Herbertshöhe had by 1913 increased to twelve lines and thirteen extensions, while the Rabaul network grew from six lines and seven extensions to twenty-two lines and thirty-five extensions. This was the only telephone system to be established in German New Guinea.[2].

The Herbertshöhe-Rabaul telephone line was established purely for the purpose of linking these two important commercial and administrative centres. Considerable use was made of it during the years preceding the transfer of the capital, but it came to possess a greater significance. As mentioned in Chapter 3, the Germans had developed their own wireless technology in competition with the Marconi Company, and the great Telefunken concern was given powerful backing by the German state. It was natural that the Germans would install their national equipment in the chain of long-range wireless stations that they built in their Pacific colonies in the last years before the war. The South Sea Phosphate Company had convincingly demonstrated the value of wireless telegraphy in the vastness of the Pacific with its private station between Yap and the phosphate mines on Angaur Island, on the southern tip of the Palau group in the Carolines; by 1911, Yap was linked with the world cable service through the Celebes, Guam and Shanghai submarine cables. Military considerations were involved and the international situation was fast deteriorating when the German

---

1 According to the *Lloyd Guide to Australia* (1906), a post office was in existence at Nusa, on Neu Mecklenburg, New Ireland, in 1906, but this cannot be substantiated.

2 In his book *District Officer* (Pacific Publications, Sydney, 1968), G.W.L. Townsend states that there was a telephone exchange at Madang (Friedrich Wilhelmshafen) in 1914, and that this was destroyed by Australian troops during the occupation. But I can find no mention of this exchange in the records.

government made its decision to construct wireless stations at key points in the Pacific: Yap, Nauru, Samoa and German New Guinea.

The Germans swiftly put the first three stations into service. As they were equipped with massive Telefunken sets, extraordinarily large in relation to their power by today's standards, they were viewed with grave concern by foreign military planners, particularly the British. The New Guinea station was the last to come into operation. It was erected for the government by the South Sea Wireless Company. Months of work by hundreds of conscripted labourers were wasted in 1912 on site preparation for a planned station in the North Bainings that was eventually abandoned; it was not until July 1914 that the first stage of the Bitapaka station was completed. It went into operation on low power while planning continued for the erection of masts and the installation of additional equipment which would greatly increase its range. Bitapaka was connected to the Herbertshöhe-Rabaul telephone line, and it was clearly a target of the first importance when the world went to war in August 1914, for while the German stations remained in operation they could be used to direct the movements of the powerful German naval units known to be at large in the Pacific.

On 6 August, Britain asked the Australian government to seize the wireless stations at Yap, Nauru and Bitapaka as a 'great and urgent Imperial service'. The Australian response was astonishingly rapid. A Naval and Military Expeditionary Force of 1 550 men under Colonel William Holmes was hastily assembled; it consisted of one battalion of infantry, six companies of naval reservists, a signals section, two machine-gun sections and an Army Medical Corps detachment. They embarked on the armed merchant cruiser *Berrima* and sailed for German New Guinea on 18 August, with a strong naval escort.

Meanwhile, on 12 August, the destroyers *Warrego*, *Yarra* and *Parramatta* of the Australian Naval Squadron landed a small force at Herbertshöhe which cut the telephone line to Rabaul. That afternoon, three officers, six seamen and two mechanics from the *Warrego* occupied the Herbertshöhe Post Office and did as much damage as they could in the space of one hour. They then withdrew, leaving behind them a letter to the German Governor demanding that Bitapaka cease operations immediately.

Dr Hahl was in Germany. The Acting Governor, Dr E. Haber, had withdrawn the seat of government to Toma, behind Herbertshöhe on the outbreak of war. On 7 August, a field post office had been established for the use of the scanty military forces available to him. It was obvious to Dr Haber that he had little chance of defending the colony, but he was not prepared to let Bitapaka fall intact into enemy hands.

The *Berrima* and her escort reached Palm Island, off Townsville in North Queensland, and there, by pre-arrangement, met the cruiser *Encounter*. On board the *Encounter* were six radio operators of Amalgamated Wireless (Australasia) Ltd., and three AWA wireless transmitting and receiving sets, part of a group of twelve operators with six sets that had left Sydney on 7 August on the cruiser *Melbourne*. At Rossel Island, south-east of New Guinea, the *Melbourne* kept a rendezvous with the *Encounter* and other units of the Australian navy. Six of the operators — S. Ambler, H. Firth, E.J. Giles, H. Maxwell, A. Peek and W. Shaw — transferred to the *Encounter* with three wireless sets; the *Encounter* then set off for Palm Island to meet the *Berrima*. The *Melbourne* sailed to Noumea, New Caledonia, where two operators set up a station; a landing party from the cruiser captured the Nauru wireless station; the Yap station was destroyed by the British cruiser *Hampshire*, and Samoa was occupied by New Zealand military forces.

On 11 September 1914, the Australian Naval and Military Expeditionary Force arrived at Blanche Bay. It was a formidable assembly of ships and men, headed by the battle-cruiser *Australia*, which was more than a match for the *Gneisenau* and the *Scharnhorst*; but for her presence the German cruisers might well have attacked the Force. It also included the cruisers *Sydney* and *Encounter*, the destroyers *Yarra*, *Parramatta* and *Warrego*, the submarines AE1 and AE2, the *Berrima* and a number of supply ships and colliers. Governor Haber had only a handful of troops in the area — two regular army officers, about 60 white reserve officers and men, mostly civilians, and some 240 native police — and it was expected that if any defence was attempted by the Germans, it would be of Rabaul only.

The priority task was the capture of Bitapaka Wireless Station. The exact location of Bitapaka was not known to the invaders — it was about six miles inland from Kabakaul Bay — but two parties of naval reservists, each twenty-five strong, were landed at Herbertshöhe and Kabakaul to locate it and put it out of action. The Herbertshöhe force, commanded by Lieutenant Webber, encountered no opposition, but the other party, under Lieutenant Bowen, met with stiff resistance. The road from Kabakaul to Bitapaka passed through dense tropical forest, ideal cover for the German force of less than seventy lying in ambush. It launched a fierce attack on Bowen's party, and at 9.20 a.m., G.V. Williams, Able Seaman, was mortally wounded by a German bullet, the first Australian casualty of World War One. Bitapaka was occupied at 7 p.m., by which time Captain B.C.A. Pockley, Lieutenant-Commander C.B. Elwell and Able Seamen Moffatt and Street had also fallen. The Germans lost a white NCO and thirty black police in the fighting; it was a heavy casualty list for so small a number of combatants.

That was the end of serious German resistance. On 12 September, a party from the *Berrima* occupied Rabaul, and five days later Dr Haber surrendered German New Guinea, on favourable terms afterwards criticized in many circles. Local laws and customs remained in force, civilians who took an oath of neutrality were permitted to go about their normal occupations, and a number of German officials were retained as advisers. Following the surrender, detachments of the Expeditionary Force occupied the other towns of German New Guinea (except Finschhafen, which was never garrisoned); the last, Morobe, was taken on 8 January 1915.

Before Bitapaka was captured, the Germans had succeeded in removing and burying essential parts of the wireless equipment, thus immobilizing the station. The AWA team from the *Encounter* therefore installed a 1½ kilowatt Marconi transmitter and receiver at Government House, Rabaul, to enable contact to be maintained with the fleet. The station was run by Corporal G. Smith, Signaller, assisted by the AWA operator W. Shaw, J. Fitzpatrick, telegraphist of HMAS *Australia*, and two ratings. Power was supplied by a captured German AEG dynamo and converter driven by a Bolinger crude-oil engine. AWA operators Peek and Giles accompanied the force that occupied Friedrich Wilhelmshafen, and installed another set there. They remained for a year before returning to Sydney.

The Government House installation was a temporary measure, and when the occupying troops discovered a large quantity of Telefunken equipment that the Germans had buried at Bitapaka, part of it was used to erect a new station in Rabaul; a five-kilowatt transmitter using a two-cylinder Skandia motor as power unit, and a crystal receiver. Meanwhile, in November 1914, the engineers D. McDonald and C.W. Hardinge arrived at Rabaul with a number of technicians from the Australian Coastal Radio Service, to restore Bitapaka.

The original Telefunken design for the high-power Bitapaka station called for the erection of four steel lattice aerial masts, each 250 feet high. Extreme range was not now required, so the design was altered. A main mast, 315 feet high, was erected, equipped with an 'umbrella'- type aerial containing thirty-two wires, held at an angle of eighteen degrees by steel wire outhauls, connected to the operating building by two lead-ins. A smaller mast, 155 feet high, carried an aerial for 600-metre transmissions. Power was supplied by two monstrous 60 h.p. Swiderski semi-diesel engines, driving a pair of 55-kilowatt DC generators. Two Telefunken transmitters were installed, one giant of 60 kilowatts and the other of five kilowatts. The station opened for traffic with the call-sign, VJZ, in September 1916, under the control of L. Luscombe. Smaller AWA-supplied stations were erected at Morobe, Kieta, Lorengau, Kavieng and Eitape during 1915 and 1916, and traffic from these and from Nauru, Ocean Island and Tulagi was relayed to Australia through Bitapaka, Woodlark Island (established in 1915 by the Navy) and Townsville.

During the course of the war the colony was administered under military rule. The events of the early months of the war had naturally severely disrupted everyday life in German New Guinea, but by early 1915, things had largely returned to normal. In time of war, it was important that the German plantations should continue to produce their valuable crops, and the principal aim of the military administration was to preserve and strengthen the economy. This aim was achieved. The output of the two most important plantation crops, copra and rubber, increased. The German system of field administration was largely retained. District Officers and Policemasters took over the German outstations. The *luluais* and *Tultuls* were retained in office, and more were appointed. Native police continued in their role — although their uniforms were changed — and more were recruited. Head tax was retained, but the German law that permitted employers to physically punish their native labourers was abolished. A style of administration evolved during the six-and-a-half years of military rule that was more akin to traditional German methods than to the benevolent pattern practised in Papua.

Colonel Holmes, the commander of the Expeditionary Force, was the Administrator for four months before he was sent to the war in Europe (where he was killed in action in July 1917). He was replaced by Colonel S.A. Pethebridge, who was made a Brigadier-General and a Knight before his death in office in January 1918. It was during his term that the military administration was consolidated. Brigadier-General G.J. Johnston was Administrator until May 1920, and another Brigadier-General, T. Griffiths, filled the position during the final years of military control.

With the coming of war, the Norddeutscher Lloyd steamers ceased to operate in the Pacific. Throughout the German era, a strong commercial link had always been maintained with Australia, which remained the cheapest source of sugar, coal, meat and petrol, but the subsidized steamers of NDL had forced the Australian company Burns Philp out of this lucrative trade. Now it was its turn. The *Moresby* was in Rabaul loaded with plantation goods as early as October 1914, followed shortly afterwards by the *Matunga*. The Australian Commonwealth government increased the subsidy payment to the company, to provide a mail service to German New Guinea and the Solomons, and Burns Philp rapidly expanded its activities into general trading and plantation ownership and management, achieving a dominant position that it never afterwards lost. The BP steamers ran regularly throughout the period of military administration. Throughout 1915, the *Matunga* made voyages from Sydney direct to Rabaul and return, taking nine days for each leg, and providing the fastest mail service so far enjoyed in New Guinea. Early in 1916, the route was changed. The *Matunga* commenced a monthly run from Sydney to the British Solomon Islands, Rabaul, Kawieng, Friedrich Wilhelmshafen and back to Sydney via Rabaul, the Solomons and Brisbane. The SS *Mindini* made a similar monthly voyage, omitting the call at Friedrich Wilhemshafen. In addition, the *Marsina* and the *Morinda*, hitherto serving only Papua, extended their route to Rabaul, one ship arriving every three weeks. Burns Philp took over the fine facilities established at Rabaul by Norddeutscher Lloyd.

The internal shipping service was of vital importance to the prosperity of German New Guinea during these years. All plantation produce for shipping to Australia was sent to Rabaul, the only overseas port. After the surrender, the military authorities took over the NDL and New Guinea Company vessels employed on the internal services. These included the *Sumatra*, the *Meklong*, the *Siar*, the *Samoa*, the *Nusa* and the *Madang*, and the former official yacht the *Komet* was also pressed into service under the name *Una*. By mid-1916 the *Madang* was making two scheduled voyages per month between Kawieng and Namatanai; the *Siar* made a monthly run to Kieta and the *Sumatra* to Madang, Eitape and Manus. (Many of the German names of ports and towns were anglicized after the surrender — Friedrich Wilhelmshafen became Madang, Herbertshöhe, Kokopo, etc.; Finschhafen, however, with others, remained unchanged). The internal distribution of mails was just as dependent on the movements of small ships as it had been in the time of the Germans.

The military administration developed a system of government by departments that was largely continued when Australia was eventually granted a Mandate. Among these was the Department of Post Office and Telephones. There was some expansion of the existing German telephone system in Kokopo and Rabaul, but no new exchanges were installed. Most of the old German post offices and agencies were reopened in 1914-15; Buka reopened in a new location in 1925, Finschhafen closed in January 1915, and reopened in 1922, as did Maron. A new post office was opened at Talasea in New Britain in June 1920.

The Australian Naval and Military Expeditionary Force did not take stocks of stamps or postmarkers with them when they invaded German New Guinea. Large quantities of current German stamps were destroyed by the postal authorities prior to the surrender, but a number of the 'Yacht' series of stamps first issued in 1900 were handed over by the Rabaul postmaster, Carl Weller, and further small stocks were located in a number of other centres. As a temporary measure, these stamps were overprinted with the letters GRI (Georgius Rex Imperator) and new values, in Australian currency. Until these overprinted stamps were available, mail was inscribed by hand 'on active service — no stamps available'. Australian stamps taken to German New Guinea by individual servicemen were also accepted for postage. Only a small quantity of German stamps was available, and as stocks began to run out, German registration labels were overprinted and used as registered stamps. Marshall Island stamps were likewise pressed into use, overprinted. On 15 March 1915, these provisional issues were replaced by current Australian stamps, overprinted in black 'N.W. Pacific Islands', and these remained in use until 1925.

The postal traffic between Australia and German New Guinea was heavy. In the *Government Gazette* for 1 December 1914, it was advised that the *Morinda* had arrived with 20 000 letters, newspapers and parcels. 'On account of the Commonwealth Military Authorities preventing a lot of newspapers being forwarded, the number received was small in comparison to previous mails', the notice read. The *Morinda* carried some 10 000 mail items when she returned to Australia. As the war progressed, traffic increased.

The future status of German New Guinea was in doubt for most of the war. It was at first expected that the colony would become a part of the British Empire, but the situation changed after the United States entered the conflict. That great idealist, President Wilson, was rigidly opposed to the extension of European colonialism. Japan, South Africa and New Zealand wanted to annex the former German colonies they had occupied during the war, and Australia considered it essential to retain control of German New Guinea. The debate was long and wordy and was not resolved until the Versailles peace conference in 1919. Australia's Prime Minister, W.M. Hughes, fought hard for outright annexation but the Allies agreed that former German colonies would instead be administered by the powers in occupation, under Mandates. The League of Nations was established for the maintenance of international peace, and the member states agreed to forswear warfare as an instrument of national policy. A new era of world harmony and prosperity was seen to be at hand. Unfortunately, the dream was too fragile to stand up to reality and the League tragically failed.

Australia was granted a Mandate over New Guinea by the League. The Prime Minister told Parliament that this had been forced upon Australia, but the general feeling seemed to be that the arrangements were almost as good as annexation. In accepting the Mandate, Australia also accepted the doctrine of the League that the government of dependent peoples was a 'sacred trust' of the civilized nations of the world, but the implications of this attracted little public comment.

The Mandate granted, two major issues remained to be settled: the fate of the Germans in New Guinea and their property, and the future administrative arrangements to be adopted. In retrospect, it is plain that both issues were badly resolved. There was much controversy over these matters. There were those who argued that the interests of the New Guinea people would best be served by an administrative union with Papua, where the 'Murray Tradition' was already winning wide recognition for its paternal, but humane character. More thought that the Papuan administration so 'coddled' the people that there was little chance of business enterprises, dependent upon native labour, succeeding, and it was all too obvious that majority opinion favoured the exploitation of the natural resources of New Guinea, rather than the welfare of her people. There was less argument over the other major issue. As early as 1916 Pethebridge had recommended the expropriation of German property and the repatriation of German nationals, including missionaries. This view was generally accepted by the government, but there were differences of opinion about the way expropriation should be handled.

To settle these matters, the Commonwealth government in 1919 appointed a Royal Commission on Late German New Guinea, to make recommendations for its future administration and on the action required to achieve expropriation and repatriation. The Lieutenant-Governor of Papua, J.H.P. Murray, was appointed Chairman; the other Commissioners were W.H. Lucas, Islands Manager for Burns Philp & Co., and Atlee Hunt, Secretary of the Department of Home and Territories. It was a curious choice, if impartial recommendations were really wanted. Murray had made no secret of his desire to be Governor of the combined territories; Lucas could hardly be expected to be objective in his opinions, and Hunt was known to be a supporter of business interests. Moreover, Hunt and Lucas were suspicious of Murray and his ambitions.

Throughout the proceedings of the Royal Commission it was apparent that the views of Murray differed fundamentally from those of Hunt and Lucas, and finally two reports were written, one by Hunt and Lucas which recommended a completely separate administration for German New Guinea but one organized in a way similar to that in Papua; and Murray's minority report, which was written with the clarity and logic to be expected of a man with his background. An experienced administration already existed in Papua, he argued; amalgamation would secure economy and efficiency; Papuan methods would be more likely to secure the welfare of the New Guinea people than the commercially-orientated methods of the Germans (which he felt had been followed by the Australian military administration), and these would accord with the spirit of the 'sacred trust' the nation would soon be assuming. Murray disagreed, too, with some of the majority recommendations on the expropriation and repatriation questions. He was particularly opposed to the expulsion of German missionaries in the wake of the planters and businessmen. This was the only significant victory he had. The Australian government unfortunately accepted practically all the recommendations in the majority report. The New Guinea Act 1920 came into force on 9 May 1921, and from that date military administration ceased and a civil administration of the Mandated Territory of New Guinea began, under Brigadier-General E.A. Wisdom. It was completely separate from the administration in Papua. (Ironically, also, in view of Murray's misgivings, *every* subsequent Administrator was to be a military man). An Expropriation Board, with wide-ranging powers, was set up, with Lucas as its chairman. Its task was to take over German plantations and companies, the erstwhile owners being sent back to Germany. The process was carried out harshly, and little official regard was paid to the anguish of German families forced to leave a land they regarded as their home to face the uncertainties of life in a Fatherland many of them barely knew, and ravaged by the most terrible war in history. Australia was to come to regret these decisions.

CHAPTER FIVE

PAPUA: THE MURRAY TRADITION

The initial flurry of excitement over the safety of the Port Moresby Wireless Station and town subsided with the surrender of German New Guinea and the later destruction of the German Pacific Naval Squadron, and life quickly returned to normal. The First World War did not have a profound effect on Papua, although the loss of manpower was keenly felt in administration and commerce. Some 140 men went away to fight (out of a total white population in mid-1916 of 1 036), among them almost half of the Public Service, of whom eight were killed.

Murray, and those in private enterprise, had to accept replacements from Australia who in several instances failed to match the standards of those who were away, but this was a common enough problem in time of war. Shipping services were frequently disrupted during these years — by strikes as much as the fighting — and there were material shortages of all kinds, but the war was far away, in Europe, and intruded only lightly on local affairs.

Papua was, of course, in a very different situation from German New Guinea during the course of the war. The one territory was an Australian possession, carrying on normal activities only slightly hampered by wartime rules and regulations; the other an occupied enemy colony, completely subject to military rule. Australians in Papua were free to attack the administration and the policies of Governor Murray, war or no war; the Germans did what they were told to, and kept their opinions to themselves.

A small but bitterly vocal section of the Australian commercial community in Papua never ceased its attacks on Murray and his policies during the war years. The pages of the *Papuan Courier* (this newspaper succeeded the *Papuan Times*, which expired in 1915) carried letters vilifying Murray in terms that would be deemed libellous today. The view of Murray held in many circles, that he over-protected the

Papuans and ignored the legitimate requirements of business, was not confined to Australia.

Despite everything, Papua carried on. In 1916, work began on the remodelling of the Port Moresby telephone system; this was completed in 1917, at a final cost of £1,319. The line was extended to Katea and several other plantations, the farthest being eleven miles from the exchange. The extensions were made at the expense of the plantations concerned, the line carried on trees from the town boundary, to save costs. By the end of the war there were 69 lines connected to the Port Moresby exchange, and 60 extensions; the mileage of telephone wires totalled 43 miles, 47 chains. The system was under the control of John George Boileau, who joined the Public Service in June 1916, as Telephone Mechanic and Postal Assistant. The exchange operated around the clock and was worked by three Papuan operators, trained by Boileau. The line staff was also Papuan, and averaged four in number. In 1917, a fourteen-year-old lad from Elevala village joined the staff as a trainee linesman. His name was Mavara Hekure, and he was to remain in the service until his retirement, forty-five years later.

In 1916, the government decided to provide better quarters for the Port Moresby Post Office, still confined to a small, ill-lit room in the Treasury and Customs building. The volume of mail traffic had greatly increased over the preceding ten years; in 1907-08 the post offices of Papua received 105 187 items (letters, packets, newspapers and parcels) and dispatched 63 833, and in 1916-17 the figures were 243 144 and 146 258 respectively (the heaviest year was 1913-14, when 486 221 items were handled). The bulk of this mail went through Port Moresby. The Treasury building had been erected on high stumps, for coolness, and the area beneath was now enclosed by the Public Works Department, and fitted out for postal business. The Postmaster, J.P. Fitzgerald, transferred into the new quarters in 1917, together with the postal clerks E. Grant and H.F.S. Russell and their Papuan assistants. A new post office and customs bond store was also built that year at Kulumadau on Woodlark Island (and a road constructed to the wireless station at Kwaidan that had been erected for the Navy in November 1915; it was opened to the public in June). The Treasurer, R.W.T. Kendrick was still the nominal Chief Postmaster although in practice he left the management of postal affairs to Fitzgerald. There were thirty-nine white officers in the Department of the Treasury. Ten were employed in the Treasury Central Office, eleven in the Customs section, five in the Government Printer's office, eight in the Government Store (one stationed as Treasury Agent in Sydney, Australia) and four in the Postal and Telephone section.

During the war, a number of new post offices was set up. Bwagaoia was opened in May 1916, following the removal of the headquarters of the South-Eastern Division from Kulumadau to Misima. Prior to this move, the postal work at Kulumadau had been conducted by the ARM; it was now necessary to hand over the work to a temporary Postmistress, which led to the cessation of the Commonwealth Savings Bank Agency — the CSB had begun operations in Papua in 1912 — and the money-order business. Tiveri replaced Nepa in May 1917; in July 1920, the office returned to Nepa and closed, permanently, six months later. Vailala opened in August 1915, as a receiving office only; it was closed in July, 1918.

Imili, opened in January 1916, existed for only a few months, because of a gold-rush that failed. The office at Kanosia, opened in October 1908, was closed in July 1917, because a suitable person could not be found who was willing to take over when the Postmaster resigned; Rigo office, opened in June 1913, closed in July 1919, for the same reason. In February of that year the Abau post office opened to serve the local plantation industry. Baniara post office, opened in April 1917, closed in October, 1918 — the postmaster was the ARM, who was absent on patrol for such long periods that it was found impossible to keep it open.

The Burns Philp-subsidized mail steamers continued to run throughout the war, interrupted frequently by maritime strikes, the great 1918 influenza epidemic and sundry incidents such as a fire which put the *Morinda* out of action for some months in mid-1917. There was one major catastrophe: the loss of the SS *Matunga* in August 1917, to the German merchant cruiser *Wolf*, in the vicinity of Woodlark Island. The steamers of KPM, the Dutch company, continued to call, irregularly, at Port Moresby until February 1918, when their visits abruptly ceased. Internal mail services suffered grievously from the loss of the BP coaster *Misima* in 1917; the only service to the western stations for a long time thereafter was provided by the ketch *Kerema*; the *Rambler* ran along the north coast, but she was too small to carry the tonnages offering. In 1920, the ARM Nepa, C.R. Muscott, complained bitterly about the delay in forwarding supplies and mail to his remote station; during the previous fourteen months he had received only five mails. The RM of the Eastern Division, C.B. Higginson, wrote in his *Annual Report* that twice during this time his division had been threatened with famine because of supply shortages.

Murray had been using the auxiliary ketch *Elevala* for his official inspections, but she was really not up to the job. Only seventy feet long, she was staunch but slow, not designed to carry outstation supplies like mats of rice, cases of tinned meat, sacks of sugar or bulky canvas bags of mail, which the old *Merrie England* had swallowed with ease. Navigated on most of her voyages by Leonard Murray, the *Elevala* was constantly on the move, but it was a relief to all concerned when a new government yacht was built and delivered late in 1918. She was 113 feet long with a loaded draft of 7 feet; two Union engines each of 80 h.p. gave her a speed of ten knots, and she could carry 50 tons of mails and cargo. She, too, bore the proud name, *Merrie England*, but her career was disastrously short: in March 1919, she caught fire in Port Moresby harbour and was a total loss. The *Elevala* was again pressed into service, until the arrival of the lovely *Laurabada* in February 1924.

The work of exploration and the extension of government influence went on although it was hampered by the absence of so many experienced officers. During the war, the series of cross-patrols was continued linking all mainland stations. Much of Papua was under effective control by the war's end, and although the doctrine of 'peaceful penetration' was accepted and practised by Murray's officers, blood was sometimes shed. In 1916, a Patrol Officer, J.F. Kirby, died of arrow wounds received while he was attempting to make murder arrests.

After the war, the affairs of the Mandated Territory of New Guinea attracted a good deal more attention than those of Papua. In New Guinea the dramatic discoveries on the Morobe gold-field made that territory known to the whole world, and led to the employment of aerial transport on a scale so intensive that by the early 1930s New Guinea was the world leader in this field. Prospectors searching for gold discovered the heartland of New Guinea, the magnificent, heavily-populated valleys of the Central Highlands, and again world interest was captured. Papua seemed to be a dull place by comparison.

European commercial opposition to Murray came to a head in 1920, sparked by a comment made by the Lieutenant-Governor that white labour was less efficient in the tropics than in cooler climates. This truth should have been self-evident, and the comment was surely trivial, but it was seized upon by Murray's enemies. A public meeting was held in Port Moresby to discuss this, and other, grievances, and was chaired by the implacable W.C. Bruce. It called for the removal of Murray and his replacement by Staniforth Smith, in whose hands white interests were deemed to be safe. In September, the Citizens Association of Port Moresby again called for Murray's removal, and sent a telegram to the King begging him to take immediate action. It was the nadir in Murray's relationship with his white critics. From 1921 onwards, things gradually improved, although the early years of the 1920s were hard ones for Papua. A short but fierce fall in copra and rubber prices from 1920-2 had certainly not helped the temper of the planters and merchants, and the application in 1921 of the Navigation Act to both Papua and New Guinea made matters a lot worse. This Act, blatantly protectionist, made it practically impossible for foreign vessels to trade with the territories; all exports and imports now had to be consigned to Sydney and there reshipped to the final destination, creating a burden which came close to crippling the already struggling plantation economy of Papua. Murray was shocked by the decision to bring Papua under the provisions of the Act, and his public opposition did much to improve his relations with the white community. It was not until 1925 that the Act was lifted; in this year Murray was knighted, to the general acclaim of the white residents. The collapse of the New Guinea Copper Mines company in 1927 and the Depression of the 1930s again brought Papua to the brink of ruin, but by this time Murray was secure, a revered father-figure almost immune from criticism.

The restrictions of the Navigation Act were, of course, a bonanza for Burns Philp & Co. Its near-monopoly of the lucrative shipping trade between Papua and Australia was bound to be resented by commercial interests fighting to survive and denied the benefits of foreign competition, and as the economy of the Mandated Territory of New Guinea began to eclipse that of Papua, shipping services declined. Two BP vessels, *Morinda* and *Marsina*, were used on the Australia-Papua mail route until 1922, then the *Marsina* was switched to the Mandated Territory run. The *Morinda*, of only 1 972 tons, carried on the service to Papua alone until 1928, although other BP ships called at Port Moresby and Samarai from time to time. The Pacific mail contracts between Burns Philp & Co. and the Commonwealth government were continually renewed during the 1920s and 1930s. Moans from the public about the frequency of the service never ceased, and in October 1926, the Australian Parliamentary Joint Committee of Public Accounts, under the chairmanship of Sir Granville Ryrie, visited Papua to investigate the situation. The majority report recommended that a single three-weekly steamer service from Sydney should be provided to Papua and the Mandated Territory, the ports of call being Brisbane, Townsville and Cairns on alternate trips,

Port Moresby, Samarai, Rabaul, Kavieng and Madang, and back to Sydney by the same route. A minority report opposed amalgamation of the Papua and New Guinea services.

For once, notice was taken of a minority report. The *Morinda*, later replaced by the *Mataram*, continued to make monthly voyages to Papua, while the Mandated Territory was served by three-weekly voyages by the *Marsina* and the *Montoro* until mid-1931, then by the new *Macdhui* (launched in 1930) once a month and the *Marsina* once every six weeks. In October 1931, a new three-weekly service was introduced by the *Macdhui* and the *Montoro*, serving both territories, and this continued during most of the 1930s. Once the Navigation Act restrictions were lifted, foreign shipping again visited Papuan ports. Royal Dutch Packet Company steamers began calling at Port Moresby once a month during their voyages from Saigon and Java to New Zealand and Sydney; on their return voyages, the ships ran from Sydney to Port Moresby direct. Ships of another old-established company, the Bank Line, commenced calling to pick up bagged copra for Europe. Fifty years on, Bank Line cargo vessels were still running to Papua and the Mandated Territory.

Although the overseas mail contract remained firmly in the hands of Burns Philp & Co., other companies provided subsidized mail services within Papuan waters, the most important being the British New Guinea Development Co., which began operations in Port Moresby in 1910, and the Steamships Trading Co., which opened for business in 1924. The BNG Co. won a contract in 1919 for a coastal mail service once every six weeks to all ports, including Thursday Island, employing the 200-ton steamer *Tambar*, but lost it to Steamships in 1922. The Steamships contract provided for monthly voyages to all south coast ports at a subsidy of £375 per quarter, paid by the Commonwealth government. The vessel used, the 99-ton *Queenscliffe*, was sixty years old and she broke down with painful regularity, completing less than half her contracted voyages. The protests from the public were loud and clear, and Steamships made hasty arrangements for a replacement steamer. The new vessel, *Papuan Chief*, was the smallest ever built by the famous Belfast firm of ship-builders, Harland and Woolf. A squat, ugly ship of 225 tons, she quickly won a unique place in the hearts of the people who lived in the villages, settlements and plantations that she served, until her sale to Japanese interests, as scrap, in 1940.

It should not be supposed that a cruise in the steamy heat of the tropics on a little coal-burning coaster like the *Chief* was a pleasurable experience. She rolled terribly, she was slow and she was very dirty. The traveller John Vandercook wrote in 1938:[1]

> The rusted decks were covered with black dust, the worn paint of the housings were smeared everywhere with soot, the solid iron rails, the grubby canvas hatch cover, everything once touched blackened and greased the hands. Our cabin was exactly six feet square. Its doorless narrow doorway gave on a deck hardly five paces from end to end and so narrow you could stretch an arm from wall to rail. At the rear of the cabin were two wooden bunks, the lower too close to the upper, and the upper too close to the ceiling. They were plank-hard, springless, and provided with only thin straw

1 John W. Vandercook, *Dark Islands*, Heinemann, London, 1938.

mattresses covered with a sheet that had seen use since its last washing, and an anaemic pillow filled, by the feel of it, with metallic discards from the engine-room ... a grimy, wretched, battered little ship ...

The Secretary of the London Missionary Society in Australia, New Zealand and Papua, H.L. Hurst, was less jaundiced in his view of the little steamer:[2]

> The *Papuan Chief* is more than a ship, it is an institution. It is known by Papuans and white folk alike up and down the coast of the Territory. As soon as it is sighted the cry goes up from village to village — 'Sail-ho-*Papuan Chief!*' ... the cry is one of the cheeriest for many a missionary, magistrate or planter along these shores. It means letters, papers, books. It means stores — food, kerosene, machinery.

Another traveller on the *Papuan Chief* in the later 1930s was Caroline Mytinger. In her book *New Guinea Headhunt*[3] she described a voyage of five days along a 290-mile stretch of the coast during which the *Chief* made sixteen calls at plantations and stations with mail and supplies.

Steamships put a number of vessels into service over the years, mainly small auxiliary sailing craft — the *Veimauri*, the *Nuisa*, the *H. and S.*, the *Vaiviri*, the *Maira*, the *Panther*, the *Chinsurah* — and they all carried their share of mails, but none gained the fame of the *Papuan Chief*.

The government continued to use a mixed fleet of small craft — the *Kismet*, the *Minnetonka*, the *Nivani*, the *Vailala* were some of the best known. Like her predecessors, the new *Laurabada* regularly carried mails on Murray's voyages of inspection. It was always difficult to maintain close contact with remote Daru, in the Western Division, and the stations, plantations and oil company settlements along that dreary western coastline. Mails were dispatched, therefore, by every available vessel — principally the *Royal Endeavour*, the *Maira* and the *Angas*, and the *Papuan Chief*. Sailings of the *Laurabada* were notified for public information, and it was the responsibility of the Port Moresby Postmaster to ensure that the mails were on board when the ship sailed. Sometimes there were slip-ups, and then Sir Hubert Murray became angry: 'His Excellency wants an explanation why no mails were despatched to the West by *Lauarabada* on 23 April', Leonard Murray wrote to the Chief Postmaster in May 1935. 'Great disappointment was expressed by all round the West at our failure to bring any mail'.

Complaints about the frequency of mails to Daru were common. When the Papuan Oil Development Co. and Island Exploration Pty. Ltd. commenced oil exploration work in the west during 1936, complaints increased. The two companies were subsidiaries of the giant Shell and Vacuum oil combines, and they were not accustomed to communications delays. Daru and district by this time had a white population of around eighty, all but a few oil company employees, and although most supplies came via Port Moresby a lot of mail was received and dispatched through Thursday Island, approximately fifteen to twenty hours sailing for the small craft

2 H.L. Hurst, *Papuan Journey*, Angus & Robertson, Sydney, 1938.
3 Caroline Mytinger, *New Guinea Headhunt*, Macmillan, New York, 1947.

based at Daru — the *Amy*, the *Aramai*, the *Dogai*, the *Ada*, ʰthe *Goodwill*, the *Vari Vari* and others.

Small ship travel along the Papuan coast could be dangerous. On 10 June 1930, the *Vaiviri*, of 32 tons, was overwhelmed by a terrific south-easterly wind during a voyage from Port Moresby to Kerema. On board were F.J. Berge, Mrs Berge and their four children, nineteen Papuan passengers, and a Papuan crew including the master, the experienced seaman Igua Kevau. Berge, Resident Magistrate, was on posting to Kerema, headquarters of the Gulf Division. He perished with his four children, as did thirteen of the Papuans. Mrs Berge was saved by the heroism of Igua Kevau and one of his crewmen, Gari Dai, and their bravery was later recognized by the Royal Humane Society. Everything on the *Vaiviri* — all the Berge's possessions, station supplies and a number of bags of mail — was lost.

As the effects of the depressions of the early 1920s and then the 1930s started to bite, Murray and his Government Secretary, H.W. Champion, were forced to consider extreme measures in order to maintain a reasonable standard of administration. Costs were trimmed wherever possible, at first in small ways. In 1922, the Collector of Customs and Postmaster at Daru, J.H. Irving, was transferred. He was not replaced, on grounds of economy, and the Resident Magistrate, E.R. Oldham, was obliged to handle this work as well as his own which he did with a not very good grace; the RM at Misima, A.H. Symons, had to take over the post office also. Minor measures such as these could not begin to cope with the harsh realities of the savage Great Depression that was about to hit Papua and the rest of the world. 'I have little but disappointment to report', Murray wrote in his 1929-30 *Annual Report* — the very size of which was reduced to the 'smallest possible compass' for considerations of economy. By 1933, the Commonwealth subsidy, originally £50 000 per annum, was down to £34 000, public works had virtually ceased, Public Service salaries had been reduced and recruitment had come to an end. Murray's cherished programme of exploration and pacification by 'peaceful penetration' suffered greatly because of a shortage of money and experienced field staff, although funds were scraped together to enable the great North-West Patrol, led by Charles Karius, ARM, and Ivan Champion, PO, to cross New Guinea from the Fly River to the Sepik in 1927-8.

Throughout these dreary years, internal revenue steadily declined, but then a ray of light pierced the overall gloom. A new issue of stamps was received with such enthusiasm that in 1929-30 postal revenue increased by £381 over the previous year; in the following year revenue shot up by £3 164 to £6 646, almost entirely due to sustained interest in the stamps by the world's philatelists. On 14 November 1932, the famous 'Lakatoi' series was replaced by an extremely handsome pictorial series, in sixteen denominations from one half penny to one pound; by 30 June 1933, revenue from the sale of the new stamps amounted to £7 293. Overall revenue from all sources in that Depression year exceeded the previous year's by nearly £3 000, entirely due to the new issue, a striking illustration of the significance of a well-executed stamp series to a small, struggling economy. The designs were chosen by a committee appointed by Sir Hubert Murray, composed of the Chief Medical Officer, Dr. W.M. Strong, the Government Anthropologist (F.E. Williams) and the Chief Postmaster (E.C. Harris, also the Treasurer).

The stamp-buying public, however, was fickle; post office revenue fell by £7 712 in 1933–4 as the sale of the new pictorial series slowed. Business again picked up in 1934-5 with the issue on 6 November 1934, of four commemorative stamps marking the fiftieth anniversary of the declaration of the Protectorate of British New Guinea. A rumour spread throughout the philatelic world that a syndicate of dealers in Auckland, New Zealand, was planning to corner the supply of the one penny value of the new issue; the Honorary Secretary of the Australian Stamp Dealers Association, S. Orlo-Smith, wrote to the Minister for Home and Territories on 25 September, to seek assurance on the matter. His letter was referred to Sir Hubert Murray, who asked the Chief Postmaster for his comments. 'Nonsense', said Harris. The only way the New Zealand syndicate could obtain a corner on the penny stamps would be by negotiation with himself; this had not occurred, nor would it.

There was heavy demand — 'quite unprecedented' in Harris' words — for a series of four stamps issued in July 1935, to commemorate the Silver Jubilee of King George V. 'This department, unfortunately from the revenue point of view, has had to reject repeat orders from all parts of the world for many thousands of these stamps', Harris reported. The one penny stamps were completely sold out by 5 October, and the threepenny stamps by the twenty-third.

The Papuan Treasury benefited even more handsomely from the sale of the four stamps in the issue made on 14 May 1937, for the coronation of King George VI. World philatelic interest in these (which were similar in design to the coronation issue in Nauru and the Mandated Territory) was extraordinary. Postal receipts in 1937-8 reached £31 097. The stamps were withdrawn from sale on 31 December 1937, and although the face value of those in the series was only eleven pence, sales totalled £23 894.

King George V had been a noted philatelist, his collection world famous. Being King, it was not difficult for him to add to the royal collection. In a letter from Buckingham Palace to the Postmaster General dated 9 November 1914, Sir E.W. Wallington had conveyed a request from the King that a corner block of four stamps of all new stamp varieties issued in the future by the Commonwealth government be sent to him. (They would be paid for by Treasury Warrant Authority.) In 1921 stamps issued in Papua and the Mandated Territory were included. When King George V died, the new King decided to carry on the royal collection, and the Governor-General in Canberra was requested to ensure that the previous arrangement was continued.

The stamps that had attracted this world philatelic interest in Papua in 1929-30 were not in fact of new design. They were the then current 'Lakatoi' issues, of three pence, six pence and one shilling denominations, overprinted with the words 'AIR MAIL' in black, and then with the outline of a high-winged monoplane bearing the same letters across the wings. For the air age had finally caught up with the ancient land of New Guinea.

The story of aerial transportation in New Guinea is exceedingly rich and detailed.[4] Practically all of the significant developments in aviation took place in the

---

4 James Sinclair, *Wings of Gold: How the Aeroplane Developed New Guinea*, Pacific Publications, Sydney, 1978.

Mandated Territory, not Papua, and will be briefly discussed in Chapter 6. But the first aeroplane to fly anywhere in New Guinea flew in the skies of Papua, in October 1922. It was a Curtiss Seagull biplane flying-boat, brought to Papua by Captain Frank Hurley and piloted by Captain Andrew Lang. Hurley intended to use the aeroplane as an aid in exploration; in this he largely failed, but he will always be honoured as the man who introduced the aeroplane to New Guinea. (It is fascinating to note, however, that in his *Annual Report* for 1920-1, the RM of the Western Division, A.P. Lyons, wrote that the Mabadauan people held a Christmas festival in 1920, during which several novel dances were performed, the principal being an 'aeroplane dance', each performer carrying a toy monoplane obtained from Thursday Island with which he imitated the flight of the machine. Did the Mabadauan people actually see an aeroplane in the skies over Thursday Island in 1920 or earlier? History has no answer.)

The coming of the aeroplane to New Guinea foreshadowed a revolution in communications and the carriage of mails that was surprisingly slow to eventuate in Papua. Regular, everyday use of aeroplanes began on the Morobe gold-field in the Mandated Territory in 1927, but they were still something of a curiosity in Papua (except for Port Moresby) until the mid-1930s.

The first attempt to introduce a scheduled airmail service in Papua and the Mandated Territory was made in November 1928, by P.J. McDonald and his partner, the pilot Ray Parer, one of the two pioneers of aviation on the Morobe gold-field (the other being 'Pard' Mustar). McDonald and Parer formed a little company, Morlae Airline, with their principal asset a De Havilland DH9C biplane of limited capacity. They asked both the Papuan and Mandated Territory administrations to support their request for a Commonwealth government subsidy of £12 000 spread over three years to enable them to provide two flights a month between the gold-field and Port Moresby, carrying 100 pounds of letter mail each flight. They suggested that if a surcharge of two shillings and six pence per half ounce were made, the return from the carriage of 1 000 letters per month would cover the outlay. They proposed flights to meet the monthly voyages of the *Morinda*, and to take mails and passengers to Wau or Lae, to return to connect with the ship on her voyage back to Australia. Mails from the gold-field to Sydney would thus be delivered in seven days, less than half the time taken by the BP mail steamers travelling via Rabaul. It was an imaginative proposal and there was ample precedent for the granting of a subsidy, but despite support by both administrations, the request was refused.

Parer had already demonstrated that the route proposed was feasible, despite the primitive nature of the equipment available. On 12 January 1928, he flew from Ela Beach, Port Moresby, to Lae in a DH9, in company with Charles Pratt in a Bristol Fighter, the first time aeroplanes had flown across the island of New Guinea from coast to coast. No official mail was carried by either aeroplane, but it is likely that both Parer and Pratt carried letters for friends. The first official airmail was carried by Captain P.H. Moody in his Ryan monoplane, *L'Oiseau de Tropicale*. He flew from Ela Beach to Lae on 17 March 1928. In October 1927, Squadron Leader E.C. Wackett carried mails to and from Samarai and Port Moresby, and to and from Kerema and Daru during the course of the survey flights made by two Supermarine Seagull amphibians of the Royal Australian Air Force for Anglo-Persian Oil and the

Commonwealth government. In 1928, the Department of Agriculture of the United States sent an expedition to New Guinea to search for new species of sugar cane with which to revive the declining sugar industry in its southern states. Led by the pathologist Dr. E.W. Brandes, the Sugar Expedition covered vast areas of Papua and the Mandated Territory in its Fairchild seaplane, and on 12 July air-dropped mail to the newly-established Police Camp on the Turama River. On 25 August, the Fairchild flew from Lae to the Sepik, stopping *en route* at Madang to deliver an official mail from Port Moresby. No air mail postage fee was charged for any of the mail delivered on these several flights.

Following the rejection of the Morlae subsidy application, Parer made two flights between Port Moresby and the Morobe gold-field, on 26 October and 13 December 1928, carrying mails (as well as other flights with passengers only). He was determined to establish a regular service, despite the lack of official support, but his next mail flight over this route was not until 16 April 1929. Morlae expired and Parer formed the Pacific Aerial Transport Company, and went on flying. Other pilots began to fly between the gold-field and Port Moresby; up to 30 September 1932, 132 round flights had been completed as far as can now be ascertained. Ray Parer made 45 of these flights, Lionel Shoppee 34, Orm Denny 34, Les Ross 11, Kevin Parer 3 and Charles Pratt, P.H. Moody, G.I. Thompson, F. Drayton and L.T. Holden one each. A total of 15 flights with mail was made in 1929, 3 in 1930, 24 in 1931 and 13 in 1932, to 30 September. It is impossible, now, to give any details of the mails that were carried; the only Department of Defence file on civil aviation that appears to have survived from those days notes that for the year ending 30 June 1929, all companies operating aeroplanes in Papua and the Mandated Territory together carried 13 878 pounds of mails, and most of these could have been carried within the Morobe District.

Although Ray Parer pioneered the Port Moresby-gold-field route, it was Orm Denny who developed it into a reliable service. Denny had incomparably better equipment. The largest and most efficient aerial transport company to operate in New Guinea prior to the outbreak of the Second World War was undoubtedly Guinea Airways Ltd.; it operated a fleet of single and tri-motored Junkers and Ford aeroplanes that were technically superior to most of the machines used by their competitors. The time-saving advantages of a mail service between the gold-field and Port Moresby should have been obvious to the most casual observer, and when the Burns Philp mail steamers *Montoro* and *Macdhui* began their three-weekly voyages serving both Papua and the Mandated Territory in October 1931 (each ship making one round voyage every six weeks), the potential savings in time became even more dramatic. An aeroplane connecting with one of the two steamers at Port Moresby could fly the incoming mail and passengers across to the gold-field in two hours or so; if the mail remained on the ship, up to two weeks would elapse before it arrived at its destination. Guinea Airways then decided to enter this route. A single-engine all-metal Junkers F/13 was imported, and Orm Denny was engaged as its pilot. Denny made the first flight to Port Moresby in the Junkers on 23 March 1932, returning three days later with passengers and mail. So popular was the new service that in August Guinea Airways placed a second Junkers, a W/34 specially modified to carry up to eight passengers, on the route.

Up to the end of September 1932, all mails to and from Port Moresby and Morobe were carried by courtesy of the companies and pilots concerned. No air mail fee was levied, but obviously this was a situation that could hardly continue. In September, Guinea Airways entered into a contract with the Papuan government for the aerial transport of mails. By notice in the *Government Gazette*, of 26 September 1932, the Chief Postmaster, E.C. Harris, fixed the air mail rate on letters and other first class mail matter at three pence per half ounce, in addition to ordinary postage. For the time being, no air mail fee was charged for second class mail.

The first official flight under the new contract was made by Orm Denny[5] in the F/13 on 30 September; the service was maintained, unbroken, until the Japanese invasion. The first air mail from the Port Moresby Post Office to Australia was carried on 12 April 1934, by Pilot S.D. Marshall in his little Westland Widgeon monoplane; the first air mails from Australia to Papua and the Mandated Territory were carried by Pilots Charles Ulm and G.U. Allan in the famous Avro monoplane, *Faith in Australia*, which landed at Port Moresby on the rough Paree aerodrome on 26 July 1934. The aeroplane carried 9 063 pieces of ordinary and 2 011 registered mail items for Port Moresby; on 27 July, Ulm and Allan flew on to Wau and Lae, with 15 906 ordinary and 1 942 registered mail items. On 30 July, the *Faith in Australia* left Lae on the return flight south. This official airmail flight was well supported by philatelists and the public, but it was not until 30 May 1938, that the Australia-New Guinea Air Mail Service was begun by a De Havilland 'Express' airliner operated by W.R. Carpenter Airways.

Postal articles from Papua were accepted for conveyance on air mail services operating in Australia from December 1925, on pre-payment of a special fee of three pence per half ounce, plus normal postage. At that time, air service existed between Charleville and Camooweal, Perth and Derby and Adelaide and Cootamundra, via intervening towns.

Papua was a poor country, and made limited internal use of aeroplanes. Sir Hubert Murray was suspicious of the effect they might have on native administration — he feared his Patrol Officers would lose touch with the people if they flew over them rather than walked among them — but towards the end of his life he expressed the belief that wide use would be made of aeroplanes, 'should prosperity every return to Papua'. Although the economy did pick up towards the end of the 1930s — gold once more heading the list of exports — there was never sufficient money available for the government to provide more than token aid to aviation. The Paree aerodrome, near Kila Kila village, was built and maintained by the government; a small emergency landing ground was constructed at Kubuna, in the Mekeo district east of Yule Island, in mid-1932, under the direction of W.H.H. Thompson, ARM; D.M. Rutledge, ARM; and Peter Brewer, Patrol Officer, built the Aibala aerodrome, in the Goilala district, in 1938 (the first stations in this wild region, Kambisi and Mondo Police Camps, were supplied and received mails by mule transport from the coast from 1928); and another small government landing ground was constructed at Ioma in 1938. Most of the small

---

5 In my book *Wings of Gold*, I wrongly credited this inaugural flight to pilot Frank Drayton.

outstation airstrips in Papua were built by miners, missionaries and plantation owners — Bulldog, in the Lakekamu district, and Tauri, near the river of the same name, by the Nason-Jones party in 1934; Ebei, on the Yodda, and Kiunga, on the Fly River, by the Ward Williams expedition in 1934-5; Hula, near Kapakapa, by the LMS missionary Revd H.J. Short in 1937; Eilogo, on the Sogeri Plateau, by G.A. Loudon in 1937; others were temporary, unnamed and now forgotten. All were from time to time used for the delivery of mails.

The most widely-used of the government-built outstation aerodromes was Kokoda. It was constructed under the supervision of Mac Rich, ARM, the first landing being made there on 28 September 1932, by the Guinea Airways Junkers F/13, piloted by Orm Denny and Frank Drayton. As well as half a ton of supplies for the mining engineer, J. Ward Williams — who was engaged in extensive goldmining activity in the Yodda Valley, where he later built his Ebei landing ground — the F/13 brought in mails. Rich spent a busy hour cancelling first day air covers sent in on this flight. When the Junkers attempted to take off, however, it stuck fast, the aerodrome being new, and soft from overnight rains. Denny and Drayton spent the night at Kokoda, and next day the ground was stamped hard by the pounding feet of chanting police, prisoners and villagers marching up and down the soft patches. This treatment was successful, and the fliers took off on the 45-minute return flight to Port Moresby.

Although regular Port Moresby-Kokoda flights were thereafter made, the overland mail service by police runners continued. Considering the span of years during which the service operated and the warlike nature of the people when it began, it is remarkable that only one of the runners was killed in the course of this duty.[6] In 1931, two constables, carrying mails to Kokoda, fell to squabbling over their loads, and one of them, Karo, shot the other in the back. Karo was sent to goal for this deed; years later he killed a warder and achieved the melancholy distinction of becoming the last man to be executed in the Territory of Papua, in August 1938.

Policemen — members of the Armed Native Constabulary, and Village Constables — continued to deliver mails to remote plantations and mission settlements throughout the 1920s and 1930s. Strictly speaking, the correct way to obtain a direct mail service along the coast of Papua where there were no post offices, was to apply for a private mail bag at a cost of one pound per annum, or authorize in writing the delivery of mails from a post office to a named agent. But in practice RMs and ARMs generally sent policemen with mail to outlying districts, often for considerable distances. Alice Keelan, whose husband was Manager of Gobaregere Plantation, Kemp Welch River, wrote in 1929:[7]

> The arrival of a policeman with a mailbag gave us a pleasant surprise. It was a
> Christmas mail, too, so we spent an exciting morning in opening our letters and parcels
> and living for a while among familiar faces and old associates ... if people with friends

---

6 In December 1913, two messengers bringing mails from the Dubuna copper mine to Port Moresby were murdered by Koiari tribesmen, and the mail, which contained money, was stolen.

7 Alice J. Keelan, *In the Land of Dohori*, Angus & Robertson, Sydney, 1929.

in these out-of-the-way places could only see the delight with which the arrival of a mail is greeted, they would never miss writing by one.

André Dupreyat, missionary priest of the Sacred Heart, was at Cœur-des-Anges Mission Station in the heart of the wild Goilala country in 1930, when mails arrived:[8]

> Two native policemen strode into the hut. They stood to attention, saluted, and presented arms with their old-fashioned but highly-polished rifles. We returned the salute. Then, gravely, one of them produced a small, carefully wrapped package from his canvas rucksack. This was our mail ... We thanked the two *policimani* and offered them a plug of tobacco. They presented arms once more, and left for their camp some two or three days' distance away.

Papua's first Crown Law Officer, R.T. Gore (later a greatly respected Judge) was surprised by the seemingly careless handling of the mails during his first voyage along the west coast in 1924, on the *Laurabada*:[9]

> We anchored off a fairly large village, Dubumubu. The village policeman came out in a canoe with the Kikori bag of His Majesty's mails left at the village by some vessel carrying mail, but not intending to go up the river to the government station. I thought it a very casual manner of delivering mail, but I was assured that it was quite a common practice, perfectly safe in the hands of the village constable, and the mail would arrive at its destination eventually.

The mail services of Papua remained the most important means of communication for the ordinary white resident in the decades between the two world wars. Nothing could take the place of letters and newspapers, either for the townsman or the man in the bush on station or plantation. Papuans were the mail handlers, but individual Papuans made very little use of mailing facilities, for few were literate; during the Murray era, education remained in the hands of the Christian missions, and the most devoted efforts of the mission teachers produced only a handful of partially-literate Papuans each year. A few books in simple English were published for school use, but it was not until 1929 that the government produced a monthly simple English newspaper for Papuans. Called the *Papuan Villager*, it was edited by the Government Anthropologist, F.E. Williams, and issued free of charge. The circulation was small, never more than 1 000, but the newspaper was mailed to government stations throughout Papua and each copy undoubtedly passed through many hands.

The use by the Papuan people of the other principal means of long-distance communication within their own country, telephones and wireless telegraphy, was even more limited, although again the services of Papuans were essential for their operation. For the whole of the between-wars period, the telephone exchanges were

8 André Dupreyat, *Mitsinari*, Staples Press, London, 1955.
9 R.T. Gore, *Justice versus Sorcery*, Jacaranda, Brisbane, 1965.

operated by Papuans, and Papuan linesmen did the installation work. J.G. Boileau was promoted to the grand-sounding position of Supervisor of Telephones, and remained in charge for almost all of these years. Despite repeated requests from the residents of Samarai for telephones, only Port Moresby and district had a telephone network. (A small exchange system was established at Misima in 1937, to link the administrative headquarters, Bwagaoia, with the gold mines which were then highly important to the Papuan economy.) In 1920, the Commonwealth government provided a special grant of £2 000 to extend the Port Moresby telephone system to Kanosia in Galley Reach. By 1921 the line to Katea had been taken on to Tahira, Bootless Inlet (headquarters of the New Guinea Copper Mines company) via Sapphire Creek, and by 1924, to Rouna Falls. By 1935, there was a trunk line to Sogeri, a private line around Fairfax Harbour to the Napa Napa Slipway, and extensions to the Gaol, LMS station and aerodrome. Two Stromberg Carlson magneto switchboards of 150 and 50 line capacity handled the work, while an Ericcson magneto switchboard of 100 line capacity was used for training purposes. There was a small circuit with seven connections between Obu and Aroa, in the Hisiu district, and eight connections on the 27-mile route between Rorona and Kanosia, Kanosia and Doa, and Kanosia and Veimauri.

In 1936, a new telephone exchange and workshop was completed at Port Moresby, with a 200 line switchboard to handle the increasing traffic. The average number of daily calls now exceeded 2000, with a peak load of 250 calls per hour. The service provided was often criticized by the public. J.G. Boileau was a competent technician and he gave his Papuan operators careful training, but his section was small and always limited by the availability of funds. (Cash could not be spared for such niceties as telephone posts for out-of-town extensions. For many years Sir Hubert Murray took a daily horseback ride, usually travelling far beyond the confines of the town; in September 1930, he complained to the Chief Postmaster about 'telephone wire lying so low as to be a real danger when riding. For instance, behind the race course it is in places only a couple of feet from the ground, and at others high enough to take a horseman in the face.') It was at Boileau's request that approval was given, in December 1922, for two bright young Papuan switchboard operators, Mavara Hekure and Heni Davi, to proceed to Australia for a special course of training at the Sydney Telephone Exchange, and other PMG establishments. Both men did well, and upon their return to Port Moresby, they did what they could to pass on their newly-won skills.

The public still complained about the telephone service, and angry letters regularly appeared in the pages of the *Papuan Courier*. Even the Lieutenant-Governor himself was sometimes inconvenienced. 'I have never known the service so inefficient and exasperating', wrote Leonard Murray to the Chief Postmaster in May 1929. 'Shutters fall and bells ring when no one is calling. Outside conversations are clearly audible on all the direct lines . . . most of the lines seem to be crossed. No. 122 rings day and night for 142, and vice versa . . . much business is done by telephone from Government House. This business is being impeded by bad service.' The line was hastily overhauled, but a fortnight later Murray complained again: 'The direct line to the Government Secretary is again out of action, and has been in that condition for two days. Also, a deafening series of explosions obtrudes on some lines, making their use impossible.'

By contrast to the financial restraints on the use of telephone networks in Papua, the development of wireless telegraphy was controlled by the big, efficient company, Amalgamated Wireless (Australasia) Ltd. Although the use of telegraphy in Papua was on a lesser scale than in the Mandated Territory it was nonetheless highly significant, so much so that in one of his last *Annual Reports* (1937-8) Sir Hubert Murray wrote that 'the progress which has been made in aviation and in wireless telegraphy has had the effect of practically annihilating distance in Papua and has facilitated administration, though perhaps increasing its cost'.

In a country like Papua, mountainous, laced by powerful rivers, with a vulnerable economy and a small, scattered population, roads can never be the complete answer to the problem of communication; initial costs of construction are too high and maintenance is a never-ending financial nightmare. There was only one major arterial road in all of Papua at the end of the 1930s, from Port Moresby to Sogeri, a distance of about thirty miles. Water transport was of course extremely important, and remains so, and the aeroplane quickly established its worth, expensive though aerial transportation was to a country as poor as Papua. Wireless telegraphy, as Sir Hubert said, has the power to almost literally annihilate distance, and it was fortunate that a company with the resources of AWA had the responsibility for its operation in Papua and the Mandated Territory in the years between the two world wars.

As detailed in Chapter 3, AWA Ltd. was born in 1913 to represent the interests of the Marconi and Telefunken companies throughout Australasia. The general manager of the new company was Ernest Thomas Fisk and he dominated the emerging electronics industry of Australia for the next thirty years.

Fisk was an Englishman, born at Sunbury-on-Thames in 1886. In 1906, he joined the English Marconi Company, and in 1911 established branches for the company in Australia and New Zealand. He concentrated on the development of the marine wireless service with considerable success, and when AWA was formed, the Marconi School of Wireless was organized to train marine operators, under Chief Instructor George Apperley. As we have seen, AWA operators and equipment fulfilled a vital role in Papua and the Mandated Territory during the First World War, but of more significance was Fisk's work in pioneering direct wireless communication between England and Australia in 1918. Australia until that year had been completely dependent on submarine cables, a dangerous position in time of war. As a result of Fisk's successful experiments, the Australian Prime Minister, W.M. Hughes, became an enthusiastic campaigner for an Australia-England direct wireless link. England was more interested in a relay service, to link various countries in the Empire with the mother land, and after an Imperial Conference in 1921 failed to resolve the issue, the Commonwealth government commissioned AWA to establish a direct service; in 1922, the government acquired a major interest in AWA and the company took over the operation of the Australian Coastal Radio Service from the Postmaster-General's Depar.ment. There were twenty-nine stations in the chain, nine of them in Papua and the Mandated Territory: Port Moresby, Samarai, Rabaul, Morobe, Aitape, Madang, Kavieng, Kieta and Manus — the Island Radio Service. They were supervised from Rabaul, where W.G. Clarke was the first Radio Inspector.

Port Moresby and Rabaul were the key stations in the Island Radio Service. Samarai remained the chief subsidiary station in Papua, although another was opened at Misima in December 1936, following considerable pressure from the nine mining companies working there. The Port Moresby Wireless Station was connected with the Australian coastal network through the station at Cooktown and initially employed a 5-kilowatt set operating on the 'spark' system. The Samarai station, which had been erected by the Royal Australian Navy, also used a 'spark' set.

The Papuan stations operated at a heavy financial loss — some £3 000 for the year ending 30 June 1922 — because of the comparatively small volume of traffic they handled. In an effort to reduce this loss, the then Radio Stationmaster, C.E. Tapp, was instructed to ask the Port Moresby Post Office to accept messages for transmission from the public, thereby enabling the Radio Station to close down its town office at a saving of £400 per annum. Losses continued under AWA management, although at a reduced level — around £1 000 in 1928.

Upon the takeover by AWA charges for telegrams, unchanged since 1913, were increased. The new rates were six pence per word to Australia, Samarai and Rabaul, one shilling and five pence to Mandated Territory subsidiary stations, and two shillings and six pence to Tulagi and Nauru and to Ocean Island. Cablegrams were five pence per word additional to cable rates for Australia. There was strong criticism from the public and the Papuan government, but the increases had not been made by AWA but by a committee of officers of the Postmaster General's department. In February 1925, the first power station was opened in Port Moresby and in March 1926, current from the station replaced electricity previously generated by the Wireless Station's own plant, resulting in a saving to AWA of some £50 a month. Sir Hubert Murray wrote to the Minister for Home and Territories in August 1927 citing the saving and asking for a reduction in AWA charges.

AWA was sensitive to accusations of over-charging, and when the Minister forwarded Sir Hubert's letter to the company, the Deputy General Manager, J. Moon, pointed out that a heavy loss was still being sustained on the entire Coastal Radio Service. The company wanted to transfer the Port Moresby station from Konedobu to a site in the town which would be far more convenient for the public; at the present time, those wishing to lodge messages for transmission outside normal Post Office hours had to face a 20-minute walk to the Wireless Station. The Papuan government, however, had refused to make a suitable town site available.

In that year, 1927, there were four AWA engineers and operators at the Port Moresby station: Messrs Leverett, Cusack, Stubbs and Izett. There were a number of Papuans, too, one of whom was to become a legend in AWA circles. He was Morea Mea, who joined the Company in 1926, and became the first Papua New Guinean to be trained as a rigger. He was to retire fifty-seven years later, and during his long career was never involved in a single accident. His eldest son, Igo, followed in his footsteps.

1927 was a landmark year in Australian wireless telegraphy, for in April the short-wave Beam Wireless Service with England was inaugurated. When AWA was commissioned by the Commonwealth government in 1922 to establish a direct Australia-England service, it was generally accepted that successful long-distance radio communication depended on a combination of high power and long wave-lengths, and the company directed its research into this field. But the great Marconi was still at work, experimenting with the use of shorter wavelengths, which had first captured his interest in 1916. In 1923, on board his specially-equipped steam yacht *Elettra*, he received short-wave signals from his station at Poldhu, Cornwall, at a distance of 1 400 miles from a transmitter rated at only one kilowatt, and the following year AWA engineers received powerful Morse Code signals from Poldhu, using two special short-wave sets hastily constructed and installed in the Sydney suburbs of Vaucluse and Willoughby. It spelled the end of the proposed, very expensive long-wave direct service. The Beam Wireless Service was born, and in 1928, successful experiments in international wireless telephony — the transmission of speech using ordinary domestic telephones — led to the introduction of a radiotelephone service between Australia and England, on 30 April 1930. Under the inspired direction of E.T. Fisk, AWA played a leading part in these dramatic developments.

Papua and the Mandated Territory directly benefited from these technological advances. The Island Radio Service was initially connected to the Beam Wireless Service via the coastal feeder stations to Sydney. In 1928, a direct wireless link between Sydney and Rabaul was established. By 1929, AWA had three modern wireless telegraphy centres in the Pacific region, controlled through the AWA Radio Centre in Sydney. The station at Suva in Fiji collected and distributed all traffic from three other stations in Fiji, and from Samoa, the Friendly Islands, the Gilbert and Ellice Islands, New Caledonia and the New Hebrides. Bitapaka worked Sydney direct and the AWA stations at Aitape, Madang, Manus, Kavieng, Kieta, Marienberg, Bulolo and Salamaua in the Mandated Territory, and also maintained contact with the Gilbert and Ellice Islands, the Solomons and Santa Cruz Island. Port Moresby worked with Cooktown, Townsville and Sydney, and with Samarai and two small private stations owned by oil exploration companies at Oriomo and Popo in Western Papua. A direct radio-telephone service between Rabaul and Sydney began in October 1937, while Port Moresby had to wait until July 1941 for a similar link.

Rabaul was the most important station in the Island Radio Service, but Port Moresby, too, was a vital link. The introduction of short-wave Beam Wireless transmissions meant that AWA had to re-equip the Australian and Islands stations, and the question of the transfer of the station at Konedobu to a site in Port Moresby was again raised. A new Treasury building, as before shared by the Customs branch and Post Office, had been erected in 1925, and space did not permit the previous arrangement whereby the Post Office accepted messages for the Wireless Station. AWA was thus put to the expense of reopening a town office, with subsequent employment of extra staff.

The new Deputy General Manager of AWA, Lionel Hooke, asked Sir Hubert Murray for the co-operation of the Papuan government in providing an acceptable site in town for the construction of a new station with the latest equipment, capable of communicating direct with Sydney in all conditions of weather. This would enable the AWA station at Cooktown to be closed down. Hooke also asked for Sir Hubert's support in an approach to the Postmaster General's department for a fifty per cent reduction in the landline charge of one penny per word currently raised on traffic from

Cooktown, until the new station was in operation. The net result of these economies was to be the reduction of telegram charges between Papua and Australia.

Eventually agreement was reached, and the Papuan government granted AWA a 25-year lease over a two-acre site at the corner of Musgrave Street and Ela Beach Road. Work on the new station began immediately. True to their word, the AWA directors slightly reduced rates in November 1929, before the new station was completed. Late in August 1930, a powerful new transmitting and receiving set of 5-kilowatt output — designed and manufactured by AWA, like most of the equipment they used — was shipped from Sydney, and in March 1931, the new station went into service. It was capable of high-speed operation, 100 words per minute, and eliminated the previous dependency upon land cables in Queensland. A smaller set was also installed for maritime communications.

The 1930s saw a marked increase in the use of wireless in Papua and the Mandated Territory, spurred by the development by AWA of a series of compact, relatively cheap teleradio sets that culminated in Type 3BZ, destined to serve the territories in war and peace for many years.

Prior to the introduction of this teleradio equipment, the use of wireless telegraphy in Papua was mainly confined to the oil companies, and to individual 'wireless experimenters', as they were called. As early as 1921, the Postmaster General's Department had supplies two field sets for the Anglo-Persian Oil Company in the Popo district where test oil wells were being drilled. The sets were supplied and installed at the expense of the company, and all operating costs were met by it. Messages were charged at the rate of one penny per word either way between Port Moresby and Popo; messages to and from Australia cost three pence per word, plus land cable charges. The larger of the two sets, of 1½-kilowatt output, cost £1 000 and installation another £200; the smaller, a ½-kilowatt set, cost £800 plus £150 installation. The company had to provide certificated operators and make all necessary maintenance arrangements — an estimated annual outlay of £600 and £550 respectively. As a cost measure, conveniently placed trees were used for aerial masts. The sums of money given were considerable for 1921, far beyond the capacity of the average individual or small company, and certainly too expensive for the Papuan government at a time of rural Depression. When in 1921 the Planters Association asked the government to provide a number of small wireless stations throughout Papua, they were referred to the PMG department to make their own arrangements if they so desired; as far as can be ascertained, no sets of this kind were purchased by the Association.

The first individual to apply for an 'Experimental and Instructional Licence' appears to have been the Supervisor of Telephones, J.G. Boileau. His application, dated 24 November 1921, was approved. An Anglo-Persian Oil operator, L.N. Seccombe, applied for a similar licence on 15 May 1922. Of greater significance, however, was Land Station Licence No. 42 granted by the PMG Department in April 1933, to M.C.W. Rich, to operate a 'wireless land station at Kokoda or other localities in Papua'. This was the first land station to be operated by a government officer in Papua, and the first amateur station.

Mac Rich had attended the Marconi School of Wireless in Sydney in 1920, with the intention of becoming a marine wireless operator. To his chagrin, he found that he could not be issued with a licence until he reached the age of twenty-one, so he left the school and later returned to his birthplace, Papua, where in March 1924, he was appointed a Patrol Officer in the Magisterial Service. He never lost his interest in radio, however, and wherever he was posted over the years, he experimented with home-made equipment — the amateur was then very much on his own. Rich received much advice and assistance from the officer-in-charge of the AWA station at Samarai, E.J. O'Donnelly, and from Ken Frank of the Port Moresby station, a man whose contribution to the development of radio in Papua was immense.

In 1932, Rich was posted to Kododa, and for the first time succeeded in establishing consistent communication with Samarai and Port Moresby, albeit in an entirely unofficial — even illegal — way, for he was not licensed. His equipment was hand-built, a tuned-plate tuned-grid transmitter using a Type 112A valve with 180-volt dry battery power supply on Morse Code, and a four-valve TRF receiver using Type 30 valves. In October 1932, Sir Hubert Murray made his annual inspection of Kokoda — as usual, on foot, despite the mountain terrain and his advancing age — and found that Rich had not only completed the construction of the Kokoda aerodrome but was in radio communication with the outside world. On 21 October, Sir Hubert had the novel experience of sending, via Samarai, a wireless message to the Prime Minister in Canberra:

> Have pleasure in sending first official wireless message from Kokoda 60 miles inland from Buna stop Magistrate Rich has personally established wireless communication via Samarai stop Leave on foot for coast tomorrow.

Next morning, the Lieutenant-Governor left on his return journey, camping that night twenty miles from Kokoda on the banks of the Kumusi River — good going for a young man, let alone one well into his sixties. He was on the point of retiring at 9 p.m. when a runner arrived, holding aloft the blazing firestick with which he had lighted his way from Kokoda. He bore a reply from the Prime Minister:

> Desire acknowledge receipt from you of first official wireless message from Kokoda stop Establishment by Magistrate of wireless communication noted with appreciation.

This was a significant event in the history of wireless in Papua. In his *Annual Report* for 1932-3, Sir Hubert wrote of the incident: 'We live rather out of the world in this Territory, and it was a strange experience to receive a message from the Federal capital in the middle of the Papuan bush'. There is no doubt that Rich's initiative stimulated Sir Hubert's imagination, and contributed to the rather cautious acceptance of wireless communication by the Papuan government.

While Sir Hubert was at Kokoda, Rich asked him to support an application for a land station licence, to place his operations on a proper, legal footing. Sir Hubert took the matter up with the Prime Minister himself, saying that any fees involved in the issue of the licence would be met by his government. In due course Licence No. 42 was granted, at a fee of one pound per annum. It allowed Rich to use a transmitter of up to 25 watts, giving a normal range by day of 200 miles, and by night 400 miles, from any locality in Papua. It was allocated the call-sign VLX. During his service at Kokoda, Rich handled a lot of traffic for the mining engineer, J. Ward Williams, who was expanding his activities in the Yodda Valley. Messages between Kokoda and Samarai were charged at three pence per word.

Shortly after Mac Rich began his station, AWA announced the development of a portable teleradio, for use in remote or difficult locations. With a total weight of 150 pounds, the set could be broken down into separate components, each capable of being transported by a carrier. Power was supplied by a low-output pedal generator, supplied by the Machinery and Electric Company and mounted on a steel bicycle-frame. During operation, some luckless person — nearly always a Papuan — sat on a seat and pedalled away furiously, generating the power that gave the set a transmitting range of 350 to 400 miles under favourable conditions. Reception was possible over far greater distances. Tests in the Mandated Territory in 1933 proved the practicability of the new sets in tropical conditions, and in Papua, Ward Williams was quick to install one at his headquarters in the Yodda Valley. He was soon in regular contact with his Sydney office, via Port Moresby. By mid-1936, there were thirty-six pedal sets in use in the territories, most of them in the Mandated Territory.

The weak link in the pedal radio was undoubtedly the generator. Generating power by grinding away at a set of pedals was an exhausting business, and inefficient to boot. Before the introduction of small petrol charging motors in 1937, many alternative methods of power generation were used on the outstations. Mac Rich tried most of them. He served at Kerema in 1934 and used a Smith cycle wheel, coupled to a slow-speed truck dynamo. The Smith equipment consisted of a light motorcycle wheel on which was mounted a single-cylinder four-stroke petrol engine, the whole assembly being bolted to the back wheel brackets of an ordinary push-bike. At Losuia in 1936, he employed an old four-foot diameter waggon wheel, hand-turned, belt-connected to the dynamo. In 1937, AWA introduced the Type 3A transceiver, from which was developed in 1939 the Type 3B, and the famous Type 3BZ, after the outbreak of war in the Pacific. These sets had an aerial rating of 10 watts. They were contained in three metal cases — transmitter, receiver, loudspeaker — plus batteries and charger motor, usually of Briggs and Stratton or Delco manufacture — a total weight of less than 200 pounds. The early transmitters were provided with two crystal-controlled spot frequencies, and the receiver was of the super-heterodyne type, capable of reception on 13 to 500 metres. They were fine pieces of equipment, simple to install and operate and quite cheap, considering the average prices of domestic receivers then. (Fisk Radiola Model 247, seven-valve battery-operated sets were retailing in the major stores in Papua and the Mandated Territory for around £43.) Mac Rich purchased a Type 3A in 1938, while he was on leave in Australia, for £125. This price did not include the battery charger. At Cape Nelson and Baniara from 1938 to 1940, Rich successfully employed a wind-driven dynamo imported from the United States, and then a Johnson Iron Horse from the same source. This not only provided power for the set but also electric light for his home.

Rich maintained his commercial licence — No. 42 — until the outbreak of war, and in 1940 constructed a modern set from a design supplied by the big American mail order firm, Montgomery Ward of Chicago. It catered for the wireless amateur throughout the world, and with this equipment Rich was able to use wireless telephony. He applied for an amateur licence in 1938 and was allocated the call-sign VK4VX; he held this licence until he gave up 'ham' operations in 1972.

Mac Rich was the first amateur to operate a wireless land station in Papua, but he was not the only one to appreciate the advantages of wireless telegraphy. In July 1933, the Revd J.R. Andrew of the Methodist mission, Salamo, was granted a licence, and J.R. Foldi received one in July 1935. Foldi, at the time Patrol Officer stationed at Kikori, already had a 'ham' licence and he was one of the first government officers to hire a Type A transceiver from AWA.

To encourage wider use of their teleradios, AWA was prepared to hire them to approved persons for £25 per annum. In July 1935, the Papuan government had set aside £300 for the purchase of two transmitting and receiving sets, hoping to use them as the basis of a service which would ultimately lead to the linking of all outstations with Port Moresby. The Treasurer and Chief Postmaster, E.C. Harris, was instructed to look for a suitable set. He found no acceptable equipment in America, and for some reason rejected the AWA pedal units as 'unreliable'. He favoured the pedal sets developed by Alf Traeger for the Revd John Flynn of the Australian Inland Mission, but Flynn had none to spare. Harris abandoned his search, and it was decided in the Executive Council to rely on the use of sets privately owned by government officers, who would be paid an allowance to maintain services between their stations and Port Moresby. It was a cheese-paring decision by a financially-pressed government, and as a result Papua failed to develop an administrative radio network to equal that in use in the Mandated Territory. When the advanced Type 3A and 3B transceivers became available on a hire basis, a number of officers obtained them, and the government paid them £25 per annum to operate them — the amount of the rental. Mac Rich was paid a similar sum for the use of his home-built equipment. By mid-1938, sets were being used by F.W.G. Andersen, ARM (mobile); R.A. Vivian, RM Kerema; C.F. Cowley, ARM Baniara; G.W. Toogood, PO Tauri; P.W. Brewer, PO Goilala; S.G. Middleton, ARM Kokoda; J.B. McKenna, PO Tufi; A.A.C. Hall, ARM Losuia, and M.R. Horan, ARM Rigo. A set was in use at Lake Kutubu. Many were operated by companies and private individuals. Papuan Oil Development Co. Ltd. had eleven sets in use in the Western Division and The Island Exploration Co., nine. Oil Search Ltd. operated a set on the Era River, and others were in use by Sawmillers & Traders Ltd., Port Romilly; Tiveri Gold Dredging Co. on the Lakekamu; British New Guinea Development Co. at Obu; Anglo-Papuan Plantations Pty. Ltd. at Lolorua; Yodda Goldfields Ltd.; Robinson River Plantations Ltd.; Investors Ltd., the gold exploration company backing Jack Hides, late ARM, and David Lyall in their search for gold at the head of the Strickland River; Apinaipi Petroleum Co. Ltd., Apinaipi; the Methodist Overseas Mission at Salamo; D.G. Irvine, Giligili Plantation, Milne Bay; the Anglican Mission at Godura, and J.G. Nelsson at Kulumadau. The various Archbold Expeditions made extensive use of wireless communications.

The average operator of teleradio equipment had little technical knowledge, and AWA officers installed sets and gave instruction in their use whenever required. This often involved considerable time and trouble, as Clendyn Searle, AWA officer at the Port Moresby station, found in September-October 1936. He had two teleradio stations to install, one at Aroa Plantation at Obu, and the other in the mountainous hinterland, at the government station in the Goilala where R.G. Speedie was then ARM, assisted by Patrol Officer Allan Champion. Before he returned to Port Moresby five weeks later, Clen Searle had covered 400 miles, mostly on foot. The walk from the coast to the Goilala took ten days, burdened as the carriers were with the component parts of the set. Speedie had already erected one aerial mast; the other, 74 feet long, broke in half while it was being hauled into position by a hundred chanting Goilala tribesmen. It took three more days before a replacement mast was up. From Goilala, short-wave programmes from London, Berlin, Hong Kong and Australia were received with ease.

By the time war reached the Pacific, wireless communications had thus transformed life in the Territories, banishing forever the old isolation that had made life so hard for those on remote stations and plantations, and especially for white women. The intrepid British naturalist, Evelyn Cheesman, who travelled widely in the Pacific in the between-wars years, admirably described the plight of those women, and their menfolk, in her book *Who Stands Alone:*[10]

> I discovered very soon that some women were haunted by their isolation; they resented it fiercely, daily and hourly . . . the stark greyness of these lonely lives can scarcely be imagined except by those who have experienced it . . . hundreds of men and women endured this, in the days before radio and air communications were fully developed.

Radio eased the task of exploration in Papua in the 1930s. The last great exploratory journey to be made without the aid of aircraft and radio was the Strickland-Purari Patrol of 1935, led by J.G. Hides, ARM, and L.J. O'Malley, PO. In 1936, Ivan Champion, ARM, and C.J. Adamson, PO, made another patrol into the unknown region between the Strickland and the Purari Rivers, to check Hides' findings and map the terrain.

Champion was one of the very few 'outside men' in the Papuan (or, for that matter, the Mandated Territory) service who was skilled in celestial navigation and surveying. To fix his position in the bush on this big patrol, Champion had to obtain time signals, hitherto impossible during a long exploratory patrol. He took the problem to Ken Frank and Clen Searle, and they designed and constructed a small receiver, powered by dry batteries. The entire outfit weighed 64 pounds, and enabled Champion to receive time signals from Station NPG San Francisco through the American naval station in Hawaii during the eight months of the Bamu-Purari Patrol. On occasion, he was able to receive signals from the Eiffel Tower in Paris, and from Moscow. He used the receiver for only five minutes or so each day, and at the end of the patrol the batteries were still active.

10 Evelyn Cheeseman, *Who Stands Alone*, Geoffrey Bles, London, 1965.

Champion and Adamson visited a magnificent lake set in a heavily-timbered depression among harsh limestone mountains, and called Kutubu by the tribesmen who lived along its shores and on tiny islands in the centre. In 1937, Claude Champion, ARM, Ivan's brother, was instructed to lead a patrol to Lake Kutubu and beyond. His second-in-command was F.W.G. Andersen, PO. Andersen was an experienced radio operator; he had been a member of the Ward Williams expedition to the headwaters of the Fly River in 1935. Williams took with him an AWA pedal set, and Andersen was the operator at the base camp the expedition established at Kiunga, on the Upper Fly. The standard AWA pedal set was too bulky for a long foot journey in rugged country. Once again Ken Frank came to the rescue. He designed a short-wave set so compact that he was able to fit it into a standard 12-pound biscuit tin, which he painted bright red for ease of identification. To provide power, Frank constructed a pedal machine, some 2½ feet tall, which was turned by hand and coupled to a motor cycle generator and battery. It looked strange, but it worked.

'The Red Peril, we called it', Andersen recently recalled. 'Ken said we could use pig fat to grease the gears in the hand pedal machine. After midnight, just before we left Port Moresby on the patrol, Claude and I went to AWA to get the set. Ken picked it up from the bench and dropped it onto the concrete floor! We were pretty startled, but he just said, "Well, if there's anything loose it'll show now". Back on the bench, it worked like a charm. We kept it at Kutubu base, and it worked extremely well although it proved to be very hard work to generate the power. We had a line of very fit policemen, but each man could only last a minute, turning that machine'.

Champion and Andersen established a base at Lake Kutubu and walked on through unknown country almost to the Mandated Territory border, before turning back to the Lake. Later, Ivan Champion with Bill Adamson established a permanent government outpost there.

Lake Kutubu Police Camp was from the outset supplied by Junkers seaplanes of Guinea Airways Ltd., the first Papuan station to be wholly serviced by aeroplane. Champion, Adamson, A.T. Timperley, J.B.C. Bramell and K.C. Atkinson were stationed there at various times, almost constantly on patrol, until the outbreak of war forced the closure of the station in 1940. Wireless contact was maintained with Port Moresby for the whole of this period. The government purchased a Type B teleradio for Lake Kutubu. Petrol for the battery-charger was always a problem, for the station was supplied by seaplane only once a year. It was by far the most isolated outpost in Papua. Sometimes the officers at lonely Lake Kutubu used the radio to listen to broadcasts from Port Moresby, but not very often — petrol was too precious to be wasted on entertainment.

Before the Port Moresby broadcasting station was opened, radio enthusiasts in the territories were limited to stations in Australia (mainly Queensland) and other parts of the Pacific, and had to put up with static, fading signals, hum and noise that rapidly drove the less patient into outbursts of rage. In the early years of the 1930s few domestic radio receivers with sufficient performance to overcome these problems were readily available, but as the time went by, technical standards rapidly improved, and a greater range of receivers came onto the market.

In Australia, owners of receivers had to obtain a licence from the Postmaster General's Department, for which an annual fee was charged. Early 'listeners' as they were called, also obtained these licences, in Papua. Early licence-holders included C.R. Pinny; Brother George of the Yule Island mission; L.C. Cusack of Port Moresby; Revd M.A. Warren, Samarai; W. Frederick, Samarai; F.N. Faris, Samarai; Revd C.F. Rich, Fife Bay (father of Mac and Clem Rich); and E.A. James, editor of the *Papuan Courier*. Their licences were all issued in 1923-5.

In the early 1930s, the Commonwealth government began to demand licence fees from the increasing number of people tuning in to Australian stations without licences. E.A. James keenly resented having to pay for a licence in Papua where residents had no vote, and in 1934 he took on the Commonwealth government over the issue, claiming it had no right to collect fees that would go into consolidated revenue over which the people of Papua had no control. He urged his readers to follow his lead and refuse to obtain licences. 'It is an absurdity', he wrote. 'At no time of the day is reception good, and for perhaps three or four months of the year only can Australian stations be heard, and then imperfectly.' He challenged the government to take him to court.

In due course, a charge was laid against James in the Court of Petty Sessions in Port Moresby. The Magistrate found for James and awarded costs against the government. From that date — December, 1934 — to the present, no licence fees have been levied on radio listeners in Papua or the Mandated Territory.

The case attracted wide publicity throughout the Pacific and was an embarrassment to the government. Radio was no longer a novelty but a medium sweeping the world and with enormous implications for the future. Television was a long way off — although successful TV experiments had been made overseas as early as 1925 — but radio was an accomplished fact, and the public was demanding consideration.

Late in 1933, the staff of the Port Moresby Wireless Station began to experiment with a limited broadcasting service. Local and shipping news, overseas news by courtesy of the *Courier Mail* newspaper in Brisbane, and music, were transmitted using a low-powered set with a rating of 10 watts. The broadcasts were heard at Samarai, Hisiu, Kanosia and Otamatu in Papua, and by residents of Wau, Salamaua and Kieta in the Mandated Territory. They were picked up by the MV *Macdhui* at sea, and in Sydney. It was a limited experiment, but it proved the practicability of a broadcasting service from Port Moresby, and was exceedingly popular with listeners. AWA therefore decided to open a permanent station.

On 25 October 1935, Station 4PM Port Moresby, under the management of C.F. Bale, commenced transmissions. It was the first broadcasting station in the South Pacific. It operated on 100 watts, on a wavelength of 221 metres, and was thus limited in range, but the programmes provided, for two hours daily, six days per week, were enthusiastically received.

Opening the station, Sir Hubert Murray said to a large gathering of Port Moresby residents:

We shall all benefit by this service, but, in particular, it will be a priceless blessing to those who hold the lonely outposts of these territories, the planters, miners and others, who are far removed from the centres of settlement. It is a lonely and often a monotonous life that these pioneers lead, and I am glad to think that, through the establishment of this service, they will feel less cut off from civilization, and that they are still part of the great world beyond the limits of Papua and New Guinea.

The residents of the Mandated Territory were quick to ask for a similar broadcasting station, but war was to engulf the Pacific before AWA could act.

CHAPTER SIX

THE MANDATED TERRITORY

The civil administration of the Mandated Territory of New Guinea began in May 1921, and ended with the Japanese invasion in February 1942. Born in war and dying in war, it was administered throughout the two decades of its existence by military men: Brigadier-General E.A. Wisdom from May 1921 to June 1933; Brigadier-General T. Griffiths from June 1933 to September 1934, and finally by another Brigadier-General, Sir Walter McNicoll. For the whole of these two decades, the Mandated Territory and Papua had two entirely separate administrations with only limited formal contact: two Public Services, two sets of laws, two administrative philosophies, a state of affairs that was surely extraordinary, given the small population and modest economy of the metropolitan power, Australia, and the homogeneous nature of the societies being administered. Amalgamation of Papua and the Mandated Territory was indeed proposed in 1938, but it was firmly opposed in both Territories, and came to nothing.

Compared with Papua, New Guinea was a violent territory, particularly in the 1930s when the great grassed valleys of the Highlands were being explored. Much blood was shed; patrol officers, police, and a number of prospectors and recruiters fell to spears and arrows, and two missionaries were killed in the Highlands. Many other attacks were beaten off, and it will never be known how many New Guinea tribesmen were killed by rifle fire.

There were many reasons for the differing state of affairs in Papua and the Mandated Territory. For almost the whole of those two decades, until his death in February 1940, Papua was governed by the autocratic Sir Hubert Murray, and his policy of 'peaceful penetration' was well established. There was not this continuity of direction in the Mandated Territory, where the field service lacked the traditions of its Papuan counterpart, forty years older. The Mandated Territory was also much bigger, and the tribes of the interior far larger than those of Papua, and perhaps more warlike.

Papua was explored, in the main, by the field officers of the government as part of their ordinary duty, but much of the exploration of the Mandated Territory was done by prospectors, looking for gold. The Great Depression of the 1930s which hit Papua so hard had a lesser effect on the Mandated Territory, and it was the discovery of the Morobe gold-field that made the difference.

The territory that Brigadier-General Wisdom and his administration took over in May 1921, was little known. The Germans had concentrated their efforts on the coast, where their plantations were situated. The Admiralty Islands, New Britain, New Ireland and Bougainville, all contained considerable unexplored areas, and apart from the territory penetrated by the small number of scientific expeditions sent by the Germans into the interior, the mainland, with its huge hinterland population, was unknown. The 1921-2 *Annual Report* to the League of Nations reads:

> Scarcely anywhere in the Territory is there a plantation or a Government post or a mission station more than ten miles from the ocean; the only exceptions are a post on the lower reaches of the Sepik, and a few mission stations in the Gazelle Peninsula and in the Huon Peninsula in North-East New Guinea.

At the beginning of civil administration, the Mandated Territory was divided into ten administrative districts, each under the control of a District Officer; Aitape (then spelled Eitape), Morobe, Madang, Rabaul, Gasmata (Gasmatta), Talasea, Kavieng (Kawieng), Namatanai, Manus and Kieta. The number of districts was reduced in 1932 to seven: Sepik, Madang, Morobe, New Britain, New Ireland, Manus and Kieta.

The military administration had been organized into eleven departments, the Post Office Department being a sub-department of Customs. Soon after civil administration began, this number was reduced to seven: Government Secretary; Treasury; Native Affairs; Public Health; Customs and Shipping; Lands, Mines, Surveys and Forests; Agriculture. Posts and Telephones was a section of Customs and Shipping until 1923, when it was transferred to the Treasury.

The District Officers, Deputy District Officers (who became Assistant District Officers in June 1926) and Patrol Officers of the Mandated Territory service were located within the Department of the Government Secretary until 1932, when a separate field department was established, District Services and Native Affairs (DDS and NA). This was a much bigger organization than the equivalent Magisterial Branch of the Government Secretary's Department in Papua and employed more officers, but it had the same overall responsibility for local administration in the districts. Many of the departments were not represented at the local level, and the officers of DDS and NA then acted as their agents, as was the case in Papua.

The Postal Services Branch (which included the Telephone Section) was very small. As in Papua, the Treasurer was nominally the Chief Postmaster. The Rabaul Postmaster was the senior professional, with an Assistant Postmaster from 1928. Included in the Postal Services branch was a Foreman (Telephone and Lines) and up to three mechanics. Some appointments of Wireless Officers were made in the late 1930s. Treasury officers commonly relieved the Postmaster and his Assistant at Rabaul during their periods of leave, and when the Morobe gold-fields began to boom, Treasury men acted as Postmasters at the busy offices at Wau and Bulolo. Until 1929, the Postal Services Branch was housed in the old German building, but in that year the southern wing of the Treasury building was remodelled and became the new postal headquarters. In 1934, the Public Works Department built a tower over the Post Office, capped with a high-pitched red-tiled roof and equipped with an imposing clock.

The extent of the dependence of Postal Services upon DDS and NA officers may be gauged by the number of post offices throughout the Mandated Territory. In November 1922, these were located at Rabaul, Kokopo, Madang, Kavieng, Manus, Kieta, Aitape, Gasmata, Morobe, Talasea and Namatanai, all official post offices; also at Bitapaka, Maron, Mokareng, Witu and Finschhafen, unofficial offices. As the Mandated Territory was explored and developed, new government stations were established, most of them with post offices. Sohano and Ambunt post offices were opened in 1925, and others quickly followed. Salamaua (September 1927); Edie Creek (September 1928); Wau (January 1930); Wewak (late 1928); Bulolo (March 1932); Lae (March 1932); Angoram (April 1934, replacing Marienberg which had opened in 1927); Maprik (late 1939) and Bulwa (May 1941). Most were operated by DDS and NA staff.

The first permanent postmaster was T.G. Grant, a Commonwealth officer, appointed to Rabaul on 31 August 1922. He established the postal service on a sound footing before returning to Australia in July 1924. His replacement, Eric Kingsley Abraham, was an ex-Treasury clerk; he served as Postmaster until August 1935. Known throughout the Mandated Territory as 'Abie', he was universally liked by the public and by his staff, mostly New Guineans. Upon the departure of 'Abie', A.M. Ryan became Postmaster, serving until 1940, when he was replaced by the last Postmaster, Rabaul, J.W. Smith. Officers who served at various times as Assistant Postmaster included R.L. Gane, C.H.J. Williams and C.S.P. Mater.

As previously mentioned the economy of the Mandated Territory soon eclipsed that of Papua, although the early years of civil administration were difficult, financially. The economy, firmly based on copra, suffered heavily under the restrictions of the Navigation Act and the loss of the experienced German planters forced to return to Germany after the expropriation of their properties was quickly felt. Many of the Australians who took over ex-German properties knew nothing of plantation management, and production slumped drastically. Determined efforts were made by the Department of Agriculture to retrieve the situation, with considerable success. New crops were introduced — coffee, oil palms, cotton — but copra, with gold, was the mainstay of the Mandated Territory economy. Copra production rose from 23 735 tons in 1921 to almost 74 000 tons in 1939. Copra was a bulky crop, marketed mainly in Europe, the United States and Australia, and its export required a steady flow of overseas shipping, which in turn ensured a good mail service. Until the Navigation Act was lifted, Burns Philp & Co. had a near-monopoly of the Australian business, and as previously detailed, the company never lost its pre-eminent position as the official mail carrier for the Pacific Mail service, which carried an annual subsidy of £45 000 by 1940.

The BP fleet in 1926 consisted of the *Malabar, Marella, Montoro, Morinda, Mataram, Marsina, Melusia, Makombo* and *Maiwara*, and it grew during the 1930s. The MV *Malaita* came into service late in 1933 and was employed on the Solomons run, with Rabaul as her terminal port. *Macdhui* was launched in 1930 and the pride of the BP line, the fast, modern, twin-screw motor vessel *Bulolo*, of 6 267 gross tons and a passenger capacity of 239, made her first voyage to Papua and the Mandated Territory in December 1938.

From 1925 onwards, the company faced opposition from overseas ships, mainly cargo liners and copra carriers. Bank Line vessels were frequent visitors — the *Larchbank, Springbank* and *Myrtlebank* were regularly seen in Territory waters, fine ships of around 6 500 tons engaged in charter work for the Expropriation Board, carrying bulk copra to Europe. The ex-German cargo steamer the *Calulu* ran between Australia, the Mandated Territory and the East, and carried mails. Hain and Clan Line ships began to call at Rabaul, and steamers like the *Poonbar* and *Teneriffa* for a time made voyages. The Japanese NYK Line also entered the Mandated Territory trade. The serious competition, however, came from the old-established shipping companies. KPM — the Royal Dutch Packet Company — was early on the scene, employing at first the steamer *Le Maire* on a run between Batavia and Rabaul via Papuan and New Caledonian ports, and then, in 1932, the *Van Rees*, a smart little ship of 1 846 tons, with accommodation for 65 passengers, which commenced bi-monthly sailings from Rabaul to Sydney via Port Vila and Noumea. The saloon fare, Rabaul-Sydney, was £22. In 1937, the modern, 4 000-ton *Maetsuycker* came into service, offering a twenty per cent fare reduction to government officers and their families travelling on leave, but only 10 per cent to missionaries.

Burns Philp could live with KPM, but Norddeutscher Lloyd was another matter. Early in 1929 NDL announced its intention of re-entering the Mandated Territory trade, initially with a single ship, the *Bremerhaven*, carrying copra at 65 shillings per ton between Rabaul and Hong Kong. Immediately three Australian companies, who were charging £6 per ton (Burns Philp & Co., W.R. Carpenter & Co., and Dalgety & Co.) protested to the Minister for Home and Territories, C.W. Marr, asking him to reintroduce certain clauses of the Navigation Act. This attempt to block NDL failed. The *Bremerhaven* made her first run to Rabaul in May 1929. A new NDL vessel, *Friderun*, came into service at the end of 1932, and a letter appeared in the *Sydney Morning Herald* complaining of the inroads being made by NDL ships, employing native crews at 'starvation wages', into the New Guinea and Solomons trade. But NDL persisted, in 1934 announcing a Sydney-Hong Kong monthly service to take in Salamaua, Rabaul, Sandakan and Manila, using the motor vessels *Neptun* and *Merkur*. This was more than Burns Philp could tolerate. Negotiations began, and in December BP purchased the two ships from NDL. The *Neptun* was renamed *Neptuna*, a break from the BP tradition of names beginning with the letter 'M', and kept on the Hong Kong run until the outbreak of war. The *Merkur* was placed on the Sydney-Singapore route. NDL continued to operate its South Sea Service to Hong Kong via ports in New Guinea and the Solomons, using the *Bremerhaven* and the *Friderun*.

Burns Philp & Co. were also agents for the Eastern and Australian Steamships Company. The E. and A. Line for most of the between-wars years employed the steamers *Nellore*, *Tanda* and *Nankin*, each of 7 000 tons, on scheduled voyages between Australia and the East, calling at Rabaul and later Salamaua. The company offered a three-month round trip from Rabaul to Manila, China, Japan, Australia and return for a first-class fare of £90, all found.

W.R. Carpenter & Co., BP's principal competitors in the Mandated Territory, were also substantial shipowners. From 1934 onwards, the old Motorships *Salamaua*, 9 000 tons, and *Rabaul*, 9 000 tons, ran between the Mandated Territory and England; the steamer *Suva* was later added to the fleet.

Rabaul was always the principal port for overseas shipping, although Madang, with its fine harbour, was frequently visited. With the discovery of gold at Edie Creek, and the subsequent decision to develop the dredging leases of the Bulolo Valley using giant, prefabricated dredges, Salamaua and Lae became increasingly important ports. Many of the massive steel dredge sections were delivered by the American motor vessel *Carisso*, the first overseas ship to call at Lae. Motorships of the Norwegian Wilhelmsen Line — *Templar*, *Tudor*, *Temeraire* and *Thermopylae* — began to call at Lae, and two ships of the South African Railway Shipping Line — the *Erica* and *Dahlia* — frequently visited Salamaua and other ports with cargoes of rice from Burma. Enormous quantities of petrol and diesel fuel were consumed on the gold-field, and much of it was carried in the old steamer *Pinna*, which made bi-monthly voyages between the Mandated Territory and Borneo.

Many other foreign vessels traded into Mandated Territory ports, but it was the scheduled lines that were the most important, carrying most of the freight, passengers and mails. Even after the introduction of an air mail service to Australia, ships remained the most significant carriers of bulk mails, for the aéroplanes of the day were limited in their carrying capacity.

Distribution of cargo and mails within the Mandated Territory remained, as always, greatly dependent upon small ships, of which there was an infinite variety, although the Pacific Mail subsidized ships of Burns Philp played a vital part. As mentioned in Chapter 5, the Mandated Territory was served by the two coal-burners *Montoro* (4 057 tons) and *Marsina* (1 932 tons) until 1931, when the smaller ship was replaced by the new *Macdhui*. The *Montoro* and *Marsina* provided a three-weekly service, each ship taking six weeks for the round voyage, via ports. On a typical voyage in 1927, the *Montoro* took on eight small copra boats at Rabaul, sixty native cargo handlers and a Customs Officer, and sailed to Kavieng, where cargo, passengers and mails were discharged and copra loaded. She then went to Manus, to service Lombrum and Lorengau, and to Wewak and the offshore island plantations of Tumleo and Seleo. Here, as at other localities lacking facilities, the copra boats were used to discharge and load cargo; lashed together in pairs and decked with hatch covers, the floating platforms thus formed were used as lighters, towed to and from the shore by the ship's launch. The next port of call was Madang, then Alexishafen, Singaua Plantation near Lae, Salamaua and back to Rabaul, stopping at copra plantations along the south coast of New Britain en route. At each port and plantation, mails were picked up and delivered.

Burns Philp also operated an inter-island service, using smaller vessels. The *Maiwara*, of 606 tons, went into service in May 1926. A coal-burner, with five two-berth cabins on deck, she was typical of the little steamers that spent their days running along the coastline of the mainland, and to New Britain, New Ireland, the Admiralties and the Solomons. The *Mirani* was another BP inter-island steamer. These vessels were replaced in 1937 by a new motorship of 689 tons, the *Muliama*. The *Lakatoi* joined the fleet in 1938.

Another well-known small motor vessel was the *Ralum*, owned by the Melanesia Company. She had accommodation for twelve passengers and could carry 7 000 bags of copra. W.R. Carpenter & Co. had a number of small ships in service in New Guinea waters in the 1920s and 1930s — the steamer *Durour*, the MV *Ballangot*, the *John Bolton*, *Duranbah*, *Desikoko* and the *Mako*.

The Christian missions also maintained many vessels that regularly carried mails, mostly auxiliary-engined schooners of substantial size. The Lutheran mission schooner, *Bavaria*, was a familiar sight along the north coast; the Seventh-Day Adventists had the *Melanesia* and the *Veilomani*, the Roman Catholics the *Stella Maris* and the *Gabriel*, and the Melanesia mission the big *Southern Cross*. And there were many others.

A host of privately-owned auxiliary schooners, ketches and cutters sailed the waters of the Mandated Territory, carrying odds and ends of cargo, copra, labourers for the plantations and gold-fields and, from time to time, mails. Some were in poor repair, and losses were frequent. The ketch *Wattle* went down off Salamaua in September 1928, with the loss of fourteen lives and a year later the *Talasea* was also lost. 'At the rate schooners are piling up they will soon be a rare sight in these waters', commented the *Rabaul Times*, the newspaper founded by Harry Hamilton in April 1925.

Small sailing vessels were an uncomfortable means of travel in the tropics. Margaret Matches, an American girl, made a voyage out of Rabaul in the 20-ton ketch *Bonta*, in 1928. She wrote:[1]

> There was a tiny poopdeck, just large enough for a coil of rope and myself on a small wicker stool, if I dangled my feet over the side. Three perpendicular steps led down to an infinitesimal chartroom, the whole thing about eight feet square, with a bunk along either wall, a chart table, and a chest of drawers ... I smelled the rank odour of oil, petrol, and stale copra ... roaches swarmed too thick to make the thought of food enticing.

But these ships were indispensable. 'These small ships are the "listening posts" of the Territory', wrote the editor of the *Rabaul Times* in January 1934. 'They poke their iron noses into all sorts of out-of-the-way places; they are the only means of communication between isolated plantation men and the outside. They are the medium through which lonely men are able to adjust their mental equilibrium'.

The largest fleet of small ships in the Mandated Territory was that of the Administration. For a short time after civil administration began, the government

---

1 Margaret Matches, *Savage Paradise*, Century, New York, 1930.

continued the service between Rabaul and the principal ports and settlements of the Territory begun during the war, to supplement the Burns Philp & Co. mail ships. The steamers they used were the ex-Norddeutscher Lloyd and New Guinea Company vessels the *Sumatra*, the *Siar*, the *Meklong*, the *Madang* and the *Nusa*, ranging in size from 15 to 200 tons. The earnings of these steamers in 1921 from fares and freights were £36 599, but they cost £37 777 to operate. In 1923, the *Sumatra* was lost at sea with all hands. By this time the *Siar* and the *Madang* were in need of expensive overhaul and it was decided to dispose of them. The SS *Tintenbar* was chartered as a replacement, but in April 1924, this steamer piled up on a reef. These attempts to operate a shipping service had attracted so much public criticism that the government now quietly withdrew from commercial shipping, and left the field entirely to private enterprise. The government service, however, had been a real boon to residents of the many isolated settlements of the Mandated Territory.

G.W.L. Townsend, who went to the Mandated Territory in 1921 as a Patrol Officer, made a voyage on the *Meklong* to Aitape in December, and discovered how mails were handled on outstations. He described the trip in his book, *District Officer*.[2] The ship had a white captain, mate, engineer and supercargo, Chinese in the engine room, a Malay bosun and a New Guinean crew — a typical complement for an inter-island steamer in those days. Upon anchoring in Aitape Bay, a surf boat rowed by Manus policemen went out through the waves to the ship and took aboard Townsend and three big canvas bags of mail. It was a wild, wet ride back to shore, where the bags were dumped before one Ossie Egan,[3] radio operator, who was sitting on a tin beneath a *lau-lau* tree. 'We usually tip all the mail out on the grass here', said Egan. 'The salt water always gets into the bags coming ashore, and makes a mess of things'. Two constables spread the soaked letters in the sun to dry, and they were then carried up to the government station, to the district office. Townsend wrote:

> I went up the steps and made my initial acquaintance with a very extraordinary man, Noel Tracey Collins [DDS and NA clerk]. He was lying back in a canvas chair, dressed in pyjamas and wearing Chinese sandals on his feet. 'Give me a hand with this mail, will you?' he asked. 'Chuck all the Mission and the Expro Board stuff into separate piles, don't sort them any further. The Chinese go together, one of *them* can sort them out. Official stuff over here . . . better have a drink while you work'. The mail on the floor was finally sorted with the aid of a second drink and all this time runners from the RC mission, the Expro Board offices and others had been waiting down at the office. Collins now told a constable to bring them up, and they received their packets at the steps.

After withdrawing from commercial shipping, the Mandated Territory government, like its Papuan counterpart, continued to operate small ships for administrative purposes. Eventually all the coastal and river stations were equipped with auxiliary-engined sailing craft, invariably referred to as 'schooners' despite the fact that many

---

2 Townsend, 1968.

3 Egan was soon afterwards appointed Radio Operator of the SS *Sumatra*, and lost his life with all others on board when the ship went down in 1923.

were ketch-rigged. They all carried mails. The schooners *Lady Betty* and *Wandera* were acquired in 1924, and two others, the *Eros* and the *Hermes* — 60-footers built to the order of the Administration in Australia — arrived in 1928. The *Rabaul Times* was just as critical of alleged government excesses as were the Papuan newspapers. 'White elephants!' snorted the editor. 'An unnecessarily heavy burden on the taxpayers!' The two new schooners both met violent ends. All on board the *Wandera* were saved when she struck a reef, but three whites and fourteen New Guineans were on board the *Hermes* when he disappeared without trace. These two craft were replaced in 1937 by a pair of fine 70-footers, the *Sirius* and the *Leander*. Other well-known administration vessels were the launch *Osprey*, used on the Sepik, and the *Thetis*, the *Rabaul*, the *Kaewieng*, the *Siassi*, the *Dorunda*, the *Poseidon* and the *Nereus*.

For a few years, the Administrator of the Mandated Territory enjoyed the services of an official yacht, the steamer *Franklin*, of 288 tons. Originally a naval tender at the Jervis Bay Naval College, the *Franklin* was about thirty years old when she was taken over by the Administration in December 1924. It cost over £11 000 to recondition and deliver her. Of deep draft and expensive to operate, she was as unsuitable for her purpose as had been the old *Merrie England*, and she attracted just as much public scorn. 'The most colossal white elephant ever foisted onto a long suffering public!' shrilled the *Rabaul Times*. In 1931, the yacht was withdrawn from commission, and in 1932 she was sold. She was not replaced; the Administrator was obliged to use other ships of the government fleet — often the *Dorunda* — for his official inspections.

Constables of the New Guinea Police Force were commonly employed for the local delivery of mails on the outstations of the Mandated Territory. For many years, there was a weekly runner service between Aitape and Wewak. Malutu Patrol post in the interior of New Britain received mail by police runner from Talasea. Vanimo got its mails from Aitape by runner, and when Kobakiki Base camp was established in May 1937, a runner service was maintained with Otibanda, which in turn received mails from the post office at Bulolo. Mails were delivered to the new Highlands stations in the 1930s by air, and then distributed by police runner to outlying mission stations and prospectors' camps. The Sepik River base camps received mails by launch and runner.

When district vessels were laid up for maintenance, or ran onto reefs, the police runners were always there to provide an emergency mail service. G.W.L. Townsend was transferred to the newly-opened station of Ambunti in 1924, and this became the headquarters of the Sepik District that September. It was supplied by the ketch *Aloha* from Aitape. One day the *Aloha* struck a reef, and was taken to Madang to be slipped. 'The first I knew of the mishap', he wrote, 'was when two of my police arrived at Ambunti with a couple of sacks of mail. The mail had come off the ship at Aitape two weeks previously and it had taken a week for it to be carried the 200 miles along the beach to the mouth of the River, and another week to come the 200 miles upstream'. When Townsend was transferred to Kavieng in 1927, the radio message advising him of the move had to be carried the 400 miles from Aitape by canoe and police runner, for this was before the introduction of wireless communications with the more remote stations.

A.J. Marshall was at Aitape in 1936, awaiting the arrival from Wewak of the BP steamer *Montoro*. He wrote in his book *The Men and Birds of Paradise*:[4]

> Four days before the Sydney steamer was due to leave Wewak a police runner straggled in with a message that *Maiwara* was being overhauled in Rabaul, and mightn't be along for weeks! All our swear words had been exhausted long before this: now we simply piled the gear into the canoes ... and put out to sea, under great square sails of strapped patches of fibre, the 30-foot masts creaking and straining in the wind ... we were OHMS, for one of our canoes carried the Aitape mails — several bulky bags full.

Despite the best efforts of the postal authorities and the schoonermasters, delays in the deliveries of mails were frequent, and attracted much criticism from the public. A letter in the *Rabaul Times* in April 1928 told a typical tale. 'Schooners from Rabaul came right to Namatanai and the West Coast without even bringing news of where the mail was ... it arrived a month after leaving Rabaul, after being sent on a grand tour of the Territory on a copra barge, 23 days out from Rabaul before reaching Namatanai!' Residents of Bougainville continually asked for a better service. 'Poor gorforsaken Aitape!' moaned a correspondent in March 1934. 'The December *Mirani* with Xmas cheer and mail on board was sent from Wewak to the Western Isles first ... those nitwits at Rabaul!' 'Manus is fast slipping away into complete obscurity and isolation', wailed another, 'but then a miracle came to pass, a ship from Rabaul, and so we received mail posted down South months and months ago'. 'To be without a mail or any reliable news from the outside world for over seven weeks is the latest experience of Finschhafen', another resident wrote in February 1934, 'and it doesn't claim to be an out-of-the-way place, either, less than 60 miles from Salamaua'. And so it went on.

The one sure guarantee of a swift mail delivery service in the Mandated Territory in the 1930s was the presence nearby of an aerodrome or landing ground. The breed of aviators who pioneered the aerial transportation industry in the Mandated Territory was prepared to land its stout little biplanes under conditions that would horrify the pilots of a later, more technically advanced day.

The air age in New Guinea really began with the discovery of gold at Edie Creek by the prospectors Bill Royal and Dick Glasson, in January 1926. From this discovery flowed the spectacular development of the Morobe gold-field, culminating in the formation of Bulolo Gold Dredging Ltd. to exploit the rich dredging flats of the Bulolo Valley, using giant prefabricated dredges flown in from the coast in the Junkers tri-motor G/31 freighters operated by Guinea Airways Ltd. Prospectors searching for another Edie Creek, another Bulolo Valley, penetrated the high-grassed valleys of the Central Highlands and encountered their huge populations of virile, warlike tribes-men whose very existence had until then been unsuspected. Every government, mission and mining settlement in the Highlands was there by courtesy of the aero-plane, for there was no road link with the coast — as in Papua, there were few vehicular

---

4 A.J. Marshall, *The Men and Birds of Paradise: Journeys through Equatorial New Guinea*, Heinemann, London, 1938.

roads in the Mandated Territory, a claimed total of 799 miles in 1941, much of it of minimal standard.

The story of the development of aerial transportation on the Morobe gold-field is well known. The field began when William 'Shark-Eye' Park found gold at Koranga Creek, near its junction with the Bulolo River in 1922. A 'rush' followed which swelled into a veritable avalanche after Royal and Glasson made their fabulous strike at Edie Creek, another tributary of the Bulolo. One of the earliest men on the field was C.J. Levien, something of a visionary but with the practical qualities of a man of action. The field was supplied from the coastal port of Salamaua, a terrible eight to ten day journey for the thousands of carriers who toiled to keep the field alive. Levien quickly realized that its future was limited unless the transportation problem could be solved. He pinned his faith on the aeroplane, proof of his vision, for the machine was then a cranky, uncertain thing. He persuaded the pioneer goldmining company, Guinea Gold No Liability, to purchase an aeroplane, a De Havilland DH37 bi-plane fitted with a Rolls-Royce Falcon engine of 275 h.p., with a payload of only 600 pounds. A.E. 'Pard' Mustar was engaged as pilot, and A.W.D. Mullins as engineer. From this tentative beginning grew Guinea Airways Ltd., one of the most successful airline companies in aviation history, with its fleet of then-advanced aircraft including the work-horse, all-metal Junkers single- and tri-motor freighters and the Ford tri-motors. Second into the aviation field was that tough little dare-devil, Ray Parer. A great many individuals and companies followed, pilots such as Les Holden, Lionel Shoppee, Les Ross, Kevin Parer, H.D.L. McGilvrey, Les Shaw, W.E. Gardiner, Charles Pratt, P.H. Moody, Frank Drayton, Les Trist, Bill Wiltshire, Jerry Pentland, Orm Denny, Ian Grabowsky, George Mendham, Tommy O'Dea, R.O. Mant, and so many others, and companies such as Holden's Air Transport, Pacific Aerial Transport, W.R. Carpenter and Stephens Aviation. The most serious challenger of the premier company, Guinea Airways, was W.R. Carpenter & Co., which inaugurated the Australia–New Guinea Air Mail Service in May 1938.

It is now history that the town of Bulolo was the first in the world to owe its existence and growth solely to the aeroplane. In all, eight mighty dredges were flown from Lae, on the coast, to the gold-fields in the hinterland, by Guinea Airways Junkers, from 1930 to 1939, and in the process world aerial transportation records were shattered, time and again.

The first airmail contract to be awarded anywhere in Papua or the Mandated Territory was granted to Guinea Airways by the Administration in June 1927. It was for a period of twelve months and provided for the payment of two pence per letter, and the ordinary air cargo rate for other mail matter, for mails to and from the field from points outside. Internal mails, between Lae, Salamaua, and Wau and Bulolo, were not included in the agreement, but were in fact carried free of charge for many years. On 1 March 1928, a mail and general carriage contract was granted to Guinea Airways, to run for three years. Under it, first class mails were carried for two shillings and eight pence per pound, and other classes for nine pence. In March 1931, the contract was extended for a further twelve months, at one shilling and six pence per pound first class, and six pence for other classes, a reflection of the increasing efficiency of aerial transport as better aeroplanes were introduced. The contract applied to overseas mails only; local mail was still carried, free, by the air transport operators. Holden's Air Transport Service and Pacific Aerial Transport Company then took the Administration business from Guinea Airways. The Pacific Aerial Transport tender price was a flat four pence per pound for all classes of mails, a level that Guinea Airways considered unrealistic. Mandated Airlines Ltd. (a W.R. Carpenter company) and Stephens Aviation then secured the major contracts until March 1939, when Guinea Airways again was successful, at the expense of Stephens.

By 1940, a network of aerodromes and landing fields existed throughout the Mandated Territory. Many were no more than emergency landing grounds; many were temporary, hastily cleared, often unnamed and quickly forgotten. Some are still in use today. It is impossible to give a full listing, but the more important included: Lae, Wau and Bulolo (the major aerodromes), Salamaua, Slate Creek, Rabaul, But, Chimbu, Roamer, Kaiapit, Nadzab, Zenag, Sangan, Mogei, Wahgi, Upper Watut, Upper Ramu, Telefomin, Aiyura, Asaro, Bena Bena, Kainantu, Finintegu, Bulwa, Heldsbach, Wabag, Alexishafen, Juni, Keluwere, Kerowagi, Kudjuru, Kundiawa, Sunshine, Menyamya, Madang, Malahang, Mount Hagen, Otibanda, Garaina, Roaring Creek, Wampit, Wewak, Ogelbeng. Asaroka, Boana, Bukaua, Ono, Sandy Creek, Surprise Creek, Waria, Wom, Tring, Nago and Maprik. Because of the aeroplane, men living in the most remote corners of the land could expect to receive regular deliveries of supplies and mails. Where the landing-grounds were too marginal for the bigger aircraft, there was no shortage of small machines, principally De Havilland Moths.

The March 1939 contract, shared by Guinea Airways and Mandated Airlines, was a tightly-scheduled agreement, specifying the rate to be paid by the Administration for the aerial conveyance of mails between named aerodromes. The rate per pound, for all categories of mail, varied from one penny between Salamaua and Lae, to two-and-a-quarter pence between Salamaua and Surprise Creek. The Bulolo–Wau rate was three-quarters of a penny. Wau to Port Moresby was eleven pence; Madang–Wewak ten pence; Wewak–Salamaua one shilling and eight pence; Madang–Mount Hagen eight pence; Upper Ramu–Madang two-and-a-quarter pence and Madang–Aiyura, four-and-a-half pence. Rates for other airstrips varied between these figures.

The changing contract rates for the aerial carriage of mails had their effect on the postage rates paid by the public. There was initially a surcharge on mails delivered and dispatched by air. This was progressively reduced, and in 1934 abolished within the Mandated Territory, except in the case of parcels mail. As postage rates were varied over the years by the Postmaster-General's Department in Australia, they were similarly varied in Papua and the Mandated Territory.

As mentioned in Chapter 5, a scheduled airmail service between Australia and the two Territories did not begin until May 1938. In the early 1930s, politicians and planners in Australia were preoccupied with the proposed Empire Air Service, the great aerial link between Great Britain and her far-flung Dominions. In 1935, it became commercially possible, with the development of the immortal Short 'C' Class Empire Flying Boats. Imperial Airways Ltd announced the construction of a fleet of twenty-eight of the advanced Empire machines, each with four Bristol Pegasus engines of 910 h.p., seating for 28 passengers and a mail and freight capacity of 2 tons. The first of the 'C' boats, *Canopus*, made her maiden flight in July 1936, and by 1938, the Empire Air Service had been extended, in stages, to South Africa, India, Malaya and Australia. An airmail service between Australia and the Territories of Papua and New Guinea would virtually become an extension of the great Empire Service.

After some initial disputes over the choice of a route, the Commonwealth government called tenders in January 1937. Guinea Airways was a keen contender, and made a number of proving flights over the route in a fast twin-engined Lockheed Electra airliner. Strangely, requests by the company to be allowed to carry mails on these flights were refused.[5] W.R. Carpenter & Co. announced its intention to use four-engined De Havilland DH86 bi-plane airliners on the service, if they were successful in their tender. To the surprise of many industry observers, they were. A new company, W.R. Carpenter Airlines, was formed to operate the service. The DH86 was a strange choice for a long-distance aerial route in 1938, when fast, technically superior, all-metal American aircraft such as the Lockheed Electra, Boeing 247 and Douglas DC2 were proven, and available. The De Havilland was really a survivor from the early days of flying; a fabric-covered, strut-braced, fixed-undercarriage, slow aeroplane with — according to its pilots — a 'built-in headwind'. It could carry only ten passengers, two pilots and a limited quantity of mails and freight.

Before the service could be inaugurated, a great deal of preparatory work had to be completed. The airliners were to be equipped with AWA radio and direction-finding gear, and the Department of Defence established radio-finding stations at Cooktown, Port Moresby, Salamaua and Rabaul equipped with Bellini–Tosca instruments. A modern meteorological station was provided at Port Moresby by the Commonwealth Meteorological Department. The schedule called for a DH86 to leave Sydney every Tuesday at 7 a.m., with passengers, mails and freight, and thence to Brisbane, Rockhampton, Townsville, Cairns, Cooktown, Port Moresby, Salamaua and Rabaul, the flight taking 2½ days. The return flight, by the same route, was commenced on Friday.

To prove the service, a number of survey flights were made over the whole route by the three DH86 airliners purchased by Carpenters, christened the *Carmania*, the *Caronia* and *Carinthia*. Keen interest in the forthcoming Australia–New Guinea Air Mail Service was displayed by the general public and certainly by philatelists, but the Postmaster General's Department steadfastly refused to allow mails to be carried on the survey flights. The editor of the *Papuan Courier* wrote in April 1938:

> If the airliners are running to schedule, and we understand they are, it is hard to understand why mails cannot be put aboard them. The postal authorities may say that these 'survey' flights cannot be trusted with valuable mails, but that argument falls flat when it is discovered that the civil aviation authorities permit passengers to be carried. We do not know it as a fact, but we have every reason to believe the truth of the matter is that the stamp dealers desire to post many thousands of air mail covers

---

5 A special Melbourne Cup return flight was made from Wau in the Electra in November 1930, carrying mail at the rate of eight pence per half ounce.

endorsed as being dispatched on the 'inaugural flight' of the new service, and therefore until such time as these people are ready to mail their covers no one else may use the service for mails, otherwise it may take away the value of these inaugural covers. If that is the true state of affairs, it appears to us a sad commentary on the conduct of our postal services.

True or not, the accusation attracted no official comment. When the DH86 airliner the *Carmania* took off from Sydney's Mascot aerodrome on 30 May to inaugurate the service, there were only five passengers on board — including the Minister for External Affairs, W.M. Hughes — besides Captain R.O. Mant and First Officer K.G. Jackson, because of the huge volume of mails carried, some 25 000 letters, most of them self-addressed return covers posted by philatelists. Special arrangements had been made by the Postmaster General's Department to cope with the anticipated demand, as had been done for the airmail flight of the *Faith in Australia*, in July 1934. Twelve bags of mail were finally delivered at Rabaul by the *Carmania*; five from Sydney, one from Brisbane, one from Rockhampton, two from Townsville, one from Port Moresby and two from Salamaua.

Philatelic interest in such things as first flights — and, indeed, in the various stamp issues of Papua and the Mandated Territory — was to be expected, and keen philatelists seldom missed a chance to add to their collections. On 6 June 1938, the famous American mammalogist and explorer, Richard Archbold, left Hawaii in his Catalina flying boat, *Guba 2*, bound for Hollandia in Dutch New Guinea, via Wake Island. He was about to launch the third great Archbold Expedition, and as with the previous two, both also in Papua, world interest was aroused. He received requests from philatelists in many countries begging him to carry 'first flight' covers, for this was the first flight from Hawaii to New Guinea. Archbold, a serious scientist, refused all approaches, but his pilot, the veteran Russell Rogers, was, just before take-off, persuaded by Honolulu philatelists to take with him twenty self-addressed covers, each bearing a two cent United States stamp and endorsed 'First Flight, Hawaii to New Guinea. Archbold Expedition Flying Boat *Guba*, June 1938'. The Honolulu postmaster had somehow been prevailed upon to postmark each cover, 'Honolulu, 1 p.m., June 6 1938'. The *Guba* reached Hollandia on 10 June, and the covers began their long journey back to Hawaii by steamer via Hong Kong, arriving there five months and nineteen days later. Philatelists in New York quickly offered to pay $100 and more for each cover, but there were no sellers.

The *Guba* made a direct flight from Port Moresby to Sydney on 22 November 1938, carrying mail. The Catalina was a patrol bomber and no speedster, but the flight was completed in ten hours, by far the fastest delivery of mails yet made from New Guinea.

The Empire Air Service from Australia to England was inaugurated on 1 August 1938. Airmail letters posted in Papua or the Mandated Territory could now reach Southampton in thirteen days. In anticipation, the governments of the two Territories had been requested to amend their postal rates to bring them into line with the rates agreed upon by all countries participating in the Empire Service, based on five pence per half-ounce for a letter, including the airmail surcharge.

The Mandated Territory was a leader in aviation, and it was natural that airmail stamps were soon issued. Overprinted current Australian stamps were used in the Mandated Territory until 1925, when the first distinctive Territory stamps were introduced (the 'Native Hut' stamps, as they became known) in denominations ranging from one half-penny to one pound. Nine of the stamps in this series were over-printed 'OS' (Official Stamps) in black. On 8 June 1931, the full series was issued over-printed in black with the word 'Airmail', and a crude outline of a bi-plane. To celebrate the decennium of the civil administration, the famous 'Bird of Paradise' series was issued on 2 August 1931, in three sets, one bearing the airmail and bi-plane overprint in black, and another with 'OS' in black. The 'OS' stamps were keenly sought after by collectors.

So popular were the 'Bird of Paradise' stamps that the Administration was able to make a special payment of £6 928 to the Commonwealth government with part of the proceeds from their sale, to reduce the debt owed for assets taken over from the military administration. Total sale of stamps in 1931-2 amounted to £24 515.

All the 'Bird of Paradise' stamps of the 1931 issue carried the dates 1921-31. These plus the remaining 1925 stamps, were destroyed by the postal authorities in February 1933, after the issue of another three 'Bird of Paradise' sets, this time without dates, but similarly overprinted, in June 1932. The first distinctive airmail stamps, of £2 and £5 values, were issued on 1 March 1935. These large denominations were required because of a change in the postal rates, consequent upon the rapidly increas-ing volume of gold production on the Morobe gold-field. The gold was exported by ordinary registered mail, and it was appropriate that the design featured a Junkers G/31 flying over the Bulolo Valley.

The Mandated Territory stamp issues commemorating the Silver Jubilee of King George V consisted of two of the 1932 stamps, overprinted, and they were widely sold, as was the Coronation issue of May 1937, which in 1937-8 brought almost £40 000 in revenue to the Mandated Territory. In March 1939 fourteen new denominations were added to the two- and five-pound Bulolo stamps, the last stamp issues to be made in the Mandated Territory of New Guinea.

Telephones were used in the Mandated Territory to a much greater extent than in Papua, but by the standards of today the telephone was a neglected means of com-munication. It was for the townsman only, and almost entirely for the white towns-man, although New Guineans kept the systems working. When civil administration began, there was a manual telephone exchange at Rabaul with approximately 120 connections, and a trunk line service to Kokopo and the Bitapaka Wireless Station. There were, of course, no land telegraphic lines or telegraphic cables.

For the whole of the life of the Mandated Territory Administration, the Telephones section was directed by one man, E.M. Hawnt, from his appointment in May 1921, to his death in 1942 on the Japanese prison ship *Montevideo Maru*.

Ted Hawnt was a dedicated telephone man. His official title was 'Foreman (Telephones and Lines)' but he was more generally known as 'Our Telephone Chief'. C.E.J. Burns served for two months as Foreman in 1924, but this was the only break in Hawnt's record. S.G. Farnham was appointed Temporary Assistant, Telephones and Lines, in 1924, and in 1928 R.L. Gane became Linesman and Mechanic before becoming a Postal Assistant in 1934. A.J. Clarke received the appointment in 1935, and another Linesman and Mechanic, T.R. Walsh, was appointed in 1936, as the telephone system slowly expanded. In July 1937, S.C. Kensett became the third Mechanic and Linesman, Postal Services. There was one Apprentice Telephone Mechanic, E.L.S. Till.

Rabaul, capital of the Mandated Territory, was naturally the principal telephone centre. As the economy picked up and the town grew, so telephone connections increased. The businessman and the private citizen paid £15 per annum for a telephone, and all users continually complained of the service provided by the operators at the Exchange, most of whom were Tolai. 'What's the matter with our telephone service?' asked a correspondent in the *Rabaul Times* in February, 1926. 'Subscribers pay £15 per year, and are entitled to civility and service . . . one obtains neither.' The editor took the matter up in January 1927. 'Our telephone service leaves much to be desired . . . there is large scope for improvement . . . one often wonders how long the patient Rabaul subscribers must endure the trials of endeavouring to communicate with Kokopo numbers during business hours. The constant traffic to the wireless station at Bitapaka during daytime makes communications impossible.'

The situation improved somewhat in February 1928. New telephone cables were installed, providing a metallic circuit to replace the existing earth return circuit. Another switchboard came into operation to serve 150 subscribers. Complaints about the operators continued. It was hard for easy-going young Tolai men to share the impatience of subscribers, some of whom were abrupt and rude in their treatment of the operators. The only remedy would have been an automatic exchange, and even a city the size of Melbourne had taken until March 1929, to fully achieve this. It was not until September 1931, that the problem of the overloading of the Rabaul–Kokopo trunk line was partially overcome by the introduction of a schedule of hours during which no calls were accepted for Bitapaka. By this time the miracle of AWA wireless telephony had made it possible for telephone subscribers in Australia to call twenty-two European centres and many other parts of the world from the comfort of their living-rooms: small comfort to the citizens of Rabaul. Telephone subscribers never ceased their complaints. 'Subscribers may be interested to learn', wrote the *Rabaul Times* editor in February 1934, 'that much of the indistinct functioning of the local telephone service is due to faulty switch cords. New ones are on order from England. We can only hope they arrive soon, and thus obviate some wrathful subscriber from the possibility of being charged with the homicide of one of the "Hello" Boys!'

A new telephone line was laid between Rabaul and Kokopo in 1934, and in that year Ted Hawnt went to the Morobe gold-field, to investigate the possibility of a telephone system there. Telephones had been in use on the gold-fields since 1929. New Guinea Goldfields Ltd. had a private line between Wau and Edie Creek, and from Wau to a number of mining camps. Bulolo Gold Dredging Ltd. had its own private telephone system within the Bulolo township and to the outlying dredging camps. The NGG and BGD systems together totalled 18½ miles of lines by 1930. A small private system at Salamaua was later taken over and expanded by the Administration, and at Lae, Guinea Airways Ltd. maintained a company service. In mid-1931, BGD Ltd. installed radio-telephones at Lae and Bulolo, mainly to provide reliable weather information for the Guinea Airways Junkers pilots. In 1933, a similar link was provided between Lae and Salamaua. They were only moderately effective, but in July 1939, an advanced radio-telephone service was installed by AWA for the two companies, connecting Lae, Salamaua, Bulolo and Wau. Six complete alternating-current sets were provided, fitted for duplex privacy operation and employing four different transmission frequencies. Two sets were installed at Lae, and one each in the other towns, leaving one on standby. A mechanical inversion system 'scrambled' speech, and gave complete security. This AWA system was as up-to-date as anything then available in the world.

Meanwhile, in May 1935, Hawnt began the installation of a public telephone system at Wau. By the end of the year it was in operation, linking Wau, Edie Creek and Bulolo, with some 60 initial subscribers, who soon increased to over 100. The Wau Exchange was under the control of A.J. Clarke. In 1936, the administration spent £2 100 on improvements to the Wau and Salamaua exchanges. Late in 1938, Ted Hawnt installed a small telephone system at Madang.

The Wau and Salamaua Exchanges were modern and efficient, and the editor of the *Rabaul Times* drew an unflattering parallel with the Rabaul Exchange in the issue of 21 August 1936:

> Our Bellowphone System! Our local telephone system . . . causes the individual more
> irascibility, compels him to use more bad language, exhausts his patience and in many
> instances causes untold inconvenience . . . we should have the most up-to-date
> exchange system possible. The system at Wau is a service and the telephone
> instruments are a pleasure to use . . . we should consider Asiatic girls as operators . . . if
> some improvement is not effected soon, some irate subscriber will send over the wire
> such sulphuric epithets that the operator will be asphyxiated, and there will be a charge
> of illegal killing. But it would be justifiable — at times.

It may have been a coincidence, but Chinese women operators were employed at the Rabaul telephone exchange from September 1937.

The inauguration of a radio-telephone service between Rabaul and Sydney on 18 October 1937, with a charge of ten shillings per minute, did much to mollify the critics. Late in 1940, the Port Moresby and Rabaul telephone exchanges were equipped with new, modern switchboards, and the standard of service improved greatly, even though subscribers were still on occasion seen to 'curse their telephones and dance with rage', in the words of a report in the journal *Pacific Islands Monthly*.

The really dramatic developments in long-distance communications in the Mandated Territory were in the field of wireless, and again Amalgamated Wireless (Australasia) Ltd. was the dominating influence. Radio communications in the Mandated Territory were employed to a much greater extent than in Papua, both by private enterprise and by government.

As detailed in Chapter 5, the chain of wireless stations in Australia and the Territories then operated by the Postmaster General's Department was taken over by AWA on 1 July 1922. AWA career officers manned the Island Radio Service stations — Rabaul, Aitape, Kavieng, Kieta, Manus, Madang and Morobe — which were under the supervision of Radio Inspector, W.G. ('Nobby') Clarke until 1928, when he was succeeded by J.K. Twycross. Jim Twycross retired to Australia in April 1938, after over twenty years service and H. Holland became the last AWA Radio Inspector in the Mandated Territory. Sadly, Harry Holland was to share the fate of the telephone chief, Ted Hawnt, and die in the sinking of the *Montevideo Maru.*

The men of the AWA Island Radio Service formed a close fraternity, united by bonds that transcended normal professional ties. Particularly just after the First World War, they were men who grew up with the fledgling wireless industry, men whose whole existence was the magic of radio, the stuttering of Morse Code, the mysteries of this new technology. Some of them gave the best years of their lives to the service of AWA and the community in the Mandated Territory; some died in harness. They frequently lived under conditions of great discomfort on remote outstations and improvised when there were breakdowns in equipment or supplies. The surviving annals of the Mandated Territory — most were destroyed during the Pacific war — contain many examples of the work and deeds of AWA men. Those who became legends in the tight world of wireless included Syd Ambler, who served in the Mandated Territory from the First World War to 1930; Geoff Buckland; M.D. O'Sullivan, who died in 1932 after eleven years as a radio-telephonist at Bitapaka; H.D. McGuigan, one of the most senior AWA men; J.T. Allan, who left in 1937 after twenty years service; Frank Tracey, who died in Madang in 1940 (during a career of over 20 years he had served in every radio outstation in the Mandated Territory); J.L. Bain, whose death in Port Moresby ended a lifetime involvement in radio (he had helped to erect the Thursday Island and Port Moresby stations in 1912); E.A. Bishton, the man who brought radio to the Morobe gold-field; Cyril Urquhart, who finished his New Guinea career with a five-year term at Madang; Charles Beckett, another pioneer of gold-fields radio. There were many others.

It is difficult to imagine that the technicians of today's world would accept duty such as that voluntarily performed by the AWA men for many years: manning the radio and weather station on the tiny sand-spit known as Willis Island, 250 miles off the coast of North Queensland and first established in 1922. Each year, two AWA volunteers were marooned on Willis, usually with only a dog for company. For twelve months without a break they would then monitor their instruments and send daily radio reports to Cooktown, giving warning of the approach of cyclones.

Bitapaka remained the headquarters of the Island Radio Service until 1935 when a new receiving station was constructed in Rabaul, on a site previously occupied by the Native Hospital. The transmitting station was built at Malaguna, on the outskirts of town, and controlled from the receiving station by wire connections.

Rabaul was a lovely tropical township in the 1920s and 1930s, bright with colourful gardens, shaded by tall palms, the white-painted bungalows set amid emerald green lawns carefully tended by New Guinean servants. It was indeed a pleasant place for the white man to live. There was a number of hotels — the Rabaul, run by the well-known E. ('Tex') Roberts; Chin Hing Hotel, 'cheerful, bright and comfortable' in the words of the advertisement in the *Rabaul Times*; the Chee Jour Gnee, run by the famous Ah Chee, 'the Home of Tourists and Travellers'. Chinese were in fact the principal small businessmen. Ah Seng, tailor, offered white duck suits cut to order for 28 shillings, dinner jackets for 15 shillings and 'house-boys Fancy Lavalavas' for a mere 4 shillings. One of the leading general storekeepers was Alois Akun; See To Tung and Yep Loy were bakers, See To Hoi a commercial photographer, Cing Shing a watchmaker, Bay Loo a shipwright and Ching Fook a 'motor car proprietor'. They were typical of the hundreds of Chinese businessmen in Rabaul, and in Namatanai, Kavieng, Kokopo and other centres, most of them descendants of the labourers brought in by the Germans to man their plantations.

Rabaul was the commercial centre of the Mandated Territory. Motor cars quickly became popular after the war: there were over 300 in the Territory by 1927, most in Rabaul. A Model A Ford then cost £185, a Nash £260, a Fiat £235, a De Soto £285. Accidents were frequent, even in these early years. W. Easton, a Bitapaka operator, was one of two killed in an accident in October 1927; the manager of the NSW Bank died the following April, and the Administrator made an order under the new Motor Traffic Ordinance limiting the maximum speed at which a motor vehicle could travel on public streets in Rabaul, Kavieng and Kokopo to fifteen miles per hour. Some years later, the Tolai people discovered the bicycle. Japanese machines at 30 shillings each were within the means of the majority, and the roads were soon thronged with bicycles. 'The native cyclist is a menace to the travelling public!' grumped a correspondent in the *Rabaul Times*. 'They haven't the foggiest idea of riding, and are in absolute ignorance of which side of the road they should pass a car or overtake another cyclist'.

From 1926 there was a Rabaul District Motor Bus Service; a 'Picture Palace' from early post-war (the Double 'R' Picture Palace was showing the super-film *While Satan Sleeps* starring Jack Holt in October 1925); an ice-works, and from 1932, a power station (which resulted in a flood of electrical household appliances including the new-fangled refrigerator in the stores). Prior to the introduction of electric light, silk-shaded Tilley and Aladdin table kerosene lamps were used in smart Rabaul households. The latest Remington office typewriter sold for £28 in Rabaul (as against £43 in Australia) and fine French champagne was 17 shillings a quart. Ladies could purchase a Berlei Corselette, 'of Lace, Elastic and Soft Brocade, Delightfully Cool', for seventeen-and-six, and Kayser silk hose, in Mercury, Plaza or Nutone — the 'latest shades' — for nine-and-six per pair.

There was a Book Club in Rabaul, and many social and sporting clubs, where dancing was a nightly event to the music of spring-wound gramophones made by Columbia and HMV: gala Steamer Dances were held when the Burns Philp mail ships arrived. But from the late 1920s the most popular form of home entertainment was the radio. 'Radio News' was published regularly in the *Rabaul Times*, supplied through Bitapaka, and broadcasting stations in Melbourne, Sydney and Brisbane provided entertainment for the owners of radio receivers. These were invariably battery-powered before the opening of the Power Station. Popular sets sold in the 1930s included the various Fisk Radiola models, manufactured by AWA; American sets — Hallicrafters, Airzone, Scott-All-Wave, Zenith — Dutch Philips and the several Eddystone receivers, light, powerful English sets popular with AWA operators. Reception conditions in Rabaul varied greatly, from so-so to plain impossible, and AWA never did provide a broadcasting station in Rabaul as they did in Port Moresby, although they opened a station in Townsville in 1931 and another in Cairns in 1936, both of which could be received in Rabaul and other centres for most of the year.

Indifferent as the reception of programmes from Australia frequently was, the coming of radio meant a great deal to the man on the outstation. The *Rabaul Times* editor wrote in May 1926:

> In a flash his isolation has vanished and though the next steamer may not come along for a month or so, gone is the marked feeling of loneliness, the hatred of his own company, and comes in its stead a soothing mental relaxation. The day of the pioneer has faded away into the mists of the past. The day of brawn and muscle, a straight eye and a quick trigger finger is over.

AWA operators on the outstations were often called upon to repair domestic receivers. In those days the sets, valve-operated, and not proofed against the ravages of a tropical climate, were prone to a wide variety of ills. There was usually an AWA man at hand, for the numbers of stations increased during the 1930s.

The discovery of gold at Edie Creek and the amazing growth of Morobe had a vigorous effect on wireless communications. When 'Shark-Eye' Park made his find on Koranga Creek in 1922, the only radio station in the huge Morobe District was at the Morobe post, the little station established in 1909 by the Germans, where Charles Beckett was the operator. It was a long journey from Morobe to the gold-field: seventy miles by canoe to Salamaua, and three days by runner to Edie Creek. As the rush of miners swelled to a flood, so the wireless traffic at the normally sleepy centre of Morobe increased by leaps and bounds. The miners were soon demanding radio communications at Edie Creek and at short notice from the Administration, AWA shipped a small ¼-kilowatt 'spark' transmitter, designed as a lifeboat set, to Salamaua, plus a receiver, petrol engine and ancillary equipment. The man chosen to install and operate the new station was E.F. Bishton.

Ted Bishton (or 'Bish', as he was commonly known) was a veteran AWA man. Born in May 1898, he became a telegraph messenger at the GPO, Sydney, at the age of fourteen. He began to study wireless telegraphy at AWA's Marconi School, and when the First World War began he joined the Army and served as a wireless operator in Mesopotamia and India before being invalided back to Australia, where he completed the AWA course the war had interrupted. In 1920, he was asked if he would go to Rabaul as a wireless operator. Since New Guinea was then still under military administration, Bishton and two other volunteers from the Marconi School, Dinny Morgan and Jim Widdup, were required to enlist in the Australian Naval and Military Expeditionary Force (like all the AWA men who served in New Guinea during the military administration). The three new Petty Officers sailed to Rabaul on the *Melusia*, and there their paths divided. Morgan eventually returned to Australia, but Widdup remained in New Guinea, as did Bishton, until the Second World War. Widdup rejoined the Posts and Telegraphs Branch in 1954.

Bishton's career for the next few years was typical of those of the men who stayed on after the AWA took over the Island Radio Service. After a week at Bitapaka, he was transferred with Roy Barker to Manus, travelling there at the steady pace of six knots per hour in the Administration steamer the *Siar*. Bishton and Barker relieved two RAN wireless operators at Lorengau. G.H. Reed, who took over the station in 1928, described it in an article in the AWA house magazine, *The Radiogram*:

> The station is located on a flat a few hundred yards from the beach and, except for a slight screening to the westward, is ideal from a wireless point of view ... a short description of the wireless bungalow will suffice. It is of the one-room, native-built type, with a sacsac leaf roof, very cool in warm weather, and very porous in wet. The back verandah is utilized as a bedroom, and overlooks a crocodile-infested river a few yards below. Several domestic pets have ventured too close to the river of late, and departed this life.

Few of the AWA outstations were any more elaborate.

After twelve months at Lorengau, Bishton went on leave and upon his return made a voyage as Wireless Operator on the *Sumatra*, carrying heavy-hearted German planters and their families to Hollandia in Dutch New Guinea. Their plantations expropriated, these Germans were on their way back to Germany, where most of them were swiftly reduced to pauperism. They were supposed to be compensated by the German government for the value of their properties at the time of expropriation, but by their return to the Fatherland the incredible inflation of the immediate post-war years was raging out of control, reducing the value of their compensation to virtually nothing.

Upon the conclusion of this sad voyage, Bishton went to Kieta in Bougainville, where he remained until mid-1923, when he was relieved by Harry Holland. He returned to Manus, his last posting before being sent to Morobe. Manus was still operating with an old-fashioned 1½-kilowatt Marconi 'spark' transmitter, with power provided by a 6 h.p. Bartram engine; after G.H. Reed relieved Bishton, a modern AWA Type R valve transmitter of 25 watts was installed, powered by a little Chapman Pup motor. These transmitters were used at a number of outstations.

AWA men on the outlying stations had a lot of spare time on their hands, for the hours of daily operation for each station were fixed and maintenance of the equipment was normally a simple matter. Each operator had his own way of killing, or using, time. Some read detective stories or western tales; the well-known Charles Sturgeon worked out complicated mathematical problems and experimented with short-wave transmissions. Jack Boto drank beer. A.J. Marshall visited Aitape in 1935 and wrote[6] that to Boto 'sobriety was sinful, and his favourite view was over the top of a foam-capped mug. His whole philosophy revolved around beer and its ingredients; he claimed that he had discovered it was food long before modern scientists and dieticians'. Ted Bishton was at heart an entrepreneur. At Manus he gardened and reared ducks, pigs and sheep for sale; at Edie Creek he took out a Miner's Right and went goldmining; later, at Kavieng, he purchased copra plantations and ran cattle.

The transportation of the 'lifeboat' set from the beach at Salamaua over the high mountains to Edie Creek was something of an epic, even for that era of supply by carrier. The equipment arrived on the *Montoro* in August 1926. The heaviest com-

6 Marshall, 1938.

ponents were the engine and generator, each weighing approximately 100 pounds. Lashed to carrying-poles, each made a heavy, awkward load for two carriers. The other components were packed into one-man loads, protected by wrappings of heavy canvas. The complete wireless station required 74 carriers, and three months' supply of tinned and preserved foods for Bishton called for 30 more. Escorted by four police constables provided by the Morobe District Officer, Major S.S. Skeate, the long cavalcade left Salamaua on 14 September for Edie Creek, via the Buang track through the valley of the Snake River. More carriers were recruited as they marched. They sweated over the high razor-back ridges, crossed flooded mountain streams — the generator was dropped during one crossing — and fought off attacks by tribesmen. The journey occupied five weeks and six days: the regular time for carriers was eight to ten days.

At Edie Creek, Ted Bishton swiftly brought his new station, which had the appropriate call-sign VGF, into operation. The entire station, including the 1½ h.p. Cooper engine, was housed in a single tent twelve feet by ten. Edie Creek, over 6 500 feet in altitude, could be bitingly cold and the tent provided only flimsy shelter. The Cooper engine was mounted with the generator onto a hardwood log 10 feet long and set into the ground to reduce vibration. The aerials were simply slung between convenient trees. On 1 November 1926, Station VGF opened for business.

Bishton was rushed off his feet by the eager miners, long starved of speedy contact with the outside world. He began operating at 6.30 a.m. each day, and was frequently still going at 6 p.m., although atmospheric conditions often made transmissions impossible after 8.30 a.m. He worked through Station VZK Morobe, but it quickly became apparent that a more conveniently-located station was required to handle the gold-field traffic. The logical site was Salamaua, the field's port, and the administrative headquarters of the Morobe District. A modern six-valve 500-watt transmitter set was dispatched to Salamaua on the *Marsina* with AWA operator E.G. Betts, in July 1927. With H.O. McGuigan, Betts established Radio VJQ Salamaua, which henceforth handled all Morobe District traffic. At Morobe, Charles Beckett locked up the old AWA station, and abandoned it. It was never again used. By this time, Bishton was due for leave, so Beckett walked in to Edie Creek and took over from him. In 1928, the little 'spark' set was replaced by a Type R transmitter.

As the 1920s drew to a close, Edie Creek declined in importance as a mining centre, while Wau grew. It was decided to relocate the Edie Creek station at Wau. While financial considerations were not all-important, it was still necessary for the radio stations at least, if possible, to pay their way: AWA lost £9 000 on the Island Radio Service operations over the 1924-6 financial years, and this the Commonwealth government had to make good under the terms of the 1922 agreement.

In February 1929, a Guinea Airways Junkers W/34 delivered a cast-iron engine bed weighing 400 pounds to Wau for the new AWA station — the heaviest single item yet carried in an aeroplane on the gold-field. However, the transfer of the station from Edie Creek was not completed until January 1932. Charles Beckett remained there as Operator.

The steady growth of the towns of Lae, Wau and Bulolo in the 1930s, as the great gold dredges began to tear up the rich gravels of the Bulolo Valley, resulted in a further

expansion of wireless communications. In 1931, Bulolo Gold Dredging Ltd. established a station at Bulolo, and in 1934 Guinea Airways Ltd. opened stations at Lae,
Wau and Salamaua. These sets were installed by the Guinea Airways electrician and
wireless expert, Harry Balfour. In 1935, Upper Watut Gold Alluvials No Liability
erected a station at their head-quarters on the Upper Watut.

Although the major thrust of oil exploration took place in Papua, there was
considerable activity in the Mandated Territory and the field parties made wide use of
radio communications, particularly after the introduction of the AWA pedal sets and
the subsequent Type 3A and 3B teleradios. The Ormildah Oil Company purchased an
AWA 500-watt short-wave set as early as January 1928, to maintain contact between
its headquarters in Rabaul and its Sepik River properties. This was the first station to
be established on the Sepik. It was short-lived; Ormildah abandoned its activities near
Marienberg in May 1930, and the Operator, I. Hyde, transferred the equipment to
Madang. In 1937, Oil Search Ltd. employed two Type 3A stations on the Sepik, one in
the Mai Mai district and the other in the Upper Sepik; Island Exploration Co. Pty. Ltd.
installed a set at Atembla, and had three mobile stations in use in the Madang
District.

The major user of wireless communications in the Mandated Territory was the
Administration. The development of the pedal and teleradio equipment made it
possible for the outstations to be linked with their district headquarters and Rabaul at
relatively small cost, and in 1933 the first (pedal-operated) set was installed by AWA
operator Jim Widdup connecting the Kieta station with Buka Passage.[7] Widdup
operated the set for a time while he trained the Kieta District Chief Clerk, A. Barnes, in
the mysteries of Morse Code. The station was opened for general public use on
1 March 1934. A radiogram could be sent to Buka Passage from any part of the
Mandated Territory with wireless facilities at the normal rate of six pence per word,
plus a surcharge of two pence. As with most of the pedal sets, considerable trouble was
experienced with power generation and this continued until the introduction of small
petrol motors and accumulators. A set was installed at Talasea, with a young Tolai,
Nelson Tokidoro, as operator, and in 1935 N.E. Weldon, a keen radio enthusiast who
was also an assistant surveyor for the Administration, installed pedal sets at Vanimo,
Wewak, Marienberg and Ambunti. On 26 February 1935, at 5.40 p.m., Colin
McDonald, ADO Ambunti, sent the first radio message from his remote station to
Rabaul, where it was received by the Administrator. Two days later, McDonald was
shot to death in his sleep by Constable Sipi of the New Guinea Police Force, who had
earlier had an argument with the ADO. Sipi was later hanged.

By mid-1936, the Administration had installed thirteen stations, primarily for the
conduct of official business but also available to the public. They were located at
Ambunti, Angoram, Buka Passage, Gasmata, Kavieng, Kieta, Namatanai, Otibanda,
Rabaul, Salamaua, Talasea, Wewak and at the Upper Ramu Post in the Central

---

7 In his book *Patrol into Yesterday* (Cheshire, Melbourne, 1963), J.K. McCarthy states that
the first outpost to have wireless communications was Kobakini Base camp. McCarthy
and John Black, Cadet PO, arrived there in June 1933 on the way to Menyamya, and
found that Patrol Officers Ted Sansom and Bill Bird had installed their private set, with
which they maintained contact with Wau.

Highlands. The sets were all supplied by AWA and operated by Administration officers, who received training in Morse Code and general radio procedures. AWA continued to operate the Island Radio Service on behalf of the Commonwealth government at Rabaul, Kavieng, Kieta, Manus, Madang, Salamaua, Wau and Wewak (the Aitape station was transferred to Wewak in 1936). Well-known AWA outstation Operators in the 1930s included T.K. ('Meggs') Colquhoun, C.H. ('Slam') Sturgeon, J. Bassett, Len Coleman, Frank Barclay, H.S. Burgess, F.J. Nibloe, Don McMillan and Kevin Minogue.

From time to time, teleradios were employed on Administration and other small vessels.[8] Sir Walter McNicoll, the Administrator, was a strong advocate of wireless communications. Appointed in September 1934, he was keen to see as much as possible of the Mandated Territory and on 1 October 1935, he left Wewak in the old Administration schooner *Thetis* on a voyage up the mighty Sepik River to the limit of navigation, a distance of some 700 miles. Accompanying him were J.K. McCarthy, ADO, and a detachment of police. At Angoram, they transferred to the big schooner, *Hermes*, commanded by J.A. Andrews with N.E. Weldon as navigator and wireless operator. During the course of this expedition, the Administrator kept in constant radio contact with headquarters at Rabaul. It was immediately following the Sepik voyage that the *Hermes* disappeared at sea, together with Andrews, Weldon, a white passenger and the entire crew. A year later, McNicoll toured Bougainville and adjacent islands in the *Nereus*, and again used radio to maintain contact with Rabaul.

In 1937-8 the biggest exploratory patrol ever to operate in Papua or the Mandated Territory penetrated the unknown territory between the outpost at Mount Hagen and the headwaters of the Sepik River. The Hagen–Sepik Patrol, led by J.L. Taylor, ADO, and John Black, PO, began on 9 March 1938, and was completed on 19 June 1939. Sir Walter McNicoll took a close personal interest in the progress of the expedition, and it was at his direction that an AWA teleradio was made available to Taylor. The set, with petrol motor, fuel and batteries, was heavy to carry, but it functioned perfectly throughout the patrol. Taylor made radio contact with Rabaul every ten days in the first months of the journey, and several times spoke directly with the Administrator, on one occasion while Sir Walter was on board the schooner *Sirius*, 200 miles up the Sepik River. His calls were monitored by AWA stations and by wireless amateurs in various parts of the Territory, in particular L. Williams of Salamaua, and R. Chugg of Madang.

During the early stages of the Hagen–Sepik Patrol, a base camp was established at Wabag, and an aerodrome constructed. The area to be explored was so vast that Taylor had taken the decision to divide his patrol, and so speed up the work. John Black would lead one party and walk to Telefomin, on the Sepik Headwaters, following the southern fall of the central range. In 1935, the Fly River gold prospecting expedition of J. Ward Williams had constructed a rough aerodrome at Telefomin. Taylor would make for the same destination, travelling along the northern fall of the range.

8 The Administration schooners *Boruda*, *Leander* and *Sirius* were wireless-equipped, and included radio operators among their crews.

C.B. Walsh, a medical assistant attached to the patrol, would remain at Wabag with the radio, the balance of the patrol personnel and bulk supplies.

Taylor left Wabag for Telefomin on 26 August 1938. Two days later a police party from Wabag, out looking for food, was attacked by a strong force of tribesmen. A constable-bugler was killed; two constables and three carriers were wounded. Eleven of the attackers were shot down and killed by police rifle fire. Walsh and his party were soon besieged by furious tribesmen, in the most remote government outpost in the Mandated Territory. Without radio communication, their situation would have been perilous. As it was, Walsh was able to call for aid. The District Officer of the Morobe District, E. Taylor, flew to Wabag with police reinforcements, and order was soon restored. Taylor returned to Salamaua, leaving I.F.G. Downs, PO, with Walsh. While awaiting the return of Jim Taylor and John Black, Walsh and Downs explored the headwaters streams of the Yuat River.

The great Hagen-Sepik Patrol completed the broad exploration of the Central Highlands of Papua and the Mandated Territory that began after the amazing walk across New Guinea from the Upper Ramu to the Papuan coast, by the prospectors M.J. Leahy and M. Dwyer, in 1930. The exploration of the Central Highlands quickly followed. In 1933, a party led jointly by ADO Jim Taylor and M.J. Leahy walked from the Upper Ramu, centre of a small-scale gold strike, through the vast valley of the Wahgi, to Mount Hagen and beyond. They found an enormous number of people, the greatest concentration found so far by whites in New Guinea. They carried a battery-operated wireless receiver for the reception of time-signals, to enable their surveyor, Ken Spinks, to build up a map of the country as they travelled, and they were supplied throughout by aeroplane, at prearranged intervals.

The Central Highlands discoveries captured world attention. In quick succession, the Administration and the Christian missions established a string of stations throughout the Highlands, all supplied by aeroplane and many eventually with wireless communications. The Lutheran missionaries had been the first to begin Highland exploration, but they kept their findings within mission circles. There was a Lutheran station at Lihona, near the head of the Ramu watershed, as early as 1926, and by 1931 the Lutherans had established the first mission station in the Highlands, at Kambaidam (transferred to Onelunka in 1933). In 1934, major new stations were located at Kundiawa, Kerowagi and Ogelbeng. This year saw the entry of the Catholics, with stations at Mingende, near Kundiawa, and at Mt Hagen. In 1935, the Seventh Day Adventists built a station at Kainantu and later another in the Asaro Valley. By the mid-1930s there were ten major mission stations between Kainantu and Mt Hagen staffed by white missionaries, and 74 outposts in charge of native teachers and evangelists. In December 1934, and January 1935, two Catholic missionaries, Father Charles Morschheuser and Brother Eugene Frank, were killed by tribesmen in the Chimbu Valley and there was no further mission expansion in the Highlands until after the Second World War.

Both the Lutherans and the Catholics purchased their own aeroplanes, primarily to supply the Highlands stations. They also employed wireless communications at their key centres. By September 1938, the Lutherans had radio stations at Malahang,

Ogelbeng, Kerowagi and Finschhafen, and the Catholics at Alexishafen, Mingerde and Mt Hagen.

As previously mentioned, the Administration commenced the installation of teleradios at outstations from 1933 onwards, and in 1936 employed R.G. Cox as Senior Mechanic (Wireless). Cox later became Master Engineer and Wireless Operator of the Administration vessel, *Dorunda*, and, in February 1938, an officer of the Postmaster General's Department, Alexander Waugh Munro, was seconded to the Mandated Territory Administration as Senior Mechanic (Wireless), to supervise the installation of teleradios at the remaining stations, and establish an organization to repair and service the sets, mainly AWA Type 3A and 3B models. At the time of Munro's appointment, a number of Administration stations had been located in the Highlands, at Kainantu, Bena Bena (afterwards transferred to Goroka), Finintegu, Kundiawa and Mt Hagen, and he equipped them all with sets. By the end of 1938, the Administration owned a total of 20 teleradio outfits.

Other AWA teleradios were then in use by individuals and companies throughout the Mandated Territory: W.M. Middleton at Kar Kar Island; B.O. Edgell at Manus Island; W. McGregor at Wewak; Coconut Products Ltd. at Pondo; W.R. Carpenter & Co. at But; D.S. Hore-Lacy at Garua Island; H.L. Cameron at Djaul Island; Pacific Timbers Ltd. at Rugenhaven; J. Cassel on the Upper Waria and D.M. Mitchell at Roamer, on the Lower Watut. In 1939, the private surveyor, P.D. McKenzie, employed a teleradio to transmit data from the field to his draftsman in Rabaul, using a pre-arranged code, thereby enabling the draftsman to plot and draw plans for McKenzie to sign and submit immediately upon his return, at a vast saving in time. In 1940, four more sets came into use, by the Methodist Mission at Malalia, New Britain; Cape Lambert (NG) Forests Ltd.; New Britain Timbers Ltd., and Tom Flower, timber merchant at Henry Reid Bay, New Britain. All worked through Rabaul, which was then the centre for fourteen field teleradio stations. By the end of this year, AWA teleradio stations were established in more than 180 locations throughout the Mandated Territory, Papua and neighbouring Pacific islands, a network which proved its worth when the forces of Japan began their first victorious push, in 1942.

The most dramatic demonstration of the value of radio communications in these last years of peace came in 1937, when Rabaul was struck by a series of volcanic eruptions that brought death, massive property damage and disruption of normal life in their train. Deep, rumbling earth tremors began at 1.15 p.m. on 28 May, and the following afternoon Vulcan Island erupted with a shattering series of explosions, belching forth black columns of steam, smoke and pumice dust, which rapidly turned day into night.

When the earth tremors began, an American ship, the *Golden Bear*, was in the harbour, and that night the captain took it out into Blanche Bay, and then to a safe anchorage at Nordup. The ship's radio operator, Victor Castner, decided to have a closer look at the scene, and was ashore when Vulcan exploded. He was never seen again.

Rabaul was blanketed by smoke and dust, and the AWA transmitting and receiving stations were enveloped. Radio Inspector Twycross ordered the Operator

L.C. Coleman to abandon his post, but Coleman stayed on. C.H. Sturgeon drove the AWA wives to safety on the north coast, and tried in vain to fight his way back. C.B. Alexander worked desperately to keep vital equipment working, but the sulphurous smoke and blinding dust proved too much. The stations were evacuated and Rabaul went off the air, from 6 p.m. Saturday until 12.15 a.m. Sunday.

While Rabaul was reeling from the effects of the worst volcanic eruption in living memory, the sole communication with the outside world was provided by the marine wireless on the *Golden Bear*, manned by a volunteer, S.W. Faulkner, of the W.R. Carpenter staff. He stuck to his task without a break, keeping the outside world informed, while the AWA men struggled to restore the normal service.

On Sunday morning, Twycross set off for Kokopo. The BP mail vessel, *Montoro*, was expected to dock that afternoon, and Twycross planned to establish contact with Sydney using the ship's AWA wireless. That morning Sturgeon at last succeeded in finding his way back to Rabaul, where Alexander had managed to get the emergency power generator working (the eruption had temporarily wiped out the Rabaul electrical reticulation system). At the receiving station, H.S. Burgess was in contact with Sydney.

Then, at 1 p.m., the Matupi crater erupted. This time the communications system held. On Sunday night, Twycross contacted Sydney from the *Montoro* and then went back to Rabaul. He sent a small emergency set to Kokopo, restoring the link with Rabaul.

Until 5 June, the AWA staff at Rabaul and Kokopo, working eighteen hours daily, sent some 1 700 official and private messages, totalling 60 000 words, and many thousands more were diverted through the Papuan AWA stations. To keep the Rabaul and Kokopo stations clear for the emergency, traffic between Australia and the other Mandated Territory stations was passed through Port Moresby instead of Rabaul. As a result of this clear communication channel, necessary measures to cope with the situation were speedily taken.

Two Europeans and 438 New Guineans died during the eruptions. Property damage was enormous. It was estimated that over one million tons of pumice dust fell on Rabaul; the roof of the AWA transmitting station was covered in a layer of volcanic lava over a foot thick. The W.R. Carpenter inter-island vessels, the *Durour* and the *Duris*, were destroyed. It was by any standards a disaster of colossal proportions.

It was many months before Rabaul was cleared of the effects of the eruptions. George Clark, a Morobe gold-field miner travelling to Australia on leave, arrived at Rabaul on the *Macdhui* late in June and wrote of the scene to a friend, Jack O'Neill, back on the Watut:

> Rabaul was a sight that one never wishes to see again. One looked upon desolation everywhere. For people to return to their shattered homes and start again required an enormous amount of intestinal fortitude. Really one cannot explain or describe the sight. We arrived in the harbour at night and what met our gaze in the morning, well, here's the only way I can describe it. Just picture in your mind's eye a big liner standing upright on the open downs country; a big boat loaded with cargo and humans, and *not a single drop of water in sight*. The pumice was from six inches to two feet

deep on the water, and not a ripple or movement of any kind. It gave the appearance of a perfect landing-ground . . .

The Australian government dispatched two world-recognized experts, Dr C.E. Stehn and Dr W.G. Woolnough, to Rabaul, to conduct exhaustive vulcanological and seismological investigations. As a result of their report it was decided that Rabaul would have to be abandoned as the capital of the Mandated Territory. There was a long period of bickering and controversy before Lae was chosen as the new site, but the move did not begin until after further eruptions in January 1941, and only the Administrator, Sir Walter McNicoll, and a number of departmental officers were established in Lae when the Pacific war burst over New Guinea.

2
TAIM BOLONG BIHAIN —
FROM WAR TO INDEPENDENCE

CHAPTER SEVEN

THE PACIFIC WAR

The Second World War marked an end, and a beginning, for Papua New Guinea. An end, bloody and violent, to the ways of the era of classic colonialism, where the interests of the indigenous people were subservient to those of Australia; the beginning of a brave new world and the birth of a new spirit of idealism in the relationship between the governors and the governed, and the beginning of a process of fundamental change that would result in self-determination for the people of Papua New Guinea within a span of years so brief as to amaze, even today.

Only superficial treatment of so cataclysmic an event as the war is possible in this account. Hundreds of books have been written on different aspects of the struggle in the Pacific alone, and more constantly appear.

When the forces of Japan launched their wave of conquests after Pearl Harbor, Papua New Guinea lay virtually defenceless. War had been raging in Europe and the Middle East for two years, but the Territories were far away and the impact of the great campaigns in those distant regions was slight. Australia had been quick to respond when war began in September 1939, and most of her scanty forces were overseas when the Japanese attacked. Singapore, and the Royal Navy, were seen to be Australia's bastion, and a shield, too, for Papua New Guinea.

But Papua New Guinea responded, also. In the Mandated Territory, soon to receive the initial impact of the Japanese onslaught, the Commonwealth Government authorized the raising of a local defence force, the New Guinea Volunteer Rifles (NGVR), with an authorized strength of 20 officers and 400 other ranks, all Europeans. Small NGVR detachments were speedily raised at Rabaul, Wau, Salamaua, Lae, Kokopo, Kavieng and Madang. Recruiting of the first New Guinea Contingent for the Australian armed forces began on 22 September; the quota, of 60 men, was filled in less than one month, and in February, 1940, they sailed away to the war. Another quota, of 95 men, left in August. By September 1940, 162 men had enlisted in the Mandated Territory and been drafted to Australia, and 157 Public Servants had been granted leave for military service.

Despite this warlike activity, the Mandated Territory was really defenceless. Under the provisions of the Mandate, Australia had been forbidden to erect fortifications or raise bodies of indigenous soldiers, and it was not until March 1941, that regular troops of the 2/22nd Battalion of the 8th Division AIF were dispatched to the defence of New Guinea. The 1st Independent Company followed in July. In December 1941, the total armed force opposing the Japanese in the Mandated Territory was pitifully weak: some 2 200 soldiers (mainly in the Gazelle Peninsula, centred on Rabaul); the poorly-equipped NGVR; a coastal defence battery of two six-inch guns, two three-inch anti-aircraft guns, an anti-tank battery and a small RAAF detachment with a handful of already obsolete aircraft.

Within days of the attack on Pearl Harbor on 7 December 1941, Japanese aircraft were flying over Rabaul. It was clear to the most sanguine that an assault was imminent, and on 12 December, in a superbly planned and executed operation, almost all of the white women and children in the Mandated Territory and in Papua were evacuated by sea and air to Australia, snatched from the path of the Japanese in the very nick of time. For Rabaul was bombed on 4 January 1942. Further raids followed, one by one the defending RAAF aircraft were shot down by the superior Zero fighters of the enemy, until only three remained, and on 21st January the Japanese landed at Rabaul, in overwhelming numbers. The defenders fought bravely, but they were quickly routed. Some 400 Australian servicemen and civilians ultimately escaped from New Britain, mostly in small ships, many through the efforts of J.K. McCarthy, ADO, and Ivan Champion, ARM. But most of the soldiers and the citizens of Rabaul were trapped. Over 160 were murdered by the Japanese at Tol Plantation, after they had surrendered. At the end of June 1942, 850 servicemen and 180 civilians — including the Deputy Administrator of the Mandated Territory, Harold Page, many other senior officers, missionaries, Ted Hawnt of the Telephone service and Harry Holland, the AWA Radio Inspector — were herded aboard an unmarked Japanese vessel, the *Montevideo Maru*, bound for Japan. On 1 July the ship was torpedoed and sunk off the Philippines by an American submarine. There were no European survivors.

The swift fall of Rabaul and the fate of the defenders caused bitter controversy in New Guinea and Australia, both at the time and afterwards. Ships were available to evacuate the Rabaul garrison and civilians once it had become apparent that there was no stopping the Japanese, but they were not employed. G.W.L. Townsend, who was on the spot, said in his book, *District Officer*, that as a result of the Australian government's 'shilly-shallying, no-one, civilian or soldier, ever really knew the score; no-one had any clear idea what to do in the event of an invasion; and even when the Japanese bombs began to fall in January 1942, no effort was ever made to get civilians out, or to get military reinforcements in'.

Rabaul became the principal stronghold of the Japanese and they remained there for the next three years. By May 1942, they had captured and occupied Kavieng, Lae, Salamaua, Wewak, Madang and Lorengau. They were in complete control of the Bismarck Archipelago, the Admiralties, Bougainville, and the coastal and sub-coastal regions of the Sepik, Madang and Morobe Districts. Then they turned towards Papua, and by August had penetrated as far as the Buna-Gona-Sanananda-Kokoda regions, crossed the Owen Stanley Range and fought their way to within thirty miles of Port Moresby.

At the time of Pearl Harbor, Papua was as defenceless as the Mandated Territory — perhaps more so. Papua was an Australian territory, and there was no Mandate agreement to prevent the development of adequate defences. Defence plans for both Papua and the Mandated Territory had been in existence since 1933, but practically nothing had been done to implement them, although in 1937 the Resident Magistrates of the various Divisions were instructed to prepare secret registers of European British subjects and ex-members of the Armed Native Constabulary capable of rendering service in the defence of Papua. It was not until March 1939, that Major K.D. Chalmers arrived with a subordinate officer and thirty-eight men of 13th Heavy Battery of the Australian Artillery to assume command of the Port Moresby defences, such as they were. They installed two six-inch coastal defence guns on Paga Hill commanding the approaches to Basilisk Passage. Later, a battery of 3.7-inch anti-aircraft guns was positioned on Tuaguba Hill. After the outbreak of war in Europe troops, mostly young, ill-trained militiamen of the 49th Battalion, were sent to Port Moresby together with some reconnaisance aircraft. In June 1940, the Papuan Infantry Battalion was raised to assist in local defence. It was composed of Papuan troops and Australian officers. Approval was given to raise a contingent for the 2nd AIF; as in the Mandated Territory, response was rapid.

Port Moresby quickly assumed the character of a garrison town, and in August 1940, became the headquarters of the 8th Military District, which included both Papua and the Mandated Territory. The coming of war brought inevitable regulation into everyday life. Aliens were forced to register with the authorities in both Territories; key installations and localities were closed to the public; censors were appointed; civil aircraft movements were curtailed. Emergency regulations gave the governments in both Territories power to control or restrict the activities of virtually every section of the community, and to take any measure thought necessary to protect defence works and telephone, postal and telegraphic communications. Friction between the civilian government and the military authorities in Port Moresby was probably inevitable. Sir Hubert Murray, almost at the end of his long and distinguished life, was a sick man, struggling to cope with the rapidly-changing situation. The defence plan called for wide-ranging action on the part of the government and its officers in the event of an attack, and Sir Hubert was, in his own words, 'filled with apprehension' as to the ability of his government to do everything required of it. His end was near: on 28 February 1940, he died in Samarai hospital. The Government Secretary, H.W. Champion, was sworn in as Acting Administrator, and in December, Leonard Murray become Administrator (the old position of Lieutenant-Governor had been abolished).

Leonard Murray's period of office was limited, circumscribed and unhappy. The position of a Civil Governor in a town that was the headquarters of a Military District in time of war was, to say the least, difficult. After Pearl Harbor, it became impossible. The 39th and 53rd Battalions were sent to join the 49th in Port Moresby, arriving 3

January 1942. The soldiers were young and ill-trained, the officers inexperienced. Early in February, the Japanese began to bomb Port Moresby; discipline cracked and the troops began to loot the town. It was a shameful, though brief, episode. It was clearly no longer possible to maintain a civil administration in a land apparently on the verge of occupation by a ruthless, all-conquering enemy, and at noon on 15 February 1942, civil government in Papua and the Mandated Territory ceased. The officer commanding the 8th Military District, Major-General B.M. Morris, took over, and Leonard Murray left for Australia.

By the time the Japanese made their first moves towards the capture of Port Moresby — vital to their war plans, and as a springboard for an invasion of Australia — a further, limited strengthening of the defences there had taken place, and the first of what would soon become a veritable host of American troops had arrived. In May 1942, a Japanese invasion fleet left Rabaul for Port Moresby. Unknown to the Japanese, the Americans had succeeded in completely breaking their naval code, and in a striking example of the importance of secure communications in modern warfare, American and Australian naval units, forewarned by decoded enemy wireless signals, were able to intercept the Japanese and turn them back. This Battle of the Coral Sea as it has become known was the first major Japanese setback in the Pacific war. The following month saw the defeat of the Japanese in one of the decisive battles of naval history: Midway. From this point onwards, the Japanese were on the defensive, although they were a long way from defeat in Papua New Guinea.

Although the Japanese failed in their attempt to capture Port Moresby from the sea, they came close to succeeding with their land forces. Their major thrust was launched from the north coast of Papua, where an invasion army was landed, near Gona, on 21 July 1942. It was commanded by Major-General Horii, who had led the assault on Rabaul. The tough, lightly-encumbered Japanese soldiers drove swiftly towards Kokoda, their advance only slightly hindered by forward patrols of the 39th Battalion and a few Papuan troops. By 29 July, they were in Kokoda. Before them was the high, harsh barrier of the great Owen Stanley Range, which had to be crossed if Port Moresby was to fall to Japanese arms. Many defence authorities considered that it was impossible for an army to cross the Owen Stanleys. The Japanese soon demonstrated that it could, however, be done.

Port Moresby was essential to Allied strategy: it had to be held. The Australian forces available to stop the Japanese were hopelessly inadequate, but fortunately the commander of the Allied forces in the south-west Pacific area, the Australian general, Sir Thomas Blamey, was receiving reinforcements of seasoned troops withdrawn from the Middle East. In June, General Morris (in charge of the New Guinea Force: he handed over command to Lieutenant-General S.F. Rowell in August) had ordered the construction of a road from Sogeri to Kokoda, to keep troops in the forward area supplied. It was quite impossible to build a 'road' across the Owen Stanleys, where individual peaks towered to over 13 000 feet, but there was a track in existence, that had been used for many years by the police runners carrying the mails to Kokoda, and it was this route, widened and improved with incredible effort by conscripted Papuan labourers and by Army engineers, which has become famous as the Kokoda Trail.

Fighting at the end of a long supply line, the Australians kept the Japanese engaged in energetic patrol activity during the first days of August. In mid-August the

21st Brigade of the 7th Division AIF joined the men of the 39th and 53rd Battalions on the Trail, and the 25th Brigade followed. But the Japanese had also been reinforced, and by early September had 5 000 troops in the forward zone. Fighting desperately, the outnumbered Australians were forced back to Imita Ridge, thirty miles from Port Moresby. The Supreme Commander South West Pacific Area, General Douglas MacArthur, expressed his lack of confidence in the fighting spirit and ability of the Australians and the leadership of Rowell. The Prime Minister, John Curtin, ordered Blamey to take over direct command of the operations in New Guinea. Rowell, whose detailed planning and staff work had prepared the way for the victory that was about to follow, was replaced by Lieutenant-General E.F. Herring.

By the beginning of October, the Japanese were in retreat. The Australians, strengthened by soldiers of the 6th Division, forced the enemy back over the Owen Stanleys, fighting under terrible conditions and proving they were more than a match for the Japanese. On 2 November, now under the command of Major-General G.A. Vasey, they recaptured Kokoda and pushed the Japanese back to their heavily-defended bases in the Buna-Gona-Sanananda region. After further savage fighting, Australian and American forces captured Gona and Buna, and by the end of January 1943, organized Japanese resistance in Papua had ended.

The second Japanese attempt to seize Port Moresby, made in conjunction with the attack across the Owen Stanleys, also failed. Their plan called for the capture of Milne Bay by an assault from the sea, and then an advance on the capital along the coast. The Japanese believed Milne Bay to be lightly held, and on 26 August landed a small invasion force of some 2 000 men. They encountered hot resistance from the veteran 18th Brigade of the AIF under Brigadier G.F. Wootten, the 7th Brigade of Militia under Brigadier J. Field and Kittyhawk fighters of 75 and 76 Squadrons RAAF. The Japanese were decisively beaten, and withdrew on 6 September. It was their first defeat on land in the Pacific war, and ended the legend of their invincibility.

Japan's star was now on the wane. There were still victories to be won, but defeat would follow defeat in all theatres during 1943 and 1944. Only by swiftly knocking the Americans out of the war before they could harness the matchless power of their economy could the Japanese have won, and having failed in this, the ultimate end was sure. In Papua New Guinea, bloody fighting lay ahead, but after only a year, the Japanese had been driven from Papua. Port Moresby became an enormous base from which the bitter, remorseless New Guinea campaigns of the next two years were directed.

Although the Japanese had succeeded in occupying so much of the Mandated Territory during the first victorious months of their war, they made no attempt to invade the hinterland. The Central Highlands remained in Allied hands, and in the Morobe District, the towns of Wau and Bulolo held out, supplied by carrier-line from Papua over the Bulldog Road, under conditions of extraordinary difficulty. To harass the Japanese at Lae and Salamaua, the Australians formed a unit known as Kanga Force following the Coral Sea battle. Kanga Force was very small: the NGVR survivors, the 5th Independent Company, a mortar platoon and a platoon of the 1st Independent Company. Commanded by Major N.L. Fleahy, Kanga Force was flown in to Wau in May 1942. Far too weak to do much more than annoy the Japanese, it constantly raided Japanese positions with remarkable daring and skill, on one occasion entering Salamaua itself, killing over a hundred Japanese. The savage little war was fought almost unnoticed throughout the big Papuan campaigns; in October 1942, the 2/7th Independent Company joined the now much-depleted force.

Kanga Force had become a sufficient threat to the Japanese to warrant determined action. In January 1943, a body of 2 500 seasoned soldiers of the crack Japanese 51st Division, commanded by Lieutenant-Colonel Maruoka, left Salamaua and advanced swiftly over the mountains towards Wau. Kanga Force had again been reinforced, with units of the veteran 17th Australian Infantry Brigade, whose commander, Brigadier M.J. Moten, took control of it. Maruoka's soldiers, lightly armed and supplied in the Japanese manner, achieved almost complete surprise and penetrated to the approaches of Wau before the defenders, fighting desperately succeeded in driving them back.

Kanga Force ceased to exist in April 1943, when Major-General S.G. Savige established the headquarters of his 3rd Division in Bulolo. The Allies now began to close in on the Japanese at Lae and Salamaua. A great air base was constructed in the Markham Valley, barely forty miles from Lae, and American forces landed at Nassau Bay, south of Salamaua. Lae and Salamaua were pounded mercilessly by never-ending attacks from the Markham base, and Japanese supply barges were sunk. Starvation threatened the Japanese. In September, Australian and American forces captured Lae and Salamaua, encountering fierce opposition from Japanese rearguards; the main body of the enemy had already withdrawn. An untold number of them died in an attempt to cross the great barrier of the Saruwaged Range; without doubt, many soldiers were killed by villagers.

After the fall of Lae, the 7th Division captured Kaiapit and continued up the Markham Valley into the Ramu, and the bloody fighting best remembered by the Shaggy Ridge action occurred. The 9th Division moved up the coast, headed for Madang. After fighting of extraordinary ferocity, Finschhafen fell in October, and Sattelberg in November. By mid-January 1944, the 9th Division was at Sio.

The remorseless encirclement of the Japanese, aimed at the reduction of the stronghold of Rabaul, continued. The Americans were pouring in men, equipment and supplies and there was now little chance that the Japanese, at the end of a long and savagely battered supply-line, could hold the territory they had won so spectacularly in 1942. American marines landed at Torokina in Bougainville in November 1943; at Arawe and Cape Gloucester, New Britain, in December; at Los Negros in the Admiralty Group in February 1944, and in New Ireland in March. The Japanese fought with fanatical bravery, often to the last man, and many thousands were killed. In April, Madang fell to the Australians.

The Japanese position was now hopeless. Their forces were isolated, their men in danger of starving, their equipment failing. Nevertheless, they were still full of fight. After the fall of Madang, the Allied offensive came to a halt while the divisions rested and refitted. In October and November 1944, the Australians took over the American bases in the Sepik, on Bougainville and New Britain. While the Americans pressed on with the campaign in Dutch New Guinea, their ultimate objective the home islands of Japan, Australian forces continued the job of finishing off the surviving Japanese in New Guinea, now something of a backwater as the tide of war rolled forward. There was bitter fighting on Bougainville; the Japanese on the Gazelle were cut off, and in the Sepik the enemy defended Wewak with frightening tenacity. The Japanese commander, General Adachi, surrendered at Wewak in May 1945; of the 100 000 men who had originally made up his army, barely 13 000 survived.

When the Japanese laid down their arms following the dropping of the atom bombs on Hiroshima and Nagasaki in August 1945, there were still defiant soldiers in various parts of the Mandated Territory prepared to fight on, forever, if their Emperor so willed it.

The campaigns in Papua and the Mandated Territory were small in scale when compared with the gigantic struggles of the war in Europe. The cost in human terms was nevertheless great. Perhaps 300 000 Japanese fought in Papua New Guinea and of these some 170 000 were killed, or died of disease and starvation. The Americans lost thousands of men and the Australians approximately 14 500. Only small numbers of Papua New Guineans served as soldiers and eighty-one of these died. Many villagers, innocent bystanders, were killed — the exact number will never be known. Whole districts were devastated in the fighting, villages destroyed and the meagre possessions of the people lost. Tens of thousands were forced to labour for an Allied cause that hardly concerned them. The fighting over, the soldiers departed to their homelands across the sea, and in the war-shattered regions in Papua New Guinea, the people began to rebuild their lives.

The war in Papua New Guinea was essentially a war of communications and supply. It was a mobile campaign, shifting rapidly from one district to another; it was fought over vast distances, usually under conditions of great physical stress. Only those who soldiered in the jungles and mountains of PNG against a skilful, ruthless enemy know how tough it really was. Time and again the vital necessity of swift, secure communications to ultimate victory was proven during the Pacific war. At one time or another, every conceivable system of communication was used: runners, dispatch riders, canoes, carrier-pigeons, telephone lines, radio, semaphore, aircraft, mirrors, long lines, the telegraph and the post.

The outbreak of the Second World War did not at first greatly affect postal operations in PNG, apart from the early imposition of censorship, which was accepted readily enough apart from a few grumbles. (In Papua, the Treasurer was appointed Censor and the Postmasters at Port Moresby and Samarai became Assistant Censors, as did the Resident Magistrates of the Eastern, South-Eastern, North-Eastern, Northern, Gulf, Delta and Western Divisions.) The W.R. Carpenter Airlines air mail service continued, although the DH86 *Caronia* was soon impressed into the RAAF, leaving the company without a reserve aircraft. Then one of the surviving two, the *Carinthia*, crash-landed into the sea near Kavieng, on 15 March 1940. There was no loss of life, but the aircraft was destroyed. This was a serious blow: replacement aircraft in time of war were desperately hard to obtain. Only *Carmania* remained to fly the mail service; the volume of mails and passengers carried dropped drastically as scheduled departures fell into arrears, and all seats were fully booked for months ahead. The only DH86s available as replacements were old machines, 'A' models built in 1935, in operation on Malayan routes out of Singapore. Two were purchased and went into operation on the PNG mail route in June and July 1940. But the RAAF now urgently required light transports, and defence needs were paramount. Both replacement aircraft were taken over, the first in July and the second in December 1940. The *Carmania* faithfully carried on, but the service was soon in a shambles. The volume of sea mails to PNG rapidly increased.

Fortunately, W.R. Carpenter Airlines were able to obtain approval from the Commonwealth Government to import a pair of second-hand Lockheed 14-H2 airliners from America. These were fine modern aircraft, superior in every way to the antiquated De Havillands. The two Lockheeds began flying between Australia and PNG in May and July 1941. The old *Carmania* went the way of her sisters in June 1941, into the inventory of the RAAF, and the company named the Lockheeds *Carmania* and *Caronia*, in tribute to the aeroplanes that had served them, and PNG, so well.

The Lockheeds maintained the air mail service until the Japanese invasion. Flying at a cruising speed of 225 m.p.h. with twelve passengers and an air hostess, they brought a new concept in air travel to PNG. Carrying three times the mail load of the DH86, they gave the Territories the best mail service they had ever had. The De Havilland airliners were not forgotten, though. The last two stamp issues in Papua were air mail ones: a commemorative set, inscribed 'Air Mail Postage' featuring a DH86 over Port Moresby, and a regular air mail set showing a DH86 in flight over the Papuan Gulf. Both were issued on 6 September 1938. An additional denomination of one-and-six was introduced in July 1941.

When the civil administrations of Papua and the Mandated Territory were suspended in February, 1942, all their stamps were withdrawn. Those civilian post offices not already closed by Japanese occupation, were closed. Military post offices were established by the Australians and Americans (and during 1944 by the New Zealanders) in the various towns and regions, as the fortunes of war changed. No attempt will be made to list what eventually became a multitude of military post offices, for the Pacific war was a special episode in PNG history, and the military postal system had little effect on developments after the war. One military organization that operated in Papua and the Mandated Territory, however, is clearly relevant to this account: the Australian New Guinea Administrative Unit, better known as ANGAU.

The suspension of civil government left a serious hiatus in administration in Papua and the Mandated Territory. Although the Japanese quickly overran huge areas, whole districts never saw the presence of a single enemy. The task of government in a colonial dependency was a job for the specialist, not for the soldier, and there were specialists available: the officers of the pre-war administrations. Some had enlisted, some had been captured and others evacuated, but many remained. In February 1942, the New Guinea Administrative Unit and the Papuan Administrative Unit were formed, and on 10 April they were combined into the Australian New Guinea Administrative Unit, with headquarters in Port Moresby. For the first time in history, both Territories — outside the areas under Japanese control — were under one administration, and it had taken war to bring it about. Major-General B.M. Morris, who had just handed over command of the New Guinea Force to Rowell, was appointed General Officer Commanding ANGAU in August 1942, and in March

1943, Brigadier D.M. Cleland became the Unit's hard-working and much admired Deputy Adjutant and Quartermaster-General.

ANGAU was a military unit, and where military needs clashed with the interests of the Papua New Guinean people, they invariably prevailed. But ANGAU was largely staffed by men who had been civilian administrators before circumstances forced them to become soldiers, and although no proof can be offered, it is certain that ANGAU was more understanding in its treatment of the indigenous people than a purely military administration would have been. Nevertheless, military requirements often called for unpalatable measures. The great majority of the senior positions in ANGAU were filled by ex-field officers of the two pre-war administrations; ANGAU District Officers were almost invariably men who had filled similar positions in Papua or the Mandated Territory, and the average ANGAU Assistant District Officer was similarly experienced. ANGAU administrative districts conformed as far as was practicable to the pre-war ones. There was a good deal of internal dissension in the ranks of ANGAU between the officers of the old Papuan and Mandated Territory administrations, but this lessened as ANGAU grew, and men who had been private citizens, and selected Army personnel, joined its ranks. Eventually, ANGAU contained three times as many men as the old administrations combined, with a peak strength of just over 2 000 officers and men.

ANGAU had two main functions: operational and administrative. In its operational role, it directly supported the Army and frequently took part in military activities, including reconnaisance patrolling and fighting. The pre-war native police forces were amalgamated under the title Royal Papuan Constabulary, and came under ANGAU control. These men fought in many an action alongside ANGAU and the Army. ANGAU had primary responsibility for the everyday administration of the districts not under Japanese control, and, as the enemy retreated, ANGAU moved in and attended to the needs of the people in the war-ravaged regions. It was also ANGAU's task to maintain production of copra and rubber, both of great strategic importance, until the formation of the Production Control Board in May 1943; Cleland was appointed Chairman. It was ANGAU's role in the recruitment and management of labour to serve military needs, and the activities of the Production Control Board, that has drawn the greatest criticism in recent years, but the requirements of those perilous times demanded the actions taken.

In order to carry out its various tasks, ANGAU was organized in the military manner into a number of sections: headquarters, with a general staff; medical; dental; finance; legal; educational; amenities; supply; labour; District Services and Native Affairs; marine; transport; agriculture; signals and postal. It is the work of the ANGAU Signals Section that is most relevant to this account, for in the fast-moving Pacific war, radio and telephonic communications were of far more significance than were the postal ones.

The PNG campaigns — indeed, the Second World War itself — could not have been fought, on either side, without the various Signals organizations of the armed forces involved. In the case of ANGAU, the Signals Section was responsible for the provision of wireless communications and telephones in all areas in PNG where the Australian Corps of Signals was not operating. Up to the end of 1943, Army Signals personnel were providing communications to a number of localities throughout Papua and the Mandated Territory under ANGAU control, but it was then decided that this should become an ANGAU responsibility. ANGAU administrative officers were, where necessary, given training in radio procedures and maintenance by Signals men, and by 31 March 1944, five outstations had been taken over by ANGAU, working into a Control Station at headquarters. Officers at another seven outstations were also in regular radio contact, using normal Army signals channels. By the end of 1944, ANGAU was operating two wireless networks, in the Northern (Mandated Territory) and the Southern (Papua) Regions, with a total of thirty stations.

On 22 May 1944, a school was established at ANGAU headquarters to train Papua New Guineans for posting to the network stations as Wireless Operators. This Native Signals School was a decided success. The first course was completed on 21 August, and 42 pupils were graduated: 24 wireless operators, 12 linesmen and 6 switchboard operators. Other courses followed. The course included instruction in wireless operation, both W/T and R/T; maintenance, battery charging, message writing and general signals procedures. The average speed attained in sending and receiving in Morse Code was 12 words per minute, and some pupils reached 15-20. So encouraging were the results, that ANGAU formed a Native Line and Construction Maintenance Section, with 16 personnel who were attached to 18 Australian L. of C. Signals, for practical training in line construction and maintenance. By the end of October 1944, this section had already constructed several line routes and an internal line network and telephone service in the ANGAU Southern Region; by this time, too, Papua New Guinean operators were serving on all stations in the regional network. On 21 September 1944, graduates of the Native Signals School took over operation of the main ANGAU telephone switchboard.

As the various districts were recaptured from the Japanese, ANGAU established new signals stations. Five were opened in the Northern Region Network during January and February 1945: two in the Madang District, one in Manus and two in New Britain. Native operators in the network were at that time graded as 'good' on average, with some 'exceptional'. Another station was established in March, at Emirau in New Ireland, and in May and June at Torokina, Green Island and Lavongai, New Hanover. In April, sets were installed on four of the small ships operated by ANGAU.

Most of the stations used AWA Type 3B teleradios, and the Type 3BZ, a development of the 3B specially modified to withstand the effects of a harsh tropical climate. The modifications were carried out by Clarence Healey of AWA, and the Type 3BZ became available for issue in June and July 1942. It was immediately ordered by both the Australian and American Signals Corps; the first units were delivered to the Americans. A school was established at Sogeri to train American signals personnel in the use and maintenance of AWA equipment which was unfamiliar to them. As the Pacific war drew towards its end, more and more Type 3BZ sets were acquired by ANGAU, and when civil administration resumed, the smooth-running ANGAU network was progressively transferred to civilian control, in many cases with the Papua New Guinean operators. The value of relatively efficient internal wireless communications to a civilian authority struggling to restore orderly government in a war-torn country like PNG can hardly be over-estimated.

The AWA Type 3B teleradio sets, and the 3BZ, have yet another claim to fame in the history of telecommunications in PNG, for it was mainly these sets that equipped the intrepid little band of early-warning intelligence gatherers that has become known as the Coastwatchers. There was a strong link, too, between ANGAU and the Coast-watchers, and a number of Coastwatchers later served in ANGAU.

The coastwatching organization was formed after the First World War as a substitute for a coastguard service like the American one which would have been far too expensive for a thinly-populated country like Australia with its great length of coastline. The object of the organization was to ensure as far as possible the systematic surveillance of the coast and the prompt reporting of any unusual activity in time of war: the movement of ships or aircraft, enemy landings or suspicious behaviour. Controlled by the Royal Australian Navy, the coastwatching organization was at first confined to Australia. Reliable civilians — usually local officials such as policemen, schoolteachers or postmasters — resident in coastal regions who were prepared voluntarily to report to the authorities, were appointed. An official 'Outline of Coast-watching Organization' issued by the Department of Defence, detailed the reporting method used:

> It is not proposed that any person be placed in charge of the Coastwatching Organ-ization in any section of the coast. Postmasters of coastal telegraph or telephone stations will, however, be in a position to exercise supervision or reporting as, from whatever source a report may emanate, it will be through the most convenient coastal telegraph or telephone station that it will be transmitted. Postmasters at these stations are supplied with the Coastwatching Guide.

In 1928, the organization was extended to Papua, the Mandated Territory, and the British Solomon Islands. There were, of course, no telegraph or telephone networks linking these vast territories in 1928, and the only means of rapid communication with Australia was by wireless telegraphy. It was essential that information from Coast-watchers be transmitted in code. There were Admiralty Reporting Officers at a few key posts in the Territories, and it was planned that Coastwatchers would report their findings as quickly as they could to these officers, who would encode the messages and forward them by AWA wireless telegraphy to Australia. It was obviously a makeshift arrangement, for few Coastwatchers had access to wireless equipment in 1928, and a lot of time could elapse before a message from the field reached an Admiralty officer. Nor was it possible to rely on Postmasters, for as this account has shown, there were few in the Territories. The obvious class of local official to be appointed Coastwatchers were the Field Officers of the Magisterial Branch in Papua, and the Department of District Services and Native Affairs in the Mandated Territory, most of whom were ex officio postal officers in any event. This was done. In Papua, the Resident Magistrates of the Western, Delta, Gulf, South-Eastern, North-Eastern and Northern Divisions were appointed, and also the Assistant Resident Magistrates at the island and coastal stations of Kairuku, Rigo, Abau, Misima, Kulumadau, Losuia and Baniara, and the ARM of the inland station of Ioma, in view of its isolation. The same principle was followed in making the initial Mandated Territory and Solomons appointments.

Since the organization only became active 'in time of war or proclaimed imminence of war' in the words of the Coastwatching Guide, not much attention was paid to it by busy field officers in the years before the Second World War. As officers were transferred from one station to another in the normal course of service life, the Coastwatching Guide would be handed on and left, often unread, in the station safe. Sometimes there were embarrassing losses, such as that which occurred at Abau, in 1933. Leo Flint, the ARM and Coastwatcher, died suddenly on duty. A temporary appointment was made until the replacement ARM, O.J. Atkinson, could be sent to Abau, and because of the death of Flint, Atkinson was not briefed on his coastwatching responsibilities, which were confidential. After an outgoing Coastwatcher handed over his Guide to the incoming, he was required to furnish a certificate of transfer, which was sent on to the Navy Office in Melbourne. In 1936, a routine enquiry from the Navy Office led to a frantic search at Abau for the Coastwatching Guide, and Leonard Murray wrote an apologetic letter to Melbourne: 'The ARM now in charge states that he has searched his safe, also all current and old records, but that the Coastwatching Guide can not be traced. He offers the opinion that it may have "been destroyed by rats, judging by the rat-eaten condition of some of the old records here".'

This must have been very discouraging to the Navy Office, but the war in Europe was soon to bring an end to such complacency. By the end of the 1930s there were some 800 Coastwatchers throughout Australia and the Territories. The introduction of the pedal radio and teleradio sets meant that information could now be swiftly relayed from the most remote and isolated locations, and the network was far more valuable than it had been in the 1920s. In Papua and the Mandated Territory, a number of planters and missionaries was appointed Coastwatchers in an attempt to fill gaps in the early-warning chain, but the coverage was still skimpy.

When the war began, E.A. Feldt was Mining Warden of the Morobe gold-field, based at Wau. He was also an ex-naval officer, and in September 1939, he rejoined the Navy and was appointed Staff Officer (Intelligence) at Port Moresby, under Commander R.B.M. Long, Director of Naval Intelligence, the man who with his civilian assistant, W.H. Brooksbank, had been most responsible for the development of the coastwatching organization. Under Long, Feldt was charged with the responsibility for the collection of intelligence throughout the south-west Pacific area, which involved operational control of the Coastwatchers.

In his book, *The Coastwatchers*, published in 1946, Feldt described how he strengthened and extended the organization, so that it was ready when the Japanese invasion began:

> On 21 September 1939, with the war sixteen days old, I set out with a sheaf of printed coastwatcher instructions to visit every man in the islands who had a teleradio. My travels took me by ship, motor boat, canoe, bicycle, airplane and boot throughout the Solomons, the New Hebrides, Papua, New Guinea, New Britain, New Ireland and their satellite specks of land. I saw nearly everybody and nearly everybody saw me ... by December 1939, I had enrolled all existing teleradio operators, taught them how to code, what to report, and that speed in reporting was the prime essential. With an eye to the future, I also instructed about a hundred others in reporting, although most of

these had no means by which a message could be passed to us except by runner to the nearest teleradio — often a matter of days.

To further improve the system, additional teleradios were supplied by Naval Intelligence to Coastwatchers at a number of strategic points. Each Coastwatcher was issued with a crystal cut to a special frequency, known as X, and at any hour signals could be picked up at key stations in Rabaul, Tulagi, Port Moresby and Thursday Island. The radio sets — AWA Type 3Bs at this stage of the war — were maintained by AWA technicians.

And so, when the Japanese began their war in the Pacific, there were in existence sixty-four teleradio-equipped coastwatcher stations in the south-west Pacific area, in Feldt's words:

> . . . a secret and highly unorthodox military unit which, out of the foresight of the Australian Navy and the determination of a handful of enemy-surrounded planters, missionaries, government officers and miners, grew into the organization that supplied information from the heart of Japanese-occupied tropical islands in the Southwest Pacific, to the two Allied Headquarters of the Pacific Theatre.

Throughout the war, the organization was known by the codeword *Ferdinand*, after the gentle bull of Walt Disney, who hated fighting. Coastwatchers were there to silently and secretly observe and report on enemy activities, not to fight — although circumstances forced many of them to do so. The organization was only a part of what became known as the Allied Intelligence Bureau, or AIB, which included a number of Australian, Dutch, British and American units dedicated to sabotage, propaganda and the collection and reporting of intelligence.

This is not the place for an examination of the work of *Ferdinand*; the story has been told in many books and accounts, most notably in Eric Feldt's inspiring book. The incredible speed of the Japanese advance in the opening months of the war meant that a number of coastwatchers were overrun before they could escape — 27 coast-watchers were killed during the war and 18 captured (of whom only two survived) and 60 native members of *Ferdinand* guerrilla forces were killed or captured. The position of the Coastwatchers in the early months was made doubly hazardous by their civilian status; if captured, legally they could be treated as spies, and executed. They were mobilized into the Royal Australian Navy in early 1942, but military rank seldom saved them if they were taken. *Ferdinand* remained in operation for the whole of the Pacific war, although purely intelligence work ceased when the Australians began the mopping-up of the surviving Japanese forces after taking over the American bases in October and November 1944. *Ferdinand* then went over to offensive operations, and the 'M' Special Unit Native Infantry Battalion was raised to assist in this bloody work.

There was scarcely a campaign in the south-west Pacific Area where the Coast-watchers did not provide intelligence useful, and frequently vital, to Allied success. Many were decorated. Probably the most striking tribute to the Coastwatchers was that paid by the American, Admiral Halsey, to the work of two of the most famous, Paul Mason (a planter) and Jack Read (a government Field Officer), on Bougainville.

Intelligence from Bougainville had saved Guadalcanal, said Halsey, and Guadalcanal had saved the South Pacific.

As the war progressed, men from other services became Coastwatchers and by the war's end, some 421 had served in *Ferdinand*, including those in base positions: 163 officers and men, Royal Australian Navy; 11 Royal New Zealand Navy; 169 Australian Army; 10 RAAF; 8 British Solomon Islands Defence Force; 7 United States Marine Corps; 34 US Army; one Women's Royal Australian Naval Service, 13 civilians and 5 AWA men, who were made Honorary Chief Petty Officers of the RAN Volunteer Reserve.

Upon the outbreak of war, the Australian War Book provided for the control of all commercial wireless stations to pass to the Navy Office, through the PMG's Department. In Papua and the Mandated Territory, AWA continued to operate as usual, subject to the requirements of the National Security Regulations, until the Japanese entered the war and civil administration was suspended. As already mentioned, the AWA Radio Inspector for the Island Radio Service, Harry Holland, was captured when Rabaul fell, but all AWA operators in the Mandated Territory succeeded in evading the Japanese and returning to Australia, some after truly remarkable adventures. Typical were the experiences of W.R.B. Thomas, AWA operator at Kavieng, in New Ireland.

Kavieng was attacked by dive-bombers and fighters on 21 January. The town was quite defenceless, and the District Officer and Coastwatcher, J.H. McDonald decided to evacuate it, with a group of civilians that included Thomas. Three miles from Kavieng, McDonald assembled his people at a secure bush camp, and during the following week Thomas maintained contact with Port Moresby and Wau, using McDonald's Type 3B teleradio. Enemy activity then forced them to destroy the set and leave the camp; after perilous wanderings, the party arrived at Samo Plantation, 200 miles from Kavieng, where Coastwatchers A.F. Kyle, ADO, and G.M. Benham, PO, were holed up. Kyle and Benham had been chased by Japanese patrols since abandoning their station at Namatanai, and had hidden their teleradio — swift movement in the jungles of New Ireland was quite impossible when encumbered by a teleradio, with its heavy accumulators and changing motor. The set was discovered by a party of soldiers escaping from the Rabaul débâcle; they brought the transmitter section to the plantation, together with a Fisk Radiola domestic receiver that had been air-dropped by *Ferdinand* on receipt of the two Coastwatchers' last radio report; this was apparently the first such supply-drop to be attempted in the south-west Pacific area. The transmitter leads had been torn off, and the Radiola damaged in the drop; Thomas repaired them and within two days was again in contact with Port Moresby. He handed over the equipment to Kyle and Benham, and later succeeded in escaping by sea in a cranky old launch, with sixteen others of McDonald's party. Kyle and Benham were captured by the Japanese, and executed.

When the Japanese attacked Lae, the Administrator, Sir Walter McNicoll, was in residence there, following the transfer of the capital of the Mandated Territory from Rabaul after the volcanic eruptions of January, 1941. Lae was badly battered by the enemy bombers; the Guinea Airways powerhouse was completely destroyed and the AWA radio building and equipment riddled by shrapnel fragments. Civilians were ordered to evacuate the town, and McNicoll asked the two operators who ran the AWA station to erect an Administration-owned Type 3A teleradio at a camp five miles from Lae. Contact was established that night with Port Moresby, and with Rabaul and Wau.

On 22 January, Radio Rabaul went off the air. The Administrator, who was a sick man, with the Government Secretary flew to Wau — from where they were later flown to Australia — and on the following day, all civilians were advised to make for Wau also, or the government station at Kainantu, in the Upper Ramu, on foot. The AWA men arranged for the final destruction of the Lae radio equipment, handed over the teleradio to the NGVR detachment that was remaining, and joined the exodus. Lae fell on 8 March.

The Upper Ramu station became the assembly point for survivors of the Japanese assaults from many parts of the Territory. The Central Highlands came under attack from marauding Japanese bombers and fighters, but this huge hinterland remained in Allied hands for the whole of the war.

Hugh Taylor, AWA operator at faraway Lorengau, Manus Island, had a long way to go to reach the Highlands, and by a devious route. When the war with Japan began, Taylor very prudently deposited at Tingo village, eight miles inland, a carrying-box containing an AWA Type 242 transmitter, his personal Eddystone Four receiver (because of its performance and light weight), HT batteries and aerials, and a supply of fuel, spare parts and two six-volt accumulators. On 25 January, Lorengau was attacked by formations of Japanese seaplanes. The AWA station was destroyed, although Taylor managed to remove and later bury the transmitter and receiver.

A Japanese landing seemed imminent, and after conferring with the officer in charge of the small AIF detachment stationed on Manus, the District Officer, D.H. Vertigan, decided to fire the town and withdraw into the interior. They walked to Tingo, retrieved the radio equipment hidden there by Taylor, and from a camp further up in the mountains, kept in radio contact with Port Moresby and Wau. Early in April, the Japanese landed in force. It was time to leave. They walked to the south coast and set sail in a launch and the ketch *Emily*, for Bagabag Island, north of Madang.

At Bagabag, Taylor again contacted Port Moresby and Vertigan was advised to head for the Upper Ramu with his party. They landed at Bogadjim, south of Madang, crossed the Finisterres, walked up the Ramu and across the Bismarcks and reached Kainantu late in April. Taylor maintained his contact with Port Moresby and soon after reaching Kainantu they were instructed to keep on walking, to Mount Hagen, for evacuation to Australia.

Taylor's odyssey was matched by that of the veteran Cyril Urquhart, who was AWA operator at Madang when the war began. There was an NGVR unit at Madang, with a teleradio link to an AIF detachment at Bulwa, near Wau (the NGVR had a number of radio links in these early months). On 18 January 1942, a warning was received from Bulwa that a Japanese force was about to land at Madang. This proved false, but on 21 January, Madang, along with Kavieng, Lorengau, Salamaua, Lae and Bulolo, was attacked by waves of Japanese bombers and fighters. Urquhart stayed by his radio throughout this raid, broadcasting a warning, undeterred by the bursting bombs and exploding cannon-shells. Rabaul fell, and Madang would soon follow.

Civilians left the town and started on the long trudge to the Upper Ramu and Mount Hagen; the NGVR stayed behind. Before leaving, Urquhart, with the help of the NGVR men, destroyed the Madang radio station. He took an Eddystone dry-battery receiver from the deserted W.R. Carpenter store, his Type 3B teleradio, batteries, fuel and charging motor, and set up a temporary station at Wagol Plantation while the movement of the civilians was organized. During the trek to Mount Hagen, he contacted Port Moresby and Thursday Island each night, reporting progress. It was a hard journey; Urquhart was a short, plump man nudging fifty, and like a number of others in the party, he suffered.

The evacuation of the refugees from Mount Hagen was an epic, carried out with complete success under conditions of discomfort and great danger. The plight of the little band waiting at Mount Hagen was not at first realized by the authorities in Australia who were preoccupied with one crisis after another as the Japanese stormed across the Pacific. It was not until a Catholic priest and amateur pilot, Father John Glover, and a mechanic, Karl Nagy, made an extraordinary flight in a creaky, patched-up DH60 Moth to the Papuan coast, followed by a canoe-voyage to Thursday Island, to ask for help, that official arrangements were made to fly the refugees — seventy-seven men and one woman — out.

The job was done by Qantas, in two ex-Qantas DH86A aircraft that had been impressed into the RAAF. They were hastily fitted with long-range fuel tanks and additional instruments. Flown by three volunteer crews — Captains Orm Denny (veteran New Guinea pilot), Eric Sims and Rex Nicholl; Radio Operators F.S. Furniss, R.J. Anderson and L.W. Louttit; Engineers D.E. Chambers and R. Carswell, and with Father Glover and Tommy O'Dea, another New Guinea old hand — the De Havillands made eighteen flights from 13 to 24 May 1942, between Horn Island at the tip of Cape York Peninsula and Mount Hagen, and flew out all the refugees. Cyril Urquhart advised Thursday Island by pre-arranged code as each aircraft departed Mount Hagen — the skies were commanded by Japanese fighters — and went out himself on the last flight.

Driven out of the Mandated Territory, AWA stayed on the job in Papua. During the frantic days of January 1942, the AWA stations at Samarai and Misima were abandoned, but the main Port Moresby station carried on without a break throughout the war. Furious Japanese bombing attacks led to the relocation of the station to a safer site; the Radio Station, built at the corner of Musgrave Street and Ela Beach Road, was close to oil dumps and food stores, and the tall aerial masts were a constant invitation to the enemy pilots.

The Port Moresby station was vital to the Allied cause in the early months of the war with Japan. As the Mandated Territory was overrun and Rabaul was captured, Port Moresby was the surviving key station in the region, operating the secret X frequency used by the Coastwatchers. The defence forces then based at Port Moresby depended entirely on AWA facilities to maintain contact with Australia, for their communications equipment was at this stage limited to a few field transmitters and telephones.

At the request of the defence authorities, AWA established a station at Rouna, nineteen miles from the town, equipped with major units from the Port Moresby station. This handled Army traffic until August 1943, when what was to become the largest Signals Office in any AIF operational area was established at the foot of Horsley's Gap, a few miles from Port Moresby. This office was initially established in a tent by an advance party of 1st Australian Corps Signals under the command of Lieutenant-Colonel L.J. Wellman. The switchboard was installed in a slit trench. On 25 August, a secondary office was established at Bisiatabu, through which communication was maintained with the 7th Division on the Owen Stanley Range. The office at Horsley's Gap became the nerve centre for the whole of the forthcoming New Guinea campaigns.

AWA handed over all available spare teleradio equipment to the Army, which distributed a quantity to the NGVR. It was the original NGVR radio network that was developed, with Army, Navy and Air Force networks, into the New Guinea Air Warning Wireless Company.

As the tempo of the Japanese bombing attacks increased — over a hundred raids were made on the AWA stations in the Port Moresby region — the 200-watt general purpose transmitter, and the J3719 transmitter that had been removed from the Samarai station when it was abandoned, were taken to a temporary safe location outside the town, leaving the Port Moresby station with barely sufficient equipment to continue operating. Naval headquarters were removed to a large private house at Wonga, five miles from the town centre, and the property of a leading merchant, J.R. Clay. By arrangement with the Navy, the principal AWA station was relocated on the ground floor of the Clay house. The Wonga station stayed in operation throughout the war and for some time thereafter, and remained the key reporting station for the Coastwatchers. The officer-in-charge was Ken Frank of AWA, who subsequently provided invaluable assistance to the post-war provisional administration during the initial re-establishment of the territorial wireless network.

It is an undeniable fact that without the resources of AWA and the existence of the teleradio outstation network and the Coastwatcher stations equipped by it, Australian defence forces in Papua and the Mandated Territory at the outbreak of the Pacific war would have been virtually without communications. The nation was woefully short of skilled technicians and engineers. Many were serving overseas. Before the war Australia had obtained almost all her specialized telecommunications, long line and associated 'carrier' terminal equipment from overseas contractors; AWA manufactured a wide range of first class radio communication units, but had not ventured into long line telephony. The first two years of the war in Europe amply proved the vulnerability of radio communications to interception by enemy intelligence. It was not until the Japanese crippled the American Pacific Fleet at Pearl Harbor that the Australian government was shocked into a realization that communications with the north of the continent, and with Papua and the Mandated Territory, were desperately inadequate, and vulnerable. The initial successes of the Japanese caused a wave of fear, even panic in Australia; the rapid collapse of British forces, the sinking of the vaunted capital ships, *Prince of Wales* and *Repulse* followed by the fall of Singapore seemed evidence enough that Australia's turn would soon come. How could the north, so vast and underpopulated, be held against a Japanese invasion? Defence planners came to a sad conclusion; the north could not be defended: a stand would be made along the so-called 'Brisbane Line', just north of the Queensland capital. The British were no longer in a position to help defend Australia, and in a historic decision, Australia turned to the United States. The massive build-up of American military might in Australia began.

American involvement in the defence of Australia changed overall strategy, and there was no more talk of the 'Brisbane Line'. Early in 1942, urgent steps were taken to consolidate, duplicate and expand existing channels of long line communication from the eastern state capitals to northern Australia. The work was done by the Postmaster General's Department, assisted by both the Australian and United States Signals Corps, and involved the design and manufacture in Australia of a great deal of the long line and associated equipment that previously had been purchased overseas. Of particular significance to the defence of Papua and the Mandated Territory were new channels provided between Townsville and Cape York, and Adelaide and Darwin.

As the fast-moving war in the Southwest Pacific Area developed, so did the communications networks of the armed forces. War is unpredictable, and it was the fortunes of war that shaped the development of these, not the requirements of peacetime. As a result, few of the communications installations of the war years, other than those in northern Australia, proved to be of long-term benefit to Papua New Guinea. Port Moresby swiftly expanded into an enormous military base; by mid-1943 the Australian and American signals corps had laid more than 2 000 miles of wire and installed forty-seven telephone exchanges in Port Moresby and district, but little of use remained when civil administration was resumed.

No attempt will be made to describe the intricacies of the military communications systems used in PNG during the war, except for the crowning achievement of the Signals Corps, the construction of the Long Line from one coast of the mainland of New Guinea to the other. It was superb technical and human feat.

The trans-New Guinea Long Line telephone and telegraph system resulted from the urgent need for safe, secure communications between the Allied headquarters in Port Moresby, and the front line following the Japanese campaigns in mid-1942. Radio communications would not do; although relatively easy to supply, and undoubtedly efficient, radio could be readily intercepted by the enemy with possibly catastrophic results, as the Coral Sea battle just concluded had once again demonstrated. Powerful forces were being committed to battle in the Mandated Territory, and the need for secure communications was essential to their proper deployment. As the Australians pushed the Japanese back over the Owen Stanleys, Signals Corps personnel constructed a single wire telegraph line to Kokoda, which was extended to Dobodura during the Buna campaign. It was a useful, but limited, telegraph link, often broken. Defence strategy at this time called for forward headquarters to be established as the enemy retreated. Following the recapture of Buna and Gona, it was decided to transfer some American and Australian Air Force and Army units from Port Moresby to the Dobodura district, in preparation for air attacks on Japanese strongholds in New Guinea. Inonda, about thirteen miles from Dobodura, was selected as the site for the headquarters of the First Air Task Force of the United States 5th Air Force. The question of communication between Port Moresby and Inonda then arose.

A number of conferences were held late in 1942 between Australian and American signals engineers to discuss the problem and the best means of overcoming it. The Americans were frankly sceptical of the Australian proposal: the construction of high-grade long line communications over the Owen Stanley Range. American engineers did not believe that such a line could be built, given the unprecedented physical difficulties that existed, but the leader of the Australian team, Lieutenant-Colonel N. McCay, insisted that the job could, and would, be done.

The Australian Corps of Signals had been completely reorganized following the return of the AIF from the Middle East, under the direction of Major-General C.H. Simpson. As a part of the reorganization, General Simpson gradually built up a headquarters staff of experts in every field of communications. One of these was Lieutenant-Colonel McCay, who had been considered one of the most efficient transmission engineers in the PMG's Department. With great difficulty, McCay succeeded in persuading a reluctant Australian Government to agree to the release of three key PMG engineers, who had volunteered for active service: Major J. Reed, Major I.M. Gunn and Captain E.C.A. Brown. McCay gave Brown the job of establishing, from first principles and transmission and theoretical calculations, whether or not the proposed long line system was feasible.

Brown was amply qualified for such a task. He had joined the PMG's Department in 1926 as a Junior Mechanic, and in the years before the war worked in Britain, Hungary and France, and in the PMG research laboratories in Australia, before qualifying as an engineer. He lectured in transmission theory in Victoria and Tasmania, and gained a great deal of engineering experience in the field. It was this combination of theoretical knowledge and practical experience that eventually enabled him to reach the confident conclusion that the long line was feasible and could be provided, given the necessary resources.

Many unique problems would have to be overcome. Never before had a long line been taken through such hostile terrain. The steep slopes of the Owen Stanleys were covered with dense rain forest, many of the trees eighty to a hundred feet high and shallow-rooted, liable to come crashing to earth at any time, for no apparent reason. Grades were excessive, humidity was extreme and windsqualls common. Not only would initial construction be extraordinarily difficult; maintenance would be a constant nightmare. But, given the resources, the job could be done. In March 1943, the decision was taken to proceed with the Port Moresby-Inonda multi-channel long line. Construction, installation, maintenance and future development of this and all other Australian signals communications in New Guinea would be under the direction of Captain E.C.A. Brown.

While an engineering team which included Brown worked on the design of the long line, manufacture of suitable heavy PVC-insulated copper wire with a breaking strain of 200 pounds was begun. Light, barrel-type insulators, weighing no more than four ounces (for materials would have to be carried to the site) were made in Australian potteries to Signals Corps specifications, and special tree-spikes, weighing eight ounces, were produced. The design finally employed called for standard PMG-type open wire construction from Port Moresby to Ilolo, and from Mason's Corner to

Inonda. The rest of the line, following the Kokoda Trail over the Owen Stanleys, would be slung from tall trees in the rain forest, using the light insulators attached to the special tree spikes by galvanized-iron wire with a breaking strain of sixty pounds. The theory was that falling trees would break the wire and carry the heavy-gauge PVC-insulated conductor lines to earth without breaking them, allowing transmission of telegraph and voice traffic through the system until repairs could be made, even though the lines were down. There would be some loss of quality, but no break in transmission. Later experience proved this theory entirely correct.

The decision to proceed having been taken, the mass of materials and equipment required was assembled and tested at Port Moresby. One of the most formidable of the many problems confronting Brown and his team was that of the transport of the heavy conductor wire and other materials and tools through the deep forest of the Owen Stanleys. There was a jeep road to Ilolo, a distance of twenty-one miles, but the only way through the mountains was on foot. Four hundred carriers and labourers were recruited by ANGAU, for the success of the project depended vitally upon the assistance of Papua New Guineans. Arrangements were made to drop supplies and materials by aircraft of the US Fifth Air Force and the RAAF, but it was still found necessary to employ a constant chain of carriers throughout the exercise.

The initial line from Port Moresby to Ilolo was constructed in thirty-two days, using steel telescopic poles designed and manufactured in Melbourne. Work on the crossing of the Owen Stanleys began on 12 May 1943. The Ilolo-Kokoda section was divided into three parts, and a detachment from 18th Australian Line of Communications Signals under the command of Major W. Geddes was allotted to each, together with medical orderlies of the Australian Medical Corps to care for the labourers and Signals personnel. Each party began work on the same day, 12 May, steadily advancing into the virgin forest, the labourers clearing a path for the line while the signalmen spiked the insulators into suitable trees, about fifteen feet above the ground. Huts in the forest, used during the construction of the existing single-wire telegraph line, were again pressed into service, and others erected. Rain and wind hammered at the men as they slashed their way through the forest, and the medical orderlies were kept busy dressing cuts and abrasions. The heavy conductor lines had to be hauled into place by brute force. Despite all obstacles, the work proceeded almost without a break. Contact was maintained with Kokoda and Port Moresby throughout using the old line, and as each section of the new line was completed it was carefully tested.

Twenty-nine days after the start, the line was through to Kokoda. There the US Fifth Air Force Signals took over from the Australians, and carried it to Mason's Corner, and by conventional pole construction to Inonda. Meanwhile, Australian and American technicans were erecting the terminal buildings at Port Moresby and Inonda, and installing the Western Electric CS5 three-channel carrier units that were to be employed. The CS5, manufactured in the United States, was recognized as the best then available anywhere in the world, and although the distance between the terminals was 152 miles, regarded as the extreme operating limit for the CS5 when using a stable permanent line, tests proved that the Owen Stanley Long Line — anything but stable — was highgrade. The system came into operation on the night of 5 July 1943. Two of the three channels available were reserved for use by the US Fifth

Air Force, and by the AIF and the US 41st Division; the third provided a bearer for an Australian-built four-channel VF telegraph system, later replaced by a Western Electric 12-channel system, as traffic increased.

There is little doubt that the flexibility and complete security of the Port Moresby-Inonda Long Line had a significant effect on the Allied war effort in PNG. It was always expensive to maintain, but in time of war cost was a secondary consideration. Forty stations were established along the route, each staffed by maintenance parties who kept the line clear and standing, reporting daily by telephone. Until the end of 1943, basic equipment and tools were always in short supply, and a number of the personnel at the line stations lacked the proper training for their important and demanding work. In his final report on the project, Brown noted that line maintenance left much to be desired; some inexperienced linesmen had been known to go out on a fault without wire, sleeves, jointing tongs, clips or belts. The situation gradually improved as personnel with Middle Eastern experience became available, and late in 1943 the US Services of Supply organization, which prodigally poured in tools and equipment, began to make its presence felt. Material shortages were soon a thing of the past, thanks to the Americans.

By the time the Owen Stanley Long Line was complete, the Allies had gone over to offensive operations in the Mandated Territory. Secure communications were urgently required to the rapidly advancing forward headquarters and it was decided to extend the line along the north coast of Papua to Lae, using another CS5 carrier system, with a repeater station at Morobe. The job of constructing the Inonda-Morobe section fell to 18th Australian Line of Communication Signals, while 19th Line of Communications took on the longest section, Morobe-Lae, which involved the most difficult single construction problem of the extension, the crossing of the formidable Markham River.

The Markham crossing was undertaken by a unit of 4th Australian Field Company, Royal Australian Engineers, commanded by Captain I.G. Tulloch. The long line was completed to the south bank, and only the great brown river, swollen by heavy rains in the mountain headwaters, barred the route to Lae. At the mouth, near where the crossing was to be made, the Markham was almost a mile wide, flowing at a rate of six to eight knots through a score of braided channels separated by sand bars. It would have been impossible to cross the river with a single span, but fortunately there was an island in the main channel, roughly two thirds across. Tulloch decided to run a heavy suspension cable across the river, anchored by large trees on each bank and supported by an intermediate mast which would be erected on the island. The long line would be carried beneath the suspension cable, on wire droppers.

The erection of the island mast posed the greatest engineering problem. The island was low, and covered by water during the spring tides. Concrete bases were laid on land for the mast and anchorages, in excavations sheeted with corrugated galvanized iron. The mast itself was constructed of two 40-foot lengths of twelve by twelve inch oregon timber, spliced together with heavy bolts. To erect the ponderous mast, a 30-foot lever spar was employed, haulage power being provided by an amphibious truck. The two spans to the mast measured 1 001 feet and 1 614 feet respectively, the long line dipping to within 20 feet of the river level.

The eleven Engineers and forty native labourers who built this vital link took sixteen working days to complete the task, finishing on 2 January 1944. It was unfortunate from the point of view of the technicians who would soon be struggling to restore communications in post-war PNG that the mast and cables were designed for a probable life of only eighteen months. But this was sufficient for military needs. On 22 January, the entire carrier system linking Port Moresby with Lae became operational; on 26 January, a storm of fearsome power swept over Lae and the lower Markham, damaging the terminal building; the suspension cable across the river was hit by lightning, and the span was broken. But the system was quickly restored.

While the Moresby-Lae system was being consolidated, the United States Signals Corps carried the line on to Finschhafen, where they were developing the colossal base at Dregerhafen, using spiral four cable, a type not previously used in PNG or Australia.

Following the completion of the long line, the Australian Corps of Signals turned to the question of linking PNG and Australia by submarine cable. The old, disused Melbourne-Launceston cable was recovered and after much trouble (a considerable quantity was lost in the Gulf of Papua) the cable was laid between Cape York and Delena, on the south coast of Papua, and from there was taken on to Port Moresby. The telegraph link between Allied Headquarters in Melbourne, and the front line in PNG was thus completed, even as the Japanese were facing their final defeat.

To mark this historic occasion, Lieutenant-General Sir Leslie Moreshead telegraphed to Blamey, in Port Moresby:

> This message marks the linking of New Guinea with Melbourne by direct line
> communication. It is a step forward in permanent secure communication made
> possible through the defeat of the Japanese by the troops of the New Guinea Force and
> by the enterprise and energy of the Australian Signal Service.

Unfortunately, the submarine cable across Torres Strait failed soon afterwards, and since the war in PNG was virtually over, no attempt was made to make repairs. It was by this time recognized that maintenance of the long line was no longer a viable proposition. Only the urgent demands of war could justify the expense involved, and in any case, advances in communications technology since the war began in 1939 had already made it obsolete. Under the spur of wartime necessity, the British had developed their revolutionary Wireless Set No. 10 first used in the invasion of Normandy. This set, utilizing microwave radio transmission, was the forerunner of the microwave transmission links in use all over the world today. The potential of this new technology was quickly realized by the Signals Corps, and experiments conducted in PNG with No. 10 sets before the war ended proved that it would be possible to provide trunk communications by microwave systems to most of the main centres. But hostilities were concluded before action could be taken.

Among those who quickly realized the importance and value of microwave radio transmission were N.J. McCay and his subordinates. Following the completion of the long line, Brown had been officially commended for his part in the project and promoted to the rank of Major, and on 18 May 1944, he was directed to establish a specialist training school at Balcombe, Victoria, as Chief Instructor. Here he remained until the end of the war, but his involvement with PNG was far from over. When civil administration was resumed, the PMG's Department was asked to select two experienced officers to tackle the immense task of restoring posts and telecommunications facilities throughout a war-torn PNG. One of the officers chosen was B.J. O'Brien, the Superintendent of Postal Services, Queensland, and the other E.C.A. Brown, whose discharge from the AIF was arranged with unusual rapidity.

THE RESUMPTION OF CIVIL ADMINISTRATION

On 25 October 1945, Colonel Jack Keith Murray arrived at Port Moresby to assume duty as Administrator of the Territory of Papua New Guinea. By an oversight, nobody was at the airport to greet him officially. This, Murray was soon to find, was typical of the muddling and inefficiency that marked the early years of the Provisional Administration.

Civil government was restored to Papua, and to that portion of New Guinea lying south of the Markham River, on 30 October 1945, and by 24 June 1946, had been progressively extended to the rest of the mainland, and to Manus, New Britain, New Ireland and Bougainville. The Papua New Guinea Provisional Administration Act 1945 provided for a single administration for the two former territories of Papua and the Mandated Territory, which was from the outset located at Port Moresby, the only important centre that survived, though badly scarred, the Pacific war.

The war had brought suffering and destruction to PNG and her peoples, but also the promise of a bright new future. Tens of thousands of Australians had served in PNG during the war; many servicemen owed their lives to the devotion of the 'Fuzzy-Wuzzy Angels', as the carriers on the Kokoda Trail had come sentimentally to be called. There was a general awareness in Australia of the debt the nation owed to PNG, a recognition that after the war, money would be spent on compensation and reconstruction. Australia had a Labor government for most of the war years, and this shared the mood of the country in the traditional Labor sympathy for the underdog. By 1945, Labor had formed, in broad terms, a policy on the post-war administration of PNG which was outlined in July by the Minister for External Territories, E.J. Ward, in a now-famous speech: 'The Government regards it as its bounden duty to further to the utmost the advancement of the natives and considers that can be achieved only by providing facilities for better health, better education and for a greater participation by the natives in the wealth of their country and eventually its government', said Ward. Compensation would be paid for war deaths and losses, a comprehensive programme of rehabilitation and development of the Territories would be followed, and new labour laws would be introduced. 'In future', Ward continued, 'the basis for the economy of the Territory will be native and European industry, with the limit of non-native expansion determined by the welfare of the natives generally'.

The extent of the influence of the Australian Army's remarkable brains-trust, the Directorate of Research and Civil Affairs, headed by the almost legendary A.A. Conlon, on Labor's PNG policy has often been argued. There seems little doubt that it was considerable. The Directorate was by any standard a unique organization, and it is extraordinary that it was sponsored by the Army. Certainly Blamey, Commander-in-Chief in PNG, relied mainly on Conlon and the Directorate for advice on all matters concerned with civil government, and Conlon had a close personal relationship with the Prime Minister, John Curtin, and with E.J. Ward and other leading Labor politicians. The creation of the Australian School of Pacific Administration, to train officers for PNG service, was largely due to Conlon's work. Members of the Directorate — some of Australia's leading intellectuals — worked in a wide variety of fields and had potent influence in many key areas. It can be said that Conlon and his Directorate provided much of the philosophical content of Labor's PNG policy, but it is an unfortunate fact that no hard plan of action had been formulated when the time came for the resumption of civil government, despite Ward's glowing promises.

The immensity of the task facing the Provisional Administration was apparent to J.K. Murray when he arrived in Port Moresby in October 1945 with a number of senior officers, among whom was the telecommunications expert, E.C.A. Brown (B.J. O'Brien, expert in postal administration, arrived shortly afterwards). A group of officers had been sent to Moresby the preceding August, 'to make preliminary arrangements for the restoration of civil government to the Territories, to determine in principle the method of transfer from military to civil control, and the supplies and equipment which the civil administration would require from stocks helds by the Army, and to devise means by which services essential to both civil and military needs would be carried on so that transfer would be effected as smoothly as possible', according to the 1945–6 *Annual Report*. In a period of three weeks, this party agreed on some basic principles for handling the transfer, but that was the extent of the preliminary planning.

The situation in PNG was that, as J.K. Murray later said, 'The Army had everything, the civil authority nothing'. All the main centres apart from Port Moresby had been destroyed and would have to be rebuilt, and Moresby itself had been transformed into a huge military base with none of the amenities — shops, hotels, accommodation, transport — required in civil life. The military authorities controlled everything: services, shipping, electricity, construction, communications. There were material shortages of every conceivable kind. The lack of detailed basic planning for the take-over was felt in almost every area; all too often, vital decisions were made on an *ad hoc* basis, regardless of the long-term consequences. All departments of the Provisional Administration were seriously under-staffed; there was a grave shortage of officers experienced in administration, and with technical or professional qualifications. There was, moreover, friction between officers of the old Papua and Mandated Territory administrations, who in turn often resented the presence of men from the ranks of the Army, ANGAU and the Commonwealth Public Service who joined the Provisional Administration. There was covert opposition to the 'new deal' for PNG promised by Labor, and to the Administrator, J.K. Murray, responsible for its implementation — feelings shared by most of the pre-war white residents as they began returning to take up their previous vocations.

Enormous quantities of equipment vital to post-war reconstruction were sold for a song through the Commonwealth Disposals Commission, were lost, stolen or simply abandoned, sometimes before the Administration was aware of their existence. As the Army relinquished control, materials and installations that would have been extremely valuable to the civil authorities were all too often removed or demolished in haste or ignorance. Doubtless the Commonwealth achieved a saving in the defence vote by such precipitate action, but it was at the expense of efficient administration.

E.C.A. Brown and B.J. O'Brien, officers of a Commonwealth Department of admitted competence, found the PNG scene hard to accept. They had, at first, no support staff, no office or residential accommodation, no inventory of the posts and telegraphs installations; equipment and materials were scattered throughout PNG, and very little transport was at their command. They found, too, little understanding among senior departmental officers of the special needs and requirements of their Branch, especially in the field of telecommunications. No town plans were available, and no firm policy had been decided on the re-establishment of towns — in particular, the future of Rabaul was in question. Two sets of laws, one for Papua and one for the former Mandated Territory, were in existence, each antiquated in many important areas and often in conflict. Enormous administrative difficulty and confusion resulted. The financial and accounting picture was also clouded: there was no separate Department of Posts and Telegraphs, and the Treasurer retained ultimate control of all financial matters, for as was the case pre-war, Posts and Telegraphs was still a branch of the Department of the Treasury. Procurement procedures for obtaining essential supplies and equipment from Australia were involved, time-consuming and notably inefficient. In all, it was a gloomy prospect.

It was quickly apparent to Brown and O'Brien that the proper solution of the complex problems that had to be overcome was beyond the capacity of the Provisional Administration to solve adequately, and they recommended to the Administrator that the Postmaster General's Department be requested to take control. On 14 February 1946, J.K. Murray wrote to the Secretary, Department of External Territories:

> In view of the very extensive resources in personnel and material of the Department of the Postmaster General of the Commonwealth . . . I recommend that the postal and telecommunication activities of this Administration become a responsibility of the Commonwealth Postmaster General's Department — the organization and relationship to be broadly those existing within a state of the Commonwealth.

No decision was forthcoming, and indeed debate over the question of PMG control of Posts and Telegraphs in PNG was to continue for years. In the meantime, Brown and

O'Brien made the best use possible of existing facilities, but came to the conclusion that all planning and development for the future should be in conformity with the standard practices employed in the Australian PMG's Department. During the frantic months that followed the restoration of civil government, they were forced to rely heavily on the postal and telecommunications systems of the armed forces. To overcome immediate problems, O'Brien arranged for the existing military postal services to carry on, handling civilian mails until civil post offices could be opened, following which the military offices would close. On 30 October 1945, the Port Moresby, Samarai and Daru Post Offices were reopened.

Unfortunately, B.J. O'Brien was forced by ill-health to return to the PMG's Department in Australia in January 1946. One of the top postal administrators in the Department, he eventually became Director of Posts and Telegraphs in Queensland, and in the coming years his advice and assistance continued to be sought by those responsible for postal affairs in PNG.

The entire burden of Posts and Telegraphs now rested temporarily on Brown's shoulders. An engineer, his knowledge of postal services was theoretical rather than practical, and it was fortunate that in May 1946 an experienced PMG postal officer, W.J. McPherson, accepted the position of Postmaster, Port Moresby. His administrative ability quickly won him promotion and he finally became Superintendent of Postal Services.

When McPherson took over the Port Moresby Post Office, his principal aide was a Papuan, Gavera Lohia of Hanuabada. Gavera had spent his entire working life in the Postal Branch, beginning work in the mail room of the Post Office in July 1920, as a seventeen-year-old, on a wage of ten shillings a month. He was now the senior Papua New Guinean in the Posts and Telegraphs Branch. During the war, Gavera served at the ANGAU post office at the 17-mile, and then at the 3-mile. Another Papuan assistant greatly valued by Wally McPherson was Michael Dawadawareta, who in 1962 was to become the first National Postmaster.

In the years immediately following the war, most overseas mail for PNG arrived by sea at intervals of between four and six weeks, in vessels carrying the familiar house-flag of Burns Philp & Co. The *Bulolo* and the *Malaita* were joined in 1952 by a new ship, the *Malekula*, and although over the following years the sea lanes to PNG were to be thronged with the ships of many nations — in far greater numbers than before the war — BP remained the official mail carrier until 1970, when the company retired its fleet. Mails were still dispatched by small craft to every part of the coastline in these early years. The organization of a coastal service proved a difficult task. Most of the small ships that had served the Territories during peace and war were worn out; many had been lost. A service was begun in May 1946, by the Commonwealth Directorate of Shipping, using the 300-tonners *Mary Rose* and *Doma*. It rapidly expanded. A number of Army trawler-type vessels was taken over by the Administration for use in the maritime districts. Stout, seaworthy 66-foot double-enders, they were fitted with Gray, Hercules and Cadillac marine engines designed for temporary wartime use, and expensive to maintain. All were eventually re-engined, mostly with Gardners, and became familiar sights in every port and along the entire coastline of PNG. Bearing names such as the *Huon, Thetis, Comworks, Poseidon* and *Morobe*, they were

frequently the sole means of supply to outlying districts. Some served PNG for thirty
or more years.

But the aeroplane, and to a lesser extent the motor vehicle, would shortly trans-
form the communications scene in PNG. As already noted, aeroplanes were widely
used in the Mandated Territory and to some extent in Papua, before the war, but
principally on the Morobe gold-field and in the Highlands. In post-war PNG, the
aeroplane would become a familiar sight in the remotest districts, and the map of the
Territory would soon be thickly spotted with aerodromes and landing grounds.

For reasons never publicly explained, the pioneer aviation company, Guinea
Airways Ltd., was refused permission by the Commonwealth government to resume
internal operations in PNG after the war. W.R. Carpenter & Co., too, was denied a
licence to fly again the Australia-PNG air mail route. The Carpenter airline was
bought out by Qantas, the Australian international carrier, which commenced a once-
weekly mail and passenger service between Sydney, Port Moresby and Lae on 2 April
1945, using C47 aircraft. By July, the service, christened 'Bird of Paradise', was
operating three times a week. By 1949, there were five weekly flights, extended to
Rabaul, Wau and Madang. Over this period, Qantas also built up a comprehensive
network within PNG, servicing the little airstrips that appeared all over the Territory
as new government outposts were established; mails were carried on all services.

Qantas had a number of competitors who also carried mails, the most important
being Mandated Airlines, the W.R. Carpenter-owned company, which had been
allowed to re-enter the domestic field. Another sizeable concern was Guinea Air
Traders, flying out of Lae. It was a Guinea Air Traders Lockheed Hudson that was
involved in the worst disaster in the history of civil aviation in PNG. The Hudson
crashed near the mouth of the Markham River on 18 April 1948, with the loss of
thirty-seven lives. In 1947, the Australian war-time fighter ace, Wing Commander
Bobby Gibbes, started his Gibbes Sepik Airways with one small Auster monoplane,
which he expanded into a sizeable fleet over the next ten years.[1] There were at least ten
other small aviation companies operating in the farthest corners of PNG in these early
years. Few of these early operators survived.

There was close co-operation between the Postal Branch and the RAAF and US
Army Air Force. RAAF planes on service flights to Territory centres allocated space
for civilian mails, and the introduction of a weekly service to Manus was by courtesy
of the Americans. The RAAF also continued the control and maintenance of major
aerodromes. As civil administration was extended and new stations were opened,
maintenance of the secondary landing grounds of the Territory became the responsibility of the Department of District Services and Native Affairs.

DDS and NA was also responsible for the dispatch of police mail runners over a
number of routes. The famous old Port Moresby-Kokoda service carried on until
October 1949, when Qantas commenced a weekly DH84 Dragon air service from Port
Moresby to Popondetta and Kokoda. A weekly runner service between Higaturu
(replaced by Popondetta after it was destroyed during the eruption of Mount
Lamington volcano in 1951), Ioma and Tufi began in early 1946; it stayed in operation

---

1 The Gibbes Sepik Airways story is told in my *Sepik Pilot* (Lansdowne, 1977).

until 1953. Ioma, one of the most isolated stations in Papua, was still being served by police runner as late as 1958. Another service began in 1946, between Port Moresby and Abau, and this was carried on to Rigo until 1952, when improved sea and air services rendered it unnecessary. A service between Port Moresby and the Kanosia district, which began in August 1946, ceased in the following February for the same reason. Another, in the Bougainville District between Sohano, Wakunai and Kieta began in 1948 and remained in operation until the late 1950s.

DDS and NA continued to have the close involvement with postal matters as it had pre-war. By mid-June 1948, thirty-two post offices had been re-opened throughout Papua New Guinea: Port Moresby, Samarai, Daru and Abau in 1945; Aitape, Angoram, Bwagaoia, Higaturu, Kairuku, Kavieng, Kieta, Lae, Losuia, Madang, Manus (Lorengau), Maprik, Namatanai, Rabaul, Rigo, Salamaua, Sohano (Buka Passage), Wau and Wewak in 1946; Bulolo, Gasmata, Goroka, Kerema, Kikori, Kokoda, Kokopo, Milne Bay and Talasea in 1947. Salamaua was in existence for only a brief period, opening in January and closing in April 1946, when the station was finally abandoned in favour of Lae as the headquarters of the Morobe District. Twenty-four of the post offices had money order and COD facilities, and all were telegraph offices. The Royal Australian Navy was still at this time operating an office at Finschhafen.

Of the above offices, only Port Moresby, Lae, Rabaul and Bulolo were controlled and staffed by the Postal Services branch; the others were run by officers of DDS and NA, subject to direction and annual audit by Postal Services. An extreme shortage of trained, experienced staff was the greatest single difficulty facing the Postal and Telecommunications branch. In the early months of the Provisional Administration, most senior staff were recruited from the ranks of the PMG's Department, on a secondment basis. The first qualified telegraphist to arrive was Ian Fisher, in 1946. He was sent to Rabaul, where he remained for the next twenty-five years. Positions in PNG were, however, hard to fill. Married accommodation was in short supply, and remained so for many years. Transport was limited and inefficient, available vehicles being relics of the war. Equipment in use throughout PNG was mostly ex-military, often in rundown condition and obsolete, or on the verge of obsolescence. Money was tight, and salaries inadequate. All positions in the Public Service of the Provisional Administration were held on an acting basis until 1 July 1949 when the Papua and New Guinea Act 1949 came into operation, providing for the administration of what was now the Trust Territory of New Guinea in administrative union with the Territory of Papua. A new classification of the Public Service providing increased salaries and benefits did not come into effect until 1951, although retrospective to 1 July. In all, general conditions of service in PNG were not sufficiently liberal to attract and hold many technical and professional officers from the secure ranks of the PMG's Department. Small wonder that the European staff wastage in 1946-7 amounted to 35.5 per cent (and the rate was even higher among PNG staff).

In many ways the staff position in the Telecommunications branch was even more critical in the early post-war period. Most returned DDS and NA officers were at least familiar with postal procedures, and new Cadet Patrol Officers were given brief, but sufficient, instruction by Wally McPherson and his officers at the Port Moresby

GPO before going out to the outstations. Technical instruction was a different matter. Cadets could be, and were, taught to operate the Type 3B and 3BZ teleradios used on the outstation networks but installation, maintenance and repairs were tasks for specialists. The planning and operation of a multi-channel telegraph system is not something that can be done by a hastily-trained amateur. Professionals were required, and E.C.A. Brown found just enough of them in the ranks of the Australian Signals Corps to be able to take over, and suitably modify, the existing defence installations and networks as the Army moved out. Few of his recruits had Public Service backgrounds, but all had served for varying periods in PNG and were accustomed to working with Papua New Guineans. This was an important qualification, for Brown intended to train as many indigenous people as possible as Telephone Linesmen, Switchboard Operators, Technicians and Postal Assistants. ANGAU had shown that this could be done. For many reasons, formal training did not begin until June 1946, but in the meantime, Mavara Hekure rejoined the Telecommunications branch. Mavara had been one of the first Papuans to receive technical training in Australia, back in 1922, and, encouraged by Mavara, a number of his relatives and friends with pre-war experience as operators and linesmen now came forward. They were sorely needed.

Europeans, both in government and private enterprise, continually grizzled and complained about the state of telephone services, where they existed, in the early post-war years. Perhaps there would have been less groaning had the public been aware of the difficulties facing the engineers and technicians.

The first task was to provide telephone services to the various Departments of the Provisional Administration, mostly located at Konedobu. The existing magneto telephone exchange established by the Army at the Port Moresby GPO, and the five satellite exchanges connecting with various outlying establishments such as the aerodrome, were taken over and converted where possible for civilian use. Considerable engineering was required. All existing systems had been designed for the temporary needs of war; most of the wire and cable reticulation had been abandoned by the armed forces, and no route plans were available. The GPO exchange was brought into service in November 1945 — the first post-war telephone exchange in PNG. For the first two months, it was staffed by ex-members of the Signals Corps, while on-the-job training as Switchboard Operators was given to a number of carefully selected male and female Papua New Guineans. An early decision was taken to adandon the Owen Stanley Long Line. Its maintenance was quite beyond the resources of the Posts and Telecommunications Branch, invaluable though it would have been in this chaotic period. The standard line to Ilolo was in reasonable condition and it was retained to provide a trunk line party service as far as Sogeri and the Koitaki rubber plantations. Other minor routes in the Port Moresby region were repaired. Much of the line work was done by cable jointers and technicians from the PMG's Department. In the process, a great deal of wire and cable was salvaged from the abandoned military networks, and stockpiled for use all over the Territory.

By mid-1947, local magneto exchanges were in operation at Sogeri, Rabaul, Lae and Madang, with another in the course of establishment at Kavieng. At Port Moresby, permanent aerial lines and underground cables had replaced most of the temporary wartime construction, and efficiency levels had risen. During 1946-7, 1 632 miles of aerial and underground cable were laid or reconstructed throughout PNG. There was a total of 762 subscribers connected to the various exchanges, 442 of them in Port Moresby. In addition, 14 private branch exchanges were in operation, with a further 168 extensions. The construction of telephone lines between Lae, Bulolo and Wau, and between Madang and Alexishafen, were awaiting the availability of staff and transport. Work had begun on the Rabaul-Kokopo trunk line. The construction and installation of the new Rabaul exchange had been complicated by uncertainty about the future of the town, and by the need to make as much use as possible of the existing Japanese cable and line reticulation system, which was of poor quality by Australian standards.

A radio telephone circuit was provided between Port Moresby and Rabaul, coming into service on 26 November 1946. By June 1947, an omnibus high frequency radio circuit was in operation between Moresby, Lae, Madang and Rabaul, and this was interconnected with the local telephone network in 1948, and with the overseas radio telephone service offered by the Overseas Telecommunications Commission.

As mentioned in Chapter 7, the ANGAU outstation teleradio network was taken over by the Provisional Administration, with many of the Papua New Guinean operators. It was expanded as new government stations were opened, and was essential for effective administration, serving as it did also the needs of coastal shipping. Sets employed on the outstations were mainly the tried and tested AWA Type 3B and 3BZ units, operated from accumulator-type batteries charged by small petrol-driven generators, which gave continual trouble and were the cause of hearty swearing in patrol post, sub-district and district offices throughout PNG, for most of the initial stations were operated by officers of DDS and NA.

A base station was established in Port Moresby in 1945, to control the outstation network, using an AWA 100 watt transmitter located in the GPO building which then housed the AWA control, to facilitate the interchange of traffic. In 1946 E.C.A. Brown gave a series of lectures to DDS and NA staff attending the Australian School of Pacific Administration in Sydney, on teleradio operation and procedures.

Technical staff recruited in Australia maintained the teleradio sets and associated equipment, and Papua New Guineans who had been trained by the Australian and US Signals Corps were located and employed. As the network grew, many plantations and mission stations sought permission to purchase teleradios and enter the system. A few compact ATR4A and 4C portable teleradios were employed, notably by Administration exploratory patrols and by field parties of the Australasian Petroleum Company, principally in the Gulf and Western Districts.

By 30 June 1947, there were sixty stations in the outstation network, controlled by Radio Zone Centres at Port Moresby, Lae, Rabaul and Madang. They spanned the Territory, being located at Abau, Aitape, Alexishafen, Angoram, Awelkon, Baniara, Bieng, Bogia, Buin, Buka, Bulolo, Cumbi, Daru, Dogura, Esa'ala, Finschhafen, Gasmata, Gizarum, Goilala, Goroka, Higaturu, Hohoro, Ioma, Kainantu, Kairuku, Kanosia, Kariava, Kavieng, Kerema, Kerowagi, Kieta, Kikori, Kundiawa, Losuia, Manus Island, Maprik, Milne Bay, Misima, Morobe, Mount Hagen, Murui, Mumeng,

Namatanai, Oroia, Port Romilly, Pondo, Raua, Rigo, Samarai, Sarno, Sio, Sohano, Talasea, Torakina, Tufi, Wabag, Wau, Wewak, Witu Island and Yodda. Of these stations, forty-one were operated by DDS and NA officers — or their wives. Within the following twelve months, the network grew to 103 outstations, and Samarai had been made a Zone Centre.

The outstation network was, of course, open to the public. Initially, it was a 'point to point' service, but it soon connected into the telephone system. It was used extensively for the passing of aircraft movement reports, and meteorological data for the Department of Civil Aviation.

The local telephone and radio telephone network was an integral part of a plan for an intra-Territorial telecommunication system drawn up by Brown in close collaboration with Ken Frank, and approved in principle at conferences in Australia in November 1946, attended by representatives of the departments of the Postmaster General, Civil Aviation, Interior, Navy and the Overseas Telecommunications Commission. The plan provided for the establishment of regional, zone and group trunk switching centres throughout PNG, to which radio telegraph and telephone terminals, and the local telephone exchanges, would be connected. The nature of the geography of PNG made the provision of normal line connections impossibly expensive; trunk telephone and telegraph communication channels between the major towns would depend in the main on high frequency radio links. The provision of communications between PNG and Australia and beyond would be the responsibility of the Overseas Telecommunications Commission (OTC).

Amalgamated Wireless (Australasia) Ltd. was quick to re-establish all major services between PNG and Australia, and within the Territory, when the war ended. The Island Radio Service was soon operating stations at Port Moresby, Rabaul, Madang and Samarai. The Port Moresby station, initially located at Wonga, was in the charge of Ken Frank, who gave Brown invaluable assistance and support in the first trying months. On 1 October 1946, the Overseas Telecommunications Commission was formed, with responsibility for the operation and maintenance of telecommunications services between Australia and other countries, with ships at sea and between Australia's external territories. The arrangement between AWA and the Commonwealth government that had so successfully endured since 1922 came to an end. PNG was little affected. Services were virtually unchanged, and staffing arrangement largely unaltered. Ken Frank became officer-in-charge OTC in PNG, and remained in that position until his death in a car accident near Charters Towers, Queensland, in August 1951. OTC established centres at Lae and Rabaul, and later at Kavieng, Manus and Wewak. There was close co-operation between Posts and Telegraphs and OTC, but telecommunications within PNG remained under P. and T. control.

Brown's telecommunications plan envisaged the formal training of Papua New Guineans in the skills necessary to support a national service, and, as noted above, on-the-job training began immediately. In June 1946, a small training school was established at Boroko, under the joint direction of V.G. Brown, Senior Technician (Telephones) and H.R. O'Brien, Line Inspector, seconded PMG officers. S.C. Kensett,[2]

---

2 See Chapter 6. Kensett joined the Postal Services Branch of the Mandated Territory Administration in July 1937.

Senior Technician, and H.L. Thompson, Line Foreman, later joined the staff. The school was destined to have a short life, but while it was in existence, it was successful. During the 1946-7 financial year, it produced six Telephonists, twenty-four Linesmen, three telephone and two radio Technicians, and also four Postal Assistants. The training programme was from the outset limited by the same restraints that governed the other activities of the P. and T. Branch — shortage of staff, finance and accommodation. Brown planned to establish regional training centres, but this proved to be impossible. It was principally the withdrawal of the training staff for other urgent tasks that caused the formal training programme to cease in 1950.

For a brief period, the P. and T. Branch had the responsibility for operating the first post-war broadcasting station in PNG, Radio 9PA Port Moresby. Established in February 1944 as a joint Australian-American Armed Forces Amenities station, it was handed over to ANGAU later that year, and used to broadcast in the Motu language to Papuans working away from their villages for the Army. It continued to operate after the war until 1 July 1946, when it was taken over by the Australian Broadcasting Commission.

In September 1947, E.C.A. Brown gave up the frustrating struggle to create an efficient telecommunications service in PNG with inadequate staff and support, and returned to the saner environment of the PMG's Department, where in due course he became the youngest-ever Director of Posts and Telegraphs in Tasmania and then Director in Queensland. He finished his career in 1975 as Assistant Director-General (Buildings) at the PMG Headquarters, in Melbourne.

Brown left PNG with the personal thanks of J.K. Murray for a job well done, for despite all obstacles he left behind him a working communication system built up from the debris of war, and a plan for the future that required only the necessary resources to be brought to fruition.

Brown's position was filled by V.G. Brown, Senior Technician, on an acting basis, until August 1948. V.G. Brown then returned to the PMG's Department, and an engineer from South Australia, T. Henry, was appointed Divisional Engineer. He, too, left and was replaced in October 1950, by W.C. Gee, an English engineer with impressive professional qualifications, who had previously worked in the British Colonial Postal Engineering Service and latterly in Hobart, Tasmania, under E.C.A. Brown. Gee was to remain in PNG until shortly before his death in 1958.

E.C.A. Brown's involvement with PNG did not, however, end with his departure to Tasmania. In May 1948, he returned, by arrangement between L.B. Fanning, Director-General of the PMG's Department, and J.K. Murray, as technical advisor to the Administration, for a period of three months. Towards the end of this period of duty, he wrote a confidential 'Report on the Re-establishment of Postal and Telecommunication Facilities in Papua-New Guinea', dated 18 June 1948. Addressed to the Administrator, J.K. Murray, it was highly critical of many aspects of the Provisional Administration and its organization, the Public Service, salary levels and general conditions of employment, and the overall lack of planning for reconstruction and future development. He repeated his earlier advice that unless the PMG's Department took control of posts and telegraphs in PNG, 'the modern Postal and Telecommunication needs of this Territory will never be efficiently established nor maintained'. One of the many recommendations in the report called for the appointment of a Director to administer posts and telegraphs in PNG. The whole thrust of the report and its recommendations was that a modern and efficient posts and telegraphs system would never be established unless the resources in men, money and material were made available, and only the PMG's Department could do this.

Such a plain-speaking report was bound to encounter resentment in some circles, and few of Brown's recommendations were adopted. Later developments, however, were to prove that his voice did not go entirely unheeded. In 1948, a top-level Economic Development Committee was set up by J.K. Murray 'to enquire into and make recommendations in connection with the economic advancement of the Territory'. It was chaired by the Secretary for Forests, J.B. McAdam, and included as its members R.E.P. Dwyer, Director of Agriculture; E.P. Holmes, Secretary for Lands and C.J. Millar, of the Department of District Services and Native Affairs. In their report, dated 7 September 1948, the Committee supported Brown, and strongly recommended that P and T should become the direct responsibility of the PMG's Department. Once again, nothing happened.

At this stage in 1948, the PMG's Department was willing, but not anxious, to take over posts and telegraphs in PNG, provided a guarantee could be given that expected heavy financial losses in the initial establishment period would be made good. Until the whole question of the transfer was settled, L.B. Fanning was reluctant to release technical and professional staff on secondment for service in the Territory, for they were badly needed for post-war expansion in Australia. There was fundamental disagreement in PNG over the question of transfer. J.K. Murray was whole-heartedly in favour, but there was considerable opposition in senior departmental circles in Port Moresby. Debate on the question dragged on, and the uncertainty about the future of the Branch began to affect the morale and performance of its officers. However, on 28 July 1950, the then Minister for External Territories, P.C. Spender, finally approved the transfer, but only on the grounds that posts and telegraphs was 'a highly technical service' requiring enormous resources and expertise not currently available to the PNG Administration, to successfully operate.

Despite this decision, no immediate action followed. To work out the details of the transfer, a conference was planned of all Commonwealth and Territory departments concerned and in May 1951, the Government Secretary, S.A. Lonergan, wrote to the Secretary for External Territories, J.R. Halligan, suggesting that it would be very desirable for experienced officers from the PMG's Department to examine the situation in PNG and report, prior to the conference. This suggestion was accepted. The officers chosen for the task were B.J. O'Brien and E.C.A. Brown.

O'Brien and Brown carried out their examination in October and November, and submitted their report on 6 December, 1951. Not surprisingly, their principal recommendation was that 'the postal and telecommunication activities of the Administration of Papua New Guinea become the responsibility of the Commonwealth Postmaster General's Department at the earliest possible date'. Many of the criticisms and recommendations contained in Brown's report of June 1948 were repeated and developed.

O'Brien and Brown did not pull their punches, and described the PNG situation as they saw it, without regard for the sensibilities of senior officers. This perhaps helps to explain the opposition the report encountered in PNG. They wrote:

Insofar as the Administration itself is concerned, it would appear that many senior executives lack the drive and foresight to meet the need of a post-war organization in its relation to posts and telecommunication activities which is totally different to that which satisfied pre-war requirements. This is particularly evident in positions requiring specialized or technical knowledge combined with a high degree of administrative ability . . . at this date it appears obvious that the present Administration lacks the resources in relation to finance, personnel and materials to establish an efficient postal and telecommunication service. No senior executive in the Administration is conversant with the requirements of such a service, or has the ability to maintain or further develop the present service economically.

J.K. Murray again supported the transfer proposal, as did S.A. Lonergan and the newly-appointed Public Service Commissioner, E.A. Head. The Treasurer, H.H. Reeve, was strongly opposed, as was W.C. Gee, Divisional Engineer. 'One cannot but reach the conclusion', wrote Reeve, 'that there is evidence of a preconceived view that a transfer of control would be desirable'. Reeve agreed that the postal and telecommunication services of PNG were not as satisfactory as those provided in Australia, but submitted that this was largely the result of a lack of 'an enlightened approach and co-operation by the PMG's Department'. He was concerned at the financial implications of setting up another Commonwealth department in PNG, pointing out that the Commonwealth Department of Works and Housing consumed twenty-five per cent of Administration funds, had deferred the progress of the Territory to the extent that physical potential was diverted to the establishment of the department, and had resulted in a staff build-up of some 900, almost three-quarters of the strength of the Administration itself.

Following the submission of the O'Brien-Brown report, preparations began for the planned inter-departmental conference to settle details of the transfer. But now the situation changed, dramatically. In the general election of 10 December 1949, Labor was defeated by the Liberal Country Party coalition under R.G. Menzies, and in May 1951, P.M.C. Hasluck became Minister for Territories (the Department of External Territories was replaced by the Department of Territories in 1951). Hasluck immediately began to press for greater progress in PNG. He was not satisfied with what had been achieved since 1945, and was openly critical of the performance and standard of the Public Service. He felt that the Administrator, J.K. Murray, was too old, too tired, too inexperienced in the arts of government to provide the leadership and drive expected of the occupant of the top position in PNG. Murray, too, was a Labor appointee, and it was in the nature of politics that the government of the day in Australia would want to have an Administrator in PNG of their own political persuasion. In September 1951, Brigadier D.M. Cleland — who had served with such distinction with ANGAU during the war — was appointed Assistant Administrator. In June 1952, J.K. Murray was dismissed; Cleland replaced him, at first in an acting capacity and from January 1953, as Administrator.

One of the first problems that Cleland faced after his appointment as Acting Administrator was the future of the Posts and Telegraph Branch, which had been hanging in the balance for upwards of six years and was by now the cause of increasing frustration and discontent among its staff. On 10 July, a matter of days after his appointment, Cleland cabled Hasluck, asking him to postpone the inter-departmental conference due to begin five days later. 'Am not convinced proposal in best interests and would prefer time consider merits and study O'Brien report before submitting any further recommendation', he wrote. The conference was deferred, pending receipt of Cleland's views, which were requested as a matter of 'extreme urgency'. On 18 July 1952, Cleland asked for the transfer proposal to be dropped. He recommended that Posts and Telegraphs be reorganized as a separate department, with essential key personnel to be provided by the Postmaster General, by arrangement, on a ministerial level. Priority housing would need to be provided by the Administration and essential equipment requirements planned on a three-year basis, in recognition of the long delays normally experienced between the time of ordering technical equipment and its actual delivery.

Cleland pointed out that while P and T services were certainly not as efficient as they should be, they had been progressively improved since the initial transfer proposals had been made in 1946, and were now equal to those provided in many country areas in Australia. Once the uncertainty about the future of the Branch was removed by the creation of a separate department, the incentive to forward planning which had admittedly been flagging in recent years would be restored, and efficiency would be increased. Cleland was particularly opposed to the setting-up of additional Commonwealth departments in PNG which were not directly responsible to the Minister for Territories who had a particular duty to the people of PNG, especially in relation to the Trust Territory of New Guinea. This was an argument with particular appeal to Paul Hasluck; he accepted Cleland's recommendation.

As Cleland had noted, the postal and telecommunication services of PNG had certainly improved since the war, even if they were inadequate when compared with those of more advanced countries. Staff, although well under establishment, had increased in numbers. The Superintendent of Postal Services, Wally McPherson, now controlled a European staff of thirty: an inspector, a senior postal clerk, six postmasters and a number of clerks, postal assistants, telephonists and typists. Five of these officers McPherson had secured, on secondment, from the PMG's Department. His Papua New Guinean staff numbered 56, including postal assistants, telephonists, clerks and messengers. Postal Services were now operating the post offices at Port Moresby, Rabaul, Lae, Samarai, Bulolo and Madang; DDS and NA staff manned the rest. Charles Gee, the Divisional Engineer, Telecommunications Services, had a staff of 85 Europeans (10 on secondment); a group engineer (A.W. Boyle), a Line Inspector,

a Radio Inspector, senior Technicians, Linesmen, Radio telephone operators, radio and telephone technicians and a draftsman. There were 128 Papua New Guineans in his branch; technicians of different grades, linesmen, drivers, labourers, messengers, telephonists and storemen. All Papua New Guineans were classed as Administration Servants, and were paid a monthly wage, plus accommodation, clothing and food. The cash wage was small; a Postal Assistant Grade 5 received £14 ten shillings monthly, and a Grade 5 Telephone Technician, £17. Messengers and labourers, at the bottom of the scale, were paid £1 or £1 ten shillings. European salaries were considerably higher, ranging from £1 064 per annum for a Senior Engineer to £431 for a female Telephonist.

By 30 June 1953, additional post offices had been opened at Finschhafen (1948); Buin and Chimbu (1949); Kandrian (1950); Kukipi, Esa'ala, Ihu and Popondetta — replacing Higaturu, destroyed in the eruption of Mount Lamington volcano — (1951); and Kainantu and Mount Hagen (1953). An office was opened at Bainings, New Britain, in March 1951, but it closed in August 1953. (The Royal Australian Navy closed their Finschhafen office, and in March 1949, opened another at Lombrum, Manus Island). All post offices throughout PNG provided full postal and telegraphic facilities, except for Milne Bay, which did not handle money orders, and Ihu and Kokoda, which had no telegraphic facilities. Nowhere in PNG were there house-to-house mail deliveries, but 171 private boxes were in use at the Port Moresby Post Office.

The first issue of PNG postage stamps was made on 30 October 1952, a colourful pictorial series of fifteen stamps in denominations ranging from one half-pence to £1. Prior to this date, current Australian stamps had been used. The new series was received with much enthusiasm by the world's philatelists, and was the first of a long line of beautifully designed and printed stamp issues that have continued, to much acclaim, to the present day.

Telephone services had been greatly extended by this time. There were 1 320 connections in Port Moresby and Samarai, where a small exchange had been opened in February. In the Trust Territory, there was a total of 1 298 connections in the towns of Lae, Wewak, Rabaul, Madang, Kavieng, Goroka, Wau, Namatanai and Kokopo. A radio telephone trunk service linked Lae, Rabaul, Madang, Port Moresby and Samarai. The outstation radio telephone network had grown to a total of 201 stations, controlled from eight Zone Centres: Port Moresby (35 stations), Samarai (27), Lae (21), Madang (40), Rabaul (43), Kavieng (7), Wewak (19), and Lorengau (9).

Post and Telegraphs revenue and expenditure figures reflected the progress that had been made by the Branch. In 1950-1 (the first fiscal year for which separate figures are available) revenue amounted to £140 000; it had increased to £316 000 by 1952-3 (the figure was swollen by receipts from the issue of the first PNG postage stamps). Expenditure in 1950-1 was £184 000, and in 1952-3, £255 000.

The Overseas Telecommunication Commission retained responsibility for PNG's international communications, but in January 1950, came to an agreement with the Administration to share some of the costs of establishing and operating a number of stations. By August 1951, the OTC stations at Madang and Samarai were staffed by the Branch, and the Coastal Radio Service was operated by it as agents for OTC. Wewak and Kavieng were staffed by OTC, as agents for the Administration. At Rabaul, a combined transmitting station was staffed by OTC and Branch technicians; both operated separate receiving stations. These arrangements were not intended to be permanent, but they indicated the degree of co-operation that existed between OTC and the Administration.

Paul Hasluck accepted Cleland's recommendation on 8 October 1952, and directed that 'immediate steps' be taken to re-organize the Branch as a department. But the establishment of a new department is not a matter than can be speedily accomplished in any Public Service, and two years were to pass before a Director was appointed.

W.C. Gee wasted no time in submitting a proposal to the Treasurer for the organization of the new department. His proposal, dated 27 October, was for a Department of Posts and Telecommunications with a total European staff of 136, headed by a Director and divided into three Sections: Postal, under a Superintendent of Posts; Engineering, under a Divisional Engineer, and Accounts, under an Accountant. McPherson was substantially in agreement with the proposal. Gee recommended immediate action to secure the Accountant — a new position — to handle the financial aspects of establishing the new department. Gee was about to go on leave, and he asked for permission to approach the Assistant Director-General (Personnel) PMG's Department in Melbourne to seek his assistance in selecting 'first class men' for the key Accountant and Cost Clerk positions. At the same time he would go into the question of technical aid to install planned automatic telephone equipment at Port Moresby and Rabaul. Since delivery of the equipment required would take at least eighteen months from the date of ordering, he asked for approval to place a firm order with the British firm of Ericsson Telephones Ltd.

This was certainly rushing things; Charles Gee saw himself as Director of the new Department, but such haste was premature. H.H. Reeve refused to allow Gee to proceed with the selection of an accountant, and pointed out that until a firm decision about the organization of the new department was reached, no commitments could be made on behalf of the Administration. However, Reeve supported Gee's proposal overall as a basis for future planning, but recommended that Posts and Telegraphs become a self-contained Branch *within* the Department of the Treasury. Gee thereupon wrote directly to the Administrator, pointing out that it had been operating as a separate Branch since 1945, with highly unsatisfactory results.

The Treasurer's recommendation was not accepted. Posts and Telegraphs was to become a separate department within the PNG Public Service, and for month after month during 1953 discussion and argument continued, in Port Moresby and Canberra, over the details. Paul Hasluck made an early decision on staffing which clarified matters to some extent: wherever possible, appointments of technical and professional officers were to be made on a permanent basis, rather than by transfer or secondment from the PMG's Department.

W.C. Gee was not offered the Director's position. Born in 1897, he was too old for the job, and remained Divisional Engineer, on secondment. Early in 1954, the Department of Territories advertised widely in Australian newspapers, and overseas, for a Director of Posts and Telegraphs in Papua New Guinea. At the same time, applications were called for the position of Accountant.

CHAPTER NINE

THE DEPARTMENT OF POSTS AND TELEGRAPHS

Chance often plays a whimsical part in deciding human affairs. On a hot day in March 1954, a dusty car pulled up outside a hotel in the country town of Condobolin, New South Wales. Two men emerged, and went into the coolness of the bar for a beer. Bill Carter, Divisional Engineer of the Parkes Division, PMG's Department, and Tudor Davies, one of the engineers attached to the division, were returning from an inspection of a job in progress west of Condobolin, and they were tired and thirsty. As they drank, they talked over the events of the day and, idly, Davies said to Carter, 'I suppose you've put in for that job in New Guinea?'.

This was the first that Carter had heard of the search for a Director of Posts and Telegraphs in Papua New Guinea. Davies had seen an advertisement in a newspaper some time before, and on their return to Parkes, he looked at home for the paper, without success. On impulse, he and his wife then searched the garbage tin and there it was, stained and sodden, wrapped around kitchen refuse. The advertisement was just readable, and next morning Davies brought it to the office, and presented it to Bill Carter. The final date for receipt of applications in Canberra had expired, but it was clearly a challenging position, professionally, and moreover carried a salary greater than Carter could hope to achieve in PMG service for years. Carter was a young man — he had been born in Sydney on 22 September 1923 — and he knew that many engineers with vastly more experience than he could claim must have applied. But he talked the matter over with his wife, Anne, and they decided that he had nothing to lose. He sent in a late application to the Department of Territories, which was accepted, and soon forgot about the New Guinea job, for his work as Divisional Engineer, Parkes, was absorbing and Anne and he loved the town, and the country life.

But Carter's destiny lay in PNG: he was appointed Director of Posts and Telegraphs. 'It was one of the best appointments I made', Paul Hasluck wrote in his book, *A*

Time for Building.[1] 'Carter was virtually the creator of the post-war PNG postal and telecommunications system. He did a stupendous job . . . Facing difficulties that must have seemed scarcely credible to him against the background of his experience in the Australian Postmaster General's Department, he went to work quietly, cheerfully, methodically and with technical skill . . . for myself, impatient and exacting as I am, the best tribute I can give is that, once Carter had started the job, I seldom had to worry about the Postal Department again and only needed to back him in his direction of it.'

William Frederick Carter was educated at Sydney Technical High School and Sydney University. In 1941 he became a cadet engineer with the PMG's Department and graduated as an engineer in 1945. He later studied Industrial Management at night courses at Sydney Technical College. During his cadetship, he served as a signalman with No.2 L. of C. Signals, Australian Military Forces. Apart from two years of maths and physics at Sydney University, his professional training was provided by the Department, for at this time Australian universities did not provide suitable courses in telecommunications engineering. Cadet engineers were a much favoured species, guaranteed a job with the Department on completion of their training, although there was a grave shortage of technicians and professionals in those wartime and immediate post-war years. Carter remained with the PMG's Department in Sydney until 1948, when he was transferred to Dubbo, NSW. His big opportunity came in 1949, when the expansion of mining operations at Broken Hill in the far west of the state began. Broken Hill was then Australia's biggest mineral export earner. The PMG project involved the provision of improved telecommunications on a wide scale.

Carter was given full responsibility for designing, costing and installing the most expensive aspect of the project, which involved re-cabling the whole of Broken Hill. He also contributed to all other aspects of the PMG project, which included the local and trunk exchange and the Broken Hill RT network, which was the first of its kind in Australia. His responsibility included the maintenance of all telecommunications west of the Darling River, including the ABC studio and transmitter. He set up what amounted to a remote office of the PMG's Department, and was soon on close terms with the powerful men who ran Broken Hill: the Mine Managers' Association, and the Barrier Industrial Council. It was invaluable experience for a young engineer-cum-manager. On behalf of the PMG's Department and after negotiations with the Barrier Industrial Council, Carter employed migrant labour from Europe on the project — 'New Australians' they were then called — and was the first employer to use them in the closed, union-dominated world of Broken Hill. At first having the title of Project Engineer, Bill Carter was later made Divisional Engineer, and was for practical purposes his own boss.

As a result of the post-war expansion of PMG activities, it was decided in 1950 to redivide New South Wales into eleven PMG divisions, one of the largest of them based on the town of Parkes. Carter was transferred there as Divisional Engineer, to set up the new division. He was in charge of a staff of professionals, technicians and office-workers that varied in number between 250 and 300 — a far bigger European staff, in

1 Paul Hasluck, *A Time for Building*, Melbourne University Press, 1976.

fact, than was employed by the Posts and Telegraphs Branch in PNG, and with heavy responsibilities. It was undoubtedly his record of efficiency and achievement in Broken Hill and then in Parkes Division that won him the position of Director of Posts and Telegraphs in PNG, despite his lack of years, and the calibre of the other applicants.

Employment procedures within the Department of Territories were then so cumbersome that many a valuable man gave up and went elsewhere after waiting, fruitlessly, for months after submitting applications for advertised positions. The months went by without word too, for Bill Carter, and he and Anne finalized plans with the architect who was about to build them a permanent home in Parkes. Then one morning the Monitor (head telephone operator) of the Parkes Telephone Exchange came into Carter's office. The night before, she had been talking to a friend at the Port Moresby Trunk Telephone Exchange (a common habit with switchboard operators in the stilly watches of the night, the world over), and the friend had asked her, 'What sort of a bloke is this Carter? We hear he is our new Director!'. It was not until some months later, however, that Bill Carter was officially told that he had won the appointment.

If Carter was Director, he did not at this stage have a department to direct; at the time of his appointment, October 1954, P and T was still, formally, a branch of Treasury. Before flying to Canberra for talks with Hasluck and the Secretary for Territories prior to proceeding to Port Moresby, Carter visited the District Postal Inspector at Parkes for some information about the operation of a postal service, a subject about which he was entirely ignorant. A telecommunications engineer, he would nevertheless, as Director, also be responsible for the postal side. The three most important aspects, said the Inspector, were the proper control of mail contracts, the naming of new post offices — they must never clash with existing names — and the Form 100, the complicated and imposing form used to account for cash and account-able documents, and sacred to all postmasters. Carter borrowed a Form 100, took it home and studied it thoroughly, and, as he later said, 'went to PNG as a fully-fledged postal expert'.

The reality of the postal and telecommunications services of PNG came as an unpleasant surprise to Bill Carter, fresh from the big Parkes Division and the efficient, well-funded resources of the PMG's Department. Soon after his arrival in Port Moresby he toured the Territory with Charles Gee and Wally McPherson, an exhaust-ing inspection of all postal and telecommunications assets in all districts, towns and major outstations. He talked with European and native staff, and with the officers of DDS and NA who were handling post offices and radio telephones in almost all of the minor centres on behalf of P and T. He found that apart from the old GPO building in Port Moresby, the services were housed in flimsy, ramshackle buildings, constructed during the war, and that these were often tacked onto district or Treasury offices. None was fit to be described as permanent. Carter saw at first hand the conditions in which his staff worked and lived — no worse than those suffered by the officers of most other departments, but certainly no better — and he returned to headquarters convinced that a massive injection of funds would be required if the new Department of Posts and Telegraphs was to do the job for which it was being formed.

In a letter to the Assistant Administrator, Carter outlined his impressions following the tour. 'To say the least, I was shocked at the lack of efficient and available services', he wrote, 'although I must admit I was pleasantly surprised at the work which was being done by such a small and, in many cases, inexperienced staff'.

The days were not long enough for all that Bill Carter had to do but he quickly achieved his initial objective. His first priority was to assess needs, finalize the initial organization of the new Department, and obtain essential key staff. He drew up a Departmental functional chart, providing for a department of five divisions — Postal Services, Engineering, Telephone, Accounts, and Personnel — each headed by an officer who would be responsible to the Director for the efficient operation of his division. The Telephone Division carried the functional responsibility for the non-engineering aspect of telecommunications. 'The general plan of action with regard to initial formation of the Department', Carter wrote in a statement submitted with the Chart:

> will be to recruit, in the first instance, the officer-in-charge of each Division. Each of these officers will then be required to examine the specialized requirements of their respective divisions and in conjunction with the Director, an organization for each division will be designed. It is essential that, in the initial stage, the organization be considered as experimental and capable of flexibility, as the complexities and work loads encountered in the formation stages of each division will most likely vary once a division is fully established and running smoothly . . . it may be necessary to recruit some officers from the PMG's Department by secondment . . . obviously, the full requirements of the permanent organization are difficult to forecast at this stage.

The proposal was accepted in November 1954. By this time, T.D. Sexton had been appointed, on secondment from the PMG's Department, to the position of Accountant, Department of Posts and Telegraphs. Tas Sexton was a qualified PMG postal accountant, with little experience of other branches of the profession. Treasury officers had hitherto done most of the accounting work for the P and T Branch, but the new Department was to be responsible for its own internal accounting. Sexton was soon working with Treasury officers on the takeover of accountancy functions, and he quickly proved his ability and his capacity for hard work.

Postal Services was, of course, already under the efficient control of W.J. McPherson. McPherson was very pleased to welcome Sexton, for as well as running his division, he was also looking after Telephones, and undertaking much of the internal accounting work of the Branch, frequently working up to eighteen hours a day. In spite of this load, Wally McPherson had managed to find the time to compile and issue PNG's first post-war telephone directory, and a book of instructions for Postmasters that remained in use for many years.

Carter saw a need for the strengthening of the Engineering division. He asked for the abolition of the existing positions of Divisional Engineer and Group Engineer, and the creation of four new positions: Chief Engineer, to be filled by Charles Gee, and three Regional Engineers, to be stationed in Port Moresby (Papua Region), Rabaul (New Guinea Islands Region) and Lae (New Guinea Mainland Region). One of these positions would be taken by A.W. Boyle, already serving as Group Engineer.

Carter attached a good deal of importance to the Personnel Division. As well as the usual Public Service aspects of the job, the man in charge of this division would be responsible for staff welfare, and training co-ordination — in particular, the training of Papua New Guineans, for Carter had been surprised to find Europeans doing many jobs that past experience had shown could be efficiently done by qualified natives.

Applications were called in Australia for the key positions: two Regional Engineers, and Superintendents of the Personnel and Telephone Divisions. In the meantime, Carter and Sexton flew to Canberra, Sydney and Melbourne to discuss a range of questions with PMG, Treasury and Territories officers. These included policy, staff recruitment, accounting and the funding procedures and costing methods to be employed in PNG. The Postmaster General agreed to place Carter in the same category as the Directors of Posts and Telegraphs in the Australian states and to send him copies of all official publications, circulars and instructions as they were issued. Australian experience would obviously be of considerable value to PNG, and Carter wanted access to the accumulated technical knowledge of the PMG's Department.

Bill Carter returned to Port Moresby with his wife, on 21 January 1955. They moved into a home in Lawes Road that had been purchased for them by the Administration from a leading businessman, E.E. Kriewaldt, for married accommodation in the capital was still extremely scarce. On 25 January, the Administrator, D.M. Cleland formally revoked the appointment of the Treasurer, H.H. Reeve, as Chief Postmaster, and appointed Carter in his stead. Two instruments of appointment were required, for two separate Posts and Telegraphs laws were still in force, one in Papua and the other in the Trust Territory of New Guinea.

When Provisional Administration began in 1945, the existing Post and Telegraph Ordinance 1912-26 of Papua was extended to New Guinea under the title Post and Telegraph Ordinance 1912-16 (Papua, Adopted). Both ordinances were based on the Australian Act that came into force after Federation in 1901. (From time to time over the following years, regulations were issued under the two Ordinances, setting and changing postal and telephone rates, and so on, for both territories. It is a curious fact that the Ordinances themselves remained virtually unchanged until 1973, when PNG took over the responsibility for her own postal and telecommunications administration. After Independence they were consolidated, still practically unchanged, into a consolidated Act, but by 1981, a new, updated Act had still to be introduced.)

By June 1955, the initial organization of the Department of Posts and Telegraphs was ready for presentation to the Department of Territories for approval by the Minister. Carter had now had sufficient experience of the Territory to be able to forecast his senior staff needs with some precision. It had already been decided that all senior appointments would be made on a permanent basis, secondment from the PMG's Department being accepted as an alternative only as a last resort. Carter's own position was somewhat ambiguous; he had understood that he was on secondment, but now, months after his appointment, he was asked to sign a backdated letter of resignation from the PMG's Department.

The Department of Posts and Telegraphs was formally born on 1 July 1955. On this day all the positions, 152 Europeans and 364 Papua New Guineans, in the Posts and Telegraphs Branch of the Treasury Department were transferred to the new

Department. One of the new Regional Engineer positions was filled in September 1955, with the appointment of R.T. Pearson, who in June 1956, moved to Rabaul to take over the New Guinea Islands Region. Tom Pearson was to remain with the Department until 1973. He was Assistant Director, Constructions, when he left it to join the National Broadcasting Commission. The second advertised position remained unfilled until July 1956 — the engineer originally appointed failed his medical examination. V.B. Hodgson arrived then to take over the Papua Region. Vern Hodgson, too, was to render great service to the Department before meeting his death, years later, in a helicopter crash while on duty in the Eastern Highlands.

After the arrival of Vern Hodgson, A.W. Boyle moved to Lae as Regional Engineer, New Guinea Mainland. Bill Boyle, who returned to Australia in 1959, concealed high technological intelligence and competence behind a brash facade that few penetrated. Although his service with Posts and Telegraphs was relatively short, his influence on the early development of telecommunications in PNG was significant, if often indirect.

On 30 June 1955, the day before the Department came into being, post offices throughout PNG were required to return to the Department of the Treasury all their cash, books of accounts and stocks of accountable items such as stamps and postal notes. Tas Sexton had speedily discovered that the Treasury books of postal accounts had not been capable of reconciliation for years past; postal business was a side-line for Treasury, and no real effort had been made to maintain accurate separate accounts. This would no longer be tolerated. By 1 July, every post office had received a sealed bag from the Accounts division of the new Department of Posts and Telegraphs, containing fresh stocks of cash and accountable items. From this day forward, Tas Sexton was always able to balance his accounts.

On 25 July 1955, William Sydney Peckover applied for the position of Superintendent of Telephones. Born in Drummoyne, New South Wales, in May 1922, Peckover became a telephonist in the Main Trunk Exchange, Sydney in 1939, and remained in that position until August 1942, when he enlisted, serving until June 1946, in the Army telephone section. On his discharge he returned to the PMG's Department, working at Sydney and Canberra where in 1951, after qualifying as a Traffic Officer, he was placed in charge of the Canberra Trunk Exchange. As a result of his varied experience, he was selected to make investigations into large trunk exchange service problems and to suggest methods of improvement. At the time he applied for the job in PNG, Peckover was studying Management at Sydney Technical College.

On 28 September, the Minister for Territories approved the appointment of Peckover as Superintendent of Telephones. He attended an orientation course at the Australian School of Pacific Administration in February 1956, and took up the position in March. Bill Peckover was to later become Assistant Director and Acting Director of the Department, in a remarkable, lasting partnership with Bill Carter. The Department was fortunate indeed that two such men, differing in style, temperament and approach, but akin in their ability, dedication and imagination were on hand from the beginning. Both men were specialists in telecommunications, and even this was fortunate, for in the coming years telecommunications would come to overshadow the postal services as independence for PNG drew nigh.

The Department's charter was the provision of efficient postal and telecommunications services throughout PNG, sufficient not only for the needs of the day, but also for the future. It was a charter requiring the everlasting trio of resources: men, money and materials. During the early years of the Department, these resources were sadly lacking. During these years, the best that could be done was to improve and upgrade existing facilities and plan for the years ahead, and always the greatest limiting factor was finance.

The PNG Administration was financed by annual grants from the Commonwealth, and by internal revenue. In 1950-1, the total revenue was £6.22 million, of which £4.35 million was provided by Commonwealth grant. In the year of the creation of the Department of Posts and Telegraphs, 1955-6, the Administration revenue was £12.29 million, £8.45 million from the Commonwealth. By 1964-5, the end of the first decade of the Department's existence, total Administration revenue exceeded £45 million, the Commonwealth contribution amounting to £28 million. It can thus be seen that although the percentage raised from internal resources steadily rose, the Commonwealth grant was the major source of revenue to the Administration. During this decade — and, indeed, for the rest of the years of Australia's presence in PNG — the annual Administration budget could not be finalized until the amount of the Commonwealth grant was known, after the Budget sitting of the Australian Parliament. All departments operated on funds allocated for specific purposes; cash allocated on one vote could not be spent on another without the specific approval of the Treasurer. Nor could votes be exceeded without Treasury approval, which was seldom given. Funds not spent by the end of the financial year, 30 June, could not be held and used for the next year's continuing programme, but had to be returned to general revenue and lost to the department, unless the Treasurer allowed them to be re-voted into the budget for the following year. It was a system that would have driven a commercial enterprise into frenzy, but in spite of annual protests not only from Administration departments but from bodies such as the Legislative Council, re-established in 1951, and the Town Advisory Councils, it was retained, virtually unchanged, until the end of Australian control.

Posts and Telegraphs was more severely affected by the system than most other departments, particularly in respect of the purchasing of telecommunications equipment, which was generally manufactured to order with a lead time of between one and three years before delivery. Long-term planning was rendered almost impossible under the restraints of the system of funding.

From the time of his appointment, Bill Carter tried to obtain a clear-cut decision on the attitude of the Administration towards his department. Was the department to be recognized as a business undertaking (as is Australia Post and Telecom today) at least paying its own way, but preferably as a profit-making enterprise, generating funds for some of its capital needs as well as returning revenue to the Administration? Was the department to be purely an arm of the Administration, providing services in the many underdeveloped regions of the Territory as a part of overall policy, regardless of operating losses?

In a letter to R.W. Wilson, Assistant Administrator, on 29 March 1956, Carter recalled that on his appointment it had been agreed that 'accelerated assistance would be forthcoming in the way of both finance and staff, to rectify the degraded position into which P and T had fallen as the result of the neglect and disinterest of the immediate post-war years. He wrote:

> During the past eighteen months, I have thoroughly investigated the present and future requirements of the department so that services provided may meet demand and be of acceptable standards. Financial and staffing proposals have been submitted by me based on these investigations. Unfortunately, adequate assistance has not been forthcoming in either staff or finance during the past eighteen months, and there does not appear to be much provision during the next eighteen months. There is now some doubt in my mind as to just what is the formal Government policy with regard to restoration of Posts and Telegraphs services, or what responsibilities and functions the government requires the Posts and Telegraphs Department to undertake.

It would be many years before a formal statement defining the functions of P and T was issued, and, in the meantime Carter continued to fight for money and staff. Wilson replied to his letter, soothingly, saying that because of budget and recruiting difficulties, 'expansion of departmental activities cannot take place at the same rate which some Departmental Heads might legitimately desire'. Carter thereupon wrote to the Administrator, pointing out that 'if the present policy is continued towards the Department in not recognizing that some additional assistance is urgently necessary, I am faced with an impossible task in administering the Department's functions'.

Carter was fighting a losing battle. In a memo to Cleland, dated 30 April 1956, the Assistant Administrator noted:

> This was discussed with the Director and the Public Service Commissioner last Friday, when the PSC pointed out that the Minister had particularly referred to the necessity of seeing that expansion of communications was not to be at the expense of other departmental activities, which he regarded as a higher priority ... I am afraid the fact remains that the Department of Posts and Telegraphs cannot get much more than the allocation of that part of the total resources already provisionally provided in the draft estimates.

In the face of these attitudes, it was apparent that Posts and Telegraphs could not hope for the increase in funds required to compensate for the neglect of past years, and in fact the level of funding provided over the first decade of the Department's existence forced Carter and his officers to patch and improvise, rather than take advantage of the new technology then emerging. The Department's share of the total Administration budget expenditure in the four years prior to its establishment averaged 3.4 per cent; in 1955-6 it increased to 4.5 (£546 500), then slipped to an average of 4 per cent over the next four years, and to 3.8 per cent over the last half of the decade, with 1964-5 the worst year of all: 3.4 per cent, or £1.55 million. It was not until June 1962, that the then Treasurer, A.P.J. Newman, authorized P and T to call forward tenders for the supply of equipment without a prior 'funds available' certificate, provided the total of all commitments for a succeeding financial year did not exceed 75 per cent of the preceding year's allocation. This eased the situation, but was a long way short of a final solution to P and T's problems.

Sinake Giregiré

MV Lauraba,
Papua 1924–44.

The auto Telephone Exchange, Rabaul, 1957.

Corporal Tommy Huntington, San Bernado, California, and Corporal William Marka, Vinita, Oklahoma, driving the spike and securing the insulators to the tree in the laying of telephone wire from Kokoda to Dobodura by the 440th Signal Construction, Bn. Co. B, June 1943.

View of the telephone wire showing the method of running the line through the jungle section of the Kokoda-Dobodura line being constructed by the 440th Signal Construction, Bn. Co. B, June 1943.

AWA Radio Station, Port Moresby, 1931.

Gabriel Bakani showing damage done by vandals at Mt Otto Repeater Station.

Port Moresby, c. 1910.

SS *Morinda,*
typical of the
Burns Philp
vessels running to
PNG.

Nelson Tokidoro
at the Telegraph
Office, Rabaul,
1957.

Joseph Auna, Traffic Officer-in-training, PMG, Melbourne (1967–8).

André Tripet, Managing Director of Helio Courvoisier of Switzerland, presenting Sinake Giregiré with a souvenir folder of stamps printed by his firm.

Graham Wade,
Stamp Designer.

Chris Lama,
Clerical Assistant,
making up first
day covers at the
Philatelic Bureau,
Port Moresby.

Bill Carter, Israel Edoni, Dale Kamara and Joseph Auna, at the NBC Reporter Centre.

Mary Manning, Instructor, with student Telex Operator.

Geoff Hutton with students at Boroko Training College, 1962.

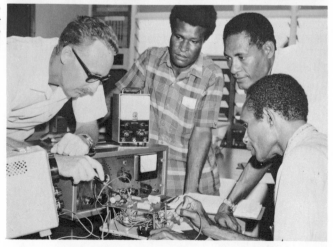

Andrew Michael Fabila, Line Foreman Grade 1 with P and T.

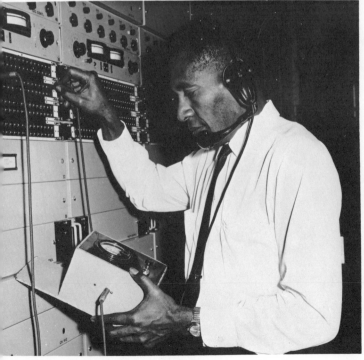

Haro Tariva carrying out testing on patch panel voice frequency telegraph equipment, while on a training course at GPO, Brisbane.

Frank Anderson, Staff Clerk, shows Dale Kamara the manner in which leave is recorded on staff record cards.

Patrick Owen, Gavera Lohia, Oscar Davura, Michael Dawadawareta and Maclaren Beaga sorting mail at Port Moresby Post Office, 1960.

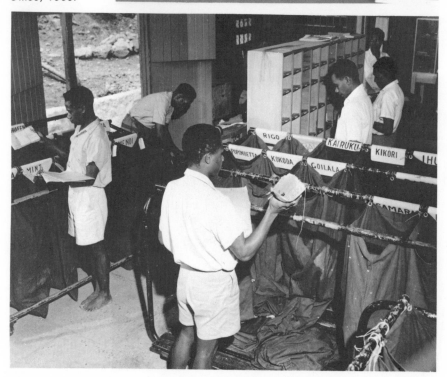

Joseph Natera, Trainee Communications Officer, sending radio telegrams from Mt Hagen Telegraph Office.

Kaibelt Diria, Maori Kiki, Israel Edoni, and John Billitokome at the APNG cable opening, July 1976.

Postmaster R. Phillips loading outward mail with Ovasuru Liriope and Michael Dawadawareta at Port Moresby GPO.

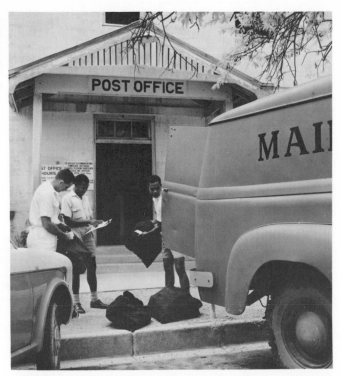

Linesmen in training. Okurai Rumba Rumba, Aia, Raka, Fred Messeri, Joe Supset and Padumio are working under instructor Jim Lappin.

Trainee technicians receiving instruction on cathode ray tubes from J.J. Thornton, at the Technicians' Training School, Port Moresby.

Sorting second class mail, Port Moresby Post Office, 1947.

An Assistant District Officer in charge of a Department of Native Affairs patrol operating a portable trans-receiver.

Postmaster J. Cardew, Henao, Iwam and T. Conboy sorting mail at Lae Post Office.

Patrick Tomausi.

Mike Harrison and
Israel Edoni.

George Tokiene.

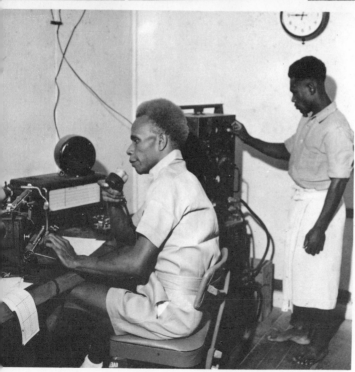

Kaibelt Diria.

Mt Shungol, an important link in the Port Moresby-Lae trunk route.

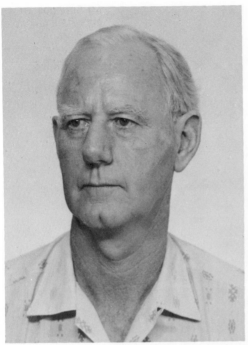

Tom Pearson.

Doug MacGowan.

Bill Peckover.

E.C.A. Brown.

Sir Hubert Murray.

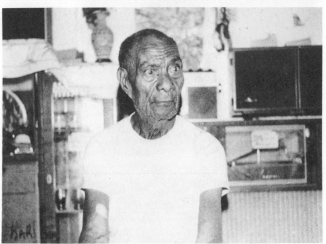

Mavaja Hekure.

Sir William MacGregor.

Repeater Station, Mt Ialibu.

Initial survey of Mt Scratchley (Vern Hodgson, killed in a chopper crash, May 1970).

Bill Carter with Morea Mea and Tom Tara.

Morea Mea receives his award from Wiwa Korowi.

Israel Edoni receives his awards from Wiwa Korowi.

Gavera Lohia and Bill Carter.

Lifting the parabolic dish on to the tower, Boroko Post Office.

Mt Scratchley Microwave Repeater Station.

Outstation teleradio equipment (3BZ), 1948.

Old Boroko Post
Office.

Bill Carter found it galling that all revenues collected for postal and tele-communications services — even the proceeds of the sale of PNG postage stamps — were paid directly into consolidated revenue and not retained to help finance the modernization and expansion of the Department. Indeed, when he became Director, government departments and authorities were not charged for telecommunications or postal services — telephones were provided without charge, official telegrams were transmitted free and official correspondence carried without stamps, a situation that endured from the beginning of civil administration in 1945 to 1 July 1956, when charges were finally levied.

Although the financial position thus remained highly unsatisfactory, some progress was made in relation to staff. As mentioned in the previous chapter, Paul Hasluck was dissatisfied with the standard and performance of the PNG Public Service as he found it when he became Minister for Territories in May 1951. In 1953, he issued instructions for a progressive re-organization of all departments, in order to improve the capacity of the Service to meet its expanding responsibilities. By 30 June 1954, four departments had been re-organized and a new Department of the Public Service Commissioner created, and in the following year the large departments of DDS and NA and Education were re-organized and the Department of the Government Secretary was replaced by the Department of Civil Affairs. The Department of the Treasury was greatly reduced in size: the Transport Branch, Stores and Supply Branch and the Government Printing Office were all transferred into Civil Affairs, and the Posts and Telegraphs Department's organization benefited from the current examination of the Service.

Bill Carter now found himself with a department with 277 classified positions. This did not mean that he was immediately able to fill them; recruitment of new officers was still dependent upon the availability of funds and accommodation, and in fact only thirteen additional European officers were employed in 1955-6. But at least an enlarged staff establishment had been created.

In March 1956, Carter wrote to each of the officers of P and T on secondment from the PMG's Department, asking them to consider accepting permanent appointment to the Territory service. There were at this time twenty-three such officers, their terms of secondment due to expire at various intervals between June 1956, and December 1957. Their combined experience and knowledge was vital to the operation of the Department. Among them were W.J. McPherson and W.C. Gee; A.W. Boyle, Regional Engineer; T.D. Sexton, in charge of the Accounts division; T.M. Weston, Supervising Technician (Telephones), whose service in PNG went back to 1947; J.H. Lappin, Line Inspector for PNG, who began his service in June 1948, and D. McDonald, an experienced Postmaster. A number of these officers accepted appointments to the Department, including Sexton and Weston, and others, like McPherson, Gee and Boyle, elected to stay on secondment. In one way or another, the PMG's Department was to continue to be a valued source of supply of skilled officers for the Department of Posts and Telegraphs.

There was, of course, a solid corps of European and Papua New Guinean officers and employees who had served from the beginning of civil administration, and earlier. The senior European officer was A.J. Clarke, who had been appointed Linesman and

Mechanic in the Telephones Section of the Mandated Territory Administration in 1935. Jim Widdup, first appointed in 1920, rejoined P and T in 1954. Another, J.P. (Paddy) Morrisey, had begun his service as a clerk in the same administration, in 1936. Radio technician J.P. Cook and telephone technician D.G. Caldwell began in the early post-war years, as did V.K. Clark, D.W.A. Mills, Keith Armistead, Ian Fisher, E. Pyne, Frank Mallumby, H.C. Tremayne, E.V. (Wally) Smythe, Harry Thompson, L.C. Raebel and others, who were to spend their careers in PNG. Some of the early European female postal clerks and assistants became known throughout the Territory, among them Miss M.M. Scott, Mrs H.L. Hawken and Mrs C. Gane. They remained in P and T for many years.

The names of some of the early Papua New Guinea employees of the Department who stayed with it for their working lives, have already been mentioned in this account. They include Gavera Lohia, the grand old man of the postal services; Mavara Hekure, Nelson Tokidoro and Michael Dawadawareta. There were many others, men such as George Tokiene, who started as a clerk/telegraphist with DDS and NA in Kundiawa in 1941; Amos Tamti, who worked with the Coastwatchers on Bougainville during the Pacific war; Mauri Taru, Tom Taru, Lawson Morove, Maso Ivare and Robinson Taugunawiri. But the men who were in later years to fill many senior positions in the Department after Independence were still at school in 1955.

The infant Department had been born, and the long struggle to improve the postal and telecommunications services of PNG began.

CHAPTER TEN

THE DEVELOPMENT OF POSTAL SERVICES TO INDEPENDENCE

When the Department of Posts and Telegraphs was born on 1 July 1955, there were 42[1] post offices throughout Papua New Guinea, all controlled by Europeans and almost all of poor, or temporary construction. By July 1975 — on the eve of Independence — the number had risen to 106, and all were manned by Papua New Guineans and were sound, permanent buildings. This span of twenty years saw the postal business of PNG increase from a total of nine million articles handled in 1955-6 to a peak of 61.8 million in 1973-4, followed by a slump to 52.5 million in the year of Independence, as the new, modern telephone and telex services continued to attract increasing support from the public, at the expense of the post.

In 1955, there were few literate Papua New Guineans. The postal services were then used almost exclusively by Europeans, although most of the villages in the coastal and island districts had their 'scribes', usually retired policemen, teachers or mission evangelists, who would write letters on behalf of villagers wanting to contact relatives or friends working on distant plantations, or in the towns. The volume of this mail was small, though very significant. By the time of Independence, more than half the village children of primary school age were receiving some education. Every district had its high school, or schools, and the Universities of Papua New Guinea and of Technology, and many technical institutions were producing increasing numbers of literate graduates. The people of PNG had long since discovered the postal services of their country, and were using them freely.

The role of the post in a developing country transcends the mere provision of a public service. In a very real sense, the post in PNG has been an instrument of social and economic change. In a country beset by daunting problems of geography, distance

---

1 For names of post offices in existence to the middle of 1953, refer to Chapter 8. Gasmata was closed in November 1953 and Konedobu on 1 July 1955.

and cultural diversity, the post has been a powerful element in the development of a sense of national identity, to an extent hard for foreigners to appreciate. It has been the post that has released the PNG villager — and most of the people of the nation are still villagers — from the age-old bondage of his isolation. Even today, few ordinary Papua New Guineans are within reach, physical or financial, of a private telephone, but few are far away from a post office. Wisely, the government has resisted the temptation to use the postal services as a convenient source of revenue. The aim has always been to recover costs, but postal rates remain lower in PNG than in most parts of the world. The trend in government and commercial circles, as in most other countries, is towards a greater use of telecommunications and a decreasing reliance on the written word, but it is unlikely that the man-in-the-village will abandon the post.

As mentioned in Chapter 8, the first post-war Postmaster was W.J. McPherson. McPherson joined the PMG's Department in Australia in 1927, and by 1939, after wide experience in a number of post offices throughout New South Wales, was a Relieving Postmaster, a tough and demanding position. He enlisted in the AIF and rose from the ranks to the position of Brigade Major during the war, winning the MBE (Military Division) and attending several military schools, including the Staff College, Duntroon. He served in many localities in PNG during the conflict and was considering a business career there when he was offered the job of Postmaster, Port Moresby. McPherson accepted the position, on secondment from the PMG's Department, on the understanding that his chances of rapid promotion were good if his services were satisfactory. They were: he was promoted to Chief Clerk of the Postal Services branch and then to the position of Officer-in-charge, which he still held when the Department of Posts and Telegraphs was created. Bill Carter then confirmed him in the position of Superintendent of Postal Services. The relationship between the two men was established right from the beginning. 'At the time I started', Bill Carter said recently, 'all I knew about postal services was that you licked a stamp, put it on the envelope, posted it in a letter box, and it would end up where you addressed it to. I soon learned from Wally that there was a lot more to it than that! He was a good man, and I had no hesitation in asking him to carry on as head of the new Postal Division.'

McPherson saw the growth of postal services from the early post-war beginnings to almost the end of the initial establishment period of P and T. A dogged, hard-working man, he established the Branch on a sound footing and provided the basis for the later rapid expansion of Postal Services. Strict but fair with his staff, he took a particular interest in the progress and welfare of the Papua New Guineans working in the division. When he arrived in Port Moresby, McPherson worked initially under the direction of E.C.A. Brown, who was then in sole charge of the Posts and Telecommunications Branch of the Treasury Department following the departure of B.J. O'Brien to Australia because of ill-health. After Brown rejoined the PMG's Department, Treasury split the administration of the branch into two divisions, Postal Services and Telecommunications, and until the Department of Posts and Telegraphs was created, McPherson was responsible directly to the Treasurer (as Chief Postmaster) for the operation of postal services. McPherson recalls:

> The going was pretty tough in the early days. There were only nine post offices when I arrived, apart from the GPO. There was hardly any staff. Paddy Morrisey — quite a

character, a pre-war man — was Postmaster at Lae, and the other offices — Abau, Daru, Samarai, Madang, Rigo, Kairuku, Wau and Wewak — were all manned by DDS and NA. With the help of Gavera Lohia, a wonderful bloke who was a tremendous help, we trained some good native staff and locally recruited a few European women to work on the counters after they were given some basic instruction. In the shortest possible time, with the meagre facilities then available, we managed to get the whole Postal Services Division functioning in a fairly smooth fashion. I was relieved in the position of Postmaster GPO by Bob Elliott from Melbourne and with the day-to-day running of the Port Moresby Post Office out of my hair, I was free to commence setting up the administrative side. This we did in the offices located on the top floor of the GPO building. My personal staff, recruited locally, consisted of a clerk and a typist, both female, who had no previous experience in office work. A rough start, but they very quickly displayed ability and a flair for this kind of work. Most of the mails in 1946-7 came by sea — it was nothing to have seven or eight hundred bags sitting on the wharf, and we had nowhere, really, to store it except for an old tin shed at the back of the post office. We didn't have any transport of our own then. The Transport people would send down a truck for the mail when they had one to spare, and we'd work half the night sometimes, sorting it, everyone pitching in.

We were really dependent on DDS. They had more staff than anyone else and we could only open new post offices if we could find the necessary funds, and if the Director of DDS agreed. As business grew, we got up more staff from the PMG and began to take over the bigger offices like Madang from DDS and NA. When DDS opened new stations, like Telefomin, Lake Kutubu, Mendi and Menyamya,[2] we forwarded their mail in 'free bags'. In the early stages we didn't bother then with paperwork, and often they never worried about sealing the outgoing mailbags with the official lead seals. Young cadets and *kiaps* (DDS and NA field officers) would arrive from South to go out to the DDS outstations, and we'd give them some postal training at Port Moresby before they went. I'd give them a bit of a lecture, then the postmaster would give them the minimum they needed to know to run an outstation post office. We didn't expect them to use things like a Form 100, of course. We lost a hell of a lot of mailbags to the outstations. The *kiaps* would use them to pack up their gear when they went on patrol. We usually had plenty of mailbags then, though, because we got far more mail from Australia than we sent out. But eventually we had to get replacements from the PMG's Department, which we had to purchase. The PMG boys were always a terrific help, and I could always call on B.J. O'Brien in Queensland. We had a fair bit of trouble with pilfering, particularly from the registered mails — Burns Philp had a lot of trouble, I remember. But this happens in postal services everywhere, not just in PNG.

Old attitudes still lingered in Port Moresby in those years. Some returned white residents of the old Papua found it difficult to accept that there was a new spirit abroad. Papuans now resented language and peremptory treatment from whites that once had been all too common, and when the first Papuan began to serve the public at the front counter of the GPO, a job hitherto performed exclusively by whites, some residents protested angrily.

Friction between white and black was slow to ease. As previously mentioned, Wally McPherson was also responsible for the operation of the Telephone Exchange

---

2 Telefomin was opened in 1948, Lake Kutubu in 1949, and the other two in 1950.

prior to the arrival of W.S. Peckover in 1956, and telephonists were located in the Postal Services Branch. A 3 a.m. one morning, McPherson was awakened from a sound sleep by the ringing of his telephone. Wondering who could be bothering him at such an outlandish hour, he picked up the phone. It was Thomas, a young Papuan who was the Night Telephonist at the Port Moresby exchange: 'Sir', Thomas said, highly agitated. 'Mr — has just called me a black bastard!' 'Oh', replied McPherson, 'did he, and what did you say to Mr — ?' 'I said to him, "Mr — , if I am a black bastard, sir, you are a white bastard". Then I pulled out the plug, and I rang you, sir.'

Incidents of this kind were quite frequent then, and McPherson's sympathies were with Thomas. But the telephone service had to be maintained. 'Thomas', he said, 'you had no right to act like that, you should have just said, "I'm sorry, sir, I must refuse you service. Good morning". Still, it was a good idea to ring and tell me about it. Don't permit anyone to speak to you in the manner that Mr — did. Now make the appropriate entries in your night journal, and I'll take the matter up with your Postmaster first thing in the morning.'

Next morning McPherson was astounded to find that there was no law or regulation then in force covering the verbal abuse of telephonists by users. He consulted W.W. Watkins, the Secretary for Law, and in a matter of hours a draft regulation was produced for ratification by the Administrator. McPherson summoned Mr — and told him, very firmly, that his telephone would be instantly removed if any further complaints of his behaviour were received.

The question of the home delivery of mail in the towns arose early in McPherson's time, and was resurrected on many occasions over the following years. The establishment of Town Advisory Councils in a number of the larger centres of PNG during 1950-1 gave citizens a formal avenue for pressing demands for home deliveries. McPherson took a firm line on this question. Houses in the towns of PNG did not carry street numbers; there were too few literate Papua New Guineans available to serve as postmen and it would be far too expensive to employ Europeans; the risk of loss of mail through pilfering of letterboxes would be too great, since a big percentage of married white women were in employment, leaving houses empty during the day.

When Bill Carter became Director, he served on the Port Moresby TAC on the instructions of the Administrator, Brigadier Cleland. He, too, came under fire from TAC members and the European public on the issue of home deliveries, but he steadfastly supported the policy established by McPherson. 'Posts and Telegraphs can't afford European postmen', he said in a press release in July 1958, 'and when we find native employees who can read, we have far more important jobs for them to do than tramping around delivering mail'.

Old-timers were not mollified. 'Why not native posties?!' wrote the columnist 'Tolala' (Gordon Thomas, ex-editor of the *Rabaul Times*) in an article in *Pacific Islands Monthly*:

> Delivery of mail in the old days used to be looked upon as something almost sacrosanct, and the more isolated the addressee the more meticulously was that obligation carried out. Well do I remember many occasions when, being ten to thirty

miles from the district office, a day after the arrival of the mail at the station there would appear at the foot of my verandah steps a policeboy with a couple of carriers with mailbags.

The good old days, however, were long gone, and no amount of nostalgic reminiscence would recall them. Mails never were delivered to homes by postmen, black or white, in PNG, and this policy has continued to the present day. Instead, mail boxes have been widely installed in both official and agency post offices throughout the nation.

The rapid expansion of the post office box system was not achieved without difficulty. The boxes themselves were expensive, and hard to come by. The PMG's Department provided the initial boxes, but the demand in Australia was so great that the needs of PNG were afforded a low priority. In England and Australia these boxes were historically known as 'private' boxes, not post office boxes. When introduced into PNG, existing postal rules made it illegal to publish or disclose the names and addresses of box holders. This was an impediment to their widespread use. P and T wanted to encourage the use of boxes as a practical alternative to home deliveries, and eventually the rules were amended to allow the names and addresses of post office box holders who were telephone subscribers to be listed in the PNG telephone directory.

As a further encouragement to prospective hirers of post office boxes, annual rates were held to a very low figure. The first boxes were installed during the 1951-2 financial year: 87 at the GPO, Port Moresby, and 60 each at Lae and Rabaul. Annual rental charges were £6 for a large box, £4 for a medium one and £2 for a small. In 1975, over 20 000 boxes were in use throughout PNG, and hiring charges had been reduced in real terms: $6, $4 and $2 respectively. Similar restraint was shown when setting the base rate for 'private bags' to subscribers living in remote areas. When introduced the rate was £1 ten shillings; by 1975 it was only $3 per annum.

Postage, telephone and telegraph rates charged in PNG were set by regulations under the two Posts and Telegraphs Ordinances. In 1951, new regulations repealed all existing postal regulations, and all but one telephone regulation, generally increasing rates previously charged to bring them into line with those applying in Australia. The inland surface letter postage rate was fixed at 3½ pence for the first ounce, and 2½ pence for each additional ounce or part thereof. Air mail letters were charged at the ordinary rate, plus an air mail fee of 3 pence per half ounce. Standard rates were increased at intervals during the following years, and in the process PNG departed from Australian practice and developed a unique internal mail classification and rating structure, far less complex than those used in other countries. The world trend today is towards just such a simplification of mail classification and rating.[3]

As a recognition of the responsibility of postal services in a developing country in the social welfare field, internal rates were maintained at the lowest economic level. (Indeed, as will be later recounted, philatelic profits have, as a matter of policy been

3 In respect of overseas mails, PNG is generally obliged to follow the exceedingly complex structure set up by the Universal Postal Union. However, over the years, the Department managed to interpret UPU structures in such a way as to allow the development of a comparatively simple overseas mail rate.

used to offset any losses on postal services.) On the eve of Independence, the internal rate was only seven cents for a letter up to two ounces in weight. Letters despatched to Australia and its territories attracted the same charge, although the maximum allowable weight was reduced to one ounce. The countries of the world were at that time divided into five zones, depending on their distance from PNG. The air mail letter rate per half ounce varied from ten cents to Zone One countries to thirty cents to those in Zone Five — Europe, the United States, West Indies etc. (The seven cents rate — which became seven toea when PNG adopted its own currency — was maintained for ten years, an extraordinary achievement in a decade of high inflation. In March 1981, it was increased to ten toea. At this time, a letter could be sent, by air mail, from PNG to Australia for fifteen toea for up to twenty grams weight; the return rate was thirty-five cents, for up to only ten grams!)

This low postage rate certainly encouraged the people of PNG to make greater use of the post. It is interesting to compare the attitude of PNG's postal administration to that of other South Pacific countries when the metric system was introduced. New Zealand, for example, converted precisely, one half-once becoming fourteen grams. PNG gave the customer the benefit of the doubt, converting one half-ounce to twenty grams. Australia, on the other hand, converted one half-ounce to ten grams for postal rate purposes.

As mentioned previously, few Papua New Guineans used the postal service in the early post-war years and in fact the volume of indigenous mail was then so low that it was commonly accepted at post offices unstamped. By the late 1940s however, the volume began to increase, and the free service gradually disappeared. At intervals during the late 1950s and early 1960s, the Department conducted a number of campaigns designed to encourage and assist Papua New Guineans to write more letters and take greater care in addressing them, efforts that definitely paid dividends. By mid-1959, the number of postal articles handled throughout PNG had risen to 13.7 million. It is clearly impossible to state what percentage of this figure comprised Papua New Guinean mails, but experienced postal officers agree that it was considerable, and rising.

It was in November 1959 that Wally McPherson left P and T to return to the PMG's Department in Australia. (He was relieved by Divisional Inspector L.J. Meiklejohn until the arrival of S.M. Jay in June 1960. Jay resigned in 1965 and Meiklejohn again became head of Postal Services.) McPherson's relationship with Bill Carter had been cordial and marked by mutual respect, but he was on secondment, and he could not remain so indefinitely.

Although McPherson had been Superintendent of Postal Services, Carter, as Director, of course retained the final say in matters of policy. Carter was determined to improve mail services throughout PNG; to build new post offices to replace the collection of ramshackle makeshifts then existing in all the districts; to encourage the use of the post by the indigenous people; to introduce technical advances — post office boxes, for example — wherever possible; to issue new and better stamps, and perhaps most importantly, to train Papua New Guineans to take their rightful place in the management and operation of Postal Services, and the other divisions of P and T.

These goals were mostly gradually achieved. Papua New Guineans did come to use the post. Post office boxes proved to be a great (and continuing) success — so much so that before long demands for home deliveries practically ceased. The construction of new post offices was a long, drawn-out business. Funds were never sufficient, and in some districts Bill Carter enlisted the aid of sympathetic District Commissioners to cause post offices to magically appear, although not on approved works programmes, through subtle manipulation of district funds. Mail services steadily improved during the 1950s and 1960s, as shipping services developed, air routes expanded and roads were built.

In the early 1950s, the major percentage of PNG's overseas mails was still being transported by sea. As mentioned in Chapter 8, Burns Philip & Co. had been quick to restore its Pacific Mail subsidized service, and by mid-1957 had five ships on the PNG run, serving Lae, Madang, Kavieng, Rabaul, Lorengau, Wewak and Kieta as well as Port Moresby and Samarai. In 1952, the New Guinea-Australia Line commenced a new scheduled service with two small motorships previously used on the China coast, the *Shansi* and the *Sinkiang*. They were joined by the MV *Soochow* in 1954. Many other shipping lines also began to send vessels to PNG ports, some of them familiar names from the *gudpela taim bipo*; China Navigation Co.; Eastern and Australian Steamship Co.; Australia-West Pacific Line; Indo-China Steam Navigation Co.; Pacific Shipowners Ltd.; Pacific Far East Line; Koninklijke Paketvaart Maatschappij Line; Karlander (NG) Line; Austasia Line; Stoomvaart Maatschappij Nederland; Koninklijke Rotterdamsche Lloyd; Crusader Line; Bank Line. In the mid-1960s, three Japanese firms began sending their ships to PNG: Mitsui-OSK Line, KKK Line and the NYK Line. Some companies dropped out of PNG services; others came in. By the early 1970s PNG had shipping links with many ports in the Pacific, Europe, the United States and the East, and at least one ship arrived each week from Australia.

Small ships continued to carry mails within PNG waters, although the rapid growth of aerial services gradually reduced their role. The early post-war service initially provided by the Commonwealth Directorate of Shipping — the Papua and New Guinea Coastal and Inter-Island Shipping Service — expanded to the point where by mid-1952 some fifteen vessels, each of 300 tons, were in operation. The service was badly handled by the Administration, and a great deal of money was lost. In an endeavour to retrieve the situation, the service was handed over to the Production Control Board to manage. In effect, the actual operation of the ships was taken over by the major mercantile and plantation companies on a cost-plus-10-per-cent basis, giving them a virtual monopoly, free of financial risk, of the rich inter-island trade. When Paul Hasluck became Minister for Territories, he swiftly acted to end this cozy arrangement. Captain J.H. Evans — 'Frog' Evans as he was universally known — was appointed shipping manager and over a period of time the ships were all sold to private concerns. Evans was later awarded the MBE in recognition of his work during these years. The Administration continued to operate its mixed fleet of trawlers and workboats for government purposes and commonly carried mails, but for the remainder of the colonial era allowed private enterprise to operate the coastal and inter-island services.

By the standards of the Western world, the roads of PNG are few, and mostly of poor quality. Although employed wherever it was practicable, they were of limited importance in the distribution of mails until the mid-1960s, when the Highlands

Highway, linking Lae on the coast with Mt Hagen in the far hinterland, was opened for general traffic. Mails were henceforth transported by truck to the many stations and settlements served by the Highway, although letters were mostly dispatched by air. This road, still the longest and most economically significant in PNG, was extended to Mendi, in the Southern Highlands, in the early 1970s. Madang and Lae were tenuously linked by road, and important road construction was undertaken in the Sepik. The Lae-Wau road was completed by Army engineers during the war. At Independence, there was a claimed 16 458 kilometres of road throughout PNG, most hardly more than four-wheel-drive tracks and apart from the Highlands, few of the districts of PNG were at that time linked. There is still no trans-New Guinea highway.

Aircraft were therefore of far greater importance than roads in internal mail distribution. By Independence, there were 414 recognized airfields throughout PNG, ranging from the two principal aerodromes — Jackson's Airport, Port Moresby, and Lae — capable of accepting aircraft as large as Boeing 747s and Fokker F28s respectively, to little private airfields accommodating light single-engine machines. These airfields were served by a multitude of aircraft, operated by many companies and individuals. All carried mails. The national airline, Air Niugini, provided international and main trunk route services, and three companies ran regular, as well as charter, services: Talair Pty. Ltd., Douglas Airways and Panga Airways Ltd. Charter companies, based in most districts, were, and remain, exceedingly important elements in PNG's internal communications. At Independence, the following charter companies were registered: Airfast Helicopters Ltd.; Bougainville Air Services; Carpentaria Exploration Co.; Catholic Mission, Siar-Manga; Catholic Mission, Yule Island; C. and B. Chee Pty. Ltd.; Co-ordinated Air Services Pty. Ltd.; Helitrans PNG Pty. Ltd.; Lutheran Mission, New Guinea; Missionary Aviation Fellowship; Kokomo Air Services; Pacific Helicopters Pty. Ltd.; Franair; Seaplane Charters Pty. Ltd.; South Pacific Aero Clubs, Port Moresby and Lae; Summer Institute of Linguistics; Wirui Air Services Pty. Ltd. There were few regions in PNG beyond the reach of the charter companies, and all carried mails when required.

In the immediate post-war years, all classes of mails, including parcels, were delivered by air within PNG without additional cost to the sender or addressee wherever this was practicable. Mails were carried by the airlines at freight rates on internal routes and were classified as 'mail carried by air' rather than as 'air mail'. By mid-1956, letter class mails were being carried free of surcharge by air within PNG to the post office nearest to the office of delivery. Other articles and parcels class mails were carried by air free of surcharge, if not over one pound in weight. A surcharge of one shilling per pound was levied after the first pound. All classes of mails from overseas, or posted within PNG for overseas destinations, were carried by the first available sea or air service.

From 1 December 1956, parcels posted overseas, prepaid at surface rates for delivery at PNG destinations to which air carriage was the only means of conveyance, were surcharged at the rate of ninepence per pound. This caused a storm of protest from the many residents of inland towns and settlements throughout the Territories. It particularly annoyed the business houses, large and small, who used free air transport within PNG to avoid air freight charges on much of their stock. When decimal currency was introduced the surcharge was first dropped to five cents per pound and then abolished. All classes of mails posted within PNG for delivery overseas continued to be carried within the country by first available sea or air transport. By Independence, aircraft were carrying the bulk of the nation's internal, as well as overseas, first class mails.

As mentioned in Chapter 8, Australia-PNG air services were provided initially by Qantas after the Pacific war, following the takeover of the W.R. Carpenter airline. Qantas introduced four-engined Douglas Skymasters onto the route in March 1950, replacing the DC3s hitherto used. Trans-Oceanic Airways made an unsuccessful attempt to establish a service in competition with Qantas in 1951-2, using four-engined Solent flying-boats. Qantas also built up a complex internal route network in PNG. In 1960, it was forced out of PNG by the two-airline policy of the Australian Government, which limited Qantas to international routes (PNG being considered as territories of Australia). Both Trans-Australia Airlines and Ansett-ANA entered the Australia-PNG service, using Douglas DC6Bs, later Lockheed Electras, and, finally, Boeing 727 jets. TAA took over Qantas' internal PNG routes, and to maintain its competitive position, Ansett-ANA bought out Mandated Airlines, which had itself earlier swallowed two other companies, Gibbes Sepik Airways and Madang Air Services. In May 1968, all assets of Ansett-ANA were transferred to Ansett Airlines of PNG which in 1970 took over Patair, a charter company. On 1 November 1973, Air Niugini was born, 60 per cent owned by the PNG Government, 24 per cent by Qantas and TAA, and 16 per cent by Ansett. Air Niugini took over all internal routes previously operated by TAA and Ansett, using their DC3 and Fokker F27 aircraft. It also began to operate fifty per cent of the Port Moresby-Brisbane services, using Boeing 727s leased from the two Australian companies.

As a result of these, and many other, developments — only the more significant have been sketched above — PNG at Independence enjoyed daily air mail services to Australia and regular services to the British Solomon Islands Protectorate, Jayapura in West Irian, Manila, Vila and Fiji, as well as a most comprehensive internal route structure. Qantas was soon to return to PNG operations, for the country was now an independent nation, and so outside the restrictions of the two-airline policy. The delivery and distribution of mails to, from and within PNG was thus swift, certain and regular.

By the time Wally McPherson left PNG in November 1959, the number of post offices had increased to forty-five. The majority were still controlled by officers of the Department of Native Affairs (the reorganized DDS and NA), but thirteen were now staffed by Postal Services: Port Moresby, Lae, Rabaul, Madang, Samarai, Bulolo, Goroka, Wewak, Kavieng, Kokopo, Konedobu, Sohano and Mt Hagen. Post offices were then divided into three categories: official, staffed by P and T; and non-official,[4] operated by private individuals, missions etc., on behalf of P and T; and agency, run by DNA as agents of P and T. The workload involved in operating an agency post office

---

4 The term 'non-official post office' was dropped in October 1970. All post offices other than official offices were henceforth called 'agency offices', regardless of whether they were run by Patrol Officers, private people, missions or local government councils.

increased considerably during the 1950s as the volume of mails increased, and by the end of the decade, Native Affairs officers were demanding to be relieved of Posts and Telegraphs duties, which were now so heavy that in busier centres DNA functions were being adversely affected. From 1959, a concerted effort was made to increase the number of official post offices, and to convert agency offices to non-official status. It was difficult to find responsible people or organizations in the outlying centres generally served by agency offices prepared to take them over from DNA. It was hard, too, for Carter to find the staff, and the funds, to increase the number of official post offices. Funds were provided by the Treasury, and there was little that the Department could do to increase the amounts allocated. It was never easy for P and T to recruit enough experienced postal and telecommunication officers from Australia, but something could surely be done to fit Papua New Guinean staff to take over post offices. Bill Carter says:

> When I made my first tour of PNG after my arrival in 1954, I was amazed at the number of routine tasks being done in every district by Australians, jobs that could easily have been done by Papua New Guineans with a bit of training. Not just in the post offices — linesmen, technicians and so on. Dark faces were few and far between, particularly in places like post office counters where there was direct contact with the public. Right away I decided that we'd have to start training Papua New Guineans, just as soon as we could.

As recounted earlier in this book, a few selected nationals had received specialized training in Australia before the war. During the war, ANGAU had trained many wireless operators, switchboard operators and linesmen, and the training school established in June 1946 by E.C.A. Brown had been quite successful before staff and funding problems had forced its early closure. No further attempts had been made to provide formal training for the native employees of P and T, although Wally McPherson and a handful of dedicated postal men — men such as L.J. Meiklejohn, R.S.J. Phillips, A.H. Johnstone, M.P. Hooley, A.W. Morley, R.A. Miller, W.W. Nicholls, J.P. Mowen, P.W. Scully, Noel Lyons, H.C. Tremayne, F.G. Cleary — and a few officers in the Engineering and Telecommunication divisions gave on-the-job instruction to promising PNG employees wherever possible. But only 50 nationals throughout PNG were employed in postal services at June, 1958, apart from labourers, messengers and so on. Clearly, considerable effort would be required to produce the National Postmasters of the future.

The Department of Posts and Telegraphs had begun the formal in-service training of indigenous staff as early as 1956, ahead of most other departments of the Administration. Only the Departments of Public Health and Education were then providing some formal instruction for their members. A small school was set up in a tiny room at the rear of the Konedobu Telephone Exchange, with an enrolment of ten trainee radio telegraphists. The instructor was I.F. Mollinger. In another room, Peter Cottell taught the first class of telephone technicians, while Geoff Hutton taught radio theory on the verandah of one of the few remaining pre-war cottages in Cuthbertson Street, which rumour had it was once used as a house of ill-fame. By mid-1958, twelve telegraphists and three technical trainees were in full-time formal training. In this year, tenders were called for the construction of the first stage of a Training College at Boroko, Port Moresby.

Available funds were sufficient only for the most basic buildings and facilities. Stage One of the College was completed in 1959. It was planned to provide Australian-standard courses of from two to five years duration, depending on the category, for trainee telegraphists, teleprinter operators, radio technicians, telephone technicians, linesmen, telephonists and postal assistants. Initial enrolment included sixteen telegraphy trainees and eleven technicians. Peter Cottell, Geoff Hutton and Jim Lappin were the first instructors. Hutton became the first Acting Principal, in 1960. These men were primarily technicians, with no formal teaching qualifications. In 1961 the veteran Mavara Hekure joined the staff as an Assistant Instructor, serving for a year until his retirement in August, 1962, after forty-five years in Posts and Telegraphs. (The Department had lost another stalwart in 1961, with the retirement of the senior serving Papua New Guinean, Gavera Lohia, who in 1954 had been awarded the Long Service Medal.)

Postal training did not begin at the College until 1960, although the on-the-job training of postal officer assistants that had been given in the field for years was supplemented by a correspondence course conducted from postal services headquarters during 1959. The first postal instructor was R.A. Miller. The duration of the initial course was set at three to four years, depending on the standard of education of each trainee. A Standard 9 pass was the minimum acceptable requirement for entry. A number of the first trainees were clerical assistants from the new Auxiliary Division of the Public Service, with higher qualifications. But P and T had few local officers with even Standard 9 education, so arrangements were made for short eight-week initial courses for selected postal officer assistants who lacked this qualification, to supplement the long courses.

Basic problems began to emerge as the Training College gradually expanded and new courses were added. Suitably qualified trainees were desperately hard to find right through to Independence. The Christian missions provided the bulk of what education was offered to young Papua New Guineans in the 1940s and 1950s; the great Administration effort did not really begin until the early 1960s. In 1960, only 1 800 Papua New Guineans were in secondary school; by 1970, the number had increased to almost 18 000, but this was still a small percentage of the youth of the nation. The picture was hardly much brighter in primary education; in 1970, only 80 000 children were enrolled in Administration and 132 000 in Mission primary schools. The variation in the quality of the instruction given was extraordinary. The University of Papua New Guinea did not begin courses until 1966. All departments of the Administration scrambled for the graduates of the education system and P and T found it hard to attract trainees in competition with such departments as Education, Public Health, Agriculture and Native Affairs. Moreover, the Department soon found that the actual level of education of many who did opt for careers in P and T was so poor that courses in basic education subjects had to be added to the curriculum of the Boroko Training College.

Certain minimum standards had to be set for the trainees. This was essential in a technical department like P and T. A radio technician could either repair a radio, or he could not. He could understand basic electrical theory, or he could not. There were no half measures. A postal clerk at the very least had to be able to read, to accurately sort mails and give customers correct change. Such standards had to be maintained, but experience soon prompted the College to drop rigid terms of training that had no regard for individual ability. By 1966, postal trainees were required to have Form II or Form III passes for entry, and the course was set at one to three years, depending on individual progress. There were at first very many failures, but the numbers of successful postal graduates steadily increased over the years leading up to Independence. From time to time, new buildings were erected, updated teaching equipment installed, and new methods introduced — a story covered in more detail later in this book. The initial postal training course had been attended by only eight trainees; in 1972-3, 48 students graduated as Postal Officers grade three, and 30 as Officers grade four.

A wide variety of postal courses was offered at the Training College during the 1960s, possibly the most significant the special three-month advanced management courses for selected trainees in the duties and responsibilities of positions up to Postmaster, first introduced in 1963. Following the course, the students were sent into the field for further on-the-job instruction, understudying Postal Clerks, Assistant Postmasters and Postmasters. On successful completion of the programme, those graduates with the necessary education standard were eligible for promotion to positions up to Postmaster grade 1. Michael Dawadawareta had shown that Papua New Guineans could do the job, given the training and opportunity. Michael became the first National Postmaster in 1962, when he took over control of the Daru office. He was trained on the job and through correspondence courses, for he lacked the educational advantages of many of the younger national officers of P and T. He was only moderately successful as a Postmaster, but he showed the way.

The year 1960 was an important one for P and T training. The Department had then been in existence for five years, and Bill Carter thought the time was appropriate for an objective examination of its management and performance, to find ways of improving productivity and achievement. He sought and obtained permission to approach the PMG's Department in Australia and in due course F.R. Schadel of the Organization and Methods Branch of the Australian Post Office Headquarters, Melbourne, was instructed to proceed to PNG and carry out a Review of the Department of Posts and Telegraphs of Papua and New Guinea. Schadel, a man with a solid background in this wide field, began the review in July 1961, and completed it in November 1962. During his review of the Postal Services Division, Schadel was accompanied by R.G. Ord from the Australian Post Office, an expert in postal administration.

The wider recommendations of the 1962 Report will be considered later. In relation to training, the main recommendation was for the creation of a separate training branch for P and T with a number of positions, headed by an officer with formal teaching and/or training qualifications. It was accepted and acted upon. J.R. Rampling was recruited as Principal of the Training College. John Rampling was a trained teacher and had served as a personnel, and later training officer with the Commonwealth Public Service. Although he was entirely ignorant of the technical operations of P and T, he quickly achieved a close rapport with his Papua New Guinean students.

A powerful impetus to the wider education and training of Papua New Guineans was given by the 1962 United Nations Visiting Mission, headed by Sir Hugh Foot. The report of the Mission — the most influential of all the post-war UN missions to PNG — was basically aimed at accelerating the pace of political, social and economic change in a country fast heading for self-determination. It called for a much greater effort to educate Papua New Guineans to replace Australians in the running of the country, and for the establishment without delay of a university. It was a highly controversial document, received in many circles with indignation, even dismay, but a great deal flowed from it, including the involvement of the World Bank (International Bank for Reconstruction and Development) in the affairs of PNG, and of the Department of Posts and Telegraphs in particular, an involvement discussed later.

The Foot Report jarred the Australian Government, and particularly the Department of Territories, out of their complacency over their PNG policy. The Report achieved, almost overnight, a change in pace and emphasis that men of fore-sight in PNG — such as John Gunther, Ian Downs and Bill Carter — had been advocating for years.

It is true that constitutional change was being considered even before the visit of the 1962 UN Mission, but a sense of urgency was lacking. Following the visit, progress in this field was rapid. In March 1964, elections were held throughout PNG for the first House of Assembly, to replace the old Legislative Council. For the first time, Papua New Guineans were members. In this month, too, the Currie Commission on Higher Education delivered its Report, recommending the immediate establishment of a uni-versity. The University of Papua New Guinea began its preliminary year in 1966, and its first undergraduate courses in the following year, with Dr. J.T. Gunther as Vice-Chancellor. An Administrative College had been established in 1963, to provide high-level training for Public Servants.

It was beginning to be generally recognized that time was running out. PNG was on the road to self-determination, and a national educated élite was lacking. A 'crash' training effort would be required if PNG was to avoid reliance on overseas aid indefinitely. But an independent PNG would not be able to afford to pay this élite — or, indeed, its Public Service — at Australian rates, as had been hitherto the case. The year 1964 which saw such progress in constitutional development and higher edu-cation, also saw the painful decision taken to reconstruct the Public Service, and the introduction of new salary scales for national officers which were much lower than overseas rates. Introduced in great haste, arbitrarily and without prior discussions in the new House of Assembly, the new salary scales were received with great bitterness by Papua New Guineans.

It was, however, out of this time of change and adjustment that fresh oppor-tunities came for young nationals in the public service, including the Department of Posts and Telegraphs. The increasing emphasis on training was precisely in accord with Bill Carter's ideas. He sought and found opportunities for national officers of P and T to attend courses in Australia, and overseas. The pace of change continued to accelerate. The House of Assembly was reformed and enlarged in 1968. Political parties began to emerge and the names of politicians became known throughout PNG: the Pangu Pati, the United Party, Michael Somare, Matthias Toliman, Tei Abal, Julius Chan and many others. Sinake Giregire, a charismatic young Eastern Highlander, became Ministerial Member for Posts and Telegraphs, and political considerations became important in the operation of the Department, as in the Public Service generally. The year 1971 saw further criticism by a UN Visiting Mission of the rate of progress being achieved in PNG, and a promise by Gough Whitlam, Leader of the Opposition in the Australian Parliament, of early Independence for PNG should his party achieve office in the forthcoming elections. In August 1971, the Public Service Board of PNG announced that the rate of 'localization' (replacement of expatriates by Papua New Guineans) in the Service would be rapidly increased, with preference for promotion being given to adequately qualified national officers over expatriates. Training institutions throughout PNG struggled, vainly, to cope with the flood of applications from ambitious young Papua New Guineans. In January 1973, the Department of Posts and Telegraphs established a Localization Division at Port Moresby, headed by A. Cox, to speed the process of localization and help national officers plan their futures.

It was in this climate of change that postal training developed from the mid-1960s to Independence in September, 1975. The Training College at Boroko continued to provide courses at low and middle levels, with considerable success; by mid-1971, seventeen out of the thirty-one Postmaster positions in P and T were localized; all were filled by Papua New Guineans by Independence.

Australian postal men at every level of P and T contributed to the progress achieved. With few exceptions, they were happy to assist national officers to prepare themselves for rapid promotion, even though their own positions were thus endangered. Certainly, the adoption by the Australian Government of a compensation scheme for loss-of-career made it easier for these men to accept the inevitable, but their good-will was essential to smooth localization.

Despite the need for rapid progress in this field, no compromise was at first made with performance and discipline. National officers as well as expatriates had to do the job efficiently. Standards were enforced by frequent visits by postal inspectors. Breaches of departmental instructions and procedures were at first common. During the 1972-3 financial year, 82 officers of the Postal Services Branch were fined and 16 dismissed for different departmental offences, out of a total of 384 national and expatriate officers employed.

The increasing rate of localization of the Public Service drew a lot of criticism from sections of the European public of PNG. Unfortunately, quite a number of the young national officers who first took over postal positions in the field succumbed to temptation and ended up in gaol on charges of stealing from the mails or the till. This fuelled the prejudice of those who held that Papua New Guineans were incapable of filling positions of trust and responsibility. The stress of economic necessity undoubtedly helped to urge some officers along the wrong path. Wages were low, living costs — particularly in the main centres — high. It was hard to make ends meet. When Gigiba Agia, a promising young officer who had successfully completed several P and T courses, was gaoled for nine months in June 1965, for stealing registered mail, he offered in his defence the fact that his cash wage was only £3 and three shillings per week. Out of this small sum he had to provide for rent, food and clothing as well as find no less than twelve shillings a per week for bus fares to and from work. Small wonder that he stole.

The situation was still serious as late as 1971. The then manager of the Postal Services Branch, A.W. Morley, was about to go to Australia on leave, and Bill Carter asked him to examine the postal investigation procedures in use in New South Wales, to determine whether any of them could with profit be adopted in PNG. Morley spent several weeks on the task. He found that postal theft was a problem common in New South Wales and the other Australian states, and one that had never been fully overcome. Nor has it been overcome in PNG, but as time went by, the problem was contained, and postal theft reduced to manageable proportions.

Morley — known throughout P and T as 'Hookey', a nickname gained during his footballing days — played a notable part in the localization of the Postal Services Division. He came to PNG as a young man of indifferent education, looking for a job. He joined P and T in 1954 in the lowly capacity of Junior Postal Officer, the very bottom of the ladder, and by dint of hard study qualified for entry into the Second Division of the PNG Public Service. From 1956 to 1962 he was Postmaster at Madang, which was then the supply and mail centre for the whole of the Highlands, and most of the Sepik. It grew rapidly during these years, and in terms of postal business, the post office was the busiest in PNG. It was common to have 1 000 bags of surface mail awaiting sorting and transport by air into the Highlands. With the opening of the Highlands Highway for general road traffic in the mid-1960s Madang declined, and Lae became the second town of PNG. During his years at Madang, Morley trained many of the young postal officers, Australian and national, who went on to take over post offices all over PNG. In October 1962, he took over the Rabaul post office. His reputation within the Department steadily increased, and in 1969 Carter brought him to Headquarters to take over the position of Manager, Postal Services from L.J. Meiklejohn. In 1972, following a reorganization of P and T, he became Assistant Director, Postal. He retired in 1975.

From the beginning of his service as Manager, Morley worked with the full support of Carter to localize the division. He located six of his best Australian postal men at key locations throughout PNG, each with a defined district in which he was 'trouble shooter', adviser and friend to National Postmasters. The six operated in two teams. The senior of them was the head of the Post Offices branch, Maurie Hooley. Under him, Barry Misson and Arthur Ottoway looked after the postmasters in Papua; Bill Green, Phil Scully and Vince Flanagan were responsible for New Guinea. Of this team of experienced advisers, Scully, Flanagan, Green and Misson stayed on in P and T after Independence. (Scully and Flanagan were still there in mid-1981, two of the last six expatriates in Postal Services.) At all times, the National Postmasters in the districts remained fully responsible for the management of their offices, but with the comforting knowledge that expert help was close at hand if needed. It was a highly effective system which did much to bolster the confidence of officers thrust into responsible positions sometimes before they were fully ready, because of the urgent need to localize the Public Service as Independence drew nigh.

The officers who rose swiftly through the ranks to important positions within the Department by Independence are today quick to acknowledge the debt they owe to Australian instructors and postal men. The careers of three notable officers illustrate the training methods used to bring nationals to the top.

Patrick Tomausi, an intense man passionately devoted to Postal Services, was born in the Milne Bay district. After an unsuccessful attempt to qualify as a medical practitioner at the Papuan Medical College in 1961 and 1962, he joined P and T early in 1963. In 1964, he graduated as a Postal Assistant — top student of his year — from the Boroko Training College. He was appointed to the Auxiliary Division of the Public Service, and in 1965 became the eighth national officer to take charge of a post office, at Daru, on an acting basis. Soon afterwards he took over the Mendi post office and then in 1966 the large office at Sohano, in the Bougainville district. At Mendi and Sohano he was the sole officer and of necessity operated the outstation teleradio service on behalf of the Telecommunications Branch. He was also the local customs officer, a situation typical of outstations where the volume of business did not warrant the posting of a specialist officer. He was at least spared one time-consuming duty commonly performed by postmasters at small offices in Australia: operating a Commonwealth Savings Bank agency. From the very beginning, Bill Carter and Tas Sexton, head of the Accounts branch, refused to accept these agencies in PNG post offices. Their aim was always to run P and T on sound commercial lines, insofar as this was possible in the context of overall Administration policy. The commission paid by the bank was very small, certainly not enough to make the operation of agencies worthwhile.

From Sohano, Patrick Tomausi went to Konedobu as Assistant Postmaster under W.W. Nicholls. It was largely the training and advice that Bill Nicholls gave to Tomausi that prepared him for his permanent promotion to full Postmaster, and Tomausi today remembers him with gratitude (Nicholls died in 1979). In 1967, Tomausi established an official post office at Mapnik, taking over the agency office hitherto run by the Department of District Administration (the former Department of Native Affairs) on behalf of P and T. Here he remained for over three years. He was given a lot of support by the Postmaster at Wewak, Noel Lyons. In 1970, A.W. Morley called Tomausi to Port Moresby to attend a course in advanced postal administration at the Boroko Training College, together with Lionel Haembo, Kelly Middle, Richard Kavu and Misob Mallanggen, other young nationals on the way up.

As a reward for good performance at the course, Tomausi and Kelly Middle accompanied Bill Carter to a Scout Jamboree at Sydney, where they operated a Scout post office.[5] On returning to Port Moresby, Patrick Tomausi became the second Papua New Guinean to be promoted to the very responsible position of Postal Inspector. In this capacity he spent the next two-and-a-half years visiting post offices all over PNG.

It was during this period that Tomausi began an experiment at the Losuia post office, in his home district. Like Carter, he wanted the village people of PNG to experience the convenience of post office boxes. He arranged for a number of boxes to be provided, one for each of a number of villages in the Losuia Sub-district. The key for each box was held by a village councillor, who collected mail on behalf of the villagers. The people responded eagerly to this initiative, and Tomausi made similar arrangements in the Buin Sub-district of Bougainville, and at Maprik, where he had earlier served as postmaster. (In the Highlands, tribesmen of the Wahgi Valley had discovered for themselves the advantages of post office boxes and held a number at various offices.)

Tomausi continued to ascend the promotion ladder. He was selected to attend another management course in 1973, this time at the Administrative College, and in that year went to Sydney, to the Australian School of Pacific Administration. On his return, he again served as Postmaster, at Boroko and Konedobu, before moving to the Philatelic Bureau where he became the acting Manager-in-training and, in July 1974, Manager.

Tomausi's career demonstrates well the mix of practical and academic training given to promising young national officers in the Department of Posts and Telegraphs. As mentioned above, he was the second Papua New Guinean to be appointed a Postal Inspector. The first was Dale Kamara.

Kamara began a brilliant career with P and T sweeping the floors of the Port Moresby GPO. The son of a Methodist pastor, he was taught by his father at a Mission primary school until the age of twelve, then he attended Administration schools until 1955. He went on to the Vunamami Vocational School for three years and Kerevat High School for five, graduating in 1963, one of the best educated young Papua New Guineans of his time. Ambitious, though with no clear idea of what he wanted to do with his life, Kamara began a course at the Port Moresby Teachers College, but quickly realized that this was not for him. A chance meeting in a Boroko street with a friend attending the P and T College led him to apply for training as a technician in the tele-communications field. The course was already in progress and another would not begin until the following year. Only postal training was available. While waiting for the course to begin, Dale Kamara swept floors at the GPO.

He was immediately successful at the Training College and in 1965 he completed a twelve month Public Service Certificate course at the Administrative College. Also at the College were a number of young men with strong political convictions, prominent among them Michael Somare, Albert Maori Kiki and Joseph Nombri.

---

5 Some of Carter's major contributions to PNG were made outside the Department of Posts and Telegraphs. He had joined the Apex Club at Parkes, New South Wales before going to PNG, and in Port Moresby was responsible for the formation of an Apex Club, the first service club to be formed in the Territory. He became its Foundation President, and in 1964 was made an Apex Life Member.

In 1966, at the request of the then Administrator, Sir Donald Cleland, who was Chief Scout of PNG, Carter took on the job of Chief Commissioner of Scouts. His work for Scouting, and his wife Anne's for the Girl Guides, absorbed an enormous amount of their private time. I can vouch for Carter's persuasive powers in the cause of Scouting; in 1970, I was talked into accepting the job of Area Chairman of Scouts in the Eastern Highlands, although I was at the time rather fully occupied as District Commissioner.

Carter's concern with the community was also reflected in his sympathetic handling of personal staff problems within the Department, and in his successful efforts to provide amenities for, and to improve the working conditions of, his officers.

In June 1972, Bill Carter was awarded the OBE 'for services to the public and Scouting'.

They formed a discussion group which they named, ironically, the Bully Beef Club. Komara became a very junior member, but his interests were not political. During that year, the African politician, Tom Mboya (later assassinated), visited the College and made a strong impression upon Somare and his friends. They went on to fulfil their political destinies. In February 1966, Dale Kamara became the first of his race to attend a two-year Postal Inspectors course in Australia. His fellow students were postal officers from Queensland, Victoria and New South Wales and in this company Kamara held his own.

Back in PNG, the then manager of Postal Services, Laurie Meiklejohn, sent Kamara out to Talasea, Buka and Buin for field experience as a Postmaster. He then moved into the Postal Planning division and later took over the GPO from postmaster Jack Mowen. Towards the end of 1973 he became acting manager of the Postal Services Branch, while the then manager, M.P. Hooley, was on leave. During 1974, Dale Kamara understudied Hookey Morley in the position of Assistant Director, Postal Services. In May and June of that year he accompanied Bill Carter to the Commonwealth Postal Conference in London, and then to Lausanne, Switzerland, for the hundredth Anniversary of the Universal Postal Union Congress. They were joined there by Richard Kavu and Julius Tamah, two other bright young stars of Postal Services. This experience of the cut and thrust of international postal conferences made a deep impression on Kamara and his colleagues. When Morley retired in April 1975, Dale Kamara became Assistant Director of Postal Services.

Smael Manikot, born in 1950 in the Kokopo Sub-district, is typical of the younger educated Papua New Guineans following a career in P and T. Graduating from high school in 1970, he joined the Department in January 1971, and attended various courses at the Boroko Training College, which he passed with ease. In 1973, he took a position in Postal Planning at Port Moresby. Alert and intelligent, Manikot was clearly an excellent prospect for accelerated promotion. His big chance came in 1974, when with Serege Dada he won a United Nations Development Programme fellowship to attend a ten-month advanced Postal Management course at the Asian and Oceanic Training School in Bangkok, Thailand. (The first Papua New Guineans to go to this school were Julius Tamah and Richard Kavu, in 1973.)

The Asian and Oceanic Training School had been set up as a result of a resolution passed by the Asian-Oceanic Postal Union (AOPU) at its first Congress in Manila in 1965, to serve the needs of member countries in the Asian and Pacific region.[6] The proposal was supported by the International Bureau of the UPU, and by the UNDP. The School was officially opened on 10 September 1970.

At the Training School, Manikot and Dada lived and studied with students from the Philippines, Thailand, Indonesia, the Gilbert and Ellice Islands, Sri Lanka and Pakistan. It was grand experience for the two young men from PNG, and the ten months at Bangkok helped to equip Smael Manikot for the rapid promotion he achieved after Independence.

6 After Independence, PNG became a full member of AOPU, the UPU and the
  Commonwealth Countries for Postal Administration (CCPA).

Many other national officers of P and T, of course, were given the chance to attend courses of different kinds overseas, particularly in Australia, under the auspices of the Commonwealth Practical Training Scheme. National officers of the different divisions of the Department studied at the International Training Institute (previously known as the Australian School of Pacific Administration) in Sydney, and in PNG the Administrative College, the University of Technology in Lae and the Regional Training Centres of the Public Service Board all played their part in training national officers of P and T.

At Independence, the Postal Services division of P and T was more than 90 per cent localized, an achievement unmatched by any other department of the Public Service and a tribute to the policies of Bill Carter and the work of the Australian postal and training men who made it possible.

THE PHILATELIC DIVISION

If one consults that august authority, the *Oxford English Dictionary*, one finds a rather bald definition of the word 'philately' — stamp collecting. A philatelist is a stamp collector, and a philatelic bureau, narrowly defined, is an organization relating to, or engaged in, the study and collection of stamps.

The philatelic divisions of modern postal services have a far wider role than this, however. In PNG, the Philatelic Division of Postal Services is responsible for the design, production, distribution and storage of postage stamps to be sold at all national post offices, and to stamp collectors throughout the world.

The hobby of stamp collecting is universal, followed by the most exalted as well as by the most humble. Kings and emperors have been stamp collectors; so have street sweepers and dustmen. People in every country of the world collect stamps, some for profit but the majority for the simple pleasure of admiring, handling and classifying the colourful pieces of paper that every nation of the world uses as the most convenient means for the pre-payment of the conveyance of correspondence.

The stamp issuing policy of PNG has remained basically unchanged for years. PNG stamps are issued to meet specific postal requirements. The special desires of stamp collectors are not catered for, in sharp contrast with policies followed by certain countries notorious in philatelic circles. Philatelists, however, contribute very handsomely to postal revenue in PNG, and the stamp issuing policy recognizes this. Currently, to keep faith with world stamp collectors and preserve the standing PNG stamps, no more than six new issues are released each year. Three usually feature national flora and fauna and traditional arts, while the remainder focus on political events, industry, sport and similar events. Definitive sets — the stamps that remain in everyday use — are replaced approximately every five years. The value of issues is kept reasonably consistent. Only PNG subjects and topics are used as the basis for stamp designs, and the stamps themselves are of high quality, printed by the world's leading stamp printers. Philatelic trickery — imperforate specimens, gimmicky issues and similar unethical practices — is avoided. The bulk of each issue is sold in the normal way of business, over post office counters. As a result of this policy, PNG has won and held a high reputation in the world of philately.

It has been said that every stamp collector considers himself an expert. Certainly, the philatelic literature is enormous, and growing, and only a brief, and general, coverage of the philatelic history of PNG is possible in this account. As mentioned in Chapter 9, the first issue of PNG stamps was made in October 1952. From the time of the suspension of civil administration in Papua and the Mandated Territory in February 1942, current Australian stamps had been in use in PNG, their postmarks the only indication that they had been issued there. Stocks of pre-war Papuan stamps held by the Australian Treasury in 1945 were eventually destroyed rather than re-issued, although any uncancelled pre-war stamp of Papua and New Guinea remained valid for postage in PNG until the end of the colonial era. After the issue of the 1952 stamps, current Australian stamps were still valid in PNG until 2 March 1953. From that date to the present, only the stamps of the separate territories of Papua, New Guinea and of PNG, have been valid.

The stamps of the pre-war administrations had been well received by the world's philatelists and as we have seen, Papua, in particular, relied heavily on postal revenue during the early years of the Great Depression. With the resumption of provisional administration following the Pacific war, the question of a new issue of PNG stamps was quickly raised. Returned pre-war residents were soon calling for distinctive PNG stamps, requests echoed by philatelists from Australia and overseas. Valuable publicity for PNG would result. The Administrator, Colonel J.K. Murray, was in favour, for reasons both of prestige and revenue. The Department of External Territories, however, did not at first agree. Public debate continued, and late in 1949 the first PNG Stamp Advisory Committee was formed at Port Moresby, its members being the then Chief Postmaster, W.N. Chester (also the Assistant Treasurer), A.J. Halls, H.H. Jackman and J.O. Lyons.

The task of a Stamp Advisory Committee is to consider designs and artwork for proposed new stamp issues submitted to them, and to make appropriate recommendations and suggestions. As the title denotes, these committees have an advisory function only, but their views are normally given considerable weight by postal authorities. In PNG, the membership of Stamp Advisory Committees constantly changed, although the position of Chairman was always filled by an officer of Posts and Telegraphs. Artists, designers, philatelists and educators were at different times members, and after the Department was formed, Papua New Guineans began to be appointed. The first was a teacher, Gau Henao, in 1961. The hundredth meeting of the Stamp Advisory Committee was held on 19 April 1971. At that time, the Chairman and Secretary were P and T officers. Members were Ralph Bulmer, Professor of Social Anthropology at the University of Papua and New Guinea; Simon Kaumi, Chief Electoral Officer for PNG; Makeu Opa, Trainee Business Advisory Officer; Sogo Sebea, trainee executive with Burns Philp & Co., and Mrs Lois Johnson, a well-known artist. During their first hundred meetings, the Stamp Advisory Committee considered over a thousand proposed stamp designs, of which 186 were printed and issued.

The selection of suitable designs and denominations for PNG's first big definitive set of postage stamps proved to be a protracted, disputatious affair. The Stamp Advisory Committee recommended that a number of designs by local artists, publicly exhibited at a RSS and AILA Arts and Crafts Exhibition in Port Moresby in August 1949, be adopted for a series of ordinary postal and air mail stamps. Colonel Murray endorsed the recommendations and the designs were sent to the Official Advisory Committee of the Australian PMG's Department for consideration. For a variety of reasons, most were finally rejected. The fifteen stamps of this first definitive set were designed by artists of the Note Printing Branch of the Commonwealth Bank in Melbourne, where they were printed. Following the decision to accept them, the Stamp Advisory Committee requested that they be given the opportunity of examining all future issues before they were adopted.

The fifteen stamps, depicting the houses, birds, animals, artifacts and people of PNG, were issued on 30 October 1952, on the seventh anniversary of the re-establishment of civil administration. Ranging in denomination from one half-penny to one pound, they were enthusiastically received by philatelists; in a matter of weeks philatelic sales exceeded £28 000. They remained in use for years. The £1 stamp, showing a Papuan about to spear a fish, was the last in the series to be withdrawn, on 28 March 1964. It was the longest-lived series ever issued in PNG. The issue of the stamps in PNG was handled by three men in the Postal and Telecommunication Branch of the Department of the Treasury who later, at different times, joined the new Department: K.C. Florentine, R. Weidenhofer and D. MacGowan.

No immediate steps were taken to establish a philatelic branch after P and T was born; far more urgent tasks confronted Bill Carter and his team. The sale of stamps to philatelists was handled by the hard-pressed Postmasters, with Port Moresby carrying the heaviest load. The 1952 definitives satisfied postal requirement until rates were increased on 1 November 1956. Two of the 1952 stamps, the two-and-one-half-penny Bird of Paradise, and the one shilling Lakatoi, were overprinted with the required new denominations of four pence and seven pence and issued in January 1957. These two provisionals were in turn replaced in June 1958, by four new definitives based on designs by R.O. Griffiths, a draftsman employed by the Australian Petroleum Company who was then a member of the Stamp Advisory Committee.

By 1958 it was apparent that a separate organization was required to handle the rapidly increasing demand by the world's philatelists for PNG stamps. The Postal (Philatelic Mail) Papua Regulations 1958 were passed, authorizing P and T to charge for philatelic services. It was also decided to set up a philatelic section of Postal Services. R.A Miller was chosen by Bill Carter to fill the new position of Controller, Philately and Training Branch.

Miller joined P and T in October 1956, after service with the PMG's Department as a Postal Training Instructor. He was postmaster at Lae in 1957 and 1958. He knew nothing of philatelics, but Bill Carter was anxious to get postal training under way at the newly-established Boroko Training College, and Miller was the only man in the Department with experience in this field. The establishment of a philatelic branch was of secondary importance.[1]

Prior to taking up the appointment, Bob Miller went to Australia on leave and spent some weeks with the philately experts of the PMG's Department, learning as much as he could. Back in PNG, he set up the Philatelic Bureau, his sole assistant being Christine Gee, daughter of Chief Engineer W.C. Gee. At the same time began the first course of postal training at the College. He was to remain controller of what later became the Postal Planning and Philately Branch for the next decade. In a May 1981 interview, Miller said:

> The Philatelic Bureau was only a very small sideline at the beginning. It took quite a time to really get it going. We poked along as best we could, but we made slow progress. I found having to submit new stamp designs to the Minister in Canberra a most frustrating business. It often took Canberra three months just to answer letters! There was authority under the P and T ordinance for the Administrator to approve new stamp designs, but at first they were all referred to Canberra. After a while, though, we began to make the decisions here. I wasn't a philatelist, of course, and our philatelic policy developed as we went along. Initially, we were pretty much guided by PMG practice, and in those days they were very conservative. When Stuart Jay took over Postal Services we began to make progress. He was a dynamic individual and he had a wide background of PMG experience. He helped us to find our feet, and we began to break away and follow our own philatelic path. We planned ahead and formed a stamp issuing policy, and, as business developed, our staff grew. We used a lot of Australian women, largely on a part-time basis, to handle our overseas and standing order accounts, particularly when new issues came out.

The first of the long and notable series of stamps that has been issued by the Philatelic Bureau was merely the half-penny tree kangaroo of the 1952 definitives, overprinted to a value of five pence. It appeared on 1 December 1959 and was made necessary by an increase in the rate for letter class mail from four to five pence. It was a tentative beginning, but as Miller and his small team gathered experience and developed confidence, stamps of sophisticated design, finely detailed and printed, began to be issued in increasing numbers. They were snapped up by collectors and philatelic revenue began to rise, from less than K26 000 (figures will be given in kina)[2] in the beginning to K322 000 in 1964-5, K745 000 in the year of Independence and, in 1980, to K1 053 000.

Such rapid progress from a puny begining could not have been achieved without the advice and support of philatelists. By 1965, the Philatelic Bureau had a staff of seven, handling 78 standing-order accounts. By 1978, standing-order accounts numbered some 16 000, from all over the world. In addition, there was a mailing list of over ten thousand. To process this veritable flood of mail order work, the Bureau then employed a permanent staff of thirty-four.

The stamp issuing policy of the Bureau took some years to evolve. There was at first criticism in the philatelic press of too-frequent stamp issues, but by 1964 the

---

1 The Branch became a full Division of Postal Services after Independence.

2 Figures to 1965 are net, and from 1966, gross. It is impossible to give precise figures for purely philatelic sales, for the post offices of PNG sold stamps to philatelists as well as to ordinary users, and for obvious practical reasons, no separate records were kept. Reasonably accurate figures can be determined by adding the amounts by which stamp sales at post offices on each first day of a new issue exceeded average daily sales, to sales by the Philatelic Bureau and agents.

current policy was, substantially, in operation. From that year, five, or at the most six, new issues were made annually. Each year's issue did not exceed a value of $3.50, except in the years when high-value definitives were replaced. To preserve the philatelic value of the annual issues, the residue of each was withdrawn from sale after six months, and destroyed, although it was usually possible to sell them in the normal way over the counter at post offices before the deadline. To advertise forthcoming stamp issues, a Publicity Section was created. A philatelic newsletter was also regularly dispatched to standing and mail order customers, and colourful brochures were released with each new issue, giving details of the background and design of the stamps, their size and denominations, the printing techniques employed, the designer, and the release and withdrawal dates.

The early issues released by the Philatelic Bureau were printed in one, or two, colour recess by the Note Printing Branch of the Commonwealth Bank. In 1961, this work was taken over by the Reserve Bank, Melbourne. An exception was made with the commemorative issue for the reconstituted Legislative Council in 1961. This was printed by Harrison and Sons, London, in multi-colour photogravure. The Commonwealth Games Issue of 1962 was the first to be produced by Helio Courvoisier SA of Switzerland for PNG, and marked the beginning of a close association that continues to the present day. Famous throughout the philatelic world for the exquisite perfection of its multi-colour photogravure printing, Helio Courvoisier concentrates solely on the production of stamps for different countries. The company has produced the lion's share of all PNG's stamps since the 1962 issue. The Note Issue Department of the Reserve Bank printed a number of important issues during the 1960s, and Harrison and Sons, Joh. Enschede and Sons of Haarlem, Holland, and The House of Questa, London, have each printed stamps for the Philatelic Bureau.

As director of Posts and Telegraphs. Bill Carter naturally kept a close eye on all aspects of the operation of the Philatelic Branch, including the design and marketing of stamps. The Stamp Advisory Committee remained an active, dedicated body — members were unpaid — and the majority of their design recommendations were accepted, but on several occasions Carter, for various reasons, ordered changes made. In the early years, too, the Administrator, Brigadier D.M. Cleland, himself a philatelist, retained final design approval. One one occasion, the Administrator rejected a proposed design showing a government patrol on the march, the carriers escorted by a constable of the Royal Papua and New Guinea Constabulary carrying a .303 rifle. Implications that could be drawn from the design — the forced labour of Papua New Guineans under the menace of an armed guard — made it politically unsuitable for a PNG stamp. It was also an unwritten and unspoken rule to avoid designs depicting bare-breasted Papua New Guinean women, although to this day such a mode of dress is usual in many regions, particularly on festive or ceremonial occasions.

Stamp designing is a uniquely demanding task. Experts in this field are few, and unfortunately it has been necessary for the Philatelic Bureau to commission virtually all of its designs from overseas specialists. To date, only two Papua New Guinean artists have had their paintings used as the basis for stamp designs. The first was Samuel Terarup Cham, a Tolai from Matupi Island who was completely self taught.

His beautiful painting of Rabaul Harbour was used by Helio Courvoisier as the basis for the design of a handsome stamp of ten shillings denomination, and printed in four-colour photogravure; it was issued on 13 February 1963.

The second, Wi Tuman, from Minj in the Western Highlands, was in 1975 commissioned by W.A. Southwood — at the time, First Assistant Secretary, Telecommunications — to paint a wall mural for his office. It was a striking piece of work based on a traditional betrothal legend. In 1978, during a visit to PNG by the head of Helio Courvoisier, M. Andre Tripet, Bill Peckover arranged for the then Minister, Sir Tei Abal, and M. Tripet to view the mural. There and then it was decided to make it the basis for a magnificent five-panel set of stamps which were printed by Helio Courvoisier and issued on 26 March 1980, to commemorate the Third South Pacific Festival of Arts, held in Port Moresby.

Many of the early issues of PNG stamps were designed by Pamela M. Prescott of Port Moresby, and by August 1967, she had been responsible for the design of twenty-three PNG stamps. George Hamori, too, produced notable designs. Paintings and photographs by a number of people, particularly F.S. Parker and M.S. Upton, were used as the basis for some of the most successful issues. A particularly striking series was the first Folk Lore issue of 1966, based on the traditional designs and myths of the Elema tribe of the Papuan Gulf. It was executed by a veteran London Missionary Society missionary, Revd H.A. Brown, who produced another series of designs of like nature in 1969. Flower stamps designed by Mrs Demaris Pearce, a resident of Lae, were issued in 1966. Tristan Walcot of Mount Hagen, Walter Jardine, Bette Hayes, Major L.G. Halls, William T. Cooper, F. and G. Hodgkinson, J. Fallas, David Gentleman, G. Quick and Terry Nolan have all designed PNG stamps. In recent years, the names of Paul Jones, Graham Wade and Richard Bates have been featured as the designers of most new issues.

A number of these artists have achieved world recognition. David Gentleman, the English graphic artist and designer, is perhaps the most famous living miniscule artist. He is the holder of the Phillips Gold Medal for Stamp Design, and is responsible for many of the best contemporary British GPO commemorative issues. William T. Cooper, an Australian, is a painter of birds whose work is represented in many private collections in many countries. He has illustrated four magnificent books on birds, including one on the birds of paradise and bower birds of PNG. Paul Jones is Australia's leading botanical artist, internationally famous for his beautiful limited edition books, *Flora Superba* (1971) and *Flora Magnifica* (1976). Richard Bates, another Australian, has more recent PNG stamp designs to his credit than any other artist. He first came to the attention of F.A. Bartu, then manager of the Philatelic Bureau, with the publication in *Australian Stamp Monthly* of a series of stamp designs that had been rejected by the Australian Post Office. Bartu (ever alert to the interests of the Bureau) and Peckover, thought Bates' rejected designs far superior to those that were accepted, and he was invited to prepare a trial series of stamp designs for PNG. The result was the National Heritage issue of 1970, four stamps depicting milestones in the history of the country from ancient to modern times. All artists, even celebrated ones, attempting stamp design, face the same daunting problems of scale, balance and clarity, and there is still no PNG artist regularly producing work in this field.

PNG has for years shown her stamps at Australian and international exhibitions and at trade fairs and philatelic displays in capital cities held under the auspices of the Crown Agents. Competition is invariably keen. At the Seventh Annual Interpex International Exhibition in New York, the award for the 'Most beautiful stamp' went to the Bird of Paradise set from the Birds Definitive Series of 1964-5. In 1973, the Italian magazine, *Il Collezionista*, conducted a popularity poll of the finest stamps from some 200 countries. Eighth prize was awarded to a lovely PNG stamp featuring the Princess Stephanie Bird of Paradise; it had been issued with others on 30 March 1973. These stamps were designed by William T. Cooper, and it is fitting that they should depict the national emblem of PNG, the bird of paradise.

Immense care was taken to ensure accuracy of detail of PNG stamps. W.S. Peckover's first direct involvement in stamp design came with the prize-winning Birds Definitive Series of 1964-5. Peckover had become very interested in the hobby of bird photography,[3] and in 1963 it had been decided to use illustrations from the classic 1888 book by John Gould, *The Birds of New Guinea and the Adjacent Papuan Islands*, as the basis for the designs of the definitive stamps. The twelve selected designs had just been prepared by the artists of Helio Courvoisier, by redrawing the Gould illustrations in much reduced format, when Peckover became interested. He considered it prudent to seek the help of the ornithologist Frec Shaw Mayer to check the designs before the stamps were printed.

Shaw Mayer was acknowledged the resident expert on PNG fauna. The curator of the Sir Edward Hallstrom Fauna Sanctuary at Nondugl, near Mount Hagen, he was small and wiry and well into his sixties, full of energy and enthusiasm and ever-ready to defend the welfare of the animals in his care. Shaw Mayer studied the designs, passed about half of them as correct and rejected one outright. This depicted the blue bird of paradise displaying his plumage in the mating ritual in an upright position, when the bird in life turns upside down to display. Shaw was doubtful of many details in the remaining designs, including the habitat of some of the birds depicted, and recommended that the opinion of the world authority on bower birds and birds of paradise, E. Thomas Gilliard, be sought.

The late Tom Gilliard was at that time Curator of the American Museum of Natural History. He confirmed Shaw Mayer's advice. Two or three of the birds depicted were actually natives of West Irian, not PNG. Fortunately, there was just sufficient time available for five replacement designs to be prepared while Helio Courvoisier proceeded with the printing of the seven stamps judged satisfactory. The new designs were adapted, with permission, from four pictures that had been published in the *National Geographic Magazine*, and one in the *Natural History Journal*.

---

3 Peckover's photographs have been used as the basis for a number of PNG stamps, the most recent being the lovely Kingfisher set of five, printed by Helio Courvoisier and issued on 21 January 1981. Peckover is co-author with Win Filewood of *Birds of New Guinea and Tropical Australia* (Reed, 1976), and is currently working with Mary LeCroy, of the American Museum of Natural History, and late Assistant to E. Thomas Gilliard, on a major series of volumes on Australian birds.

Stamps, of course, if carefully chosen and purchased, can be exceptionally rewarding as investments. Of negligible weight and bulk, investment stamps are easily concealed and transported, and are internationally negotiable. Except for the relatively small number of world-famous classics, they cannot be readily traced, since they carry no serial numbers. Historically, they have at worst held their value.

During the Second World War, most Pacific stamps appreciated in value quite substantially. At stamp auctions in Melbourne in early November 1944, four mint stamps from the German New Guinea 'Yacht' series of 1900, overprinted 'GRI' and intended for use during the First World War, were sold for the then high price of £106. Their face value was eleven shillings.

The strict stamp issuing and control policy followed by the Philatelic Bureau since its inception has prevented the public release of stamps bearing errors in printing or cancellation. Such stamps are eagerly sought by philatelists, and their value is considerable. The PNG policy has been generally successful. However, in 1960 a number of stamps was issued, double-overprinted, and these are probably the rarest and most valuable of the stamps of PNG.

In 1960, Customs clearing charges and storage fees on unclaimed parcels were introduced in the country, to take effect from 1 March. A series of Postal Charges stamps was therefore ordered from Australia, but its delivery was delayed. Late in February, as a stop-gap, a small number of sheets of current PNG stamps was overprinted with the words POSTAL CHARGES and the new value at the office of the Government Printer, Port Moresby. Somehow, a sheet or sheets of the seven-and-one-half-penny blue stamp of the 1952 issue (showing a Kiriwana yam house) were double-overprinted. The error was discovered in a sheet at the Goroka Post Office. It caused a veritable uproar in P and T circles. Searching investigation failed to solve the matter, but senior officers were convinced that somebody had bribed or persuaded some person at the Government Printing office to double-overprint the stamps. A certain officer of P and T, on leave when the Goroka sheet was discovered, quietly resigned, and remained in Australia when the news broke. As far as is known, none of the double-overprinted stamps were sold over the counter. Some have since surfaced. Their value is exceedingly high.

A number of excellent 16mm colour films has been produced by the Philatelic Division. *Miniatures Magnificent*, based on the beautiful Butterflies Definitive series, 1966, designed from photographs by M.S. Upton, won a special award at Stockholm in 1974. *Molala Harai*, based on the National Heritage series of 1969 designed by Revd. H.A. Brown, was awarded a gold medal at Rome in 1970. Other Philatelic division films, showing the culture of PNG as depicted on her Panorama stamps, include *Postmark Impressions, Tok Tok* and *Discovery of Papua New Guinea*. These films are of particular interest to philatelists, but their appeal is universal. They have helped to interpret PNG to the outside world, as well as arouse interest in her stamps.

No matter how appealing a nation's stamps are, they will not sell themselves; like any other product, they have to be marketed skilfully. Australia remains the best customer for PNG stamps, and it was in Australia that the first efforts were made to market them. The production of the 1952 Definitives issue was completely handled by the Australian Post Office, and the philatelic sales outlets of the APO were employed to sell them. After the Department of Posts And Telegraphs was formed, it assumed the responsibility for all succeeding PNG stamp issues, but the distribution facilities of the APO have continued to be used.

Until 30 June 1961, overseas customers for PNG stamps could order them by mail from the APO outlets, as well as from the Philatelic Bureau in Port Moresby. After this date, the APO ceased to handle this mail order business. Between 1958 and 1969, overseas interest in PNG stamps increased steadily, and in 1965 the Crown Agents, London, were engaged to distribute them through their Stamp Bureau, which sells the stamps of its principals to dealers in the United Kingdom and overseas. Although the services of the Crown Agents are very efficient, they are fairly costly: until 1970, their charges were ten per cent of the face value of the stamps sold and in 1973, the rate increased to fifteen per cent. APO charges, however, are higher.

In March 1969, W.S. Peckover, who was at the time Assistant Director, Operations and Administration, visited New York, to attend the Interpex Stamp Exhibition and discuss the potential American market with dealers and collectors. He returned to PNG via London and Tokyo, where he made further contacts. This was the first move in a concerted effort to increase foreign sales of PNG stamps. Earlier attempts to expand overseas markets, principally by advertising in philatelic journals, had met with little success.

The influence of Bill Peckover on the operations of the Philatelic Bureau was profound. His personal involvement with philatelics grew from his early belief that a rich potential source of revenue for P and T was not being sufficiently cultivated, and was later cemented by his growing interest in bird photography.

In 1956, Bill Carter formalized what came to be known as P and T's Management Committee, a once-monthly meeting between the Director and the heads, or acting heads, of the various divisions of the Department. Carter was a great believer in consultation, and he encouraged new ideas and debate at these monthly meetings. Although Carter made it plain from the beginning that the Committee was not intended to be a decision-making body (decisions were the ultimate responsibility of the Director), many were taken as a result of Management Committee discussions.

The two most important activities of the Committee were of the monthly reviews of cash flow, presented by Tas Sexton, and of the Works Programme, presented by Charles Gee and later by his successors, Gordon Clarke and Tom Pearson. Soon after joining P and T, Bill Peckover had begun the continuing record of statistics, expenditures and revenues that came to be known as the 'Black Book'. It was quickly apparent to Peckover that philatelic sales, then somewhat neglected, offered great revenue-earning potential and should be encouraged. He raised this question at Management Committee meetings, with little result. However, Stuart Jay, who eventually took over Postal Services, was as enthusiastic as Peckover, and philatelic activity soon quickened.

During the 1960s, Bill Carter was often called away from the Department. As well as serving on the Port Moresby Town Advisory Council (as noted in Chapter 10), Carter was an official member of the Legislative Council for five years, and of the First House of Assembly for four. He was a member of various Parliamentary Committees (Public Accounts, Public Works, House, Select Committee on Constitutional

Development) and from March 1963, to April 1964, acted as Assistant Administrator, Services, while Dr John Gunther was serving as a member of the Currie Commission on Higher Education. These responsible appointments, although a tribute to Carter's great ability, consumed much of his energy and time. Throughout these lengthy periods of duty away from P and T, Bill Peckover acted as Director. He consulted closely with Bill Carter before making major decisions affecting the Department, but he naturally had greater freedom of action during his periods as Acting Director, and was able to give Stuart Jay considerable support.

As a result of the contacts Peckover made on his 1969 overseas trip, the Philatelic Bureau entered into marketing arrangements, some short-lived, with a number of agents, in the United States and Japan. In 1970-1, philatelic sales reached a peak,[4] K856 000. The trend was not sustained. Sales declined to K561 000 in 1971-2 and slumped to K468 000 the following year — back to the level of the mid-1960s. In 1972, Peckover made another overseas philatelic tour, to Japan, the United States and the United Kingdom, and on his return, he suggested a number of marketing initiatives. Inflation was by this time becoming an increasingly dominant factor in the countries to which PNG sold stamps, including Australia. In mid-1973, it was decided to seek expert outside assistance to devise a marketing strategy for the future. The job was given to PA Management Consultants (PNG) Pty. Ltd., the parent company of which was one of the largest of the world's multinational management consultancies.

By this time, the localization of Postal Services was proceeding apace. In early 1972, the Philatelic Bureau employed twenty-six people, only eight of them PNG nationals. (One of these was Gavera Lohia, the senior serving national.) The manager was Fred Bartu, a philatelic enthusiast with a deep love and knowledge of what was both his profession and his hobby. The founding head of what had begun as the Philately and Training Branch,[5] R.A. Miller, was now in charge of Postal Systems. As the pace of localization in the Postal Services Division quickened, Bartu handed over as Manager of the Philatelic Branch to P.Z. Petrides, and became the Localization Co-ordinator. In February 1974, Patrick Tomausi became the Manager-in-training of the Branch, understudying Petrides. It was a difficult time for Tomausi, who is today grateful for the help he received from Fred Bartu. In July 1974, Patrick Tomausi became the head of the Philatelic Branch.

During the next two years, Tomausi made a number of overseas tours, seeking to implement new stamp marketing arrangements recommended by P.A. Management Consultants. He was successful in negotiating agency agreements in Japan, New Zealand, Canada, Germany, the United Kingdom and the Netherlands.

When Tomausi became manager of the branch, the process of localization was well advanced. By mid-1975, it was almost complete. Only P.J. Casanovas and F.G. Cleary still remained. Phil Casanovas joined P and T in 1964, and served initially in the Philatelic Bureau, before going into the field for long years as a relieving postmaster. He rejoined the branch in 1973. Frank Cleary worked in the Bureau from 1962 onwards, and knew more than anyone else of the operations of the Mail Order

---

4 The Training Branch had long been established as a separate entity. See Chapter 10.

5 Actual sales figures, gross.

office. He became an adviser to the Philatelic Branch, and returned to Australia in 1977. Casanovas remained as an Adviser and Special Projects Officer, the sole expatriate in the Philatelics division. (He was still the only expatriate adviser to what was now the Philatelics Division in 1981.)

Following a reorganization of P and T in 1975, the titles of a number of positions were changed and others created, including those of First Assistant Secretary of Telecommunications, of Finance and Administration, and of Postal Services. Dale Kamara, at the time of the reorganization Assistant Director, Postal, was promoted to First Assistant Secretary, and then to the new position of Deputy Secretary, Department of Public Utilities. Patrick Tomausi left the Philatelic Division and became First Assistant Secretary, Postal, when Kamara moved up to the Deputy position.

Tomausi's old position, now called Assistant Secretary, Philatelic, was taken by Alex Nonwo. Nonwo, from Lumi in the West Sepik, took an arts degree at the University of PNG in 1974, and joined P and T that November as Publicity Officer. On the twenty-fifth anniversary of the formation of the Department of Posts and Telegraphs, 1 July 1980, Nonwo was still in charge of the Philatelics Division. The Division then had three branches: Design and Production, headed by John Walup; Mail Order, headed by M. Pinjo, and Publicity and Marketing, under the direction of Paul Paiva. The staff numbered fifty, and they handled a standing order list that had been culled back to 13 000, plus an equivalent number on the mail order list. Among the staff was Michael Dawadawareta, the first Papua New Guinean to act as a Postmaster, now the Distributor of Stamps responsible for the despatch of stamps to all the post offices of Papua New Guinea.

The Philatelic Division continues to follow its well established and accepted stamp issuing policy. Revenue, which in 1980 exceeded K one million, subsidizes current losses on the overall operations of Postal Services, to the benefit of the people of Papua New Guinea.

CHAPTER 12

TELECOMMUNICATIONS: THE FIRST DECADE

A simple definition of telecommunication is the carriage of information by electrical means. Familiar instruments of telecommunication are the telephone, the telegraph, the teleprinter, the radio transmitter and receiver and the television set. But now we are in the space age, the age of the microchip, the computer and the satellite, and possibilities for the future development of telecommunication seem endless.

At Independence, PNG found herself with an ultra-modern, sophisticated tele-communication service,[1] the rival of anything to be found in the Western world, and certainly superior to those of most Third World countries. It was a system devised and constructed by the colonial power, Australia, employing the finest available world technology. And it was created over a surprisingly brief span of years, at surprisingly little cost.

At Independence, all major towns of PNG and many of the minor ones were inter-connected by telecommunications. The most remote patrol posts, missions, schools, plantations and aid posts of the nation were linked into this system by a widespread and well used outstation radio service. The telephone network was ninety-eight per cent automatic, with only five small manual exchanges remaining. National sub-scriber trunk dialling and international subscriber dialling was available to ninety-seven per cent of the telephone services in the system. Fully automatic telex and post office telegraph networks, interconnected but not integrated, covered PNG, operated through a single computer-controlled Eltex exchange in Lae, the communications capital of PNG. There were over three hundred telex subscribers, with direct access to any of the world's subscribers with access to the international telex network. Inter-

---

1 I have drawn heavily on W.S. Peckover's 'Evolution of the Papua New Guinea Telecommunications System 1955-64' for material for this chapter.

national telecommunications links with the outside world, of high quality, were in existence, and a coastal radio service for ships at sea was also in operation.

Admirable though it was, at Independence the telecommunication system was serving, primarily, the urban elite of PNG. In recent years the pros and cons of the impact of telecommunications on the lives of the people of the Third World countries have been endlessly discussed, but in PNG it has been completely accepted that the nation cannot prosper and develop without a telecommunications service. The stated policy of the PNG government is to extend the service to the villagers living in the most isolated rural districts, and as rapidly as available manpower and financial resources permit.

The story of the development of the telecommunications service that was Posts and Telegraph's legacy to the independent state of Papua New Guinea is one of triumphant achievement from a slow, frustrating beginning. As mentioned in Chapter 9, for the first decade of its existence the funds available to P and T were never sufficient to allow Bill Carter and his officers to construct a national telecommunications network. Tied to a rigid annual budget system of funding, the best that Carter could do was to provide and improve local telephone services in the main towns of PNG, plus a poor trunk line system, telegraph facilities and a high-frequency double sideband radio outstation network. It was not until the Department was successful in obtaining a World Bank loan in the second half of its existence that the great leap forward in telecommunications became possible.

On 1 July 1955, when P and T was formally born, there were seventeen telephone exchanges throughout PNG. Three — at Namatanai, Finschhafen and Mount Hagen — provided limited services. The others operated continuously. They were located at Port Moresby, Konedobu, Boroko, Badili, Sogeri, Samarai, Rabaul, Kokopo, Lae, Kavieng, Wau, Madang, Wewak and Goroka. The total number of telephone services in use was 3 288. Radio telephone trunk circuits, of poor quality, were in use between Port Moresby, Samarai, Lae, Rabaul, Madang, Kavieng, Wewak, Wau, Bulolo, Lorengau and Sohano.

All local telephone exchanges in operation in 1955 were manual magneto and central battery (CB) types, of a simple and outdated design first introduced in the late 19th century. The first telephone exchange to be installed in Papua, in Port Moresby in 1910, was a magneto exchange.

Magneto telephone handsets each contained a generator operated by turning a handle on the base which sent enough current down the line to ring a bell and drop a shutter in the exchange, thus alerting the switchboard operator. Each handset was powered by four 1.5 volt batteries, for the transmission and reception of voice signals. CB exchanges were a little more sophisticated. Batteries and generators in the handsets were not required; power for the microphones came from a central battery bank in the telephone exchange. The act of lifting the handset from its cradle closed the circuit and lit a small light at the exchange, again alerting — at least, in theory — the operator.

Magneto and CB manual exchanges in PNG worked quite well during the day, but at night it was often a different matter. Night Operators — Papua New Guineans, no different from their counterparts the world over — were all too often lulled into sleep in the small hours when traffic was normally non-existent, to the rage and frustration of the occasional subscriber. On one occasion, one of the most senior officers of the Administration was moved to leap into his car, race to the Port Moresby exchange and violently arouse the slumbering operator, thus ensuring quick service for the rest of that night, at least. Regional Engineer Bill Boyle once connected an old air-raid siren to the Port Moresby switchboard, to augment the feeble tingle of the bell. It almost frightened the life out of the Night Operator; it certainly catapulted him out of a deep, refreshing sleep, but unfortunately it did the same for the rest of Port Moresby, so Boyle was obliged to remove it.

The necessity for a third person, the Switchboard Operator, to connect two persons wishing to converse by telephone, made it inevitable that manual exchanges would be replaced by automatic exchanges. The father of automatic telephony is considered to be Almon B. Strowger of Kansas City in the United States, who in 1891 was granted a patent for a step-by-step automatic switch which, through vertical and rotary movements, was directed into a cylindrical contact bank. Further developments followed, and the Strowger technology was introduced into countries all over the world. Strowger-type bi-motional automatic switches were still in wide use in the 1940s and 1950s. By this time, however, these switches were obsolescent, if not yet completely obsolete, having been overtaken by the development of modern crossbar switching.

The first steps towards replacing PNG's manual exchanges with automatic telephone ones, had already been taken when P and T began. In 1953, a contract was finalized with the British firm of Ericcson Telephone Ltd., for the supply of the first automatic exchanges at Port Moresby, Boroko, Konedobu, Bomana, Lae and Rabaul. All but one of these new exchanges were to be equipped with Strowger-type bi-motional switches. The small Bomana exchange was to be a Rurax type equipped with simple semi-rotary switches. Preparatory cable work began during the 1953-4 financial year.

The Strowger switches specified in the contract were of the 'pre-2000' type with a forecast life of 20 years, pre-dating the then modern 2000 and subsequent types of switches. The decision to employ these obsolescent switches was taken in 1953 by the Divisional Engineer, W.C. Gee, for what then appeared to be sound reasons. Gee envisaged the training of Papua New Guineans to maintain the new systems, and it therefore made sense to use the older, simpler pre-2000 switches rather than more modern, but more complex, units. The decision to change from labour-intensive manual telephone service to capital-intensive automatic service was undoubtedly correct, as subsequent events soon proved, but the decision to use Strowger switching locked P and T into a system soon to become outdated: the 'obsolescent technology trap' as it became known in P and T.

The first automatic exchange to go into service in PNG was privately owned, installed by Bulolo Gold Dredging Ltd. at Bulolo. The first P and T automatic exchange network — Port Moresby, Boroko, Konedobu and Bomana — was brought into service on 11 March 1956, just before the arrival in PNG of the newly appointed Superintendent of Telephones, W.S. Peckover. The Lae and Rabaul automatic exchanges came into operation in 1957. The cost of this new technology was high —

the Lae and Rabaul exchanges cost more than £100 000, and were housed in new air-conditioned buildings designed to withstand the maximum anticipated earth-tremors.

One pressing task awaiting Peckover on his arrival in 1956 was the development of a priority system for determining the order in which the large number of outstanding applications for telephone service would be handled. On 26 April 1956, a priority system for telephone connection based on the then current practice in Australia, was adopted, giving first priority to emergency services (doctors, police, fire), second to 'important services' (government departments, chemists, nurses) and third to service required on medical grounds. All other applications would be considered in strict order of date of application.

The adoption of the priority system at least clarified the situation, but the demand for telephone service was so great that some prospective subscribers waited, unsatisfied, for long periods. In 1959, the Morobe District Advisory Council made a formal request of Bill Carter for the provision of a horseback/bicycle telegram delivery service to planters and farmers living between the Erap and Leron Rivers in the Markham Valley, on the grounds that it appeared these citizens would have to wait at least five years for a telephone. It was precisely to overcome this kind of problem that P and T began field trials in 1958 with ten sets of very high frequency (VHF) radio-telephone equipment specially designed for remote tropical locations. But the equipment did not prove to be sufficiently reliable to be adopted.

Prior to the introduction of automatic exchanges, a flat rate of £15 per annum for a business telephone service and £10 for a home service was charged. There was an installation fee of £2 ten shillings, and local calls were free. With the introduction of automatic telephones, an entirely new system of charges was introduced, on 1 April 1956. This provided for a 'measured rate' charge for automatic telephones of two-and-one-half pence per local call. The annual rental within base rate areas varied between £5 and £7 twelve-and-six for both business and home telephones, according to the size of the local automatic network. The flat rate system was retained for services connected to manual exchanges partly to keep procedures as simple as possible for Papua New Guinean staff. No charge was made for local calls, but a loading was added to the annual rental fee based on a calculated number of six local calls per day for 313 days for business telephones, and two per day for 356 days for residence phones, determined after a considerable period of traffic sampling. Charges increased at intervals over the following years.

As rapidly as funds permitted, manual telephone exchanges were converted, where it was appropriate, to automatic operation. By 1 July 1965, there were twenty-two telephone exchanges in PNG, located at Popondetta, Daru, Sogeri, Samarai, Port Moresby and district (Bomana, Boroko, Moresby Central, Konedobu), Bulolo, Finschhafen, Goroka, Kavieng, Kokopo, Lae, Lorengau, Madang, Mount Hagen, Rabaul, Sohano, Vanimo, Wau and Wewak. Of these, eight were automatic, eight CB and six magneto. There was a total of 5 375 direct exchange lines in operation, 3 953 of them connected to the automatic exchanges. A total of 10 064 telephones was in use. Cable reticulations in the main towns had been upgraded in readiness for the automatic exchanges, and work was proceeding in other centres. Telephone charges then varied between £8 and £12 per annum, with a unit fee of four pence.

Clearly, local telephone services had been considerably improved during this first decade, but it was now apparent that Gee's 1953 decision, to use Strowger-type equipment, had been unfortunate. Production of this equipment throughout the world had been abandoned by most telecommunications companies. Only British Ericsson was still able to supply PNG, although a government-owned company in India was producing and selling Strowger-type gear on the world market. There was still a strong demand for the equipment from Third World countries unable to afford anything better, and PNG was a small customer. She could not expect her equipment needs to be given priority. This alone was sufficient reason to move away from Strowger technology.

There was, however, a more fundamental reason. Bill Carter was from the first set upon the automation of the PNG telephone network, and the introduction of subscriber trunk dialling (STD). This would mean converting from step-by-step Strowger bi-motional switching to crossbar switching. Step-by-step switching was too slow, and took up too much non-paying trunk line time — and trunk lines, of whatever type, are very expensive. Carter had been at pains to maintain his contacts with the PMG's Department since coming to PNG, and he and his engineers had been kept well abreast of world technological advances by PMG planners and designers. Many countries, including Australia, were starting to convert to crossbar switching, with the ultimate objective of STD in mind. In 1963, orders were placed for new automatic telephone exchanges using crossbar switches for Madang, Bulolo, and Toleap, New Britain.

By this time, P and T had been reorganized, following the review of 1962 headed by F.R. Schadel. And the Department now had a National Telephone Plan. As detailed in Chapter 9, P and T was initially organized into five divisions: Postal Services, Engineering (with three Regional Engineers based at Port Moresby, Lae and Rabaul), Telephones, Accounts, and Personnel. Within a year of Peckover taking up his position, Telephones had in effect become the Telecommunications division, as a result of a transfer of responsibility for the operational aspects of telegraphic services from the Engineering Division; the change, however, was not formally recognized by the Public Service Board until 1958. Following the Review, the Department was re-organized into three divisions: Administration, Operations and Engineering. Each had a number of branches. Administration contained Accounts, Costing, Training and Personnel branches; Operations included non-engineering telecommunications aspects of radio regulatory functions, Postal Services and Philately and General Postal; Engineering branches were General Works, Planning, Installation Services, and Headquarters. The Regional Engineer offices were closed down. Grouping together similar functions in this manner followed traditional Australian and British post office practice. It was not, however, a suitable organization pattern for P and T, but despite its deficiencies it was made to work.

Of even greater importance to P and T was the National Telephone Plan. It had become obvious to Bill Carter and his senior officers that the Department of Territories in Canberra, the virtual overlord of PNG policy, preferred to seek advice from overseas experts rather than from those resident in the country. The need for a modern national telecommunications network for PNG had not been accepted in Canberra — it was not fully accepted by the PNG Administration — and Carter now decided to look for some 'overseas' expert advice of his own, to strengthen his hand when dealing with Canberra. In 1962 he began a series of discussions with the Director-General of the PMG's Department in Australia, F.P. O'Grady.

Frank O'Grady was a proven friend of P and T. He was always ready to assist the Department with professional advice and manpower, scarce though this commodity was, and in countless ways showed his genuine interest in the development of communications in PNG. In 1960, the experts of the Australian Post Office produced a Community Telephone Plan which set the objective of STD throughout Australia over the next two decades. Carter wanted the same thing for PNG. He was not content with the progressive improvement of the local telephone exchange services in the major centres. Unless these individual upgraded exchanges could be linked together efficiently, a truly national telecommunication network could not be created. Carter asked O'Grady to send engineering and planning experts to PNG, to devise a national telephone plan along the lines of the Community Telephone Plan. With such a Plan, prepared by the acknowledged experts of the PMG's Department's Engineering Planning and Research Division, Carter was confident that he could provide a case that would be accepted in Canberra.

Two experts, John Ferris and Otto Sprinz, under the direction of Ron Turnbull and Tony Newstead, went to PNG, and in 1964 the APO published its *Recommended National Telephone Plan for Papua and New Guinea.* It covered in detail both local and trunk telephone service, and touched on the international service. Part 2 of the Plan opened with these words:

> If a nation intends to progress efficiently, it cannot do so without a telecommunication network, and the development of this network has to be geared to the overall development of the country. There are two different needs to be met in the expansion of the telephone in PNG. One is to provide telephone service to subscribers in areas which are not covered by the existing system, and the other is to improve and augment the existing trunk network interconnecting existing exchanges. Both these needs require to be met to ensure future progress of the Territory.

This was music to the ears of Carter, Peckover and the telecommunications specialists of P and T, according exactly with the Department's philosophy. The plan endorsed the current policy of providing automatic exchanges at larger centres, and either manual or automatic service at smaller, and remote, locations, after evaluating all economic and social factors. The most significant recommendations were in relation to the development and automation of the trunk network.

The APO Planning experts were not impressed with the trunk network as they found it in mid-1963 when they visited PNG. Noting that fourteen exchanges were then in existence, the Plan commented that:

> ... the trunk line system interconnecting these centres is little more than an emergency communication system, judged on present day system standards, and its immediate upgrading is highly desirable from the national interest. However, there are extreme technical and financial difficulties in carrying out the improvement of the network —

some of these difficulties include the particularly rugged terrain, the absence of good roads, the inaccessibility of some of the mountains which would otherwise be suitable for repeater stations, the absence of reliable power supplies and the relatively high costs of installation and maintenance.

The scale of funding available to P and T had not been sufficient to allow Carter and his team to tackle seriously the immense task of upgrading the trunk telephone service. Most of the money provided went into the development of the local telephone and a telegraph systems. Some progress, however, had been made. Because of the nature of the geography and climate of PNG, trunk connections between local exchanges, by cable or overhead line, was physically and financially impracticable, except over short distances. The wartime Kokoda Long Line had abundantly proved this, as had postwar experience with such landlines as those from Port Moresby to Sogeri, and Lae to Wau. The trunk telephone network as it ultimately developed was therefore based on the use of radio links of various kinds. During the first P and T decade, a small number of new high frequency (HF) radio receivers and transmitters were brought into service, supplementing existing equipment and replacing a number of units dating from the Pacific War. In 1957 some low power AWA-Marconi single sideband transceivers were purchased, replacing a number of old double sideband units then in use. This was an attempt to improve the quality of HF trunk services between main centres on a single-channel basis prior to the introduction of multi-channel VHF trunk links. The first of these single sideband units went into service in mid-1958, between Port Moresby and Samarai. Some improvement resulted, but the channels were often only marginal. The first VHF radio trunk line, single channel, between Wau and Bulolo, was installed in early 1956, and in October of the following year, single channel VHF trunk lines were installed between Wau and Lae, and Bulolo and Lae.

A most imaginative step was taken with the decision to link Port Moresby with Lae by VHF radio. Between these towns, the major centres of mainland New Guinea, loomed the high barrier of the Owen Stanley Range. The straight line distance between the two towns, 375 km, was far beyond the operating limits of VHF equipment, and for the link to succeed, repeater stations would be required located at a high enough altitude for the VHF waves to be 'bent' over the Owen Stanleys.

The problem was studied at length by the P and T team headed by Bill Boyle. It was decided to build the repeater stations on two mountain tops, Mt Lawes (the station was at 1 200 feet) and Mt Kaindi (7 750 feet). These mountains were 230 km apart, approaching the extreme normal limit of VHF performance, but they were the only ones reasonably accessible and near enough to the Port Moresby-Lae line of sight.

The building of the Mt Lawes and particularly the Mt Kaindi repeater stations was a technical feat. Access roads had to be constructed to the sites on the mountain tops, to enable the complete stations, with their towers, antennae, emergency diesel power plants, fuel, batteries and buildings, to be hauled in. Mt Lawes was hardly more than a hill by PNG standards, but Kaindi was formidable, even if dwarfed by scores of other peaks. There was a road, of marginal standard, from Wau to the old Edie Creek goldfield on the flanks of Mt Kaindi, at 5 500 feet. Now it had to be taken on and up to the site of the repeater station, through the mist-shrouded, virgin forest.[2] The Mt Lawes station was completed in mid-1959, and the system came into operation on 8 February 1960. Planned to provide five telephone channels, the transmission quality of the circuit was so marginal that only three were finally available. One was used for telegraphic traffic.

The Port Moresby-Lae VHF radio trunk service was reasonably successful, and warmly welcomed by subscribers amazed at the improvement in the quality of transmission, but the technical limitations of a system working at the limit of its performance potential were soon felt. Nevertheless, P and T gained much valuable knowledge and experience from this pioneer project. Carter later used the example of this first non-HF link to demonstrate that a much higher standard of telecommunications could be provided by VHF or UHF (microwave) circuits, if the necessary funds were made available.

The National Telephone Plan for the improvement of trunk services was substantially accepted. It recommended the adoption of a 'closed-numbering scheme', whereby every telephone in PNG would have its own individual number which could be dialled direct from any point of origin in the telephone network, without the need for area codes. The closed-numbering system when allied to the parallel introduction of a single-list telephone directory made PNG practice the envy of many other countries, even as the nation's internal mail rating and classification structure was ahead of its time. Also recommended were National Switching and Transmission Plans, the concepts of which were used as the basis for detailed technical plans developed by P and T's planning expert, Graham Davey, and still in use today.

The most significant of the recommendations in this landmark document was contained in part nine, headed 'Implementation of the Trunk Network Improvement Plan'. In seven stages (but not time-scheduled, in recognition of the likely limits of finance and the physical difficulties that existed), the Plan gave first priority to a Lae-Madang link, then to Lae-Port Moresby, Goroka-Lae, Lae-Rabaul, Wau-Bulolo-Lae, Goroka-Mount Hagen via Chuave, Kundiawa, Kerowagi, Banz and Minj, and in last priority, Vanimo-Wewak-Madang. The Plan recommended the use of open wire or cable lines wherever possible, because of the high cost of constructing and maintaining repeater stations. This recommendation P and T rejected — its only major departure from the Plan. The Department was only too aware of the problems associated with open-wire long line maintenance in PNG, well demonstrated by the wartime long line to Kokoda.

Trunk telephone rates when P and T began were based on the radial distance between the 'calling' and the 'called' exchange. There was a scale of twenty-six charges — later reduced to twenty-two — ranging from five pence per three minute call where the radial distance was between five and ten miles, to £1 two-and-eleven for calls over 1 300 miles. During 1956, these rates were twice varied, bringing them into line with those applying in Australia. From 1 October 1959, PNG abandoned Australian

---

2 I was posted to Wau as ADO in early 1959, and one of my first tasks was to supervise the construction of the road. Only limited funds were available. Most of the work was done by Bill Bradley, using a little D4 bulldozer, the engine of which was not supercharged, and which developed only part of its rated power at these high, sometimes freezing, altitudes.

practice completely. The range of twenty-two trunk call charges was dropped, and a zone system introduced. Intra-zone calls were charged at three shillings per three minutes, those to an adjoining zone at six shillings, and to other zones at nine shillings. It was a simple, effective system.

The telegraph network in operation throughout PNG when the National Telephone Plan was being prepared was better developed than the trunk telephone service. A considerable effort had been made to improve the facilities in existence when P and T was born. The APO planners studied the system, and in the Plan commented:

> The costs of meeting development with a telegraph rather than a speech network are extremely attractive, and the technical difficulties in establishing a telegraph network would be considerably less. However, having regard to the type of traffic to be carried, it is evident that the demand is for speech communications generally, and a telegraph network, in spite of its traffic carrying efficiency and other advantages, would not meet the requirements of the vast majority of inhabitants ... the optimum development therefore consists of developing the conventional telephone network, which will provide later for widespread radio relays, augmented by an efficient telegraph network.

There is no doubt that the planners were correct in their appreciation of the 'requirements of the vast majority of inhabitants'. In PNG today, the telephone is used to a far greater extent than the telegraph or the post. In fact, the telephone conversation, augmented by Telex, which provides a written record, is fast replacing the letter in the top echelons of government and commerce.

From the beginning of provisional administration to 1955, all telegraph circuits in use in PNG were high frequency carrier wave (CW) radio, with operators passing telegrams by morse code. As mentioned in Chapter 8, an HF-radio telegraph omnibus circuit between Lae, Rabaul, Madang and Port Moresby was established in 1947, and OTC initially provided telegraph services to Wewak, Kavieng and Samarai, and assisted the P and T Branch at Madang and Lae. Telegraph services were provided from Radio Telecommunications Centres (RTC). By the end of 1954, the Branch had been able to take over the operation of the RTC centres at Wewak and Kavieng from OTC, and had opened another centre at Lorengau.

The P and T Branch did make a brief attempt to provide a radio telegraph service at Wewak in 1948. Nelson Tokidoro was stationed there for a period of three months, and with the technical assistance of OTC, and clerical help from DDS and NA, he handled Sepik telegraph traffic through the outstation network. He was the first Papua New Guinean to be given such a large responsibility. Nelson did not have a complete command of English, but he nevertheless provided a satisfactory service until the resignation of an operator at Madang forced the P and T Branch — perennially short of operating and technical staff — to transfer him there. OTC provided an officer — John Lennon — on secondment to keep the service operating.

In December 1955, the Department of Posts and Telegraphs established telegraph cable lines between Port Moresby and the suburb of Konedobu, using second-hand Creed teleprinters purchased from the APO. Ten years later, this remained the only telegraph cable line in use. With the exception of the Port Moresby-Lae and Lae-Madang circuits, all telegrams were still being transmitted in Morse Code.

In 1956, Siemens-Hell Printer Type 72C paper tape teleprinters, which became known to swearing P and T technicians as 'Hellscribers', went into service on the Lae-Port Moresby circuit and later on the Lae-Madang and, for a short time, the Lae-Wau circuits. They were complex machines, using a typewriter-style keyboard and long rolls of half-inch wide paper tape on which the messages were printed. For delivery to the customer, the tape strips were torn into six-inch lengths and glued to ordinary blank telegram forms. In theory, Hellscribers should have operated satisfactorily on marginal HF circuits, but unfortunately the P and T radio telegraph channels were then so poor that even this standard was seldom reached. The machines worked quite well over the VHF channels from Lae to Wau, but in general they were never satisfactory, requiring constant servicing and providing no financial or economic advantage over Morse Code operation. At the time the Hellscribers were put into service, more sophisticated, error-correcting (ARQ) equipment was available, but it was considered too expensive for P and T — in hindsight, an unfortunate decision. In 1961, Siemens 100 teleprinters began to come into service, and the Hellscribers were gradually phased out.

The telegraph service was widely used. The total number of originating telegrams passed during P and T's first year was 104 282; ten years later the figure had risen to 370 054. A phonogram service was introduced in May 1957, and was very popular. In the 1964-5 financial year, 133 913 phonograms were originated. No charges were at first made for telegrams after the restoration of civil administration. In May 1951, charges for telegrams within PNG were brought in, at the rate of three pence per word. Urgent telegrams were charged at double rate. These rates remained unchanged during the Department's first decade, although a press telegram rate of half standard rates was adopted, following much pressure from newspaper interests.

The operators in the telecommunications chain responsible for the transmission of telegrams were, of course, subject to an official oath of secrecy not to reveal any information coming to them through the course of their employment. In August, 1956, an Australian woman, Miss Patricia Robertson, was sent to gaol for three months by A. O'Driscoll, SM in the Court of Petty Sessions, on a charge of having disclosed the contents of an official telegram to a newspaper. She was the first white woman to be imprisoned in PNG, and the case sent shockwaves through the expatriate community.

Patricia Robertson was employed by P and T as a teletypist at the Konedobu Post Office. She had also been acting, openly, for months, as the PNG correspondent for the *Sun* newspaper, Sydney. Unfortunately for Patricia Robertson, relations between the press and the Administration in the mid-1950s were strained. There had been a number of clashes between DNA patrols and tribesmen, and some bloody inter-tribal fighting, during these years, and the Administration was often reluctant to release details. The journal *Pacific Islands Monthly*, was particularly critical of what it called 'this official suppression of news of tribal massacres ... this utterly stupid attitude'.

One of the worst tribal massacres in PNG history occurred in the Sepik District in August 1956. Raiders from the May River region swept down upon a settlement of their Yellow River enemies and killed twenty-nine of them in a particularly horrible manner. The news was sent by the District Commissioner, Wewak, in a telegram to DNA Headquarters at Konedobu. Patricia Robertson was on duty at the Konedobu Post Office and she received the telegram. It was duly delivered to DNA, but she also despatched a report to her newspaper, quoting from the District Commissioner's telegram.

For obvious reasons, it was standard practice for the Administrator to send urgent advice to the Minister for Territories in Canberra of such events before releasing the news to the Press. On this occasion, Hasluck first heard of the Yellow River massacre from screaming headlines in the *Sun*.

What followed was inevitable. As Director of P and T, Bill Carter was obliged to authorize proceedings against Patricia Robertson on the grounds that she had committed a flagrant breech of her Oath of Secrecy. So she went to prison. It was a highly embarrassing situation for the Administration. Expatriate public opinion was outraged by the spectacle of a white woman in gaol. The prison authorities were not amused — there were no facilities for white female prisoners. And in the mid-1950s, 'white prestige' was more than an empty phrase.

The case went to the Supreme Court on appeal. The Chief Justice, Sir Beaumont Phillips, upheld the conviction, but reduced the sentence by six weeks. This was the only such case to occur during the Australian presence in PNG, and people handling telegrams were henceforth in no doubt that swift action would follow if the contents were disclosed.

The Outstation Service was much involved in the transmission of telegrams. Telegrams for the outstations were passed by Morse Code to the nearest radio zone centre, thence by radio telephony to the addressee, and were returned along the same route. In the National Telephone Plan, the radio outstations were compared with Australia's Flying Doctor Service in the range and nature of their operations. The PNG Outstation Service was, however, far more flexible. It provided a better, broader-based service to the user than was the case in Australia.

When Bill Carter arrived in PNG to form the Department of Posts and Telegraphs, he found the outstation radio network between towns and district centres that had been developed by E.C.A. Brown, Charles Gee and Bill Boyle from the old AWA system of pre-Second World War days. This outstation network was controlled by what were called RTC centres. When Carter asked what 'RTC' stood for, he received conflicting replies. Some said the letters stood for 'Radio Telephone Centre', other 'Radio Telegraph Centre' or 'Radio Telecommunications Centre'. Keen to develop a separate identity for his new Department as speedily as possible, Carter replaced the term RTC by 'Zone Centre'. The old term, however, was still used by old hands, for years afterwards.

When P and T was formed, there were eleven zone centres, located at Port Moresby, Samarai, Rabaul, Lae, Kavieng, Lorengau, Madang, Wau, Wewak, Sohano, and Goroka. Together they controlled 233 outstations, all equipped with HF radio transceiver equipment. During 1954-5 the radio telephone trunk facility was extended to the outstations working into the zone centres at Port Moresby, Samarai, Rabaul,

Lae, Kavieng, Wewak and Madang, in theory allowing full radio telephone trunk communications between the outstations and telephone subscribers. In practice, transmission conditions often rendered telephone conversations impossible.

The outstation teleradios were located all over PNG, at district and sub-district headquarters, patrol posts, agricultural stations, hospitals, missions, plantations, sawmills and oil exploration sites. Life in the remote places would have been bleak indeed without them. They tied together isolated people with a community of interests in many districts. They made it possible for weather reports to be sent, and so allowed the coming of the small aircraft that kept most of the outstations alive. They helped to banish the fears of people living away from medical facilities. In the maritime districts, they helped peope on lonely islands to keep in touch with the small ships that brought supplies, and carried away plantation produce. Many of the stations were operated by DNA officers, but people in all walks of life utilized the facilities they provided.

The P and T technicians who installed, maintained and repaired the old AWA Type 3B and 3BZ teleradios in almost universal use after the war were masters of improvisation. Spare parts were difficult to obtain, and as the supply dried up, discarded sets were 'cannibalized' to keep stations on the air. Men like Jim Whittaker, Howard Vinning and Jim Palmer would go to extraordinary lengths to patch up the old ex-Army units used by the outstations. Palmer was held in high esteem by outstation men in the big Morobe District, particularly by the Patrol Officers on then-isolated patrol posts such as Wantoat, Kaiapit, Morobe and Garaina. Palmer even had a magic touch with the little Briggs and Stratton battery chargers that were the bane of the outstation operator's life. He was sadly missed when he died, with six others, in the crash of a Qantas De Havilland Drover aircraft off the mouth of the Markham River, in July 1951.

AWA, of course, did not rest on its laurels. The company was soon manufacturing modern transceivers, and equipment from Europe, Britain and the USA began to appear. In Brisbane, the small Crammond Radio Manufacturing Company began to design and market a range of low-powered double sideband units, with one to four fixed frequencies (over the years extended to six, then eight) for transmitting and available in 12-, 24- and 32-volt models, and for DC operation. Chief Engineer W.C. Gee was impressed by the design philosophy of Crammond Radio. In 1954 the Company won a contract to supply P and T with outstation transceivers, and the first sets began to arrive in 1955.

A small concern, Crammond Radio was able to quickly modify its designs to meet the specific requirements of P and T; to win the initial contract, the Company was able to offer a price per unit that compared favourably with prices quoted by larger concerns. P and T tried to standardize on equipment as much as possible (thereby holding down spare parts and maintenance costs), and over the next ten years, a large number of Crammond sets was purchased, and the old AWA outstation radio equipment was gradually phased out. After Gee died, his place in P and T was taken by G.W. Clark, a Divisional Engineer from the PMG's Department, on secondment. Clark liked the Crammond gear, as did radio specialist Vern Hodgson.

Crammond transceivers were widely advertised in the PNG press and in magazines like *Pacific Islands Monthly*. They were claimed to be 'completely tropic-proofed' and they sold in good numbers to private users, although P and T was always the biggest customer. Many customers, however, preferred to stay with AWA equipment, which was cheaper than comparable Crammond transceivers. (Bill Carter considered AWA equipment to be just as well suited to P and T requirements.) The end came for Crammond when it was decided to abandon double sideband (DSB) transceivers for modern single sideband (SSB) outstation transceivers and base station transmitters and receivers, a story which is told later. Crammond Radio could not compete on price and lost the P and T business.

Teleradios were used, unofficially and after normal hours, to keep widely separated people in touch in many parts of PNG. This was common practice in remote districts such as the Southern Highlands, the last of the Highlands districts to be explored. Lake Kutubu, closed during the Second World War, was reopened in 1949. Stations were then established by DDS and NA officers at Mendi (1950), Tari (1952), Erave (1953), Ialibu (1953), Koroba (1955), Kagua (1956) and Nipa (1959), and in later years at several other locations. All were equipped with teleradios, AWA 3BZs initially, and later Crammonds. Apart from the DDS and NA officers, the only non-indigenous residents of the Southern Highlands during the 1950s were a few representatives of departments such as Public Health, Education, Agriculture, Public Works and Police, and a handful of missionaries. There were virtually no roads. The aeroplane kept the district alive, as each outstation was isolated from the others. In the early 1950s, a pleasant and rewarding custom developed. Once or twice each week, before or after business hours, the Officer in charge of each station came on the air at an agreed time. The District Commissioner was thus able to speak directly with each of his subordinates; officers from all departments with matters of mutual interest to discuss were able to talk with one another. Lonely wives, their husbands on patrol, were comforted by the opportunity to talk with other women. The business of the Southern Highlands District would have been difficult to administer without these sessions.[3]

Teleradios were used in a similar way in the maritime districts, where isolation was also a social and economic factor to be reckoned with. People in the Milne Bay District were very unhappy in 1959 when teleradio operators were ordered to cease their 'Rum Sessions' as they called them. For years, the operators of some twenty-five teleradio stations — plantation managers, missionaries, government officers — in Eastern Papua and outlying islands such as the Trobriands, Misima, Rossel and Woodlark, had run an unofficial small-talk radio schedule, from 4.30 to 6.30 p.m. daily. P and T, of course, was well aware of the existence of the 'Rum Sessions', for monitoring of the radio waves was a regular, and necessary, procedure. So long as the proprieties were observed, however, the Department was loath to intervene. The rules of the game were well understood by all: no profane or indecent language could be used, and no purely commercial messages exchanged, for this would deprive P and T of lawful revenue. Then someone broke the rules, and the Department acted.

It was to ease the situation of those in lonely places that P and T introduced a 24-hour radio telephone emergency service, in September 1957, controlled from the Radio Zone Centre in Port Moresby. Hitherto, the Outstation Service had operated

---

3 I was stationed at Koroba from 1955-9 and can attest from personal experience how valuable they were.

only between the hours of 8 a.m. to 4.30 p.m. weekdays, 8 to 12 noon Saturdays, and 9 a.m. to 11 a.m. Sundays. A special emergency frequency of 5885 kc/s per second was set aside for the new service, which was available all over PNG. In a press release, Bill Carter pointed out that P and T could not guarantee that all outstations would be able to make contact on 5885 kc/s at all hours, because of atmospheric conditions, fadeouts and so on. However, extended trials had shown that stations more than four hundred miles from Port Moresby could normally make contact. Arrangements were made with the Health Department for a medical officer always to be available to deal with radio emergencies. Later, another control centre was established at Lae.

The various Christian missions, with hundreds of stations all over PNG, were heavy users of outstation transceivers. There is no doubt that a lot of traffic was passed that should, by any reasonable criteria, have gone to P and T, so contributing much-needed revenue to the national telecommunications system.

Bill Carter had the power to revoke the licences of Mission radio stations which used their channels for quasi-commercial purposes. He recognized, however, the human need of people in remote localities to communicate. Moreover, the Outstation Service was not geared to handle the increased traffic and consequent paperwork that would result if the letter of the law was insisted upon. It is a measure of Carter's commonsense approach to his job that he eventually issued instructions to his officers that Mission networks be permitted to handle all kinds of traffic — mission, business, private and government — under an agreed 'honesty' system whereby Missions made nominal payments for traffic properly classed as 'business'. This system was allowed to operate until P and T was in a position to provide a service at least equal to that provided by the Mission networks, at reasonable cost.

The year 1957 saw the introduction of remote receiver stations at zone centres situated as far away as possible from likely sources of interference from transmitters and motor traffic. The zone centre transmitters, initially AWA 100 watt units, were progressively replaced by modern TCA 250 watt units, beginning in 1961.

It will be remembered from Chapter 8 that the P and T Branch of Treasury was briefly responsible for operating the first post-war broadcasting station in PNG, Radio 9PA in Port Moresby. This was one of a number of low powered, medium frequency broadcast transmitters employed by the Army Amenities Unit in various main centres. It was the only one taken over by the incoming civil administration. Until 28 February 1946, Radio 9PA — it was the then Radio 9AA — was operated by ANGAU. The P and T Branch then took it over until the ABC began its PNG Service, on 1 July 1946; this it continued to operate until 1 December 1973, when the National Broadcasting Commission of PNG (NBC) came into being.

E.C.A. Brown, the Technical Adviser on telecommunications to the Provisional Administration, had a clear conception of the value of broadcasting in PNG. In his 'Report on the Re-establishment of Postal and Telecommunication Facilities in Papua and New Guinea' of 18 June 1948, Brown recommended that a specification be drawn up by the PMG's Department in Australia for a simple radio receiver suitable for village use, to be installed and maintained on a routine basis by properly-trained Papua New Guinean technicians. 'There is no question that broadcasts in native languages must in future play a very large part in the education and development of the indigenous people scattered throughout the Territory', he wrote. The low cost receiver especially designed for village use in PNG did not, however, eventuate. The need disappeared with the development of a vast range of cheap commercial receivers of all kinds, some quite unsuitable for local conditions, others ideal, that flooded into the country in ever-increasing numbers over the following three decades, encouraged by a far-sighted decision by the Administration to lift the import duty on radio receivers to encourage their use by Papua New Guineans. Extensive broadcasting in PNG dialects to local audiences of the kind envisaged by E.C.A. Brown began, however, during P and T's first decade, and again the Department had a considerable involvement, on the technical side.

The first of what was to become a Territory-wide network of Administration broadcasting stations was opened at Rabaul, on 19 October 1961, with Roger Wilson in charge. In April 1962, Jim Leigh took over, setting a standard for broadcasting that was to be followed throughout the broadcasting service as new stations were opened. The station was created because of the special circumstances then prevailing on the Gazelle Peninsula, in the aftermath of the violent incident at Navuneram in August 1958, when villagers opposed to the introduction of the new concept of local government clashed with Native Affairs officers and police, resulting in the death by rifle-fire of two villagers. This was the beginning of the unrest on the Gazelle that culminated, many years later, in the murder of District Commissioner Jack Emanuel, at Kabaira Bay.

Early in 1959, the Minister for Territories, Paul Hasluck, concerned at the widening communication gap between the Administration and the people of the Gazelle and other areas, began to press for the establishment of regional broadcasting stations. At this time, the ABC operated only one station in PNG, at Port Moresby. The Commission did plan to establish another at Rabaul, but estimated that this would take at least two years. This was an unacceptable delay, in view of the Gazelle situation. Eventually, the Chairman of the ABC, Sir Richard Boyer, decided that Administration regional stations of the type proposed were not within the charter of his Commission, which could not be used as an instrument of government. Hasluck directed the Administration to proceed with the establishment of the Rabaul station. For a variety of reasons, another eighteen months passed before Station 9BR commenced broadcasting. It was launched using the two Outstation Service transmitters at the Rabaul Zone Centre. The Outstation Service ceased normal operations at 4.30 p.m.; broadcasting began at 4.45 p.m.

Station 9BR was immediately successful. In December 1961, the Administrator, Brigadier Cleland, set up an inter-departmental committee to investigate and report on the immediate and long-term broadcasting requirements of PNG. The chairman was Bill Carter. Members included Bill Peckover and Vern Hodgson of P and T, D.M. Fenbury, W. Dishon, C.J. Lynch, C.P. Livingstone, and L.R. Newby and P.N. Cochrane of the Division of Extension Services.

The Report of the committee, delivered in February 1962, endorsed the concept of regional stations broadcasting in local dialects as well as the lingua franca, to be administered by a Territory authority, independent of the ABC. The committee recommended the establishment of stations in twenty localities over a period of time.

No conflict of interest between the ABC and the proposed Territory broadcasting authority was seen; the ABC would continue, as before, to provide a service aimed primarily at the expatriate audience, and set a high professional broadcasting standard for the Territory. The committee envisaged that technical staff for the Administration stations would be trained by P and T, who would also install and maintain the transmitters.

The committee's principal recommendations were accepted except for the establishment of a Territory broadcasting authority. Instead, a Broadcasting Advisory Council was set up. It was composed of two members representing the ABC, two representing the Administration (Bill Peckover and Lisle Newby) and four private citizens. The Division of Extension Services became the Department of Information and Extension Services under Lisle Newby, who became responsible for the operation of the Administration Broadcasting Service. In the beginning, P and T carried much of the load, making Outstation Service transmitters and studio equipment available until the Department of Information and Extension Services (DIES) was able to obtain its own, and providing technical staff and advice. New Administration stations were rapidly established. Radio Wewak was the second, in 1963, then Kerema (1964), Daru and Goroka (1965), Mount Hagen (1966), Samarai (1967), Bougainville (1968), Madang and Morobe (1971), Popondetta (1972), Chimbu, Mendi, Kavieng and Kimbe (1973). With the formation of the National Broadcasting Commission in 1973, the ABC and the Administration Broadcasting Service ceased to function. The NBC established regional stations in the Central District in 1974, and at Manus in 1975. During the whole of this period, the maintenance of the transmitters and studio broadcasting equipment remained the responsibility of the Department of Posts and Telegraphs, which performed the work at cost to DIES.

As mentioned above, the National Telephone Plan gave first priority to the upgrading of the national trunk line network to the Lae-Madang, Lae-Port Moresby link. 'The most important route in the Territory is the Port Moresby-Lae-Madang route', wrote the planners, '[this] interconnects three of the four biggest towns and will link them with the proposed SEACOM submarine cable at Madang, thus ensuring access to the worldwide telecommunication system.'

Although PNG's international communications were the sole responsibility of OTC, P and T was of course vitally concerned, and as we have seen, there was close co-operation between the two organizations in the initial post-war period. As early as August 1962, P and T had been informed that the proposed SEACOM submarine telephone cable between Australia and Singapore would be routed via Cairns, Queensland, and Lae, a dazzling prospect, indeed.

SEACOM was part of a plan of majestic dimensions to girdle the globe with a 23 000-mile cable network linking the countries of the British Commonwealth of Nations. SEACOM, the South East Asia Commonwealth Cable, would provide 160 two-way telephone circuits between Guam and Sydney, and 80 between Guam and Singapore. SEACOM would in addition provide new links with Japan, the United States and the Philippines through other cable systems passing through Guam, and would link the Atlantic (CANTAT) and Pacific (COMPAC) cables. It would be a giant step forward if PNG could be connected with the rest of the world by high-quality SEACOM telephone circuits.

But SEACOM would only be available at Madang, and the nation would derive comparatively little benefit from it unless Madang was linked with the other towns of PNG by an equally high quality trunk telephone system. Even before the appearance of the National Telephone Plan, Carter and his team had been looking for ways and means of obtaining the large amount of capital necessary to bring this about — a story that will be told in Chapter 13.

SEACOM would of course be the responsibility of the Overseas Telecommunications Commission of Australia. The Plan pointed out that the upgrading of the PNG trunk network would be of direct benefit to OTC, since it would enable it to gain increased utilization of SEACOM allowing it to dispense with the existing HF radio circuits between PNG and Australia.

As detailed in Chapter 8, OTC took over from AWA responsibility for PNG's international telecommunications on 1 October 1946, and continued the long-established HF radio telephone and telegraph services between Port Moresby and Sydney, and Rabaul and Sydney. In 1953, a direct HF radio telephone service between Lae and Sydney was introduced. These channels were available to the public from 8 a.m. to 10.30 p.m. Monday to Friday, and from 8 a.m. to 10 p.m. on Saturday. So popular was the Moresby-Sydney service that on 27 January 1957, it was made available each Sunday between 9.45 a.m. and 10.45 a.m. The normal rate, ten shillings per minute with a three-minute minimum, applied. Traffic continued to grow, and a second trunk channel was opened between Port Moresby and Sydney, on 19 December 1961.

While these telephone, and telegraph, channels were owned and operated by OTC, P and T had a close involvement, and at first the sound relationship that had existed between the two organizations since the end of the war was maintained. Unfortunately, it was not to last. In July, 1955, there was a conference in Port Moresby between representatives of OTC and P and T. Bill Carter and Charles Gee faced a team of six senior representatives of OTC, including the Chairman, Chief Engineer and General Manager of the Commission. The OTC team was very well briefed, and Carter found the going very hard. It was his first encounter with OTC, who had wide international negotiating experience. He told me in 1981:

> I got the impression that OTC would have taken over P and T's telecom internal radio links if we had let them get away with it. It was in their financial interests, because they could have costed the operation into the Commonwealth partners fund, make a minor contribution themselves, and come out with a profit. The move would have created some initial improvements in the service, but done nothing towards laying the foundations for an ultimately sound telecommunications trunk network for PNG.

The upshot was that it was accepted that internal communications within PNG were the responsibility of P and T. While telegraph traffic was passed between the OTC stations in PNG, this was to be regarded as an interim measure only. Once P and T was in a position to take over this responsibility, the question of the discontinuance of the OTC service would be settled by correspondence. However, for the entire period of the OTC presence in PNG — until 1 December 1973, when P and T took over responsibility for PNG's international telecommunications — OTC continued to accept telegrams at Rabaul and Lae for delivery in Port Moresby, and vice versa. The volume of this traffic was not large, but OTC refused to discontinue the practice, claiming that because it employed only Australian operators it provided a better service than did P and T, which used an increasing percentage of Papua New Guineans. In fact, OTC transmission times were usually much longer, since the telegrams had to be sent first to Sydney, then re-transmitted back to PNG. It was not until 1964, following a formal approach, that OTC reluctantly agreed to pay P and T a portion of the revenue from such traffic.

Far more serious than this, however, was the conflict generated by disagreement over the operation of the PNG-Australia radio telephone service. During P and T's first decade, trunk telephone traffic increased dramatically. During the 1954-5 financial year, 2 560 calls were originated in PNG for Australia and overseas; by 1963-4 this figure had soared to 14 882. Yet the procedure in use for connecting the calls was extremely time-consuming, and involved telephonists and technicians from OTC, the Australian Post Office and P and T. Each of these authorities acknowledged that procedures should be simplified, and in September 1961, a conference was held in Sydney to discuss the situation. P and T was represented by Bill Peckover. Current procedure was for P and T and OTC jointly to handle aspects of calls originating in PNG. Revenue, ten shillings per minute, was shared in the proportion of one shilling to P and T, six-and-six to OTC and two-and-six to the APO, which controlled inward and outward calls at the Overseas Trunk Exchange in Sydney. Peckover proposed that P and T take over full control of calls originating in PNG, with a corresponding adjustment in the percentage of revenue paid to the Department. The representative of the APO, W.A.E. Nielsen, countered this with an offer to take over the operating work presently performed by OTC, and continue the control of inward and outward calls at Sydney. Neither OTC nor the APO were prepared to consider the new revenue-sharing proposal put forward by Bill Peckover. As the junior partner, there was little that P and T could do. A modified operating procedure was finally agreed upon, to begin on 1 November 1961 and this removed the OTC technical operator from the operating chain, with the APO continuing as before. P and T refused to accept any additional workload for its operators until it received an increased share of revenue.

Despite the opening of the second Port Moresby-Sydney trunk channel in December, the rate of growth of traffic actually slowed following the introduction of the modified operating procedure, reflecting the disinterest of the Sydney operators after the withdrawal of OTC technical operators. In July 1962, Bill Carter wrote to the OTC and the APO suggested the provision of a third Port Moresby-Sydney channel, to reduce delay times for calls originating in Port Moresby. A year later, he repeated his request. On both occasions it was months before replies, negative ones, were received, and a third channel was not provided until June 1967. (In July, a second trunk channel was opened between Lae and Sydney.)

These and other fundamental conflicts with OTC caused deep misgivings within P and T and helped to prevent the development of a relationship of mutual trust between the two authorities. There was less friction, however, between OTC and P and T over the operation of the international telegraph service. Arrangements in force when P and T began remained, unchanged, throughout the decade. OTC continued to operate and maintain its transmitter and receiver stations and town offices at Port Moresby, Lae and Rabaul. Telegrams to and from other centres in PNG for or from overseas destinations were exchanged with P and T at Port Moresby, Lae and Rabaul.

Because of the poor standard of the radio telephone international service, the volume of telegraph business was heavy during this period. During the 1959 calendar year, some 94 000 telegrams were lodged in PNG for overseas countries. Of these, forty-seven per cent were handled by P and T; the remainder were lodged by senders with OTC. In the same year, a roughly equivalent number — 95 000 — telegrams were received from overseas, thirty per cent being forwarded on through the P and T telegraph network.

In June 1964, a Telex service was established by OTC between Port Moresby and Australia, operated in tandem by P and T and OTC through their own separate manual switchboards. Although it was little used at first, it was the forerunner of the great advances in telecommunications soon to come.

The only international telecommunications service that did not terminate in Sydney during the first P and T decade was a radio telephone channel between Port Moresby and Hollandia, in West New Guinea, established on 14 December 1959, for administrative purposes. It closed in May 1963.

This was the the period when the long-simmering dispute between The Netherlands and Indonesia over the future status of West New Guinea came to a head. It was a dispute in which Australia initially supported the Dutch, on the grounds that both governments had the same ultimate aim: the advancement of the peoples of WNG and PNG to self-government and independence. Early in 1958, the Australian and Netherlands governments agreed on a policy of administrative co-operation, and the appointment of liaison officers at Hollandia and Port Moresby, respectively. Following the agreement, Liaison Officers were exchanged and radio telephone links established by OTC. Radio telephone links, but using the P and T Outstation Service, were also established between the main towns of the adjoining border districts, Daru and Merauke, Wewak and Hollandia; between the adjoining patrol posts of Waris (West New Guinea) and Green River; and Mindiptana (WNG) and Kiunga. Plans were made to extend this link to the WNG posts of Ubrub and Sibil, and the PNG station of Telefomin.

But the Indonesians continued to press their claim to West New Guinea and as is well known, in August 1962 they prevailed. The Dutch, shamefully abandoned by their allies, including Australia, were forced to submit to United Nations pressure, and following a farcical 'act of free choice' in May 1963, sovereignty over what now became West Irian was transferred to Indonesia. The Dutch and Australian Liaison Officers were recalled, and the radio telephone link between Port Moresby and what was now Jayapura was removed.

It was in 1959 also that another telecommunication service between PNG and Australia began. An agreement was reached between P and T and the Australian Department of Civil Aviation for the major PNG airline operators to use the DCA Aeronautical Fixed Telecommunications Network (AFTN) for the transmission of commercial telegrams within the country relating to aircraft bookings, loadings and movements. Standard P and T rates were applied to this traffic, and the revenue collected by DCA was transferred to the Department. A like agreement was entered into by OTC and DCA, allowing the airline operators to use the AFTN for the transmission of telegrams for a similar purpose, between PNG and Australia.

In October 1961, Trans Australia Airlines established a direct teletype link between its Sydney headquarters and Port Moresby. TAA thus became the first Australian domestic airline to introduce its own telecommunications link outside Australia. Ansett-ANA later followed suit.

TELECOMMUNICATIONS: THE GREAT LEAP FORWARD

By the end of P and T's first decade, public attacks on the standard of service being provided by the Department were increasing. From one end of the Territory to the other, a shrill chorus of complaints arose. In the usual way of the gentle public, the considerable advances of the past ten years were ignored: Hell hath no fury like a citizen deprived of a telephone. Bill Carter found himself on the defensive, and detailing the solid improvements that had been made had little effect. For Carter was obliged to admit that unless a massive increase in funds was made available, there was little that P and T could do to upgrade existing facilities.

Complaints did not come merely from private individuals. In May 1964, the Northern District Advisory Council savagely criticized telephone services at Popondetta. In the same month, the Port Moresby Chamber of Commerce complained of the 'crippling shortage' of telephones in the capital. P and T was a 'farce', said the Wau-Bulolo Town Advisory Council. In March 1965, the Madang TAC described the telephone service as 'atrocious'. A droll story went the rounds, and was picked up and printed in the irreverent 'Drum' column of the *South Pacific Post*. A psychiatrist, examining a patient complaining of noises in the head, asks him:

'Do you hear voices, and not know what they are saying, or where they come from?'
'I do', the patient replies.
'How often does this occur?'
'Every day, and all the time'.
'When does it occur?'
'Every time I pick up the telephone'.
'That's remarkable', says the psychiatrist, looking sharply at his patient. 'Where do you come from?'
'Madang', is the reply.

Territorians chortled, but Bill Carter and his men were not amused. And not only the telephone service was under attack. An editorial in the *South Pacific Post* in February 1964, was outspoken in its criticism of P and T's Postal Service localization policy. The editor wrote:

> One of the worst examples of a too-early nativization of the Public Service is being illustrated in post offices in the main centres, particularly Port Moresby. There are clearly marked envelopes in the wrong boxes. There is complete confusion at most times in larger post offices where the simple purchase of stamps is an interminable procedure. The situation is getting worse . . . mail today is one of the most vital services of modern life. Inefficiency in the post offices can only spell disaster for the country's future.

The *Post* renewed its campaign in October 1965, following the announcement of new postal and telephone charges (which had remained unaltered since 1959) by the Administrator. These were expected to raise an additional £90 000 in revenue to offset the current P and T deficit of over £700 000 per annum. The automatic telephone exchange unit fee call charge went up from four pence to six pence; the internal base postal rate was increased from five pence for the first ounce to six pence for two ounces, and the rate to Australia from five to six pence per ounce. At the same time, a range of measures was introduced to simplify mail article classifications and speed the dispatch of mails. The *Post* wrote:

> While business and community spokesmen agree that the higher postal charges can be tolerated — in fact they see some merit in the simplified mail classifications — they are adamant that there is no justification for increased phone charges. They don't see why they should have to pay more for a service which, in Port Moresby at least, is so exceptionally bad . . . there is no doubt that to cope with current demands and future expansion the department must have more finance. But many of the day-to-day services of P and T don't require more finance before they can be improved. For instance, the long delays involved in trying to lodge telegrams by phone could be eliminated if the telephonists had a better command of English . . . it is, therefore, questionable whether the department should have made an additional demand on the public before making a demonstrable effort to put its own house in order as regards efficiency and service.

Bill Carter admitted that P and T was in financial trouble and that the phone service would get worse. 'The system is severely overtaxed', he said in a press statement. 'At the end of last year there were 1 000 people in Port Moresby awaiting phones. The problem is lack of finance. This year's budget gives P and T £1.7 million only'.

Ever since August 1962, when he had been advised that the SEACOM cable would be routed via Cairns and Madang, Carter and his men had been studying the implications for the Department of Posts and Telegraphs. The Department's telecommunications experts unanimously agreed that microwave technology would have to be employed if the local telephone exchanges were to be linked with one another, and with Madang, by the high quality trunk channels that would be essential if PNG were to gain the utmost benefit possible from the SEACOM cable. Millions of pounds would be required to finance the trunk system, and to improve existing services. Where was the money to come from? Not from the Administration, that was certain. The standard annual budget system under which the PNG Administration operated was unable to provide the level of funding that would be called for if a modern, effective national telecommunications network were to be constructed.

Carter, ably supported by Tas Sexton, squeezed the utmost possible from the annual budget system. He arranged for many post office and telephone exchange buildings to be constructed using the Public Works Department vote, and then spent P and T money for the equipment to put in them. Certain District Commissioners helped to eke out P and T funds by using their Minor New Works cash to finance projects that were anything but 'minor'. But there was a limit to what could be achieved by such means, and it fell far short of what was required. The June 1962 decision by the Treasurer, A.P.J. Newman, to allow P and T to forward-commit up to seventy-five per cent of funds allocated without a prior certification that money was available was a considerable step forward, but again it was not a solution. Access to a large amount of capital: that was the problem.

The answer came in one of the recommendations of the United Nations Visiting Mission of 1962. Sir Hugh Foot's mission's key recommendation, that was eventually, nearly five years later, to provide the solution to P and T's problem, was for a full review of the PNG economy by the International Bank for Reconstruction and Development, generally known as the World Bank. This was to be used as a basis for a concerted economic development plan. This recommendation was accepted, and in 1963, a World Bank Mission headed by K.R. Iverson visited PNG. In 1964, it issued a Report that was later adopted as the basis for the PNG Five Year Plan that began in 1968.

When the World Bank Mission arrived in June 1963, Bill Carter was acting as Assistant Administrator, Services, in place of Dr John Gunther, who was on full-time duty as a member of the Currie Commission on Higher Education. Bill Peckover, who was now Assistant Director, Operations and Administration (following the reorganization recommended by the 1962 O and M Review) took over from Carter.

As Assistant Administrator, Carter acted as liaison officer between Iverson's team and the Administration. He kept Peckover, and the other departmental heads informed of the activities of the team. Early in June, Peckover conceived the idea of approaching the World Bank for the capital loan so desperately needed by the Department of Posts and Telegraphs. He discussed his idea with an enthusiastic Bill Carter, and they went to Iverson and began discussions, that were to end, some years later, in the granting of the first World Bank loan made to PNG. But it was not to be an easy road.

Iverson and his team left PNG in September 1963, to compile their report. In the meantime, the National Telephone Plan appeared, supporting in broad detail the ideas that Carter and Peckover had outlined to Iverson. Dr Gunther returned to duty, and Carter resumed his position of Director of Posts and Telegraphs. In May 1964, Bill Carter left PNG to attend the Fifteenth Postal Congress of the Universal Postal Union in Vienna, as a member of the Australian Delegation. This was the first time that PNG was directly represented at a major UPU international conference.

Carter found it a disillusioning experience. As a member of the Australian Delegation, he was not able to advance the interests of PNG. He was disappointed to find that his fellow members were concerned, exclusively, with Australian postal interests, not those of the Territory. But the experience was valuable, and Carter did make a contact that was to prove of solid benefit to PNG. Before leaving Port Moresby for Vienna, he had sought and obtained approval to stop over in London after the conference, for talks with the reigning chiefs of the British Post Office.

As mentioned previously, when Carter became Director of P and T, the divisional (later Chief) Engineer was W.C. Gee. Gee was a highly qualified engineer, with a background of experience in the British Colonial Postal Engineering Service. Much of this experience was gained in Malaya, where the telecommunications network depended heavily on the use of repeater stations. Gee was a formidable person, stubborn and opinionated, but his radio engineering professional views were, rightly, respected by Bill Carter. It was during discussions with Gee before his death on the possible use of VHF and UHF (microwave) technology to solve PNG's trunk telephone problems, that Bill Carter first heard of the operations of the British firm, Preece, Cardew and Rider.

This famous old partnership of consultant engineers had been founded in 1899 by Sir William Preece, a former Chief Engineer of the British Post Office. Preece, Cardew and Rider, or PCR as they were generally known, provided technical advice and assistance to colonial administrations all over the world on a wide range of engineering projects and problems, including telecommunications. The British Post Office experts as well as the London representative of the Australian Post Office, endorsed PCR, and Carter spent a considerable amount of time discussing PNG's telecommunications problems with Sir Norman Frome and other senior executives of the firm. PCR was later appointed Consultants to the Department of Posts and Telegraphs, and in 1967 opened an office in Port Moresby under Resident Engineer Charles Isherwood, thus beginning a fruitful association that has endured to the present day.

Despite the looming obstacle of finance, P and T had already begun to plan a 300-channel microwave link between Port Moresby and Lae, to take advantage of the SEACOM cable, as early as 1963. It appeared to Bill Carter that it would be in the financial interests of the Overseas Telecommunications Commission of Australia to assist P and T to construct such a link. Without it, the SEACOM cable would land at Madang with no opportunity of hooking into the PNG internal network. Carter therefore wrote to the General Manager of the Commission, but his proposal was rejected, on the grounds that it was not within the OTC charter to invest in domestic telephone networks. It was not until P and T was preparing to take over PNG's international telecommunications after self-government that it became obvious that there was, in fact, no financial incentive for OTC to provide assistance. (This will be detailed in Chapter 14.) The Department nevertheless went on with its plans.

Experts of the APO gave technical assistance to P and T in drawing up tender invitations for the three stages of the proposed system: to survey and report on one or more sections of the route; to supply the equipment required; and to install the bearer and channelling equipment over the whole route. The preparation of this important initial microwave tender invitation was undertaken by Vern Hodgson in addition to his normal planning work. It was a job that consumed a remarkable amount of his time. Tenders were finally called in 1965.

The use of microwaves involved a departure from VHF technology, which was employed on the existing Port Moresby-Lae radio trunk link via the repeater stations on Mt Lawes and Mt Kaindi. As mentioned in Chapter 12, VHF radio waves could be 'bent' over the high barrier of the Owen Stanleys, but microwaves required direct line-of-sight transmission. A chain of repeater stations would therefore have to be constructed, on lofty mountain peaks. A whole new range of problems was opened. It would be financially impossible to construct roads to mountain tops in excess of 10 000 feet high, and remote from existing access roads. Helicopters would have to be employed. It was because of the enormity of the problem of building and maintaining mountaintop repeater stations by helicopter that the APO's National Telephone Plan for PNG recommended the use of physical lines rather than radio waves wherever possible.

The Department received an unpleasant shock when the tender offers for the construction and installation phase came in. Without exception, the prices quoted were extraordinarily high. It seemed that no telecommunications company was prepared to take even the smallest gamble on this big project in the unfamiliar wilds of PNG, and it was obvious that all estimates were heavily loaded to take account of every conceivable contingency. Plainly, P and T would itself have to construct the initial microwave systems if costs were to be kept within reasonable bounds. But valuable experience had been gained, that was later to be drawn upon.

There was, however, one heartening tender for the survey work, from that old friend of telecommunications in PNG, Amalgamated Wireless (Australasia) Ltd. The AWA offer was within the P and T budget, and the company was quickly assigned the task of undertaking a survey of the longest link on the proposed route from Port Moresby to Lae, that between Mt Scratchley and Mt Strong, a distance of 110 km. At that time, it was planned to take the Moresby-Lae route on to Rabaul with independent sideband (ISB) HF radio equipment, and to Madang by VHF. Thus, the main centres of PNG would be linked to Australia and the outside world, via the SEACOM cable.

The Lae-Madang VHF link via Mt Otto was actually in full commission long before the Port Moresby-Lae system was established. This VHF link was installed, with twelve channels, all of which were carrying telephone and telegraph traffic within a few months of commissioning. The link had a potential capacity of twenty-four channels. Channelling equipment for the additional twelve channels was immediately ordered, but in the event was not installed for another two years, becuse of manufacturing and delivery delays.

In June 1965, the first of a number of delicate purchase negotiations with the native owners of mountain top sites began. The site required was on the summit of Mt Otto, 11 613 feet high, near Goroka in the Eastern Highlands. Mt Otto was to be the first experimental high altitude station, and the first to attempt to use wind power to charge a large bank of lead-acid batteries which would feed solid-state electronics.

The man responsible for the Mt Otto negotiations was Bob Murphy, a P and T 'character'. Strictly speaking, only Lands Department and Native Affairs officers could make land purchases, but Murphy was given the task of smoothing the way. He spent months in many locations throughout PNG, in town and on the tops of mountains, arranging site purchases.

Murphy found the Mt Otto negotiations initially difficult. The owners, old men from villages thousands of feet below the summit, were not interested in money. They wanted a cow. Eventually agreement was reached, and a fine beast changed hands.

When construction of the repeater station began, it was found that the agreed site was not large enough to accommodate the entire structure. An extension of the boundary was necessary. There was some consternation in P and T ranks. As anyone who has tried to negotiate land sales with Highlanders will verify, such variations from the original deal were by no means to be taken for granted. But all went well. Bob Murphy was sent back to Mt Otto to arrange for the extension, since he was well known to the owners. To his relief, they readily agreed. They had asked for a cow in exchange for the site, but the cow had since had a calf! So it was only fair to extend the original boundary.

The planned trunk network on the PNG mainland called for the construction of ten repeater stations. Every pound of cargo would have to be lifted in by helicopter — a vastly more difficult and expensive proposition than the building of the Mt Lawes and Mt Kaindi stations, which had road access — and it was essential to cut down on weight. Much was expected of the experimental wind generators and transistorized equipment that would be installed on Mt Otto.

Meanwhile, public demands for better telecommunications did not slacken. Carter and his team continued to upgrade local telephone services as fast as finances permitted. In 1964, VHF radio telephone facilities were provided for remote subscribers in the Port Moresby region, following successful field trials. This system was extended to eleven subscribers in the Goroka district in 1967, and to fourteen at Mt Hagen the following year. The outstation sets used in these first VHF radio telephone systems were really nothing more than slightly modified taxicab radios. Within a few years, they were to be in use in many districts of PNG. An interim VHF circuit was provided between Port Moresby and Popondetta in 1964, and this was improved in 1965 to enable trunk telegraph as well as telephone traffic to be passed. Further VHF circuits were planned between outlying centres, in several districts. Automatic Swedish L.M. Ericsson crossbar exchanges for Wau and Bulolo were delivered in 1965.

The first Administration crossbar automatic exchange was cut over at Toleap in 1966. It was a small 90-line exchange. A large 800-line exchange for Madang came into operation in 1967, replacing the old magneto exchange (and silencing local critics of the telephone service). It was installed under the supervision of technician Bob Pears and engineer John Andrews. In 1968, the biggest exchange yet, equipped to service 4 000 customers and with an ultimate capacity of 10 000, was installed at Boroko by the Standard Telephone Company, under the supervision of Senior Technical Officer John Solomon. Solomon, an ex-PMG man, liked the PNG life and he accepted an offer to leave the employ of STC, and join P and T. (He was still on the job in 1981, one of the key expatriate officers working for the Department after Independence.)

The Wau and Bulolo exchanges were held in their crates for a long time after delivery. These were Swedish exchanges, and after they had been ordered, P and T decided to standardize instead on the Australian Post Office modification of the design. This decision followed lengthy consultations with senior planning engineers of the APO. Although a considerable delay in commissioning the Wau and Bulolo exchanges resulted — they had to undergo the APO modifications — the decision proved to be of tremendous benefit to P and T, which now had access to all the documentation developed by the APO during the design modification phase. Moreover, APO staff on secondment to P and T were familiar not only with the basic equipment, but also with the installation and operation procedures developed in Australia, which would in future be used in PNG.

1966 proved to be a critical year for the Department of Posts and Telegraphs, and for telecommunications in PNG. In March, the Madang end of the SEACOM cable was laid by Cable and Wireless Ltd.'s cable ship, the *Retriever*. Armed with copies of four or five World Bank Reports on projects in other developing countries as a guide, Bill Peckover and Vern Hodgson began to prepare a properly documented proposal for a Bank loan. With the knowledge gained from the preparation of the initial Moresby-Lae microwave tender and the offers received in response, Hodgson was able to calculate well-based cost estimates of the equipment required for each link in the proposed network, and the construction and installation costs for each repeater station. This initial proposal, completed in February 1966, was for the funding of a high quality telecommunication microwave 'backbone' on mainland New Guinea. The extension of this backbone to New Ireland, New Britain and Bougainville would follow later. The proposal did not attempt to put monetary values on the benefits to PNG that would flow from this construction.

Bill Carter discussed the proposal with Frank Henderson, the newly-appointed Assistant Administrator, Economic Affairs, who forwarded it with his support to Canberra. In July 1966, Peckover went to Canberra for talks on the financial requirements of P and T. Prospects for World Bank financial assistance to PNG were by this time looking good, and Bill Carter was anxious to ensure that P and T's claims were given full consideration, both in Canberra and at World Bank headquarters in Washington. To further strengthen P and T's position, Carter also instructed Peckover to discuss the loan proposal with the Economic Adviser, A.W. McCasker (appointed after the adoption of the 1964 World Bank Report). Bill McCasker, widely experienced in such matters, favoured the proposal, as far as it went. 'It needs to be supported by a costs/benefits study, covering at least twenty years, to prove whether it is a worthwhile long-term investment', he told Peckover.

So Bill Peckover went back to the drawing-board. With the aid of a copy of Australian Treasury instructions setting forth their requirements for economic proposals he set to work to try and put a monetary value for each year of the twenty years ahead on the 'benefits' (that is, revenue estimates based on traffic forecasts) of the proposed microwave backbone as against Vern Hodgson's 'costs' estimates. It was a highly speculative exercise, for Peckover had few PNG precedents to guide him. He did, however, have usage estimates made by the APO experts, John Ferris and Otto Sprinz, when they were assisting to prepare the National Telephone Plan of 1964 (estimates which had already been proven ultra-conservative by 1966). Valuable data, too, was available from recent experience in the Goroka and Mt Hagen districts following the introduction of the new VHF radio telephone units mentioned previously. There was a dramatic increase in the number of calls made when these VHF units replaced the old HF sets previously used. On the basis of these facts and estimates, plus the undoubted latent demand for efficient trunk line facilities that existed, Peckover by January had produced a documented cost/benefit study to support the earlier World Bank Loan proposal.

Bill Peckover today recalls that period as a 'tremendously interesting, but equally frustrating, time':

> The first World Bank Mission headed by K.R. Iverson in 1963 had built up hopes right through the Department, but that was more than three years before, and despite our efforts to get the necessary finance to make a start on the telecommunications network, nothing had eventuated. I can well remember asking Tom Pearson, who was our engineer in charge of Construction, to join Vern Hodgson and me in preparing the first loan proposal. Tom, too, was beginning to doubt that we would ever get finance. 'No, my boy', he said to me, 'that's yours and Vern's job. My time is fully committed. But you get the money if you can. If you do, I'll spend it for you!' He really thought we were off on what would prove to be a frustrating wild-goose chase.

It was in 1966 that a cleverly orchestrated campaign for improved telecommunications in PNG was begun in the pages of the *South Pacific Post*. A new managing editor, Keith Mattingley, had arrived in mid-1965. Mattingley, a veteran pressman, was appalled to find that there was no cheap internal press telegram rate within PNG. He was responsible for the production of a national newspaper for PNG that was forced to rely on obsolete and inefficient telecommunications. He wrote to me in June 1981 that:

> Telecommunications were chaotic in those days. Phone and telegraph links were lost completely when cloud and moisture got in the way. News from Rabaul and Lae missed editions because reporters could not get through by phone or telegram to our editorial headquarters in Port Moresby. They would start to dictate a story by phone but lose the line for five hours through fading, and a day or more when equipment broke down . . .
>
> Fortunately, we had a friend in Stan Silver, the Manager of OTC in Port Moresby, who agreed to transmit editorial copy from Rabaul to Port Moresby via Sydney on OTC's HF telegraph channels. Telephone and telegraph services to Australia and overseas were scratchy, too, often fading and breaking down. The position was becoming more desperate as community demands increased. The opening of the SEACOM cable link from Guam into Madang and on to Cairns only added to the frustration, because the Territory's trunk system wasn't hooked into it. In 1966, I decided to launch a campaign in the *Post* to try to improve things. I immediately told Bill Carter, some business leaders, and the then Administrator, Sir Donald Cleland, all of whom supported the idea.
>
> Sir Donald did not come out publicly in support, because, although never afraid to stir Canberra, he respected his responsibility to his Minister. Some of the business executives remained in the background too, for fear that the powerful Department of Territories would make things more difficult for them. Although a public servant, Bill Carter was different. He seemed to have both the Territory and his job very much at heart, and he hated complacency . . . he co-operated closely with me in the campaign, proposing many leads.

Carter was on delicate ground, but he was so convinced of the need for better telecommunications if PNG were to prosper that he ignored the convention that public servants should remain aloof from such activities. He fed Mattingley with background material, facts and figures. Editorials in the *Post* began to whip up public feeling. Chambers of Commerce in the main centres, encouraged by Carter, enthusiastically joined in the debate. At Mattingley's instigation, the South-East Asia correspondent of the Melbourne *Herald*, Garry Barker, wrote an article pointing out that the governments of both Singapore and Malaysia regarded good communications as vital infrastructure: was PNG in a different situation?

Over a period of months, Bill Carter made a number of statements that were given full coverage in the *Post*. In June 1966, he called for better communications throughout PNG. In August, he said that trunk line telephone services in PNG had reached saturation point: 'Traffic demands far outweigh the services available. There are fifteen trunk line circuits in use at the moment. There is an immediate need for 120 circuits, for 150 by 1968 and 450 by 1980, if present trends continue'.

'We need Cash Now for Local Seacom Link' shouted the headlines in the *Post*. 'The governments of Australia and PNG have known for three years that the cable would be connected to PNG, probably Madang. Why has not finance been arranged?'

The President of the Port Moresby Chamber of Commerce, the well respected H. Stubbs, said publicly that money spent to provide the SEACOM link would be 'the best investment the Territory has ever made'. Politicians Ron Neville and Ian Downs declared their strong support. The Employers Federation wanted SEACOM 'above all else'. Journalist Noel Hawken wrote an article for the Melbourne *Herald*, stressing the necessity of it. 'For thirteen hours of every weekday there is no telephone service between Australia and Port Moresby, the administrative and business capital of PNG. It operates only from 7 a.m. to 6 p.m. The weekends are worse.'[1]

Support also came from outside PNG. In September 1966, Sir Giles Chippindall, who for ten years had been Director-General of the PMG's Department in Australia, and Chairman and Vice-Chairman of OTC, publicly stated that the inadequacies of telecommunications in PNG were a hindrance to the development of old and new industries. Telecommunications must be given a higher priority in government planning, he said. The General Manager of the Dillingham Corporation, Frank Hurd, echoed these sentiments.

In the House of Assembly, Frank Martin lashed out at existing P and T telecommunication equipment, which, he said, looked like 'something out of a Meccano set. If you want to make a call from Wewak to Madang, you might as well poke your head out the window and yell. Mr Carter would probably do well to start an in-service training programme for carrier pigeons!'

'It would take at least two years to improve our links, even if money is obtained immediately, because of the current long manufacturing delay', replied Bill Carter,

---

1 The circuits to Sydney were HF radio with nominal operating times from 7 a.m. to 6 p.m., but as with all HF circuits, a lot depended on sunspot activity and its effects on the propagation of the radio signals. The circuits were seldom of commercial (usable) quality for more than seven or eight hours a day, and often were unusable for a much shorter time.

still a Member of the House. 'It appears that communications are going to get worse before they get better', the editor of the *South Pacific Post* commented, gloomily. 'Business efficiency will be severely hampered'.

It was into this climate of public clamour that a delegation, led by R.J. Goodman arrived in PNG, in March 1967, to review progress and examine possible projects for World Bank financial assistance. The World Bank Report of 1964 had become the basis for a new Australian policy in PNG. The Minister for Territories, C.E. Barnes (Hasluck had left the portfolio in December 1963), was wholeheartedly in support of the main thrust of the World Bank Report. It recommended that the Administration concentrate on the rapid economic development of favourably situated districts at the expense of the remote and poorer regions. At the same time, the Report recommended a reduction in the standard of services provided by government in PNG, and called for an increased effort by Papua New Guineans in the development of their own country. It was an economists' report, virtually ignoring political realities. The Hasluck policy of uniform, balanced development had been discarded.

The Report dealt at length with the importance of the Department of Agriculture, Stock and Fisheries to the economic development of PNG, and that Department consequently began to plan agricultural projects of various kinds which it hoped would attract World Bank finance. The Department had ample reason to be optimistic in view of the Report's recommendations; moreover, the former Director of Agriculture, Frank Henderson, was now Assistant Administrator and responsible for economic affairs. He believed the main emphasis of the Report to be correct, as did the powerful head of the Department of Territories, George Warwick Smith. Despite all this, Bill Carter considered that the case he had presented to Canberra for World Bank support was strong enough to succeed. Clearly, rapid economic growth could hardly be achieved with poor national communications.

Carter's hopes, and those of business and community leaders in PNG, were dashed when the World Bank team leader, R.J. Goodman, announced on his arrival that plans to improve the nation's telecommunications were not on the list of projects provided by Canberra. Mattingley wrote in an editorial in the *Post*:

> All sections of the community will be appalled at this statement. Mr W.F. Carter says that his Department had prepared fully documented proposals for a loan twelve months ago. PNG cannot afford to stagger along much longer with the present hopelessly inadequate 'phone links'.
>
> It soon became apparent that Goodman and his team had not seen the P and T submission that had been sent to Canberra the year before. The World Bank Mission had been well briefed on a number of possible projects (none of which had been properly documented), that the PNG Electricity Commission and the Departments of Public Health and Agriculture, in particular, wanted to develop with loan funds, but it seemed unaware of the desperate need to improve telecommunications. The Administrator, D.O. Hay,[2] publicly admitted the failings of the existing system, and the Economic Adviser, A.W. McCasker, also stressed the importance of

2 Hay had replaced Sir Donald Cleland in January 1967. Cleland retired after a period of service second only to that of Sir Hubert Murray.

telecommunications to national development. But it now seemed likely that P and T would miss out on a development loan.

There is little doubt that the Department of Territories in Canberra, and certain departmental directors in PNG, were against such a loan, and it is probable that Carter's submission had been quietly shelved. Keith Mattingley did not intend to let the matter rest. As a Public Servant, Bill Carter was limited in what he could do; Mattingley, a newspaper editor, was not. He wrote to me in 1981:

> On probing the position further in the Administration and Department of Territories, I found a definite attitude that telecommunications would not rate for a World Bank loan on this occasion for two reasons — they were a 'luxury the Territory could not afford', and, in any event, 'a documented submission had not been prepared'. Bill Carter was astounded when I told him of the claim that no submission existed on telecommunications. Immediately he sent me a confidential copy of what Peckover had prepared a long time before. Further checking led me to believe that this submission was the *only* fully documented submission for special funding which had been sent to Canberra up to that stage. And the World Bank delegation knew nothing about it! So I helped Bill Carter to get a copy direct into the hands of the World Bank people.

The P and T submission, allied with the public outcry for better telecommunications that was at its height when Goodman and his colleagues arrived, proved to be powerfully effective. On leaving PNG, Goodman announced that 'improved transport and communications are among the main priorities for World Bank help'.

Events now proceeded at a speed that was positively dazzling by the standards of international financing. Almost immediately following Goodman's return to Washington in March 1967, the World Bank asked Canberra for permission to send a two-man team to PNG to make a Bank assessment of the telecommunications loan proposal. Canberra promptly agreed. The Department of Territories and its Secretary, George Warwick Smith, had thus failed in their effort to have the P and T loan shelved. Announcing the agreement, C.E. Barnes said in September that there was an 'urgent need' for an improvement of telecommunications in PNG, to keep pace with accelerated economic development.

In the same month, a World Bank financial analyst, N. De Sirkar, and an engineer, R.L.C. Grant, began a month-long visit to PNG. They examined the P and T proposal in great detail. They were much impressed with what they saw and were told. With the help of Bill Peckover, Frank Alsop and others, De Sirkar and Grant put the P and T proposal into an entirely different format, using projected balance sheets and expenditure and revenue accounts over the anticipated repayment period of the loan, as required by the Bank. The World Bank regarded telecommunications as 'commercial-type ventures', and thus used the accepted commercial practice of projection balance sheets and 'sources and applications of funds' statements, instead of costs/benefits studies, when assessing possible loan projects.

In 1968, the first World Bank development loan to be granted to PNG was given to the Department of Posts and Telegraphs, and the great leap forward in telecommunications began.

Looking back on this turbulent era, Bill Carter is today unrepentant for the rather unconventional part he played in obtaining the loan:

> We were the only department with a full, detailed proposal ready for the World Bank economists. We got a head start on the others. The other departments — particularly Agriculture — were most upset. There was a great reluctance in Territories, too, to allow it. We got away with it, though. It was most irregular, of course, for me to send Goodman a personal copy of the P and T submission, but it worked. The granting of the loan was a great morale-booster for P and T staff, not only for Bill Peckover and Vern Hodgson who initially worked up the draft submission, but also for Tom Pearson, Tas Sexton, Gordon McLachlan[3] and others, from top to bottom of the organization.

A lot of negotiating, however, lay ahead before the loan was actually received, and when it was, there were strings attached. Most of the negotiations took place in the United States, with Bill Carter representing P and T on the Australian team. The loan sought — the equivalent in various currencies of $US 7 million — had to be formally guaranteed by the Australian government, and this required the enactment of the necessary legislation. Finally, the International Bank (Telecommunications) Loan Agreement Ordinance 1968 was passed by the PNG House of Assembly, which ratified the loan agreement reached on 28 June 1968.

Before the Ordinance was passed, the Department of Posts and Telegraphs had issued on 1 March 1968 an *Implementation Plan for the Development of Telecommunications Network*, outlining the way it was proposed to proceed if the loan was granted. In his foreword, Bill Carter stated that the plan was to be considered as an extension of the National Telephone Plan of 1964. The World Bank loan would be used, in addition to an input by the Administration then estimated to be $8.2 million, over the period 1968-73 to provide 'a fully integrated network with full closed number subscriber trunk dialling facilities'.

Carter acknowledged the assistance of the Engineering and Telecommunications divisions of the APO in the development of the Implementation Plan, and within P and T gave particular credit to the Group Engineer, Planning, Graham Davey, and the Traffic Officer, Development, Peter Simpson, who with assistance from many of their colleagues in the Department, drew up the Plan together.

The loan was granted, and the dream of Carter, Peckover, Tom Pearson, Vern Hodgson and many others in P and T became a reality. But although the loan was finalized on 28 June 1968, much had still to be done before a cent of the money could

---

3 McLachlan was the Costing and Stores Officer of P and T. A qualified accountant, with a background as Senior Costing Officer with the APO, McLachlan was recruited to introduce the APO costing system into P and T, and this he did over a considerable period of time, with great success. The documentation he and his staff produced was used by the Department's engineers to prepare estimates for future projects and other secondary purposes. For a number of reasons, but principally because it was the sort of 'historical' costing system that gathered together costs incurred in the past and gave the engineer managers no information on costs as they arose, the APO costing system never proved appropriate to the small but dynamic P and T Department. It did, however, introduce a much-needed degree of financial and stores control and order into what had been a largely neglected sector of the Department.

be spent. P and T had been in a frenzy of activity from well before the arrival of the De Sirkar-Grant appraisal team in September 1967. During that visit, the Department for the first time learned of certain special World Bank tendering requirements that appeared to threaten the equipment standardization policy developed by P and T.

These requirements were designed to ensure that manufacturers of equipment in each and every one of the developed countries which jointly owned the World Bank had equal opportunities to have their equipment purchased with Bank loan money. In East Africa, as in some other Third World countries, past insistence by the Bank on these tendering conditions had resulted in the purchase of equipment of competing types and manufacture. In one quoted instance, a single large exchange building housed three entirely different types of telephone exchange, manufactured by different companies in different countries. Each exchange required its own specialist mainten-ance staff and used different spare parts, procedures and manuals. All kinds of operational problems naturally resulted.

Fortunately, the Bank had already recognized that changes in tendering require-ments were essential if the East African situation was to be avoided. After much discussion, the Bank agreed with the P and T decision to standardize on the APO/L.M. Ericsson crossbar exchanges for PNG, and because there were three manufacturers of this equipment — L.M. Ericsson of Australia, but with Swedish parentage; STC of Australia, but with American parentage, and Plessey of Australia, but with British parentage — allowed P and T to specify this exchange type when calling tenders for future exchange extensions.

As in past years, the Australian Post Office was a good friend to P and T during this period. The APO owned (and its present-day successor, Telecom Australia, still owns) the patent rights to the modified circuitry of the L.M. Ericsson equipment, but allowed P and T to use it without payment of royalties. Over the years, the APO has kept P and T fully informed of each of the thousands of modifications to the original design. Another good friend was the head of the Telecommunications Division in the World Bank, C.P. Vasudevan, and his team of experts.

With the uncertainties created by the previous tendering policy of the Bank overcome, the Department of Posts and Telegraphs geared up for the enormous task of carrying out the works programme made possible by the Bank loan. It was obvious to Bill Carter that the magnitude of the project was such that the Department would have to be restructured and expanded. In 1968, the Public Service Board agreed to the provision of a position of Project Engineer, to be responsible for the organizing of the initial repeater station programme. The job was given to Vern Hodgson. In May 1970, the Board allowed a small restructuring exercise that removed the administrative side of Bill Peckover's position, leaving him as Assistant Director, Operations (that is, non-engineering and technical aspects) and Postal. The new position of Assistant Director, Administration, was created.

The Department was by this time rapidly developing into a business undertaking, but it was not until May 1971, that the Board finally approved an appropriate organ-ization, that brought together all telecommunications activities under a First Assistant Director. Bill Carter assigned Peckover to this job, with Tom Pearson, Graham Davey and Peter Vorpagel in the new positions of Assistant Directors, Construction, Planning and Operations, respectively.

In the 1968-9 *Annual Report* for the Territory of Papua, the P and T goals were succinctly stated:

> Broadly speaking, the planning is based upon an increase in demands for telephone services of approximately 15 per cent per annum. This includes a provision to overcome the present backlog as well as the need to provide for facilities to connect the local systems with reliable trunk circuits and with the SEACOM cable at Madang. At present, it is intended to construct a total of 47 telephone exchanges with a capacity of 22 600 lines by June 1974. Of these lines 21 810 will be connected with automatic exchanges and approximately 90 per cent will have long distance dialling facilities . . . it is expected that by the end of 1973-4 there will be 374 telegraph channels in operation [which] will also enable the introduction and expansion of a Territory-wide Telex service'.

It was an ambitious programme, but one which Carter and his Department knew they could achieve. The World Bank loan carried with it certain conditions and constraints. Worldwide tenders had to be called for all major telecommunications equipment purchased with loan funds. Consultants were required to be retained, to help in the assessment of tenders and assist in project management. (The established P and T relationship with Preece, Cardew and Rider was to prove invaluable here.) The Department was required to abandon the old annual budget, Treasury-style of accounting, and adopt fully commercial accounting. Perhaps most importantly, P and T was obliged to accept the objective of a net internal rate of return of twelve per cent on its overall capitalization *including* the World Bank component.

Bill Carter considers this obligation was an excellent thing for P and T. All in the Department quickly became 'commercially minded' as a result: the message was rapidly accepted that before a dollar could be spent on the development of the telecommunications chain, it had first to be earned.

During the next few years, the telecommunications network of PNG was improved at a startling rate. The date of completion of the works programme covered by the initial Bank loan was extended to 31 December 1972. So rapid was the rate of progress that P and T had little difficulty in negotiating another World Bank loan, for $US 10 million, on 4 May 1972; covering the period 1972-5.

It should be noted that Postal Services also benefited from the first World Bank loan. Although Bank loan funds had to be used for overseas contract purchases, funds for the internal PNG component of the project were provided by the PNG Treasury. Included in this component were buildings of various kinds.

In a number of locations, including Goroka and Wewak, a modern post office was tacked onto new buildings erected for the telecommunications project. The World Bank had no objections, since P and T did not use loan funds, and nobody in the PNG Administration appeared to be aware of what was happening. As a result, a number of towns got new post offices because of the telecommunications project.

The physical statistics of the progress made are impressive, but they hardly reveal the enormous dimensions of the achievement and the human dedication involved. At the end of the first year of the World Bank programme (1 July 1968-30 June 1969), there were 13 automatic telephone exchanges in PNG and 19 manual, with a total lines capacity of 13 490 and with 9 175 subscribers. There were 17 647 telephones connected. By 30 June 1975, there were 36 automatic exchanges and only 5 small manual exchanges, with a total line capacity of 26 360. Connected to these exchanges were 32 857 telephones and 16 949 direct lines. The automatic exchanges were located at Alotau, Arawa, Banz, Bomana, Boram, Boroko, Bulolo, Finschhafen, Gerehu, Goroka, Kagamuga, Kainantu, Kavieng, Kerema, Kerevat, Kieta, Kimbe, Kokopo, Kundiawa, Lae, Madang, Maprik, Mendi, Minj, Mount Hagen, Nairovi, Panguna, Popondetta, Port Moresby Central, Rabaul, Samarai, Sogeri, Toleap, Vanimo, Wau and Wewak. Manual exchanges were located at Daru, Lorengau, Namatanai, Sohano and Tapini, with a total line capacity of only 500. Although still dependent upon operators, these manual exchanges were more efficient than those of earlier years.

The automatic exchanges were mostly of the crossbar-switching type, replacing the now obsolete pre-2000 Strowger step-by-step exchanges which P and T inherited. The crossbar system was itself being overtaken by computer technology, still evolving, but in the late 1960s crossbar switching was the best that was generally available and is still the type most commonly employed throughout the world. It possessed a number of fundamental advantages over the earlier pre-2000 Strowger types, eliminating the rotary switches which had required constant attention and enabling more flexible interworking between exchanges. In the old exchanges, a call found its own way through the system as the digits of the number were dialled by the subscriber. The crossbar exchange, on the other hand, stored all the data of the digits of the number dialled, and selected the best path through the exchange to complete that call.

Important though this upgrading of local exchanges was, the really dramatic advance came with their interconnection with high quality trunk links — the heart of the programme. The network was developed around the town of Lae, the planned telecommunications centre of PNG.

If one studies the map of PNG, one is immediately aware that the capital, Port Moresby, is geographically isolated from the rest of the country. As we have seen, the choice of Port Moresby as the capital was an accident of history; this was where white settlement began; a superb harbour, essential in those days of communication by sailing ship, was available; and the postal and telegraph facilities of Thursday Island and Cooktown were within acceptable limits of travel. During the Pacific war, Port Moresby was the only major centre that remained throughout in Allied hands, and it became the major bastion of the Allies in their war against Japan. Lae, geographically, the obvious place for the capital of PNG, was almost totally destroyed, and its rebuilding took many years. Situated at the mouth of the Markham Valley, it is the natural gateway to the Highlands provinces, the home of almost half of the population of PNG. It is the coastal terminus of the country's major road, the Highlands Highway. It possesses at Nadzab what is potentially the finest aerodrome in PNG. Only a good harbour is lacking.

The choice of Madang as the SEACOM cable powering station was forced on OTC and its cable owner partners by the heavy siltation and resulting sea-bed mud slides in the Huon Gulf, where the Markham River discharges its turgid brown waters.[4] Originally, it had been planned to bring SEACOM to Lae, but the siltation problem made this impracticable. It is unfortunate that the Overseas Telecommunications Commission rejected P and T's arguments in favour of Lae, the logical choice, when the site for the international switching point was being determined. The already strained relationship between the two organizations was not improved by the OTC's stubborn persistence in installing the international gateway exchange at the cable terminal in Madang, using equipment that had been installed, but not used, at Guam which could not later be fully integrated into the PNG national network. But Carter and his officers did not change their plans: Lae was the natural and theoretical communications centre of PNG, and would remain so. Madang was the first town to be linked with the SEACOM cable, but Lae was the second, late in 1968.

The P and T plan was to establish the main trunk switching centre in Lae to connect the majority of calls throughout the country. It was to act as the hub of a wheel. Because of the nature of the geography of PNG, it was not possible for all centres of population to connect directly with the Lae main exchange. It was, therefore, decided to establish a number of 'primary switching centres', each connected with Lae, and each responsible for its own internal subscribers and for smaller outlying exchanges. The final establishment of the primary switching centres was at Boroko, Lae, Goroka, Mt Hagen, Madang, Wewak, Rabaul, and Arawa.

It was the linking of these primary centres and their satellites to the main trunk switching centre at Lae that was to excite popular imagination. Within the main centres, studies proved that underground cable — comparatively easy to maintain, and slow to deteriorate — could in almost all cases be employed to connect subscribers to the exchanges. No such physical linking, above or below ground, was possible outside the main centres. The job would have to be done with radio waves. As mentioned earlier in this chapter, initial plans called for the construction of ten mainland mountain top microwave repeater stations, and by the time the first World Bank loan was granted, a number of sites had been purchased and were available — Mts Ialibu, Strong, Scratchley, Shungol, Kaindi, Kegum, Kerigomna and Otto. Other purchases were in hand. The prospect of having to construct, equip and maintain repeater stations on these formidable peaks by helicopter was indeed daunting, but at precisely the right time world technology, nourished by amazing advances in the aerospace industry, came to the rescue, and enormously reduced the dimensions of the problem.

One of the conditions of the World Bank loan was that P and T should call world-wide tenders for all telecommunications plant covered by the loan. One of the tenderers was the Italian firm, Telettra Electronics, for the supply and commissioning of microwave repeater station equipment of radical design, employing solid-state thick film integrated circuits that reduced the existing five or six-step frequency conversion processes to a single stage. The Telettra repeaters were so small in size and required so little power that the equipment could be mounted in a small fibreglass shelter halfway up the microwave tower. The power consumption of a complete

---

4 I have made extensive use of W.A. Southwood's 1977 paper, 'Who's Got the Phone On?' in writing this part of the chapter.

receiver was in fact so low that primary batteries, requiring replacement only at six-monthly intervals, could be used instead of the massive banks of lead-acid batteries and the diesel generators of traditional designs. Moreover, the Telettra repeaters had a capacity of 960 channels, instead of the 300 originally envisaged. Experimental wind-chargers such as those employed on Mt Otto, which had by then proved unsatisfactory for the wind conditions encountered at the tops of the rugged PNG mountains, could be dispensed with.

There was one considerable problem: Telettra had not completed the development of the repeaters. Only prototypes were in existence. If P and T decided to adopt the Telettra repeaters, the risk of eventual failure had to be accepted. Carter and his engineers conferred with the Department's consultants, Preece, Cardew and Rider. After exhaustive consideration of all factors involved, it was agreed that the Telettra technology offered such striking advantages that the gamble must be taken. A number of visits to the Telettra factory at Milan convinced PCR engineer and partner, Doug Rumsey, that the gamble would, in fact, be low-risk.

It paid off. The repeaters were a year later in delivery than the conventional systems originally planned, but they proved to be incredibly reliable in operation, requiring minimum attention and producing superb performance.

Village people living in tiny mountainside hamlets in some of the remote districts of PNG became accustomed to the harsh clatter of helicopters during those exciting years of repeater station construction, carried out under the supervision of Tom Pearson, by this time (mid-1971) the P and T Assistant Director, Constructions. The work was constantly delayed by the adverse weather patterns so common in the high mountains of PNG, by fog, mist and rain, and by the high winds that often made high altitude helicopter flying hazardous. The machines were hampered by the strange assortment of cargo suspended in slings beneath their bellies.

Tom Pearson amply proved his worth during this heroic phase of PNG telecommunications history. He had earlier assured Bill Peckover that he would spend the loan money, should it be forthcoming, and this he now did, and obtained full value for P and T for every dollar spent. During the negotiation stages of each contract, and there were scores of them, Pearson invariably drove a hard bargain. Not even negotiators of the tough character of the Japanese were able to best him.

It was during this repeater station construction phase that the experience gained from the building of the initial Port Moresby-Lae microwave link was profitably applied. The Department could not afford to have tender offers loaded with contingency costs. Tender specifications were therefore prepared which had the effect of almost eliminating large contingency provisions. To achieve this, the Department accepted the cost of all helicopter charters, selected the sites for the mountain-top repeater stations and arranged for Lands Department and Native Affairs officers to carry out the necessary land purchases. P and T also cleared the sites and constructed the steel towers which would hold the microwave dishes. On behalf of P and T the Public Works Department built two substantial huts on most sites to house equipment and provide basic shelter and accommodation facilities for the engineers and technicians. All the stations were eventually equipped with STD telephones, to enable men trapped on the mountain tops by weather conditions to contact their families.

To Tom Pearson must go a large slice of the credit for the fact that only one of the contracts for the work done during the period of the first World Bank loan failed. Credit, too, is due to the Preece, Cardew and Rider Chief Resident Engineer, Charles Isherwood, whose brief covered not only the interests of P and T, but also those of the World Bank.

The contract that failed was later to become the subject of adverse criticism by the Auditor-General, because of a P and T decision to write off costs already incurred of some quarter-of-a-million dollars. This was instead of merely shelving the unsatisfactory equipment involved, which would have kept the Department out of trouble with its auditors.

The story of this contract vividly illustrates the pitfalls that lay in the path of the P and T negotiators during the period of the World Bank telecommunications loan project. It was for the supply of HF (SSB) Outstation Service base station transmitters and receivers, and outstation transceivers and operating consoles. The equipment would allow a base station to selectively call each of its outstations individually, without the need for stand-by call times, and would also permit the outstations to call the base station at any time, and with the secrecy of conversations preserved by 'block-out' facilities. Additionally, before writing the tender specification, the P and T engineer responsible conferred with the operations staff, and between them they managed to include in the specification just about every facility that could conceivably be wanted, then or into the future. Plainly, the new equipment would be complex.

The contract was awarded to the Australian subsidiary of a certain reputable British manufacturer, and was written around the supply of one of the company's standard SSB transmitter and receiver models for the base stations, and the manufacture of control equipment, consoles and outstation transceivers, to P and T specifications, for the rest. The largest part of the contract was the manufacture of the transceivers.

By 1973, it was obvious that real troubles were emerging. Although the base station equipment was up to Company specifications, the transceivers were another matter. P and T radio technicians were unable to make a single new outstation system work effectively. There were endless talks and discussions between the Department and the company, and many design modifications were evolved. All to no avail. P and T threatened legal action, under the 'liquidated damages' clause in the contract, and soon a senior executive from the parent company in London was on his way to Australia, and to Port Moresby for talks with Bill Carter and his men.

While all this was going on, Carter, Bill Peckover, since 1971 First Assistant Director, PCR and World Bank representatives were studying the situation. The initial decision to award the contract to the British company had been appraised by PCR and approved by the Bank. It was soon apparent that P and T was in no position to take a really hard line with the company. Lou Varney, the HF radio expert assigned by the P and T consultants, PCR, to the loan project, had been pointing out deficiencies in the design concepts of the sets ever since he arrived in Port Moresby and was, moreover, critical of certain aspects of their manufacture. He had repeatedly reported the shortcomings of the equipment, in time for the Department to have taken action. But nothing had been done. The P and T engineers had been preoccupied with the new technology and the challenge of the overall telecommunications project, and little attention had been paid to this contract for equipment using well-proved HF technology.

Meanwhile, the London senior executive, after talks with P and T technical staff and with his company's representative in PNG, Chris Christenson, faced up to a Departmental team led by Bill Carter. Both sides were aware of the strengths and weaknesses of their own, and each other's, positions. After much haggling it was agreed that the company would, at its expense, modify each set already supplied to bring it up to specification, and would also provide certain guarantees in respect of total system performance. P and T agreed to accept delivery under the contract of a considerable number of transceivers still held by the Company, as a gesture of goodwill.

It was not really a satisfactory arrangement for either the Company or P and T. Modified or not, the transceivers would obviously do nothing to further the good reputation of the company in PNG. P and T knew full well that long-term maintenance of the sets would be a heavy load, not only absorbing large amounts of money, but also the time of many skilled technicians.

During the course of the negotiations it had become apparent that the London company representative was just as unhappy about the compromise reached as were Bill Carter and his radio experts. In private, the P and T team concluded that the best solution would be for the transceivers to be scrapped, with both sides sharing the resultant loss. It was not the type of solution proper to a Public Service department, but it made a great deal of sense to Bill Carter who was trying to run P and T as a business undertaking. A dinner for the P and T team and their wives had been arranged for that evening by the company at the Gateway Hotel, to cement the reaching of agreement. Carter told Bill Peckover to approach very discreetly the senior company representative during the function, and sound him out.

This Peckover did, taking the company man aside and talking to him without witnesses. The company man, instantly and with obvious relief, agreed to Peckover's proposal, in principle. Next day in Carter's office, final details were thrashed out. The cost to both sides was approximately $250 000. The base station transmitters and receivers and the operating consoles were put into service, but much simplified outstation transceivers were purchased from another company, and proved satisfactory.

The episode did end relatively well for P and T. The British company was at the time supplying similar, but not identical, transceiver equipment to the PMG's Department in South Australia, for use in the 'outback'. Carter offered the Department the unwanted sets for half price, which considerably reduced the total final loss to P and T. Nobody in P and T talked publicly about the transaction.

While these involved negotiations were in train, the work of constructing and commissioning the Telettra mountain top repeater stations continued. Then, in May 1970, came tragedy. A helicopter carrying Vern Hodgson and senior Telettra research engineer Carlo Naggi, crashed on the slopes of Mt Otto when a drive coupling fractured. Hodgson and his companion died with the pilot, Bill Venables.

The repeater station work had to proceed. W.A. Southwood took over Hodgson's duties temporarily, and an offer was made to a talented young engineer, Doug Rowell, to come back to PNG and carry on Hodgson's task.

Rowell had previously served in P and T, from 1965 to 1967, on secondment from the PMG's Department. He decided to return to Australia to further his professional development. Before he left, Vern Hodgson had asked him to consider staying on, to act as his understudy during the forthcoming World Bank loan project, but Rowell went. He worked for a time on microwave installations in Victoria, and was then impelled to enter the exciting world of space technology at Woomera, where he became a Deputy Space Director. The United States space effort was by 1970 beginning to wind down, following the deaths of the astronauts during the Apollo 13 mission. On learning of the tragic death of Hodgson and his companions, Rowell therefore accepted the offer to return to P and T.

The death of Vern Hodgson cast a deep shadow over the Department of Posts and Telegraphs. He was liked and respected both there and in the community generally, where he was a tireless worker for the Baptist Church. His influence on the planning and conduct of the loan project had been great. Ironically, like many other senior people in P and T, he had always had tremendous faith in the safety of helicopters, which in the late 1960s were something of a perilous novelty in PNG, particularly in the type of high altitude operations required during the construction of the mountain top repeater stations. The small machines then used were flying near their limits in the high mountains, where the air was thin, and the margin for error very small. No pilot, regardless of his skill or experience, could have saved his helicopter after a drive coupling fracture at a height of more than 10 000 feet, flying close to the ground.

Hodgson's wife, Grace, did not share his faith in helicopters. She was in Australia when the machine vanished, and returned convinced that he had been killed, although the wreckage, hidden beneath the canopy of the forest, was not located for two days.

Another five helicopters were eventually 'written off' during the mountain top repeater station work, but without loss of life. The flying was extraordinarily demanding on pilots and machines. P and T chartered helicopters on an hourly basis, and they were so expensive to operate that they flew whenever they were required, weather conditions permitting. Very seldom would a pilot switch off his engine after landing at a repeater station — it was too difficult to restart them at high altitudes. So the rotor blades were kept turning until it was time to take off again. It was flying that held no appeal for the faint-hearted.

The superior quality of the trunk network constructed during those years was in large measure due to the Telettra repeaters. They were the most advanced in the world, and only PNG had them in operation. Their use, however, could not be justified in every part of the telecommunications chain. Smaller centres did not require the 960-channel bearer capacity of the sophisticated Telettra units, and to serve these, several traditional high power consumption repeater stations, cheap, but with all their inefficient complexity, were erected on small capacity routes to towns such as Kerema, Tapini and Kainantu.

Wherever practicable, as the Telettra systems were brought into operation, the equipment thus superseded was used elsewhere. Units from the original 12/24 channel VHF system that interconnected SEACOM with Lae were later employed on the link between Kainantu and Goroka in the Eastern Highlands. The equipment was still in use, though long obsolete, in 1980, nursed with tender care by Roger Cragg, P and T's senior telecommunications technical officer in Goroka at that time.

The provision of efficient trunk channels between the mainland centres of PNG happily coincided with another development of vast significance, the Bougainville Copper Project. Initial field investigation of the Panguna area by the Conzinc Rio Tinto group began in 1964, and in 1969 the decision to proceed with the project was taken. Bougainville Copper Ltd. was formed in 1969, and copper production began in 1972. In 1974, concentrates to the value of $273.5 million were produced, more than half the total value of PNG exports that year. The Company was then employing over 3 000 Papua New Guineans and almost 1 000 Europeans. It remains the largest company enterprise in PNG, its operations vitally important to the future of the nation.

The scale of the planned Bougainville Copper operations (the biggest in the world) called for the most efficient possible telecommunications, and these were simply not available when the company was formed in 1969. Before the magnitude of the copper project was known, P and T had planned to link New Britain and Bougainville by HF-SSB radio waves, but this system could not possibly satisfy the indicated level of Bougainville Copper's demands. The sea distances involved were great, and beyond the capacity of the 'line-of-sight' links used on the mainland, where it was possible to provide repeater stations. The link was made using the tropospheric scatter technique.

In tropospheric scatter (or troposcatter) systems, radio signals are scattered from the troposphere, the lower portion of the atmosphere. High-power transmitters are used to feed the signals to large antennas, with diameters up to 120 feet, for reflection from the troposphere. Transmission performance of troposcatter systems is in practice highly reliable but they are expensive. Bougainville Copper's demands — unexpected when the initial World Bank loan application was made — were in fact so considerable that the Australian government (which was particularly anxious for the project to continue) provided a special grant of $3.5 million to PNG to cover the extension of the mainland telecommunication system to New Britain and Bougainville.

The contract for the work was awarded to Page Communications Engineers Pty. Ltd., and the completed system was finally accepted by P and T in August 1971. It linked Lae with Bougainville, a distance of 715 radio route miles. Of this total, 539 miles comprised water span tropospheric scatter links. The system was one of the most technically sophisticated in the world, and provided 120 voice channels throughout, except for the span between Rabaul and Bougainville (a distance of 237 miles), which supported 60 voice channels. The system required 10 repeaters and 7 terminal stations between the westernmost terminal at Lae, and the easternmost terminals at Arawa, Panguna and Kieta on Bougainville.

The town of Arawa was created, almost overnight, as the administrative head-quarters of the Bougainville Copper Project. Page Communications also installed an automatic crossbar telephone exchange at Arawa that went into service in 1972, with an initial line capacity of the 1 000 (increased to 2 000 in 1977).

This extension of the national telecommunications system to Bougainville was a triumph for P and T. Bill Carter attempted to interest the government of the British Solomon Islands Protectorate in a further extension to that territory — even offering to finance the work, in return for a major slice of revenue from resulting traffic — but this offer was rejected.

Carter served his final term as acting Assistant Administrator while the development of the copper project was proceeding. His main task was to improve the co-ordination of activity between the mining company and the Administration. 'I think I got just as much personal satisfaction out of this sort of role as I did out of getting P and T's World Bank loan', he told me in 1981.

As the new trunk channels were constructed throughout PNG, subscriber trunk dialling was introduced, a measure that Carter had long fought for. In 1970, STD became available between Lae, Wau and Bulolo, and was thereafter extended through the trunk network, until by Independence ninety-seven per cent of telephone subscribers had the use of this facility. International subscriber dialling (ISD) was provided for the first time during 1972-73, to telephone subscribers connected to Madang, Wewak, Vanimo, Boram, Goroka, Kainantu, Kundiawa, Mount Hagen, Mendi, Minj, Banz, Port Moresby, Konedobu, Boroko, Gerehu, Bomana, Sogeri, Kerema and Popondetta exchanges, placing PNG far ahead of development in Australia. Again, by Independence ninety-seven per cent of PNG's telephone subscribers had the use of ISD.

The development of the national trunk network brought only limited benefits to the Outstation Service. By Independence, there were 20 networks in the Service, controlling a total of 1 600 HF outstations, 1 054 of them privately owned. All had access to the telephone network, and as it was improved in quality with the changeover to the SSB mode of transmission, so the outstation links were strengthened. Over these years, too, the VHF radio telephone services, first introduced in 1974 for remote subscribers in the Port Moresby region, were extended. There were 18 networks in use by mid-1975, and although there were only 170 direct exchange lines connected, they provided modern, reliable communications to people and business enterprises in isolated parts of the country. The VHF service replaced existing outstation services, but only where the outstations were within VHF range of the base station.

The construction of the major trunk bearer systems was coupled with an extensive installation programme of multiplex and telegraph equipment, again centred on what was now known as the Hodgson-Naggi Telecommunications Centre at Lae, named in honour of the two telecommunications engineers who died in the Mt Otto helicopter crash. The Telex service had grown rapidly, with 294 subscribers by Independence. Both the post office telegraph system and Telex were operated through the first computer-controlled Eltex exchange to be used in the Southern Hemisphere, opened in May 1974: the 'brain' of PNG's advanced Telex and automatic telegraph system.

The list of major contractors to the Department of Posts and Telegraphs during the 1968-75 World Bank loan project included small concerns as well as many of the world's leading telecommunications and construction companies — Mitsubishi Shoji Kaisha; Nissho-Iwai (Australia); Marconi Electronics; Philips TMC; Standard

Telephones and Cables; L.M. Ericsson; Telettra Electronics; Frederick Electronics; Olympic Cables; Racal Electronics; Vinidex Tubemakers; Electric Power Transmission; Barclay Bros.; Watkins Overseas; Austral Standard Cables; Plessey; Sagem; and Nippon Electric. Helicopters were essential to the success of the national project; they were provided by Helicopter Utilities, Airfast Helicopters, and Ferguson Helicopters.

During the whole of this time, the World Bank kept a close eye on the operations and performance of P and T. Bank experts visited PNG about once a year, and they inspected every phase of the work. A Project Performance Audit in mid-1975 considered that the Department had been 'remarkably successful, in spite of a very challenging environment. Physical achievements were substantially on target; institutional improvements included conversion of P and T to a dynamic organization operating profitably on a commercial basis'. Over the period of the first World Bank loan, 12 000 lines had been added to local telephone networks, and microwave and VHF routes now linked the most important centres. During the course of the project, 18 poor quality long-distance radio circuits had been replaced by 500 high-quality circuits with service meeting international standards, and access to the SEACOM cable had been gained from main centres. The Bank's second loan assisted in providing another 10 000 local lines, and in the replacement of 3 300 lines of obsolescent equipment. Five new microwave and VHF spur routes had been provided with 650 additional long-distance circuits on these and the earlier routes, and the national Eltex exchange was established. It was a staggering achievement in so short a time.

The full cost of the programme was not, of course, covered by the World Bank loans (which were repayable at interest rates of around eight per cent over 20 years). The Telecommunications Loan Project did not finally conclude until June 1977; the government financial contribution actually exceeded the total World Bank input. At 30 June 1975, what were classed as 'government advances' to P and T stood at K25.3 million (which included the Australian government allocation of $3.5 million for the New Britain-Bougainville extension).

It will be recalled that one of the principal conditions attached to the first Bank loan was the adoption of fully commercial accounting by P and T, and the acceptance of the objective of a net internal rate of return of twelve per cent on its overall capitalization, including the World Bank component.

When the first loan was granted, P and T was operating at a substantial annual loss. The Telecommunication deficit in the 1967-8 financial year amounted to $271 128. The total value of P and T fixed assets at the end of the 1969-70 financial year (when Telecommunication losses were $79 128) amounted to $10.3 million. This was the last loss year. By 30 June 1975, the value of P and T assets had climbed to K37.9 million, of which K34 million were telecommunication assets. A profit of K3 million was made that year, only K134 000 of it by Postal Services. Telecommunications thus made a rate of return on its net assets of almost ten point five per cent, short of the target figure of twelve per cent but nevertheless a highly satisfactory result. (The Bank was later to agree that the figure of twelve per cent was too high.) And it was obtained without increasing the postal rate or telecommunications tariffs. From the 1974-5 profit, P and T made a voluntary payment of K1 045 000 to the Department of

Finance, as the first installment of interest due (since the Department of Posts and Telegraphs was now operating on a commercial basis) on the 'government advances'.

Fully commercial accounting was successfully adopted within P and T as required by the World Bank. From the very beginning, Bill Carter had tried to run the Department along business lines, within the constraints of Public Service rules and regulations, and he welcomed the Bank direction. Tas Sexton had, in fact, been keeping two sets of books for some years past. One set were those required by the Treasury annual budget system, showing the expenditure of departmental funds vote item by item, in traditional Public Service Treasury fashion. There were no provisions in this system for profit and loss statements, balance sheets and so on. In an attempt in 1958 to identify the true commercial worth of P and T, Carter asked Sexton to open a second set of books, showing expenditures and revenues in the normal commercial manner. P and T actually had more latitude in the handling of bulk funds received from the Treasury than other departments, but all P and T revenues were paid directly into the Treasury consolidated revenue accounts, and so the 'commercial' set of P and T books were notional, not real, and could not be the subject of a normal audit. Nevertheless, they did provide a reasonably accurate indication of P and T's commercial position. Keeping these books became the personal responsibility of Frank Alsop, and they were continually used by Bill Carter as a management tool.

Immediately after the World Bank loan agreement was finalized agreement was reached with the Treasurer, A.P.J. Newman, for P and T to operate on a fully commercial basis along similar lines to the British and Australian post offices. This required the passing of new P and T legislation, and corresponding amendments to the Treasury Ordinance.

The initial draft of the new P and T Finance Bill was prepared by Bill Peckover, assisted by Frank Alsop and others, using APO legislation as a guide. This draft — as all-embracing as it could be made — was used as the basis for protracted negotiations with the Treasury Department, and these were ultimately concluded to the satisfaction of P and T. Amendments to the Treasury Ordinance freed P and T from its provisions, and allowed the Department in future to keep its own revenues.

The changeover to commercial accounting was considerably simplified by the experience already acquired from the earlier 'notional' accounts. The opportunity was taken during the transition generally to update P and T's accounting procedures. The changeover was handled with smooth efficiency, to the credit of all concerned, and particularly Frank Alsop, Tas Sexton, Gordon McLachlan and Peggy Heleweege, whose efforts at this time later earned her the award of the PNG Independence Medal.

In 1970, Tas Sexton left P and T and joined the staff of the Public Service Board. His place was taken by D.J. MacGowan, a Treasury man who had once served in the old Postal and Telecommunications Branch of Treasury. MacGowan's established contacts with the Treasury were to prove valuable to P and T over the following years. MacGowan was soon promoted to the position of Assistant Director, Management Services Division.

Tas Sexton was sorely missed in P and T at budget time, for he had been with the Department from the beginning and had, moreover, a natural ability with figures. He seemed to know instinctively when draft accounts were out of order and almost invariably took the correct action, saving the Department from embarrassment on many occasions.

The World Bank loan years, 1968-75, saw PNG achieve self-government and Independence. They were years of dramatic change, of the replacement of the old order with the new. They saw violence on the Gazelle, confrontations between the Administration and the people on Bougainville, and outbreaks of savage tribal fighting in the Highlands on a hitherto unprecedented scale. They saw constitutional change so fundamental that the rush to self-determination could not be halted, despite the doubts and fears of the villagers who made up the majority of people of PNG. They saw the rise of Michael Somare, from leader of a small, noisy, radical political party to undisputed leader of the state. They saw the flag of Australia peacefully lowered, and the flag of Papua New Guinea raised.

The nation was well served during these turbulent years by the strong communications backbone built up by the Department of Posts and Telegraphs. As the pace of change accelerated, so did the need for swift, secure telecommunications increase, and the national network was equal to the demands made upon it by politicians, district leaders, commercial interests and individuals, and by the Administration and its hard-pressed officers in the field, struggling to cope with emergency situations that never seemed to end. Their task would have been impossible without reliable telecommunications.

From time to time, however, critics both inside and outside PNG questioned the need for the ultra-sophisticated level of telecommunications provided by P and T. Some held that the vast sums of money involved could have been better expended elsewhere. Within the World Bank itself, there were opposing schools of thought over this question. One held that efficient telecommunications must exist in countries like PNG before any real development in agriculture or industry could take place. Another held that telecommunications were at best an unnecessary luxury. (In recent years, this latter view has tended to prevail.)

By 1973-5, the loan project was sufficiently advanced for senior officers of P and T to take time to think about who was using the services provided, and why. At about this period, too, serious questions were being asked in the World Bank about the 'economic' values of telecommunications and funds were being provided for research into this subject.

In early 1975, one of the Bank's senior economists, Dr. J.J. Warford, visited Port Moresby, and in discussions with Bill Peckover and the then Director of Posts and Telegraphs, Israel Edoni, it was agreed that an independent research study should be undertaken to try and ascertain the true economic value of PNG's new telecommunication system. To ensure the impartiality of the study, it was further agreed that the task of managing it would be given to the Director of the Australian National University Research Unit in Port Moresby.

The study, commissioned by the Minister of Posts and Telegraphs, Kaibelt Diria, was undertaken under the direction of Dr David D. Evans, who was appointed Project Director in July 1975. Planned to occupy a period of eighteen months, for various reasons it was over two years before the report on the study was completed. Produced in December 1977, by Dr Evans and the Australian economist Elizabeth B. Bryan, the report, entitled *Access to Calls*, is the most important study of communications in PNG ever compiled, and one of the most significant to appear anywhere in the world. A massive work in six parts, *Access to Calls* concentrates on a wide range of vital issues, including who uses telephones, why they use them, and what benefits are gained from such use. It also canvasses the myriad reasons why many Papua New Guineans who appear to have ready access to telephones do not, in fact, use them.

Unfortunately, *Access to Calls* has never been published.[5] A small number of copies was roneoed and bound in paper covers and given a very limited circulation. It seems certain also that it has been consulted by many people, as it is available at the World Bank library in Washington, but they seldom bother to acknowledge it as a source.

The transition of the old, creaky telecommunications system into a smooth, sophisticated marvel of electronics inevitably brought with it problems as well as benefits. The new technology demanded a high level of competence on the part of those responsible for its operation and maintenance. So quickly was the transformation wrought that P and T found itself even more dependent upon the services of well qualified European engineers and technicians than before. For it was quite impossible to train nationals in sufficient numbers to an acceptable level of skill in so short a period of time. Indeed, no department of the Administration had replaced all, or even the majority of, expatriates in key positions with trained nationals when Independence came. Australia simply ran out of time.

In Chapter 10 of this book, the early efforts of P and T to train national staff were outlined, and as we have seen, by Independence Postal Services were more than ninety per cent localized. This gratifying success, unmatched by any other Department, was not achieved in the Telecommunications branch.

Critics today are quick to blame P and T for its failure during the colonial era to produce sufficient skilled and experienced national technicians and engineers to take over responsibility for the maintenance, operation and expansion of its highly capitalized, modern telecommunications system. Such criticism can hardly be justified. It is true that despite the expenditure of large amounts of money, and the work and dedication of many people, the results achieved were disappointing. But the basic causes of P and T's training problems were external — the poor standard of available trainees, and the relatively low Public Service classifications of jobs within the Department — which meant that recruits faced long years of training for poor reward. The Public Service Board in PNG and the Department of Territories in Canberra showed, moreover, little appreciation of the importance of the role that national technologists would play in the development of PNG. Smart school leavers all too often opted for training as doctors, teachers or lawyers, rather than as P and T technologists: the rewards and status were far greater, and the period of training no longer.

For twenty years, then, the Department tried first one training approach and then another, adopting and discarding different methods in the search for an effective way

---

5 In 1982, agreement was reached between the Secretary, Dale Kamara, and the Institute for Applied Social and Economic Research for the report to be published in 1983.

of producing competent teletechnicians (the term adopted after Independence) from human material lacking many of the skills considered basic in more technically-orientated societies, where telecommunications trainees could be expected to have at least a background of sound secondary education, a reasonable standard of literacy, and an easy familiarity with radio, television and the other electrical appliances found in average homes. In PNG, the typical P and T trainee came from a simple village environment, had little or no knowledge of electrical or mechanical devices, and had but a shaky educational background (usually with no Chemistry or Physics, and precious little Maths). He also typically possessed an imperfect understanding of English, the perverse language in which his technical training would be conducted. Given the formidable dimensions of the problem, the wonder is that so much was in fact achieved.

We have seen how formal in-service training of P and T national staff began in 1956, and the humble beginnings of the Boroko Training College. Staff training was almost an obsession with Bill Carter. He was forced to recruit six radio telephone operators from England, at large expense, in the late 1950s. This was work that men like Nelson Tokidoro and Cosmos Hannett[6] had proved could be done by trained nationals. Technical instructors at Boroko also knew that they had the unqualified support of their Director in their efforts to train Papua New Guinean teletechnicians and linesmen.

As was the case with postal training, 'on-the-job' instruction was given to a few national officers in the Telecommunications Branch by individual expatriates before the Boroko Training College began. Staffing levels in the early years of P and T were so inadequate, and the demands of the daily task so pressing, however, that few expatriate officers were able to spare much time for this activity. The emphasis in those early years was on getting the job done; the informal instruction of PNG nationals in the demanding disciplines of telecommunications was not given a high priority by many officers. It was not by accident that the first formal in-service training courses at the Boroko College were for telegraphists, technicians and linesmen.

As mentioned in Chapter 10, the initial courses at Boroko were based on Australian standards, modified for PNG conditions. They were of two to five years duration, depending on category, and their aim was to produce well-rounded national officers, trained to a level which qualified them to join expatriates in the Third Division of the Public Service. The PNG technician was to be trained to the same standard of competence as his Australian counterpart, since each would be working with much the same telecommunications equipment.

---

6 Hannet, the brother of the Bougainville politician Leo Hannett, was taught Morse Code and radio outstation operation by Jim Widdup, who, it will be recalled, was one of the original post-First World War AWA operators in the Mandated Territory. Widdup was at the time in charge of the radio outstation network of the Catholic Mission, Bougainville. He rejoined P and T in 1954, and Hannett followed in 1955. Widdup died in July 1967. Cosmos Hannett went on to become Officer-in-Charge of the Arawa outstation radio, and was awarded an OBE in 1979, for 'public service in communications'. His career is a shining example of how on-the-job training by a sympathetic European helped Papua New Guineans to advance.

To assist trainees to improve their English comprehension and expression, the Principal of the college, John Rampling, established a language laboratory, another pioneering initiative of P and T. The laboratory certainly succeeded in improving the trainees' quality of English, but their basic educational standard was so low that the hoped-for overall results were not obtained.

It soon became apparent that the training approach was not working. In areas such as telegraphist and linesman training, reasonable results were achieved, but the vital telephone and radio technician courses proved to be too much for the trainees available to P and T to master. It was simply too much to expect that the PNG trainee, severely disadvantaged by his education and background, could match the performance of the Australian. The failure and dropout rate in some early courses reached eighty per cent. By 1963, it was clear that the training methods in use were not producing teletechnicians in the numbers that would obviously soon be required if the World Bank loan, already being planned by Bill Carter and his engineers, was granted. Once again, the Department turned to the good friend of earlier years, the Australian Post Office, for help. Early in 1964, Bill Peckover (at the time Acting Director) asked the APO to conduct a review of the P and T technical training programme. In October, Vern White, Sectional Engineer, Training, of the PMG's Engineering Management Services Section, was sent to Port Moresby to undertake the review. He submitted his report in June 1965.

White's report was a lean document of eighteen pages, but it contained recommendations for new training methods very similar to those to be brought into use in 1980. Many of the basic concepts of White's recommendations were gradually, though hardly effectively, introduced. The greatest stumbling block remained the poor standard of education of the available recruits.

Briefly, White argued that the P and T training system should be closely related to PNG conditions and requirements, rather than to those of Australia. An Australian technician was required to be multi-skilled, so that he could move with ease from one area of technology to another. But this was not appropriate for PNG, because of the different stage of development of the country and its economy, and the lower standards of education. Instead, it was recommended, P and T should provide training only in the specific tasks the trainee would be required to undertake in the field. The existing syllabuses should be broken down into small blocks of training, each related to the various levels of skill in the work situation.

Bill Carter endorsed White's report, and gave instructions for it to be implemented as far as possible (some of White's recommendations required Public Service Board action). Engineer Jim Porter, who had some background in training, was released from field duties to carry out the suggested course revision. Unfortunately, Porter could not be spared for a long enough period to watch over the implementation of the 'block' courses.

Despite the partial introduction of White's recommendations, there was no worthwhile improvement in the standard of graduates from the technician courses at the College. During the ten years 1960-70, approximately 170 teletechnician recruits passed through the P and T training system, but only 23 qualified. In 1970, with Independence five years away, P and T was still almost completely dependent upon expatriate technicians. The national trainees who failed to qualify were not all lost to the Department, of course — many were employed to great advantage in lower-level positions. Nevertheless, it was clear that P and T technical training over this period had not produced the desired results. The office of the Public Service Board controlled recruitment for all Departments, including P and T, and recruits who could have become competent technicians were all too often directed elsewhere.

There were some successes, however. Communications (formerly Telegraphists) training produced sufficient competent men to meet P and T's needs. Linesmen training, too, was relatively successful. The real failure was in the area of most urgent need: telephone and radio technician training.

It was in 1970 that Gough Whitlam made his first visit to PNG as leader of the Australian Labor Party; he promised early independence for the country should his party gain power. He returned in 1971, when his electoral prospects were looking robust, and repeated his promise. It was clear that independence would soon come, whether or not the leaders of PNG wanted it. The Mataungan troubles on the Gazelle were then at their height; Bougainville was in a ferment; there was rising violence in the Highlands. No one could doubt that the political situation in PNG was on the boil, and that Australia would soon be quitting. There was a renewed sense of urgency in the air: when independence came, where were the national officers who would be needed to take over from the departing Australians?

The position in P and T was made more serious by the very success of the World Bank telecommunications loan project, which compounded the need for well trained national technicians. In 1971, John Rampling, Principal of the Boroko Training College, decided to return to Australia. He was replaced by Leslie Canute, an Australian who had spent the previous fifteen years in telecommunications training centres in Australia, Pakistan and Malaysia; Canute arrived in July 1972. Bill Carter instructed him to develop an effective teletechnician training system as rapidly as possible.

Drawing on the 'block' courses designed by Jim Porter and subsequently modified by Senior Technical Instructors Geoff Hutton (Radio) and Gordon Nielsen (Telephone), Canute produced a report on technician training that recommended a completely new approach to P and T technical training, although the syllabus itself would be little changed and the end result would be the same: the production of technicians in the Australian mould. What was radically different from existing P and T practice was the way in which this result would be achieved.

Under the existing system, technical training was given in a formal five-year course, and if the trainee, recruited amongst school leavers, could not keep up, he dropped out. Canute advocated instead the theory of self-paced learning, with no fixed timetables. 'Each student works at his own pace, and an instructor is always on hand for individual help and tuition,' he said in his report. 'The bright students use the instructor's help infrequently, which means that he can concentrate on those who need him most.' Both theoretical and practical training were to rely largely on programmed teaching machines, similar to those that Canute had used in Pakistan and Malaysia.

Canute's new concept of technical training was exciting, and promised a solution to P and T's long-standing problems. His report was accepted, but the new system could not be put into effect immediately. The teaching machines and programmes had to be purchased and delivered, at great expense, and it was not until 1973 that the first 'Auto-Tutor' and 'Practronics' units were installed.

While planning was proceeding, the new University of Technology, Lae, announced that as from the beginning of 1974 it would be providing a five-year Diploma course in Telecommunications. P and T could expect up to thirty-five technical officer graduates a year from this course. Since the Department was planning to graduate some thirty teletechnicians each year from Boroko under Canute's new system, the future looked, for the first time, bright. In 1973, five talented young officers who had just completed their five-year courses as specialist technicians at Boroko were admitted to the second year of the Bachelor of Engineering degree course at the University. These young men — K. Maitava, N. Herritrengi, J. Moang, J. Dresok and J. Buka — all successfully graduated. Others followed in their footsteps. Paul Phillips, a young Siassi man was the first P and T officer to attempt the engineering course at the Royal Melbourne Institute of Technology. He failed, but later transferred to Lae to complete his degree in Electrical Engineering.

1971 saw the introduction of a new P and T organizational structure that combined, for the first time, the technical operations of the Department (where its telephone and radio technicians and linesmen were located) with its traffic and marketing operations (where communications officers were located). Peter Vorpagel became the first Assistant Director, Operations.

Vorpagel was immediately struck by the dearth of Papua New Guinean technicians in his Division as opposed to Communications Officers. A review of current and future requirements followed, which eventually led to a decision by Bill Carter to try to arrange for the building of a modern telecommunications training establishment. Carter and his senior officers had long recognized the need for better training facilities. The Boroko site was too small, and already developed to its final capacity. As it happened, land was available near the University of Technology at Lae, through the foresight of Regional Engineer Bill Boyle. In the late 1950s, Boyle had purchased land for a HF radio receiver station some four miles from the town centre, and much of the area was vacant.

Peter Vorpagel did a great deal of preliminary work, preparing a case for the establishment of a new telecommunications training centre, and Bill Carter turned to Tom Unwin, the representative in Port Moresby of the United Nations Development Programme (UNDP) for support. Eventually, the project was included in PNG's assistance programme for partial funding by UNDP.

In 1973, an ITU (International Telecommunications Union) team, sponsored by UNDP, visited PNG. It was later decided that a new Telecommunications Training Centre would be built on the site at Lae. P and T would be responsible for the financing, design, construction and staffing of the Centre, assisted by an ITU team of ten training experts plus a project manager, for a period of five years. The ITU experts would work closely with P and T staff on all aspects of training, train new instructors, advise on training technology and develop new courses. It was estimated that the Lae Centre would cost the Department more than K3 million. The total value of the ITU input over the period of the project was expected to be in excess of $US1.5 million.

Albert Schlegel was appointed Project Manager by UNDP and ITU, for a period of one year. He arrived in Port Moresby in November 1974, ahead of the main body of the team, due in 1976 and 1977. He was welcomed by the Minister for Posts and Telegraphs, Kaibelt Diria, and by the new Director Israel Edoni.

When Papua New Guinea achieved Independence on 16 September 1975, national officers occupied many of the top-level positions in the Public Service. Some of these men were barely qualified by ability, experience or training to carry out the full duties of their positions, but they were the best available. The education system of PNG had begun to produce well qualified nationals before Independence, but time ran out long before they were available in sufficient numbers. And national pride — to say nothing of political considerations — demanded the filling of the more visible positions by nationals, qualified or not, by Independence.

Israel Edoni was clearly the best national officer in P and T to fill the top job. The Department of Posts and Telegraphs was fortunate that a man of his quick intelligence and character was ready for ultimate responsibility at this climactic point in PNG history.

Edoni was born on Misima Island, in the Milne Bay District. He received his early education, from 1951 to 1956, at the Bwagaoia Primary T School. An outstanding student, he won a scholarship to attend Slade High School at Warwick, Queensland, in 1957. On his return to PNG with his Junior Certificate, in 1960, he joined the Public Health Department and began to train as an Assistant Medical Practitioner at the Papuan Medical College. Here he came into conflict with a senior Australian officer, and in 1962 he left the College and joined P and T. He passed with ease through the 12-months Communications Officer course at the Boroko Training College, and then was sent to Goroka, to control the telegraph office there — the first national officer to be given this responsibility. In February 1964, Edoni became one of the first to benefit from Carter's efforts to secure advanced training opportunities for local officers in Australia and overseas. He went to Melbourne, to undergo training as a Traffic Officer. He successfully completed this advanced two-year course in competition with men from all Australian states, and became the first Papua New Guinean Traffic Officer. Joseph Auna was the second, and over the following years, other national officers were trained as Traffic Officers by the PMG's Department in Australia, including Moi Eno, Aloysius Mom and Bernadi Mandrakuah.

This exposure to the wider world outside had a powerful effect on Israel Edoni, and when he returned to Port Moresby in 1966 he began to observe closely what was happening in Papua New Guinea, and in the Department of Posts and Telegraphs. A number of able young P and T officers were emerging from the training system — men such as Matoi Sevese, Andrew Mungusi and Sydney Kulupi, and, on the postal side, Dale Kamara and Patrick Tomausi, and Edoni found common ground with them. These young men were frequently critical of aspects of departmental policy: the day of unquestioning obedience by the educated minority of Papua New Guineans was fast vanishing.

Following his return to PNG, Israel Edoni was appointed Traffic Officer for the New Guinea Islands and Mainland. A programme designed to equip him with a wide work experience was devised under the supervision of the Manager, Telecommunications, John Rutherford. Joseph Auna was put through a similar programme. As the first national officers in P and T, with top management potential and professional qualifications, Edoni and Auna were under a constant spotlight, their every move watched by Carter, Peckover and other senior officers. Both, naturally enough, had problems in adjusting to their new circumstances. Both knew they were under consideration for rapid promotion.

The part played by Bill Carter, as acting Assistant Administrator, in the development of the Bougainville Copper project was recounted in the previous chapter. Carter took the position at the request of the then Administrator, D.O. Hay, after A.P.J. Newman was forced by ill health to take sick leave. Accepting the position, Carter assumed that Bill Peckover would, as usual, take over as Acting Director of P and T.

The Public Service Commissioner at the time was G. Unkles. The need to localize key positions in the Public Service as rapidly as possible was generally accepted by 1970; in August 1971, the Public Service Board announced the new policy of accelerated training and localization that included a key provision giving preference to adequately qualified national officers over expatriates for promotion to advertised positions in the Service, and removing the right of appeal against such promotions. It was to expedite the localization of the Service that the various Departments, including P and T, established Localization Divisions.

On Carter's assumption of the position of Acting Assistant Administrator, Bill Peckover did not relieve him as Director of P and T. Without reference to Carter, Unkles informed Peckover that the new Acting Director of P and T would be a national officer, and one from outside the Department: Sere Pitoi.

Sere Pitoi, from Kapa Kapa in the Rigo Sub-district, was an able man, as he was to prove when he became Chairman of the Public Service Board in December, 1970. At the time of his appointment to the P and T directorship, Pitoi was an Associate Public Service Commissioner. It is no reflection on his ability to say that he was out of his depth in a technically-orientated department like P and T, and that he relied heavily upon discreet advice from Bill Peckover.

The appointment was not welcomed within the Department. Israel Edoni and Joseph Auna, the two leading national contenders for top positions in the Department, naturally felt slighted, and it was not an easy situation for Peckover, nor for Pitoi himself. All concerned were relieved when Tony Newman resumed duty, allowing Bill Carter to return to P and T.

Joe Auna later applied under the new PSB rules for an advertised position in the PSB, and won it. He left P and T, and later climbed to a high position in the Department of Forests.

Edoni then began to understudy Doug MacGowan, Assistant Director of the Management Services Division, after a period at the University of Papua New Guinea where he began, and then abandoned an Arts degree course. Management Services was a critically important division, containing the Finance, Personnel, Supply, Office Services, Methods and Training branches. On 25 September 1973, Edoni became the Acting Assistant Director, Management Services, and his permanent appointment was confirmed in December. MacGowan stayed on for a time, as Special Adviser to the Division. During this year, Edoni became the first Papua New Guinean to attend the Advanced Management Course at the Australian Administrative Staff College at Mt Eliza, Victoria. In 1973, too, PNG became an associate member of the International Telecommunications Union, and at the ITU Conference held at Torremolinos, Spain, in October, PNG was represented by the Minister for Posts and Telegraphs, Kaibelt Diria, and by Israel Edoni and a number of others. Thrust into national prominence, Edoni was rapidly developing his confidence and range of skills.

Meanwhile, the Department was pressing on with the training of national officers, in PNG and overseas, as the telecommunications revolution fueled by the World Bank loans continued. Andy Cox and his Localization Division worked hard to obtain more openings for P and T officers on external courses held under the Commonwealth Practical Training Scheme in Australia, at the International Training Institute (formerly ASOPA) in Sydney, at the Administrative College and the Public Service Board's Regional Training Centres, and at the University of Technology in Lae.

The mix of basic training in PNG, advanced training in Australia, overseas experience and practical work in the field achieved remarkable results in a number of cases, apart from Israel Edoni's. The up-and-coming teletechnicians who gained their qualifications during these, arguably the most exciting years of P and T, were indeed fortunate. They were involved in the conversion of the nation's local telephone exchanges to crossbar switching, and they saw the introduction of the new Telettra repeaters and the move into computer-controlled technology. One of the most outstanding of these officers was Sydney Kulupi.

Kulupi, another Milne Bay man, was to have a distinguished career with P and T. He joined the Department in 1960 and passed through the five-year technicians course at the Boroko College. After two years working in Rabaul, he was selected to attend the now defunct Marconi School of Wireless in Sydney, where in 1972 he became the first national officer to obtain the internationally recognized First Class Commercial Operator's Certificate of Proficiency in Wireless and Telegraphy. In the following year, Kulupi served as a Radio Inspector in the Radio Branch, understudying the Manager, Geoff Perkins.

Perkins, a PMG officer, went to PNG in 1968 to set up the Radio Branch. Prior to his arrival, all licences for PNG radio stations were issued under the Wireless Telegraphy Act from the PMG Department headquarters in Melbourne. PMG officers were sent from Melbourne to PNG for short spells of duty, but the communications line was too long for efficient supervision of radio licensing. Perkins was given a delegation to issue licences for PNG.

With the support of Bill Carter, he established an efficient Radio Branch at Port Moresby. He was largely responsible for the drafting of the present Radio Communications Act of PNG, and also for the establishment of a modern monitoring station at Laloki.

Geoff Perkins and Sydney Kulupi were members of the PNG delegation to the 1973 ITU Conference in Torremolinos. At this, PNG became the only country to be granted associate membership (later converted to full membership, after Independence).

After the conference, Perkins returned to his old Department in Australia, and Sydney Kulupi took over as Manager. After self-government, the Branch became the Regulatory and Licensing Section of the new International Telecommunications Division. (Kulupi was still heading the Section in 1981.) In December 1973, a record number of twelve technicians graduated from the five-year course at the Boroko Training College. Four of the eight graduates who specialized in Radio — Nicholas Tari, Charles Salayan, Mathias Sageo and Billiam Sourang — were nominated to go on to the Engineering course at the University of Technology. Melchior Kivarvere, the second P and T trainee ever to graduate with a specialty in Telegraphy, was sent to the United States in 1974 for further training. In January 1974, Ansgar Palauva, the first graduate from the University of Technology to join P and T, took up a position with the Finance Branch; he later became its Assistant Secretary. Two University of Papua New Guinea graduates, Alex Nonwo and Junius Turmur also joined the Department in November, 1974. A team of six officers, two of them nationals, went to the United States to do a course on the operation of the Eltex computer-controlled exchange due to be installed by the Frederick Electronics Corporation at Lae in May 1974. Other courses followed. Ten linesmen went to the Chermside Lines Training Centre, Brisbane, for a 20-week course under the Commonwealth Practical Training Scheme. Again, others followed. Special crossbar exchange courses for national officers were in addition begun at several centres.

The localization process was now removing familiar faces from the ranks of expatriates in the Department of Posts and Telegraphs. Jack Pettifer, whose service began in the days of Treasury control of P and T, left in 1973. George Pike returned to Australia in April 1974, after 22 years in the Line Section. Allan King, with a record of 17 years in the Telegraph Section, left the following month. Tom Pearson, the Assistant Director, Constructions, left P and T to become the first Director of Technical Services for the National Broadcasting Commission. His place was taken by A.P. Vorpagel, head of the Operations Division. W.A. Southward then became Assistant Director, Operations, and Andy Cox himself returned to Australia, after sixteen years in PNG. Doug MacGowan went in 1974. Bill Peckover, then First Assistant Director, retired on 30 June 1974. He was back at work the following day, under a contract agreement as a Consultant and Adviser on technical policy on telecommunication, postal and related matters.

It was not only Australians who departed from P and T. Two of the longest-serving nationals retired in June — Tom Taru and Taitus Takabai. Between them, these two men had over 80 years of service to their credit.

The period between self-government day — 1 December 1973 — and Independence — 16 September 1975 — was a time of great stress for P and T, as it was for the other Departments of the Administration. Key staff losses through localization grew to alarmingly high levels in many professional and technical areas, leaving serious gaps that could not be filled with national officers. Belated efforts were made to slow the localization process when it was almost too late, but it was virtually impossible to recruit replacements from traditional overseas sources in a climate of political uncertainty. To try to retrieve the situation, the government — effectively,

Michael Somare and his Cabinet — decided to seek new staff from the Philippines, where there was an excess of qualified people glad to accept employment at rates somewhere between those paid to nationals and expatriates in PNG. The first 142 Filipino recruits for the Public Service arrived in Port Moresby in May 1974. Thirteen took up positions in P and T. Another intake arrived in July.

More top jobs in P and T were taken over by national officers during this period. Nick Natera became Acting Superintendent of Supply and Transport. Patrick Tomausi became the head of the Philatelics Branch, and Dale Kamara Assistant Director of Postal Services. Young men such as John Walup and Leonard Sabadi received rapid promotion. Two talented officers from outside P and T — Kila Rabona and Alu Paku — were brought in to understudy Assistant Director positions in Localization and Management Services. Little progress was made in the localization of one of the smallest, but most important, divisions of P and T: Engineering Planning. Almost all the staff were professional engineers, and until national engineers began to graduate from the University of Technology, localization could not proceed. This division was headed by J. Griffiths. Terry Woolaston was the Engineer-Manager for the Eltex exchange project. Another specialist area within P and T where rapid localization was impractical was International Telecommunications, headed by Doug Rowell. This division had come into being when P and T on behalf of PNG took over full responsibility for international telecommunications from OTC after self-government, a story that will be told in Chapter 14.

During these pre-Independence years, Edoni and Bill Carter developed a relationship of mutual respect, even though marked at times by friction natural under the circumstances. Carter was trying to pass on knowledge and confidence gained from twenty years of running P and T to the man he regarded as his heir-apparent. A teacher-pupil relationship is often not an easy one, particularly between adults. There were other national officers in P and T of obvious ability, but Edoni demonstrated a balance of qualities that to Carter made him the logical choice to head the Department. For the end of the road was fast approaching for Bill Carter.

In April 1974, he made his last overseas visit as Director, to the UPU Conference at Lausanne, Switzerland. Edoni accompanied him, and Bill Peckover took over as Acting Director. After the conference, Carter went on leave and Edoni returned to PNG and took over from Peckover.

For the three months from 1 July 1974, Israel Edoni was Acting Director of P and T, advised by Bill Peckover. It was the first time that Edoni had borne full responsibility for the Department. He made some difficult decisions and Peckover, who adopted a low-key position in his advisory role, assisted only when asked. When Bill Carter returned from leave, Israel Edoni — whose title was now Associate Director — continued as *de facto* Director, with Carter to turn to for help when required.

With the knowledge that his PNG years were drawing to a close and that he was leaving the Department in good hands, Carter was anxious not to defer his final exit. His work was done. The future belonged to Israel Edoni. On 25 February 1975, Carter stepped down, and Israel Edoni became the new Director of Posts and Telegraphs.

Bill and Anne Carter returned to Australia with their family, where Carter rejoined the PMG's Department as an engineer. He bade his old colleagues a modest farewell in a brief letter published in the P and T house journal *Inside Line*:[7]

> Today I retire from Posts and Telegraphs in Papua New Guinea, and will live and work in Australia again. Having started the Posts and Telegraphs Department in 1954-5 and remained the Director for more than 20 years, I will be taking with me many happy memories.
>
> My happiest memories will not only be about the outstanding progress made by Posts and Telegraphs during the last 21 years, but also about all the Posts and Telegraphs staff that made the progress possible. We have all worked pretty hard, but we have worked together as a P and T team.
>
> To you and your staff I say a sincere 'thank you' for your team effort. I wish you all the very best in the future.
>
> W.F. Carter, ex-Director Posts and Telegraphs

7 In 1973, Richard L. Rider, an American specialist in communications based at the University of Hawaii, was asked by Bill Carter to examine internal communications between the various levels of management in P and T, and to make recommendations for improvement. Rider made his investigation in May and submitted a lucid and stimulating report in June 1973. Among his many recommendations was one stressing the need for a well-produced P and T house journal, with the basic aim of strengthening communications between headquarters and staff in the field. *Inside Line*, launched in December 1973, was the result.

CHAPTER FOURTEEN

BRAVE NEW WORLD

On 9 December 1975, the Department of Posts and Telegraphs ceased to exist as a separate department of the Public Service of PNG. On the following day, the newly-formed Department of Public Utilities took over the responsibilities and functions of the former department, which now became Postal and Telecommunication Services, within the Department of Public Utilities.[1] The Civil Defence and Emergency Services, the Fire Fighting Services and Cemeteries of PNG were also transferred to the new department, but the P and T Services were not affected by this move.

Israel Edoni was appointed Secretary of the Department of Public Utilities. Dale Kamara became First Assistant Secretary, Postal, and W.A. Southwood First Assistant Secretary, Telecommunications. In July 1976, Doug MacGowan returned to the land of his birth (Rabaul) to take up the position of First Assistant Secretary, Finance and Administration.

In 1974, Michael Somare — then Chief Minister — announced the Eight Point Plan, a loosely defined set of economic and social principles that would guide the development of PNG. The basic intent of the eight aims of the Plan was to bring about a shift in the control of the PNG economy from Australians to Papua New Guineans. The Plan called for a fair national distribution of economic benefits, and urged self-reliance and hard work upon the people. After Independence, the Eight Point Plan was formally endorsed as the future guide for PNG development.

---

1 The Department of Public Utilities then came under two Ministers, Donatus Mola and Kaibelt Diria. The Ministry of Public Utilities included the Electricity Commission, for which Mola was Minister. Kaibelt Diria, who became Minister of Posts and Telegraphs after the 1972 House of Assembly elections, held the portfolio until October 1977, when Gabriel Bakani took over the full Ministry of Public Utilities.

The Eight Point Plan was a social and economic philosophy rather than a plan in the accepted sense, and in the PNG of today not much is heard of it. In the immediate post-Independence period, however, serious efforts were made to relate government policy to the Eight Point Plan. In a policy statement, the Minister for Posts and Telegraphs, Kaibelt Diria, said that 'the government requires the PNG Postal and Telecommunications business to be conducted in accordance with the Eight Aims. Or, in a very simple statement, P and T is to serve the community, to be self-reliant, to promote rural improvements and promote equality among our people'. He pointed out that the Department had to operate as a commercial enterprise, but went on to say that P and T had a dual role. 'It provides a social service and at the same time it is a business undertaking; consequently, it is necessary to provide some services at charges that give a reduced profit margin and offset these lower charges with charges for some services that have a high profit margin'.

As a service organization, P and T could not govern all its development priorities precisely in accordance with the Eight Aims, as Israel Edoni reminded the Loloata Workshop in May 1976. This brought together the senior executives of P and T as well as a team of advisers from the Administrative College and the Australian National University at Loloata Island, near Port Moresby. The aim of the workshop was to look at the objectives of P and T and how they could be achieved in relation to the Eight Point Plan, and to look at ways of improving the Department's efficiency.

Most of the policies that have been followed by P and T in the years since the workshop, paticularly in the provision of telecommunication services to rural areas, have been in the true spirit of the Eight Aims.

It was to be expected that the most notable advances would be in the field of telecommunications, for the trend in PNG in recent years, as in most other countries, has been towards a greater use of telecommunications and a decreasing reliance on the post, particularly in government and commercial circles. The decline in the use of the post was abrupt. In 1973-4, 61.8 million articles were handled by Postal Services; this figure slumped to 52.5 million in 1974-5, and levelled off to around 40 million in 1979-80. It has since commenced a slow climb. Much of the decline was due to the departure of large numbers of expatriates in the pre-and-post Independence period.

This sharp drop in postal business caused a corresponding decline in postal revenues. Postal Services profit in 1975-6, including the operations of the Philatelic Bureau, was K363 293. It was down to K275 151 the following year, and declined again in 1977-8. Philatelic sales over this period, however, steadily rose, and in 1980 exceeded K1 million. In the eighth Annual Statement to Parliament by the departmental head, dated December 1978, Israel Edoni stated that 'there is evidence to show that the Philatelic business is subsidizing the operation of post offices. Therefore, extension of postal facilities may in future be restricted by funds available'. Since then, profits from philatelic sales have continued to subsidize Post Office operations, although some new offices have been opened in rural areas.

The most visible result of the postal slump has been a slight decrease in the number of post offices in use. The peak year was 1972-3, when there was a total of 115 official and agency offices throughout PNG. At Independence, the figure was down to

106. By December 1980, the total was 112, 34 of them official and the balance agency; these are listed in Appendix A. Agency offices were controlled by local government councils, missions, companies and individuals under contract to the Department of Public Utilities. Twenty-three were still being operated by the successors to the *kiaps* of Australian colonial days.

The burden of this decline in postal business was carried by Patrick Tomausi. As noted in Chapter 11, Dale Kamara was appointed First Assistant Secretary, Postal, in 1975, following a departmental reorganization. In October 1976, Kamara became Deputy Secretary of Public Utilities, and Tomausi took his place. Under him were the Assistant Secretaries Post Offices (Lionel Haembo), Postal Planning (Julius Tamah) and Philatelic (Alex Nonwo).

Tomausi was faced with a situation about which he could do little. Such measures as discontinuing the international and national money order services from 1 July 1975 (the banks were providing better and cheaper money transfer services) trimmed operating costs a little, but could hardly reverse the loss of revenue. There had not been an increase in basic domestic postage rates since 1971 (and new rates were not adopted until 23 March 1981) and while this restraint benefited the people of PNG and was in line with the Eight Point Plan, it did nothing to help Postal Services to operate as a successful commercial enterprise.

During 1975-6, postal rates and charges were increased on international mail articles and some special internal services, but increased internal air, sea and road freight rates offset the revenue gained. During 1976-7, direct international air mail services were introduced to Japan, the Philippines and Germany, in addition to the existing services to Australia, New Zealand, the United Kingdom, United States, Singapore, Indonesia, Hong Kong and the Solomons. There was some saving in transit and handling costs, but again the amount was trifling. Increasingly, Tomausi looked to the revenues earned by the Philatelic Bureau to cover postal losses.

On 4 June 1976, PNG became a member of the Universal Postal Union, and on 3 November, of the Asian and Oceanic Postal Union. Membership of the Commonwealth Conference of Postal Administration was gained on 16 September 1976. PNG had come of age in the postal world.

The 1979 UPU Congress — they were held every five years — was the first at which PNG was represented as a full member in her own right. The Congress was held in September, at Rio de Janeiro, Brazil, and was attended by 1 500 international delegates. The PNG team was led by the Minister, Sir Tei Abal,[2] and included Israel Edoni, Patrick Tomausi, Smael Manikot, Julius Tamah and two expatriates, Ron Holmes, International Air Mail Adviser, and Wally Lussick, Executive Officer to Sir Tei. One of the issues to be discussed was the question of the cost of mails, a vital question for PNG in view of declining postal revenues.

The UPU Congress functions as an international forum for sorting out, and as far as possible solving, the postal problems of the world. At the 1969 Congress in Tokyo

---

2 Sir Tei Abal took over the portfolio from Gabriel Bakani in November 1978, when he was replaced by Wiwa Korowi, who was still Minister when P and T celebrated its Silver Anniversary in July 1980.

— attended by Dale Kamara and Bill Peckover as observers — an international system of 'terminal dues' had been introduced, in an endeavour to compensate countries like PNG which handled twice as much mail from Australia as the amount Australia handled from PNG. As a result, Australia had in recent years commenced to pay 'terminal dues' to PNG. The 1974 Congress at Lausanne, attended by Bill Carter, Dale Kamara, Richard Kavu and Julius Tamah, had set the rate of terminal dues at 1.5 gold francs per kilogram, but an investigation by the UPU Executive Council had since established the true cost to be more like 6 gold francs.

Travel and accommodation expenses for PNG's delegation to the 1979 Congress amounted to some K58 000, but it was money well spent. The rate of terminal dues was increased by more than five hundred per cent by the UPU, to 5.5 gold francs per kilogram for Letter Class and Other Items mail. PNG naturally voted for the increase. P and T estimated that as a result of it, PNG would earn some K3.3 million over the three-year period to December 1981. The increase was particularly welcome to Patrick Tomausi, since in that year, 1979, postmasters in PNG were granted a hefty increase in their wages.

It was in 1979 that Sir Tei Abal approved a proposal by Israel Edoni that an International Postal Affairs Division within Postal Services be established. Although the PNG Government had been granted full authority and final responsibility by the Australian Government for all internal postal, telephone, telegraph and telex services as early as 1972,[3] Australia continued to represent PNG on all major international forums until Independence. Now that the Postal Services of PNG had accepted full responsibility for the handling of the nation's regional and international postal affairs, it was plainly necessary for a special International Affairs Division to be formed. The proposal was developed by Patrick Tomausi, and he gave the job of establishing the new Division to Smael Manikot. It was formally established after Public Services Commission approval, in June 1980, under Manikot as Acting Assistant Secretary.

Manikot had gathered a great deal of international experience since completing the postal management course at the Asian and Oceanic Training School in Bangkok, with Serege Dada, in 1974. In 1975, he was promoted to the position of Assistant Controller of the Postal Planning Branch, and in November of that year accompanied the Controller, Julius Tamah, and the Special Projects Officer, G. Lund, as the PNG delegation to the Third Asian Oceanic Postal Union Congress in Melbourne. The following year saw him representing PNG at two international postal meetings in Bangkok, accompanied by Special Projects Officer Bill Green. In 1977, Manikot was in Manila on AOPU business for PNG, and at Peking, sponsored by UNDP, to study the rural postal service of China. After setting up the International Postal Affairs Division, his travels took him to Japan, Singapore, Indonesia, Barbados and Tanzania.

---

3 Les Canute became the P and T Training Controller in 1975. Geoff Hutton took over the position of Acting Principal of Boroko, and remained there until he returned to Australia in January 1978, after twenty-one years with P and T. Geoffrey Fopp, who had joined P and T in 1956, replaced him. Fopp returned south at the end of 1978.

By 1980, P and T's Silver Jubilee year, all Postal Services positions were filled by Papua New Guineans, although a few expatriates were still on duty as advisers and consultants. Postal Services headquarters were in Port Moresby, with Regional Managers at Port Moresby, Lae and Rabaul responsible for the efficient running of the post offices in their regions. But the rapid localization of Postal Services had exposed a dangerous weakness in the middle and higher management grades. The handful of men at the apex of Postal Services worked under great pressure, with inadequate executive support. These men — they included Tomausi, Tamah, Manikot, Richard Kavu, Alex Nonwo, Benjamin Rang, R. Lionel, Serege Dada, Tom Menei, John Walup, Moses Pinjo, Paul Paiva and Peter Pinu — had had the benefit of overseas travel and training, but this experience was of course not available to the average national officer.

After Independence, Australia continued to offer training opportunities for selected PNG officers, and the APO remained a good friend to P and T. One of the first to benefit was Kundi Miki, a Postal Training Instructor from the Bomana College, who attended a three-month course in Brisbane in late 1975. Other countries also offered assistance. P and T men continued to attend the Bangkok Postal Training School. The New Zealand Government conducted a six-week course on Postal Services for Overseas Countries in Wellington in January 1976. Sixteen postal officers, from African countries, South-East Asia and the Pacific attended; these included the Madang postmaster, Anthony Morea. Later that year, another six postmasters — Lausi Marere, Gregory Sali, Wapuk Kesum, Michael Uraliu, Evertius Seri and Joseph Malai — attended special postal management courses in Melbourne, Sydney and Brisbane, arranged by the Australian Postal Commission. Limited overseas postal training opportunities of this nature have continued to be available.

Valuable though this overseas experience undoubtedly is, the bulk of Postal Services training has continued to be provided in PNG, at the Boroko Training College, and, to a limited extent, at institutions such as the Administrative College and the University of Papua New Guinea. Unfortunately, postal training in the post-Independence years was not given the emphasis it should have received. It was not until August 1978, that introductory management courses for postmasters were resumed at the Boroko College.

Postal Service training and performance deficiencies were becoming so obvious by 1978 that Israel Edoni and Patrick Tomausi sought outside aid. At the request of the PNG Government, the Australian Development Assistance Bureau arranged for a senior postal training officer from what was now Australia Post to visit PNG and conduct a survey of postal training needs and priorities in the vitally important postmaster and postal supervision areas, to develop course programmes and to oversee their implementation.

The training expert chosen, Rodney Menzel, began his survey in March 1979. What he found disturbed him. Postal training had been allowed to run down. No specialized training courses of any kind were being given at Boroko for officers from the Postal Planning and Philatelic Divisions — these men were completely dependent upon courses offered overseas. Postal officer courses that were being provided were relatively low-level, based on out-of-date manuals, procedures and equipment.

Menzel was staggered to find only one postal instructor, although the establishment provided for three. Moreover, this man, Senior Instructor Mark Papau, was at the time also Acting Principal of the Boroko Training College.[4] A former schoolteacher, Mark Papau had received only three months field postal experience before taking up his training position. And two postmasters who were being considered as instructors had recently been charged with theft! Small wonder that Menzel found a 'surface only' treatment of the topics covered in the postal courses.

Menzel recommended the immediate suspension of all postal courses at the Boroko Training College. Mark Papau was transferred into a post office for on-the-job experience as a postmaster for six months. 'Before any further Postal courses are conducted', Menzel said in his report, entitled *Survey of Postal Training Needs PNG*, 'it will of course be necessary to recruit and train other instructors'.

Postal training thus ground to a halt. In his report, Menzel made a considerable number of suggestions designed to improve training methods and post office efficiency. He was critical of the frequent transfers of postal staff, finding that this adversely affected overall performance. He suggested that a new training programme be developed by a joint specialist project team from the PNG Post Office and Australia Post.

Menzel's major recommendations were accepted. In October 1979, he returned to PNG with three other Australia Post officers — Andy Holme, Ian Reddy and Dennis Ting — to work on the development of the new training programme with a P and T team of national officers: Pasco Boloti, Ben Daun, Kone Gobu, Kaiva Kako, James Kaluum, Joel Matage and two women, Rose Noke and Pauna Tito.

The inclusion of the two women in the P and T team was a notable advance. It is only in recent times that the women of PNG have begun to assume leading roles in national life. Pauna Tito was the first Papua New Guinean woman to join Postal Services, followed by Miriam Manikot, in 1973. Rose Noke joined in 1974 as a clerical officer; in 1977 she was one of three women — the others were Dorothy Wado and Margaret Isimiel — who for the first time joined with male staff in taking a Postal Officers Grade Four course at Boroko.

In January 1980, Rose Noke and Pauna Tito became the first women P and T staff members to be sent overseas for instructor training, to Bangkok and Manila respectively. Sadly, Pauna Tito was killed in a bus accident in Manila. Eleven others, all postal officers from various countries, died with her. Her body was brought back to PNG for burial, and she was a grievous loss to Postal Services.

Limited postal training began once more at Boroko in 1980, using training manuals and procedures developed by the P and T-Australia Post team. In April, eleven postal officers graduated from the new Postal Officer Grade Two course. At the

---

4 Bill Carter and his officers had been studying the possibility of employing solar cells to power repeater stations since the mid-1960s. Early cells were, however, very large and costly, and not suitable for P and T's needs. The technical breakthrough that was to make possible the solar powering of PNG's microwave communications system came with American experiments in solar cell design during the race to put the first man on the moon.

graduation ceremony, Rod Menzel said 'the new Postal Training Scheme has a magnificent future, and there is no doubt the next course will be better than the first'.

When P and T celebrated its Silver Anniversary, postal training was thus in hand once more. Menzel continues to provide supervision and advice as required, and there has been much discussion about the need for a new Postal Training Centre, perhaps sited at Lae, near the Telecommunications Training Centre.

With training once more on a productive course, Postal Services are today tackling a range of problems that have emerged during the post-Independence years, aided by advice from men such as R.A. Miller, once Controller of the Philately and Training Branch, who accepted a consultancy with P and T in January 1978, following his return to Australia. In short order, Bob Miller discovered that since Independence, Australia Post had been overpaid K30 000 because of a misunderstanding about the offloading point for PNG air mail in Australia. This was corrected. Another loss to P and T had occurred because no action had been taken to adjust gold franc terminal dues after the PNG national currency was revalued. Philatelic sales in Australia, too, had taken no note of currency revaluation. These matters were also adjusted. As a result of Miller's investigations, action was taken to improve mail circulation between PNG and Australia, and the collection of mail statistics, important in forward planning, was improved. A new sorting plan for international air mail was also introduced.

Miller in addition proposed a better procedure for the grading of post offices, one that would more accurately reflect the increased workloads and responsibilities of certain offices — in particular, Boroko, Lae, Rabaul and Arawa — that resulted from the dispatch of PNG mails directly to all parts of the world, rather than via Australia as had been largely the case in the colonial era. He suggested the need for a reorganization of the various branches of Postal Services and a reclassification of certain positions in recognition of changing work patterns. By analysis of traffic and rates, Miller demonstrated that P and T was incurring heavy losses on parcel mail to Australia, and he prepared a new schedule of rates for consideration by the First Assistant Secretary.

These, and countless similar problems, continue to crop up as Postal Services grapple with the complex task of administering a vital public service in the daunting economic climate of the 1980s.

After Independence, the steady development of the national telecommunications network continued, although at a less dramatic pace. In 1975-6, a national trunk exchange was installed at Lae, and this became the main network control centre for both the international and national telecommunications network throughout PNG. At the same time, the L.M. Ericsson Company installed a complete International Gateway Exchange at Lae to replace the Madang exchange that OTC had earlier foisted onto P and T. The old Port Moresby and Konedobu step-by-step exchanges were replaced by a new crossbar exchange at Ela Beach.

The World Bank loan project years had seen the completion of the major communications backbone, and although a number of new telecommunications projects were developed after Independence, the emphasis now changed to an extension of the system to smaller centres, and to the mass of the villagers in the rural districts. In

November 1969, the East Sepik District Advisory Council had called for the provision of a telephone link between Maprik and Hayfield. 'The only communication at present is by drum', said the Council, plaintively. Similar requests came in from local bodies all over PNG during the years of the loan project. Many of the calls were satisfied after Independence, and the work continues, new requests continually being received.

In recognition of the need to improve rural communications, from late in 1975, special emphasis was given to outstation services and small exchange projects, particularly those required to service a number of new economic ventures such as the Open Bay timber development in East New Britain, the Bialla Oil Palm scheme in West New Britain, the expansion of coffee planting in a number of areas and a general increase in rural agricultural production.

The changeover from HF double to SSB operation for the Outstation Service mentioned in Chapter 13 was greatly accelerated after Independence. Base stations were established at Port Moresby, Alotau, Daru and Mount Hagen during 1975 and 1976, serving SSB-equipped outstations in the Central, Northern, Gulf, Western, Milne Bay, Western Highlands, Southern Highlands and Enga Provinces. The following financial year saw new SSB base stations in operation at Wewak, Goroka, Lorengau and Kieta, serving the Eastern Highlands, West Sepik, Manus, New Ireland and North Solomons SSB outstations. The changeover to SSB operation was complete by the end of 1978. This was in line with PNG's international obligations in respect of the use of high frequency radio networks, now overcrowded throughout the world.

While the original Telettra microwave systems were being manufactured and installed, researchers and designers at the company's headquarters in Milan in Italy were perfecting second-generation mountain top repeaters. These had built into them facilities that allowed up to sixty channels to be 'dropped off' at any repeater station. They were put into service by P and T, and Telettra began a programme of updating every existing mountain top repeater station with the 'drop off' facility. This was completed before the end of 1980.

It is this facility that is today permitting P and T to extend efficient telecommunications services to most remote areas on the mainland, and throughout New Britain, New Ireland and Bougainville. From the mountain top stations, P and T can economically reach out to nearby towns with relatively cheap low-capacity systems. Base stations of new fully-automatic VHF radio telephone systems can feed into microwave drop-offs.

This single development means that PNG is no longer dependent on the launching, at some unknown time in the future, of a communications satellite for the South Pacific region in order to extend telecommunications services to remote regions. By the time such a satellite is in use, even the remotest remaining unserviced regions in the country will very likely have been reached by some combination of terrestrial VHF/microwave systems.

The improvement of rural telephone services was still mainly dependent upon the construction of a number of new microwave links when in 1976 the microwave radio network was extended from Mount Hagen to the Southern Highlands Province. (After Independence districts were renamed provinces). Two new repeater stations were required, at Kuta Ridge and on a rugged bluff overlooking Mendi, headquarters of the province. These were in addition to that already in existence 12 000 feet up Mount Ialibu. The new stations were constructed by Telettra engineers and P and T rigger teams. In use, microwave signals were beamed from the Mount Hagen radio tower to Kuta Repeater Station, thence by parabolic dish antennae to the repeater on Mt Ialibu and then to the new Mendi station, a large 'passive' reflector constructed of aluminium, of much the same size and dimensions as an outdoor drive-in movie screen. Microwave signals from Mt Ialibu were reflected off the Mendi repeater like a mirror, straight down to the Mendi Exchange. The distance was so short that no microwave electronic repeater equipment was necessary to amplify the signals, hence the term 'passive' repeater. Such a station also required very little maintenance.

With the commissioning of this efficient new link, the small capacity VHF systems that had been used until then were no longer required on this route, and they were employed elsewhere. So popular was the new service that in 1978 an additional 200 lines were added to the original 200 at the Mendi Exchange.

In 1978, too, a major extension of the microwave radio network from Mount Hagen to Wewak was completed after two years work by Telettra and P and T engineers, at a cost of approximately K350 000. Via repeaters between Mount Hagen, Mt Kegum, Mt Burgers, Mt Ambunti, Mt Albowagi and Wewak, the link provided initially up to 300 services, later increased to 960. Spur ('drop-off') services were extended from the new link as it was constructed, to the provincial centres of Wabag, Wapenamanda, Ambunti and Angoram, and the link to Maprik was upgraded.

Of even greater significance was the completion late in 1978 of the microwave link between Port Moresby and Alotau, in the Milne Bay Province. Intrinsically important, in view of the population to be serviced and a proposed vast increase in timber production in this underdeveloped province, the Moresby-Alotau link was the first solar powered broadband microwave system to be put into operation anywhere in the world.

By the beginning of the 1970s, the nations of the world had been forced to a recognition that oil was a finite resource that would become ever more expensive. With no proven oil reserves of her own, PNG began to consider the possibility of converting the heat of the sun into a more widely used alternative source of energy. In 1975, Gus Suarez, a Planning Division engineer, began a series of experiments which proved it was feasible to use solar power for the microwave repeater stations. The first solar powered repeater to be constructed in PNG was on the summit of Mt Nambamati, not far from Kaiapit in the Markham Valley; it was commissioned on 13 June 1976. Mt Nambamati was the experimental station used to prove the practicability of solar power for a major route, and was a considerable achievement for engineer Gus Suarez, and his chief, Assistant Secretary, Planning, Terry Woolaston.

Construction of the completely solar-powered Port Moresby-Alotau route began in June 1977, under the supervision of Project Engineer Jack White and the overall direction of Assistant Secretary, Construction, Arthur Bintcliffe. The work involved almost every section of the Telecommunications Division. Progress was rapid. Telettra engineers Pino Zollo and Virginio Archetti were talking to each other on the solar powered link between Mt Lawes — where the tallest tower on the Moresby-

Alotau route, 250 feet high, had been built — and Mt Borigoro by 4 October 1978. Colin Lancaster, a PCR engineer seconded to the Telecommunications Division, supervised the installation of the solar power system. Colin Schultz of the Operations Division and engineer Kevin Maitava worked with Telettra engineers on the radio side of the system.

Other repeater stations on this pioneer route were located on Mts Doigi, Wari'oro and Naura. The sites were cleared by linesmen and supervisors of the Bearers and Transmission Section of Engineering Services — Peter Bates, Mick Moloney, Igo Morea, Eruna Kappa, Vincent Wak, James Yal, Tawa Beube and the veteran Bert Hendry, who joined P and T in 1955 and was still serving in 1981. These men then built the towers and radio shelters, and installed the antennae. Others involved in the overall construction and installation work included Jerry Downie, Peter McKenzie, Basil Maynard, Tom Dickson, Miki Frederick, Fraser Richardson, Ray Otto, Simon Eremas, Pareke Arowa, Kedea Wari, Michael Froud, Raphael Kupe, Oscar Salcedo, Ray Amporo and Telettra engineers Dino Romano and Pietro Anibali.

The overall cost of the 960-channel Port Moresby-Alotau solar powered microwave link was some K750 000. It was commissioned into service on 11 December 1978. The new Alotau crossbar exchange, replacing an old Rurax, had a capacity of 1 000 lines. The Samarai exchange was modified by technicians Nokoma Padine and Victor Macaraeg to suit the special needs of this tiny island community, providing the 66 telephone subscribers there with 10 STD lines directed through the Boroko Exchange on its own route through the Port Moresby-Alotau system. Following the completion of the Moresby-Alotau link, a decision was taken to convert the whole PNG network of repeater stations to solar power by the end of 1981.

These new links, and others established in the years following Independence, certainly brought fast, modern telecommunications to provincial headquarters throughout the land, and to other lesser centres. New exchanges or facilities were opened in Bereina and Daru in 1977, Kupiano and Kwikila in 1978, Buin and Buka in 1979 and Ialibu in 1980. But they did comparatively little to improve the position in the villages. Some startling facts were also emerging. The population of PNG was increasing (in the 1971 Census, the population numbered 2 489 935; provisional figures for the 1980 Census put the total at 3 006 799) yet despite the impressive advances of the World Bank loan years, the number of telephones in relation to population was actually falling. A letter from Terry Woolaston, Acting Assistant Secretary, Planning Division, in *Inside Line* in August 1977, made some telling points:

> A lot of people in P and T think that we have built a very fine telecommunications system over the past ten years. That is indeed true. The service we provide links the main centres and many of the smaller centres, and gives STD service of a quality equal to any in the world . . . a lot of people now seem to think the job has been done, and we can just sit back and keep the network working. If we look a little deeper, we see that the STD network really only links up places were 12 per cent of the PNG people live. Is that good enough? . . . What P and T has done is to fix up the easy part of PNG's telecom needs, and has done very little about the rest, despite the government's policy of helping the people in the rural areas. Of course there are tremendous problems in serving the isolated communities of PNG, but we have to attack the

problems and get them solved . . . In 1974 PNG had 1.30 telephones per 100 population, in 1976 this had fallen to 1.26. The only other countries in the world where there was a fall were Mozambique and Oman. In 1974 . . . we were equal top (with Paraguay) of the 22 nations classed as 'emergent'. In 1976, we were sixth. So we are losing ground, when we are supposed to be extending our services . . . Remember that we are not providing enough of our product, Telecommunications Service, to 85 per cent of the population . . . we should do whatever we can to extend our service to the people 'out there'.

Woolaston's letter suggested a number of reasons for the relatively slow expansion of rural telecommunication services: a lack of money, complacency, a tendency within P and T to consider only the best of modern equipment as good enough to be connected into the PNG network. There were other reasons which he did not touch upon, chief of them a serious shortage of qualified national and expatriate engineers and technicians. Yet over the next few years, much was accomplished. A new system of VHF automatic telephone service was installed in Rabaul in October 1976, giving the first ever fully automatic VHF STD service in PNG to groups of subscribers in outlying areas. Similar telephones were later provided at Kaiapit, and to service the Baiyer and Wabag Valleys through the Mount Hagen exchange. As an experiment in providing communications to villages, a solar powered VHF radio telephone was installed at Borea village. Technically, the experiment succeeded, but at first the villagers made very little use of the new facility. It was largely to explain such seeming inconsistencies that P and T commissioned the survey that resulted in the landmark report, *Access to Calls*, to which previous reference has been made.

In 1978, a programme of single channel radio systems with STD public telephones was begun. By mid-1980, automatic solar powered public telephones had been installed under the programme at Gaire, Ialibu, Aitape, Angoram, Kompiam and Kundiawa. They were well received, and other centres called for their introduction.

The new Minister for Public Utilities, Wiwa Korowi, announced after taking over the portfolio in March 1980, that his first priority would be to put a telephone in every village throughout PNG. 'My ultimate aim is to provide, above all, STD facilities to all people', he said in a statement issued in May 1980. It is a very large aim, and it will be many years before it is accomplished. But in December 1980, the Minister announced that a French company, Thompson Compagnie Telegraphie Sanfil, had been awarded a K8.5 million contract to extend telephone communications from five main centres through new routes to rural areas, a project due to be completed by 1983. A route is to be provided from Wewak to Green River, and communications to Aitape, Vanimo and Anamab will be improved. The trunk routes to Kavieng and Namatanai are also to be upgraded. One of the new routes will go direct from Port Moresby to Mount Hagen. This will give P and T two completely separate microwave routes between Lae, control centre of the telecommunication network, and Port Moresby, where nearly half of its telecommunications users are located. Thus continuity of service should be ensured in the event of a breakdown on either route. There will be an extension of high quality telecommunications throughout the North Solomons, and a telephone microwave system for Ok Tedi.

Ok Tedi is an ambitious copper and gold mining project deep in the mountainous interior of the Western Province, near the West Irian border, which has been under field investigation since 1969, initially by Kennecott Explorations (Aust.) Pty. Ltd. and since 1975 by a consortium headed by the Australian company, Broken Hill Proprietary Co. Ltd. In March 1980, the PNG government gave the consortium the go-ahead to arrange finance for full exploitation of Ok Tedi within twelve months. The stakes are vast, of enormous potential importance to the PNG economy. Although the Ok Tedi copper reserves are not as extensive as those of Bougainville (some 275 million tonnes of proven reserves as against 940 million) the ore is richer, and there is an estimated 230 tonnes of gold at Ok Tedi. In March 1981, on the first anniversary of his government, the PNG Prime Minister, Sir Julius Chan, said that Ok Tedi was seen as 'the linchpin for much of our economic expansion in the future'. Efficient telecommunications will be essential if Ok Tedi is to succeed.

Another copper project of great potential magnitude is at Freida River, in the West Sepik Province, where a five-year field proving programme is under way. The company concerned, Freida Exploration Pty. Ltd., was formed by Australian and Japanese interests. In 1979, the private telecommunications company, Philips TMC (a P and T contractor during the World Bank years) asked for P and T assistance in providing an automatic telephone service to remote Freida River. After joint surveys by a Philips P and T team, a repeater site was located, and by the end of that year the single channel connection to Frieda River was made, via the Hagen-Wewak microwave route repeater station on Mt Ambunti.

Of all the problems that P and T encountered while extending telephone service to the nation, the most embarrassing was the furore that followed the introduction of monthly computerized billing. What happened was largely beyond the control of the Department, and illustrates how extremely difficult it was for a service organization, committed to commercial principles of operation, to function effectively under rigid Public Service controls.

In 1973, a National Computer Centre was established by the Public Service Board in Port Moresby, and government departments were required by the Board to use the Centre for processing financial and accounting data. P and T, although now operating under commercial accounting procedures, was not exempt. It began to introduce computerized monthly billing early in 1974, replacing the quarterly billing previously employed.

The procedures used by P and T were based on recommendations submitted by the management consultants, W.D. Scott and Co., which were accepted by P and T, the Public Service Board and the Treasury. W.D. Scott was then commissioned to implement the system. It did not prove a success.

From the outset, the new system was beset with troubles. Inefficiency and mismanagement at the National Computer Centre, allied to what was officially described in a ministerial statement to Parliament as an 'extreme lack of experienced staff' in the accounting section resulted in monumental confusion at P and T offices throughout PNG. The Department had wanted to introduce computerized billing as early as 1972, so that it could provide its customers with a bill every four weeks instead of every thirteen. This would have made the payment for telephone service easier for customers, and would have put the service within financial reach of the large number of Papua New Guineans living in the towns. But Public Service Board approval was necessary before a computerized system could be introduced, and approval was refused. Had permission been granted, the lower volume of traffic in 1972 and the more stable staff situation would have made the introduction of the programme very much simpler. At the time there was chaos. Credit control action was suspended for almost a year because of the lack of confidence of P and T in the computerized accounts. During 1975-6, outstanding telephone and telex debts soared to the incredible peak total of K12 million. When credit control action was resumed, telephones throughout PNG were disconnected for non-payment of accounts, and legal action was taken in a few cases, where this was practicable. By 30 June 1977, the debt level for telecommunication billing was down to K6.5 million.

The cost to the Department in terms of loss of public goodwill was very high. The confusion that followed the introduction of computerized billing was so great that all over PNG telephone customers were disconnected for non-payment of accounts where in fact they had in many cases paid. In Rabaul, the offices of the influential Planters Association of PNG were disconnected, twenty-seven days after the accounts had been paid and receipted. 'We are lumbered with the sheer inefficiency of the one department whose facilities are essential to almost every type of business', complained the executive officer of the Association, C.E. Holland, in a letter to the *South Pacific Post-Courier*, in March 1976. In a period of a few weeks, over 400 subscribers were disconnected in Rabaul without notice. Many came forward with receipts to prove their accounts had been paid. There was uproar. Not only was the general public affected. The Prime Minister's Department was forced to enter the fray when P and T moved to disconnect 90 per cent of government telephones in the East New Britain Province for alleged non-payment of accounts. In Lae, 600 general subscribers lost their phones. Many of these too had paid their accounts.

In Goroka, over seventy telephones were cut off, in June 1976. As well as general subscribers, the departments of Education, Interior, and Foreign Relations lost their telephones, together with the Bird of Paradise Hotel and the Goroka Local Government Council. 'Wires Crossed at P and T' wrote the editor of the *Post-Courier*:

> The P and T Department's policy of 'pay-up-or-be-shut-up-no-favours-asked-none-given' is again under heavy attack. In recent months many PNG businesses, including this newspaper, have had their phones arbitrarily disconnected even though current accounts were paid. This is bad PR and tarnishes the good image of P and T. P and T provides excellent service. Many countries are envious of the thoroughness with which it has extended communications throughout PNG and to the outside world. But now they have a gremlin in the works. Is it the computer, the clerks or the organization? Whatever it is, they must winkle it out.

The troubles continued. In July, Customs and Excise, one of the government's major revenue earning sources, lost their telephones throughout PNG, because of the failure of the Department of Foreign Affairs and Trade to pay its accounts within P and T's limit of twenty-eight days. In a public statement, Israel Edoni admitted that the operation of the computerized billing system was still not under control. 'It is still highly unsatisfactory', he said. 'The Department felt the full effects of the loss of expatriate officers during the year. They held key positions, and it will take some years to recover efficiency'.

No PNG leader relished having to admit to the damage caused by the departure of expatriates. At 30 June 1977, the total manpower strength of P and T was 2 458. Of these, 14 per cent — 304 — were expatriates, almost all employed in the professional and technical areas. They often supported young Papua New Guineans promoted into responsible positions with scant experience.

Edoni and his advisers took a hard look at the monthly billing situation. Incredibly, it took two years to convince the Public Services Commission (the Commission had after Independence replaced the Board) that the special requirements of P and T were not being met by the National Computer Centre. It was only then that approval was given to use outside assistance. Israel Edoni, Bill Southwood and Doug MacGowan had a long, hard battle to bring about the capitulation of the Commission, but events were to prove it worthwhile. In December 1976, agreement was reached with Asiadata Ltd., a Hong Kong-based computer service company with extensive experience in telephone and telex billing, to begin to process P and T's accounts in 1977.

To further improve the Department's financial position, the rate for local, national and international telephone calls was increased from seven toea to nine toea per metered pulse on 1 November 1977. At the same time, the telephone installation fee was abolished completely. This was to encourage the use of the telephone by PNG nationals and was in line with the P and T philosophy that the Department was in the business of selling telephone calls, not telephone instruments. Unfortunately, the installation fee was dropped before the billing situation was under control. In a number of cases telephones were installed and were in operation for periods up to, and exceeding, twelve months before new customers received their first bills, which caused financial embarrassment to some.

The situation was gradually brought under control. The new billing system began in October 1977. In 1979, the Department took the logical step of purchasing its own computer.

Other areas of difficulty were encountered by P and T in the early post-Independence period. For many years, the small third-level and charter airline operators of PNG (and there were many of them) had used HF radio links of various kinds and degrees of efficiency to communicate directly with other centres. This often caused frequency interference. The Department considered that small airlines should install special telephone components to enable the use of STD channels by push-button control. In May 1976, third-level radio licences issued to the biggest operator, Talair of Goroka, were withdrawn by P and T.

There were immediate outcries from the airline operators, and Israel Edoni hastened to announce that there was no intention of closing down the small-centre airline radios until discussions were held with the airlines concerned. It was not long after this that agreement was reached between representatives of the airlines and P and T on a mutually acceptable system to replace the old HF private networks.

Similar problems occurred in another area in 1977. P and T operated a Coastal Radio Service for national and international shipping, which it had taken over from OTC on 1 December 1973. On that day, the administration of the radio transmission regulatory and licensing functions were taken over from the Australian Post Office. PNG had become an associate member of the International Telecommunications Union in 1973, a full member in 1975 and, later, a member of the Commonwealth Telecommunications Organization. This membership carried with it obligations, as well as privileges. In 1975, the ITU agreed to the introduction of a new standard of ship-borne radio equipment to be carried by all ships of member countries throughout the world. In PNG, shipowners, government as well as private, were given two years warning of the new requirements, which would cost an estimated K1 200 per vessel to implement. Failure to convert to the new equipment would mean that ships would be unable to leave harbour.

The conversion of the coastal and inter-island shipping fleet of PNG proceeded slowly, despite the warning. By October 1977, 40 government and many of the 250 privately owned small ships in PNG waters had not made the change, and these comprised half the country's fleet. Another warning was given: install the equipment by January 1978, or face the consequences. There was much grumbling from shipowners, but eventually all complied.

The rapid improvement of PNG's telephone network, and the provision of STD and ISD facilities, hastened the decline of what had once been a mainstay of telecommunications: the telegram. The decline was accelerated by the increasing popularity of telex. Before the Eltex computer-controller exchange was cut over in Lae in May 1974, PNG had been one of the last countries in the world to use Morse telegraphy for internal telegraph transmission. After Eltex, PNG became one of the first countries in the Southern Hemisphere to commission an automatic telegraph exchange. Two new services now became possible — Mailgram, allowing subscribers to have telex messages delivered to post boxes, and a public telex service.

In April 1976, the then Minister for Posts and Telegraphs, Kaibelt Diria, announced that certain special categories of telegram (press, letter, collect, and government letter) would no longer be accepted. The move followed new telegraph regulations set in Geneva in 1973 by the ITU. The special categories were no longer needed, for the telephone had replaced the telegram as the prime means of international communication.

In May 1978, P and T placed order for 150 modern OKI teleprinters per year for three years with the Oki Electric Industry Company of Japan. Shortly afterwards, it was announced that owing to the increasing popularity of STD, ISD and automatic telex, telegraph offices throughout PNG would be closed down. The announcement in *Inside Line* said:

> The work now being done in Telegraph Offices will be phased into the Post Office in a gradual process over the next 12 months. This will make sending telegrams more convenient for customers. Some teleoperators will be transferred to the Post Office to manage the service. At the same time, many officers now in Telegraphs will have the opportunity to choose a new career in Postal and Telecommunication Services.

This was an inevitable development, but the announcement nevertheless came as a rude shock to the Communications Officers. Since 1972, their workload had been steadily decreasing; P and T could no longer afford to carry staff who were being rapidly by-passed by technological change.

It was a development, too, that caused much regret to Bill Peckover. He had been responsible for taking telegram acceptance and delivery away from the post offices and into telegraph offices, in the interests of better service to customers. Now the once thriving telegraph offices were falling into disuse. The telephone, and telex, had almost taken over. It fell to Peckover to wind up the telegraph offices that he had initiated.

It will be remembered that Bill Peckover, after retiring as First Assistant Director on 30 June 1974, resumed duty the following day as a 'Consultant — Special Adviser'. This appointment was arranged by Bill Carter, to ensure the sound management of P and T during his absence at the UPU Congress at Lausanne and leave, and to provide support for Israel Edoni. Carter was particularly anxious to retain Peckover's services since a number of top-level officers had by this time left P and T, or were planning to depart, including Graham Davey, Peter Vorpagel, Doug Rowell, Doug MacGowan (on sick leave) and Tom Pearson (who joined the NBC). The agreement with Bill Peckover was terminated on 14 May 1975, but he resumed duty immediately once more, this time as a Special Projects Officer, for his services were still essential to P and T.

Towards the end of 1976, W.A. Southwood, who had taken over from Peckover in 1974, in the position now called First Assistant Secretary, Telecommunications, announced his intention to resign. Although the position was advertised throughout the world, the response was extremely poor. The salary offered was insufficient to attract well-qualified applicants, and the Public Services Commission did not respond to appeals to increase it. Southwood reluctantly stayed on, but finally gave notice that he would be leaving at the end of October 1977.

Israel Edoni asked Peckover to take over his old job from Southwood. Bill Peckover accepted, but on the condition that a permanent replacement be found within twelve months, for he was looking forward to retirement in Australia, where he intended to concentrate on his bird photography and writing.

One of the first jobs Peckover tackled as First Assistant Secretary, Telecommunications, was the closing of the telegraph offices. Moi Eno of Customer Services, and Mary Manning and Peter Bourke of the Staff Development and Training Section, handled the mechanics of the changeover, and by the end of 1980, all the small offices had been closed down and the staff usefully re-employed, most within P and T but some in positions outside the Department.

The first batch of fifty OKI teleprinters arrived in February, 1979. Quiet, easily operated and maintained machines of modular construction, each was valued at K1 660. In May 1978, Jonathan Moang and Ivan Wadsworth, Telegraph and Data Engineers, had gone to Japan for P and T, to finalize delivery details and arrange for the provision of servicing tools and test equipment. When the first machines arrived, an OKI Electric engineer, Kazumasa Okamura, held a series of courses in Port Moresby in their operation and maintenance.

In February 1979, Frederick Electronics installed an Eltex concentrator in what used to be the Port Moresby telegraph office. Connected to the main Eltex Exchange in Lae, the concentrator provided 720 subscriber circuits.

By May 1979, PNG had 600 operating teleprinters. Automatic telex service was available to more than 500 subscribers to 100 countries, and another 40 countries could be reached through their operator-controlled telex exchanges.

PNG today is of course fully responsible for the operation of her own international telecommunications and coastal radio systems. As noted previously this responsibility was taken over from the Overseas Telecommunication Commission on 1 December 1973. At the same time, powers currently held by Australia under the Wireless Telegraphy Act were also transferred. It was because of the nature of the powers thus taken over from Australia that PNG sought membership of the ITU. The Radio Branch of P and T became the Regulatory and Licensing Section of a new International Telecommunications Division, to administer the functions taken over from Australia under the Wireless Telegraphy Act.

Although PNG did not assume responsibility for her own international telecommunications until 1973, serious consideration had been given to this question for at least two years previously. The desirability of setting up an independent authority outside P and T to handle this task had been discussed at great length. The trend in former British colonies that had set up separate national and international telecommunications authorities after their independence was for eventual amalgamation of the two. Carter, Peckover and senior officers of P and T, national and expatriate, had unpleasant memories of past differences with OTC as an independent authority, and there was no political support for the two-authority concept. It was quickly dropped.

Early in 1973, the political decision to give P and T the responsibility for PNG's overseas telecommunications services was taken. Negotiations with OTC over the equipment to be taken over on 1 December began.

The first round of negotiations was held in Canberra, with Roy Milne, First Assistant Secretary of the Treasury Department, and Bill Peckover, representing PNG, and the Commonwealth Treasury being represented by Harold Heinrich. Agreement was quickly reached on the transfer of OTC's Coastal Radio Service assets, for this non-profit service was subsidized by the Australian government, and Heinrich confirmed that a grant-in-aid would be made to PNG to cover the total written-down value of the assets, plus the cost of the first year of operations.

When discussions turned to the taking over of the business services assets of OTC in PNG, however, negotiations soon became deadlocked. Harold Heinrich and the OTC representatives made it plain that P and T would be expected to take over all these assets at their full written-down valuation, although Heinrich assured Milne and Peckover that Australia would provide a low-interest-rate loan to cover the transfer.

Of these business assets, with a total written-down valuation of a million dollars, Peckover concluded that only housing, office accommodation and a quantity of equipment, worth in all about $300 000, was of value to P and T. The rest was useless, apart from the Madang Gateway Exchange which would in any case only be required until a new exchange could be built at Lae. And OTC had originally given an assurance that P and T would not be asked to purchase the Madang Exchange in the event of its taking responsibility for PNG's international telecommunications.

The OTC representatives refused to budge. Neither would Peckover. The meeting ended without agreement being reached.

It was following this meeting that the Public Services Commission gave approval for the creation of a new position of Assistant Director, International Services. Carter offered the position to Doug Rowell; Carter had been impressed with Rowell's professional ability during the World Bank loan period. Rowell told me in 1981:

> It was some time late in 1973 that I was handed a heap of files by Bill Carter, who asked me whether I would be interested in setting up the International Division and negotiating the withdrawal of OTC from PNG. I was about at the end of my time on the microwave repeater station work and was thinking of returning to Australia, but this new challenge was too great, so I stayed on. Setting up the International Division was one of the great experiences of my life, but it wasn't easy. And before I could really make a start, I had to come to terms with OTC. The Commission was famous for its toughness and skill in negotiations, and I knew that they would have preferred to stay on in PNG after Independence. International telecommunications are, by their very nature, extremely profitable. At a time when manpower costs are soaring, the cost of telecommunications technology is falling and there is much more money to be made in international telecommunications than in providing service to the remotest rural districts of an underdeveloped country like P and T had to do.

Doug Rowell went to Singapore to look at the now integrated national/international telecommunications organization there, and also studied the British system. About the same time, Bill Carter went to New Zealand to see how that country administered its international communications.

He also took over the protracted task of negotiating with OTC over its withdrawal from PNG. There were no serious problems with regard to the Coastal Radio Service which OTC had provided throughout its 27-year presence in PNG. This service was not run to make a profit, but to safeguard the lives of those at sea, to provide ships with reliable weather information and as a general news and emergency service. As a member country of the ITU, Australia was obliged by international agreement to provide this service. PNG would now assume the responsibility, and the Australian Treasury made a grant-in-aid of $505 448 to cover the cost of the transferred assets. Another amount of $117 000 was provided to cover the cost of the first year of operation of the service. Financial responsibility would thereafter rest with PNG.

The real stumbling block was the question of OTC's business assets. Bill Carter assumed command of the P and T negotiating team, which included Rowell, and agreement was finally reached, but substantially on OTC's terms. Rowell recalls: 'At times negotiations became quite bloody. OTC were experts at this sort of thing, but our experience was limited'. The negotiations were complicated by the high value that OTC placed on their assets in PNG. This resulted from financial arrangements within the Commonwealth Telecommunication Organization which made it an advantage to maintain high asset cost levels in various areas, in order to establish the costs of trunk calls on international lines between various points. It was therefore not in the best interests of OTC to quickly write off or remove such items as the HF transmitters and associated gear at Rabaul and Port Moresby which had been redundant after the microwave systems were installed. The earlier decision to install obsolescent equipment that had been removed from Guam at the Madang Gateway Exchange, which could not be properly integrated into the PNG national network, had been another consequence of OTC policy. Rowell says:

> It was a bitter pill to have to swallow, that Madang Gateway Exchange. We had to pay about a quarter of a million dollars for it. One of the useless things we had to take over was a pneumatic tube system, just like they used to have in big department stores years ago to send cash to a central accounting point, and this ran from the OTC building in Douglas Street, Port Moresby, to the Cuthbertson Street corner of the GPO. It was used to transport telegrams between OTC and P and T. It was made of heavy bronze tubing and it cost us $50 000. We just sealed it up. It was never used again.

The OTC international assets were finally transferred at their written-down book value for the sum of one million dollars — the precise figure the Commission had insisted on in the first round of negotiations attended by Milne and Peckover. Loan funds for the purchase were provided by the Australian government, at a nominal interest rate of three per cent over ten years, with a three-year repayment holiday.

It should be recorded that once agreement was reached, OTC did everything possible to assist P and T in the changeover. Eleven key OTC officers remained on loan to P and T after the handover until staff could be trained to replace them. Arrangements were also made to transfer fifty-nine Papua New Guinean staff to P and T. They included riggers, labourers and messengers, and the veteran Morea Mea, who had joined AWA in 1926 and was the first Papua New Guinean to train as a rigger. OTC staff — Manager Harry Stone and Technical Officers Graham Huddy, Doug Lloyd, Rodney Pernich, Darrell Smith, Greg Taylor and John Walker — continued to operate and maintain the SEACOM Cable Station at Madang. Many of the OTC national officers transferred to P and T had been recently trained in various skills, and training continued at the Madang station.

One of the principal tasks facing P and T was the provision of a new wideband (high capacity) telecommunication link between PNG and Australia. The SEACOM cable, designed to serve Australia-Malaysia-Singapore-Hong Kong, was by this time running out of capacity. PNG had gained access to the cable before its capacity was used up, but traffic between Australia and countries to the north of PNG was also growing rapidly, and this severely limited the circuits available to handle traffic between Madang and Australia.

Three practical alternatives were available for a new wideband link; by overland microwave from Port Moresby westward along the southern Papuan coast and thence to Cairns via Thursday Island; via satellite; and by submarine cable from Port Moresby to Cairns.

The first alternative, which would have allowed P and T to easily extend high quality microwave links into the huge, sparsely-populated Western and Gulf Districts, would have been acceptable to the Department, but for various reasons was opposed by the Australian Post Office and OTC. OTC wanted a link via satellite. It already had ample capacity available in its Moree, New South Wales, Satellite Earth Station and traffic from PNG would increase the economic viability of that station.

Bill Peckover discussed the events of those days with me in 1981:

> Initially, both Bill Carter and Doug Rowell favoured the satellite. I was convinced that a submarine cable would be a better proposition for PNG, and I set out to try and prove it. One of the reasons that I enjoyed working with Bill Carter was that he didn't have a closed mind — he could change direction if he was presented with a solid enough case.

Peckover had made something of a study of satellite technology, and had recently attended a seminar in Singapore on the broadband cable versus satellite argument. He was in personal touch with the Far East representative of the world's largest submarine cable suppliers. From this representative, Peckover obtained a budgetary quote on the cost of a Madang-Cairns cable, which was not only far below estimates provided by OTC for such a link, but below their estimate for a satellite link. The Far East representative later visited PNG and assured Bill Carter and his engineers that should tenders be called for a submarine cable, his company would submit a quote in line with that given to Peckover.

Carter and Rowell were convinced. A series of management meetings between representatives of P and T and OTC began. The P and T team was led by the Minister, Kaibelt Diria, and Bill Carter, and included Doug Rowell. The Department was now fully behind the submarine cable; OTC, on the other hand, still wanted to establish the new link by satellite.

There were many advantages to PNG in the cable link. P and T had no experience of satellite technology, but cable technology was long-established, and the Department was already preparing to eventually take over the management of the SEACOM Cable Station at Madang. A cable link would allow P and T to use the microwave system between Port Moresby and Madang to take over part of the SEACOM load, and thus gain some additional revenue.

Negotiations were long and frequently heated. Neither side would budge at first, but eventually OTC agreed, reluctantly, to call tenders for a Cairns-Port Moresby cable, to be owned jointly by OTC and the PNG government.

In October 1974, a contract was let with Standard Telephones and Cables Limited, London, for the laying of a submarine cable of new, lightweight construction, manufactured in the United Kingdom. Its initial capacity was 480 telephone channels, estimated to be sufficient for five to ten years of traffic growth. It also had a television transmission capacity. The laying of the land cable between the landing point at Taurama Beach and Boroko, a distance of 10 km, was completed on 31 October 1975, on schedule. Approximately 4 cm in diameter, the cable, sheathed with mild steel armour wires, was in heavy 900-metre lengths, requiring thirty to forty men to manoeuvre it. Jointing of the first length of cable to the second was done by the STC supervisor of the project, Harry Stocker. The other twelve joints in the land cable were completed by P and T personnel — Wilfred Modudula, Moses Seimu, Peter Sansan, Angelo Aria and Paragua Piviki.

Before the submarine cable could be landed at Taurama Beach, some one hundred mines laid in the Bootless Bay-Taurama area during the Second World War had to be swept. This job was done by three minesweepers of the Royal Australian Navy, and the Navy also blasted a narrow trench through the outer reef off Taurama Beach to accommodate the cable.

The cable was brought to PNG on board the *John W. Mackay*, a venerable vessel built in 1922, the only steam-driven cable ship still then in existence. Owned by the Commercial Cable Company of London, she was under the command of Captain William Harper.

The laying of the submarine cable was completed in March 1976. The PNG end was transferred to Taurama Beach by a local vessel, through the channel blasted in the outer reef, and was jointed to the land cable already laid. The *John W. Mackay* then steamed towards Cairns, laying the 900 kilometres of sea cable in nine days, by accurate navigation following a predetermined path along the sea bed. A repeater was located every 14 km along the cable's length. The Australian land end, laid by OTC staff assisted by technicians from Telecom Australia, was joined to the sea cable at a point off the Great Barrier Reef, and the new Australia-PNG link was complete, at a total overall cost to PNG of about K12 million.

Two months of testing and commissioning followed, in readiness for the planned official opening in July 1976. However, on 20 May, the SEACOM cable between Madang and Cairns was broken when a repeater failed during a subterranean earthquake. All traffic between Australia and PNG, and between Australia and South-East Asia, ceased. The new cable — known as A-PNG — was immediately brought into service, providing a high quality alternative link until the failed repeater was restored, two weeks later.

By the time of the official opening of A-PNG, Israel Edoni was Director of Public Utilities, but Bill Carter was a guest of honour, making his first return to PNG since handing over. Doug Rowell had long since resumed his career in Australia, being replaced as Assistant Director of International Communications by A.F. Durham in late 1974. Durham in turn left in 1977, and J.M.C. Harrison became Assistant Secretary, and he was still in this position when P and T celebrated its Silver Anniversary.

Rowell had the satisfaction before his departure of commencing negotiations on behalf of P and T that led to the purchase of a five per cent equity in the SEACOM cable. Management of SEACOM was undertaken by the Commonwealth Cable Management Committee on behalf of the owner governments, Britain, Canada, New Zealand, Malaysia, Singapore and Australia. Meetings of the Management Committee were held by rotation in each of the member countries. Rowell attended the annual meeting in Montreal in 1973 to put PNG's case for a share in the ownership of SEACOM. As a result of the equity purchase in September 1976, P and T took over the Madang SEACOM Cable Station in January 1977. As a partner in SEACOM, PNG now shared revenue from the traffic passing through the cable. The seven OTC staff running the station remained, while training of P and T staff to take over continued.

The first telecommunications outlet that PNG had to the outside world that did not go via Australia was a circuit from Lae to Denver, in the United States, via the

SEACOM cable from Madang to Guam and then through the TRANSPAC 2 cable via Hawaii. The rights to the exclusive use of the two channels were purchased in June 1976, giving access to any telephone number in the United States, Canada, Mexico and Puerto Rico. Direct connection with Hong Kong was established in October 1977, with five Telex channels. In December, direct connection with Japan was gained with two telephone and four Telex channels between Lae and Tokyo. Since then, P and T has purchased the rights to direct links to Manila, Singapore and, in 1980, London.

For obvious historical, geographic and economic reasons, the main stream of international telecommunications traffic both in and out of PNG, was with Australia. As International Subscriber Dialling facilities were extended throughout the national network as it was constructed, a serious financial imbalance became apparent.

ISD was a one-way facility between PNG and Australia. The decision to provide ISD in one direction was taken when OTC was responsible for PNG's international telecommunications, in order to give telephone users better and easier access to Australia. The Australian Post Office agreed with the decision, and there was a mutual understanding that a reciprocal service from Australia to PNG would follow.

OTC forecasts that the ratio of ISD calls from PNG to Australia would peak at two calls for every one in the reverse direction quickly proved to be in serious error. So popular was ISD with telephone users in PNG that by September 1975, the ratio reached 5.5 to 1, and in December reached the all-time peak of 6.13 paid minutes on ISD calls to Australia for every paid minute for calls from Australia.

Because of the complex revenue-sharing arrangements in force between Commonwealth countries, a big slice of the revenue being collected by P and T through this traffic went to Australia. It was a hidden but substantial currency drain that PNG could not afford. The only practicable way of at least partially redressing the imbalance was for Australia to provide an ISD service to PNG.

It took two years for this simple solution to be adopted. During this period, a Royal Commission of Inquiry into the Australian Post Office was under way, and the future of OTC was in doubt. PNG's problems thus did not loom very large in the minds of the senior executives of the APO at this time.

Talks dragged on at the departmental level for month after month, without substantial result. It was obvious that the question was going to have to be resolved at the political level, and in 1974, the Minister for Posts and Telegraphs, Kaibelt Diria, visited Australia with Bill Carter and raised the matter with the Postmaster General, Lionel Bowen, who promised to take a personal interest. Later, Diria sent Bill Peckover, who had been quick to recognize the currency drain problem, to Canberra, to fully explain the P and T viewpoint to a sympathetic Lionel Bowen.

Politics now conspired to frustrate what was beginning to look like a speedy solution. General elections were held in Australia, the Whitlam government was returned, and Lionel Bowen was moved to another ministry. The new Postmaster General, Senator Bishop, was not sympathetic. The situation was becoming serious for PNG: the currency drain had reached the figure of $1 million per annum by the end of 1974. Kaibelt Diria turned to Michael Somare, Chief Minister (and *de facto* head of state), for help.

Somare wrote to Gough Whitlam, Prime Minister of Australia, in October 1975, attaching to his letter a long résumé of the history and implications of the problem, prepared by Bill Peckover. But before Whitlam could do anything, his government was sacked by the Governor-General in the dramatic political crisis of November 1975.

By this time, too, the Australian Post Office had been split into Australia Post and Telecom Australia. OTC had survived the Royal Commission — indeed, it had emerged with renewed strength. The PNG problem was still further complicated by the fact that although OTC was responsible for international telecommunications, Telecom Australia controlled the Australian STD system. Both organizations came under the authority of the Postmaster General.

Intense negotiations were now renewed, again at a departmental level, between OTC and P and T, and between OTC and Telecom Australia, over the PNG ISD issue. Eventually agreement was reached, political approval was obtained, and an ISD service between Australia and PNG commenced to operate from 1 July 1976, through the special international dialling code 0014-675. The service was made available progressively to Australian subscribers connected to crossbar exchanges, as these were installed across the country. The growth of the traffic imbalance between Australia and PNG was immediately arrested, and over the following two years was reduced to an acceptable level.

In August 1978, the Minister for Public Utilities, Gabriel Bakani, made a statement in the National Parliament:

> I feel obliged to report to Parliament that national telecommunications services will collapse if we are not able to retain a large number of the overseas telecommunications technical experts at present employed in the Department of Public Utilities . . . We have a very highly sophisticated and complicated telecommunication system, and we are critically short of national officers with the training, and more importantly with the length of experience, necessary for them to take over top and middle level technical telecommunication jobs. We do have an extensive training programme for training nationals in this work, and our country has no shortage of people with the necessary intellect and ambition. What we are short of is people with the necessary combination of education together with a suitable environmental and social upbringing that fits them for a technical career. Furthermore, it must be recognized that a newly qualified person in any discipline possesses no experience. It is experience in the real world that enables people to properly and effectively apply their theoretical knowledge to the endless combinations of situations they meet in a technical work environment, such as a modern telephone exchange.
>
> To give members some idea of the extent of the problem, there are, at present, ten national and thirty-four overseas staff in the middle and top technical jobs in our telephone exchanges. All of the nationals are in the middle level.
>
> Because of the complexity of the jobs and the numbers of people required, it will be something between ten and twenty years before we can hope to have a fully national staff in control of our telephone exchanges.

This crisis in the affairs of P and T (which indeed came close to crippling the entire telecommunications network, and which pitilessly exposed the continuing reliance of the Department on expatriate expertise) was precipitated by a decision, in June 1978, by the National Executive Council, on the advice of the Public Service Commission, to introduce new terms of employment for expatriates working in the various government departments in PNG, as from 1 January 1979.

It has already been noted that Independence came long before PNG was in a position to replace all expatriates in the Public Service with qualified nationals. Although every effort had been made to localize the Service, a great many key positions were still occupied by expatriates — mostly Australians, although there were many Englishmen from former British colonies, as well as New Zealanders, Canadians, Americans, Africans, Indians, Filipinos and other nationalities. Their services were vital to PNG.

In December 1973, the Australian Development Assistance Agency, or ADAA, was established to administer Australia's foreign aid programme, principally to PNG. Expatriates formerly employed within the PNG Public Service were transferred to the Australian Staffing Assistance Group, or ASAG, and employed under contract, their salaries paid for by the Agency as a part of Australia's aid programme. This was a temporary measure. ASAG was wound up on 30 June 1976, and many ex-ASAG officers accepted contracts with the PNG Government, roughly equivalent to the old ASAG contracts.

The new contract conditions announced in June, 1978, effectively lowered the salaries and allowances to be paid to expatriates, but offered longer contract periods and better education subsidies. To partially offset the lower salaries, gratuities were to be paid in a lump sum at the conclusion of the contract period. There was also a number of other minor variations of the old ASAG conditions.

Shortly after the announcement by the National Executive Council of the new contract system, the Australian Treasurer, John Howard, said that as from 1 July 1978, Australians living overseas and earning more than $A10 000 a year would have to pay Australian income tax. Hitherto, Australians living and working in PNG had paid only PNG income tax, at considerably lower rates than those applying in Australia. Now, it appeared as if they would be doubly taxed.

The effect of this combination of measures on the expatriates in the Public Service was shattering. The annual Congress of the Australian Staffing Assistance Association, meeting in Port Moresby a few days later, flatly rejected the contract package, insisting that the arrangements were quite unacceptable. But Public Services Commission Chairman, Rabbie Namaliu, warned that the new contract conditions were 'not negotiable'. From all over PNG came resignations from expatriates unwilling to accept the new conditions. On 31 August 1978, a Public Service Commission spokesman estimated that more than half of the two thousand, nine hundred overseas staff 'were likely to leave'. Explanations were demanded in Parliament, as the exodus of expatriates became a political issue.

The branch of the Public Service hardest hit by this proposed exodus was the Telecommunications Division of the Department of Public Utilities. As early as 1976, Israel Edoni had openly admitted the dependence of his Department on overseas staff. 'It has become clear that the localization programme adopted in the early 1970s was too ambitious', he wrote in his *Annual Report* for 1975-76. Now the problems of the

Telecommunications Division were agonizingly multiplied. Salaries currently paid to highly qualified technicians were barely adequate by overseas standards, and few men were prepared to accept less. Bill Peckover made an urgent survey of key expatriate staff within the Division, asking them to advise their intentions. Of the total of fifteen telephone exchange experts employed, thirteen said that they would leave PNG by the end of December. An overall analysis by Doug MacGowan, First Assistant Secretary, Finance and Administration, indicated a probable loss of at least fifty expatriates from the various branches of P and T, out of a total of three hundred and twenty-four employed. Those that were going included key engineers and technicians of the Telecommunications Division, most of them on secondment from Telecom Australia. MacGowan began to work hard behind the scenes to arrive at a solution to the problem, before the Department broke down.

On 23 August 1978, the Minister for Public Utilities, Gabriel Bakani, wrote to Prime Minister Somare, again stressing the seriousness of the position:

> A large percentage of the P and T Service staff have advised that they are not willing to sign contracts under the new conditions. The Department is already holding actual resignations from many of these people. Unless a compromise between these technical people and the government can be reached within a matter of days, or I immediately contract the operation and maintenance of the system to a number of foreign companies at very high cost, the whole telecommunications system will inevitably collapse within a few weeks of the departure of a critical number of top overseas telecommunications staff on or before 31 December 1978.

There was no time available in which to recruit new staff to plug the gap. In any case, recent efforts by the Department to attract additional staff from Australia and overseas had been extremely disappointing, even with the old scale of salaries and conditions then offering. Urgent talks were held between P and T Headquarters officers and the Public Service Commission. Some concessions were granted (and the Australian taxation anomaly had since been corrected) and in the event only eight instead of thirteen telephone exchange experts went. Five other technical officers and technicians also departed. By May 1979, 65 expatriate technicians and engineers had left P and T. Only six overseas recruits were gained to balance the loss, all these skilled technicians on short-term loan from Telecom Australia.

The telecommunications network did not collapse, however, although it came very close to doing so. The consequences, had the system collapsed, would have been disastrous for the country. In a letter to the Minister, Israel Edoni estimated that of the total annual revenue of about K26 million earned by P and T Services, K22.5 million was earned from telephone and other telecommunication services. Had the primary telephone exchanges ceased to operate, the rest of the system would immediately have followed. International, and domestic political, implications were obvious. It was estimated that overall costs would have doubled had outside telecommunications companies been called in to save the day.

The loss of skilled staff nevertheless had serious consequences. Writing to the Deputy Prime Minister, Ebia Olewale, in April 1979, the new Minister for Public Utilities, Sir Tei Abal, summed up the situation in plain terms:

The reduction in the level of experienced staff has led to the predicted loss of performance, particularly in our telephone exchanges. Several have broken down. Of particular concern was a fault condition in the International Gateway Exchange in Lae from 21-23 April. During this time, 50 per cent of international incoming and outgoing calls were rejected by the telephone exchange . . . Only 13 expatriate exchange staff will remain at 31/12/79. A series of advertisements for 166 positions were run in Australia during November 1978. These advertisements offered the new conditions of employment. The total response to the advertisements was 83 applications, 57 of which were found to be worthy of interview. 24 failed to appear for interview, 33 were interviewed, 12 withdrew . . . generally, the calibre of applicants was considered lower than previously experienced. On the financial side, our billings for 1979 are currently running at an annual rate of K3.4 million below budget, assuming the network does not deteriorate further.

Failures have now reached a critical stage. There is insufficient staff to attend to even major breakdowns and restoration of service is being carried out on a priority basis. Over recent days . . . Sogeri, Wabag, Mendi and Daru Exchanges have been off the air for periods of up to six weeks. Rural exchanges are being neglected in favour of repairing major exchanges such as Lae and Boroko . . . our telecommunications network provides circuits linking the SEACOM cable at Madang with the A-PNG cable at Port Moresby, which currently carry international circuits direct from South-East Asia to Australia. Any collapse of our network will cause telecommunications administrations in other countries to lose faith in PNG and it may take many years to restore this confidence.

Sir Tei went on to describe the effects of overwork on the few remaining skilled staff. Three top supervisors had already suffered physical breakdowns. In some cases, technicians were working such long hours that overtime payments exceeded their weekly salaries! The morale of P and T staff, national as well as expatriate, was taking a battering. Sir Tei proposed an immediate investigation by the government into all aspects of salary grades and allowances for all technical personnel in the PNG Public Service. In the meantime, a technical allowance (an idea largely formulated by Doug MacGowan) should be paid to all technical staff and engineers, to retain their services. Already twenty-one national technicians and two engineers, trained at such great cost in money, dedication and effort, had left the Department for greener fields.

The technical allowances proposed (K750 per year for nationals, and up to K3 000 for expatriates in specified positions) were approved. Recruitment efforts were stepped up, and further concessions were made to attract overseas staff. A review of salaries was undertaken. There was no immediate alternative to the extra allowances, for as Bill Peckover pointed out in a letter to Israel Edoni in January 1979, there was 'not one technical area in the telecommunications divisions where we are not currently dependent on expatriate expertise to ensure the system continues to be operational'.

The crisis of 1978-9 had the effect of redoubling P and T's efforts to train national technicians and engineers. Sadly, however, the new training system devised by Les Canute outlined in Chapter 13, had, for various reasons, failed to produce tele-technicians in the numbers required. In the five-year period 1973-8, only sixteen national technicians had been added to the P and T staff, and this figure included graduates from the University of Technology. The Canute system of self-paced, programmed learning through the use of teaching machines was really ahead of its time. It was soundly conceived, but could not hope to succeed given the standard of education and cultural background of the average trainee attempting the block courses.

It was in the selection of recruits for teletechnician training that the principal weakness of the system lay. The Public Service Board's grip on trainee recruiting had for a number of reasons loosened by the beginning of the 1970s, and P and T now found its own students. The Boroko Training College, however, did not consider itself a recruiting organization: its role was purely educational. In effect, recruitment of trainees was left to the Regional Engineers. A new classification, Technician's Assistant, was created. They were recruited by the Regional Engineers and their senior officers, more or less casually and often with little real investigation into background and suitability. Technician's Assistants were on the staff of the Regional Engineers, and were not under the direct control of the College, as had previously been the case. A Technician's Assistant was supposed to proceed through the block courses at the College at his own pace, as and when he and his superiors considered he was ready to move on. Periods of training at the College were interspaced with periods of practical work in the field. In theory, if a Technician's Assistant failed a 'block' he was sent back to the field until he was ready to try again. If he passed the very elementary introductory block he was signed on as a Public Servant retained on Departmental strength, thus depriving other intending trainees of a place. By 1977, P and T had in its ranks about fifty Technician's Assistants who were virtually untrainable. On the other hand, many proved to be so useful at field level that supervisors were loath to allow them to go back to the College for further block courses. This situation caused considerable friction between the College and its instructors and the men in the field. Another difficulty that Canute laboured under was a grave shortage of experienced instructional staff. From 1972 and 1979, there was never more than fifty per cent of approved staff positions actually occupied.

In 1975, Les Canute was assigned to the newly-created position of Training Co-Ordinator (changed to Training Controller in 1976) in order to free him from the responsibility of managing the Boroko Training College and to allow him to concentrate on the establishment of the Lae Training Centre. Geoff Hutton took over the position of Principal of the Boroko College.

It was in the creation of the Lae Centre that Les Canute made his great contribution to P and T training. He worked closely with the ITU Project Manager, Albert Schlegel, on the design of the new centre. He was on the scene during every phase of construction, and battled with the Public Service Commission for a realistic staffing organization. He left PNG at the end of 1979.

The National Postal and Telecommunications Training Centre, as it was finally titled, was formally opened by the Treasurer and Deputy Prime Minister, Julius Chan, on 23 October 1978. The Principal on that August day was Peter O'Malley. Technician and Linesman training, and the job of Principal, were transferred from Boroko to Lae. A new position of Principal was created for the Boroko College, since it was recognized that it would probably be some years before the Lae Centre could be expanded to absorb postal and other training still being undertaken at Boroko. Each Principal, and Canute, the Training Controller, reported through the Assistant Secretary, Staff Development and Training, to the First Assistant Secretary, Finance and Administration — a cumbersome arrangement.

By this time Schlegel had departed, and the ITU team of experts had arrived. Initially, the ITU team worked at Boroko but as buildings were completed at Lae, the team progressively transferred there. In 1976, Gordon Austin arrived to take over management of the ITU team (which by 1981 numbered fourteen). The primary ITU task was to look at P and T training requirements and then develop a suitable curriculum working with P and T instructors and using Canute's system. Although Gordon Austin tried to avoid the development of distinct ITU and P and T 'camps', this did tend to occur. There was some early misunderstanding of the role of the ITU experts, who were at Lae mainly for curriculum development, not lecturing.

By 1978, it was glaringly obvious that yet another P and T training initiative was not working. Israel Edoni, who had backed the development of the Lae Training Centre with enthusiasm and dedication, was appalled. An enormous amount of money had been spent on the centre and its equipment, and yet only a handful of national teletechnicians was being produced.

Edoni was well aware of his Department's dependence on expatriate expertise. He was realist enough to acknowledge that it would be years before there were sufficient national engineers and technicians to man the telecommunications network without outside assistance — indeed, he publicly defended the necessary employment of expatriates by his Department, refusing to bow to shallow, emotional criticism by some PNG nationalists and overseas 'experts'. But he did not like the situation.

In October 1977, Bill Peckover resumed his old position of First Assistant Secretary, Telecommunications. He was at once highly critical of current P and T training efforts. Comparing the on-the-job performance of technicians who had come through the P and T system with graduates of the Diploma courses from the University of Technology, he found the quality of the latter to be clearly superior. He proposed to Edoni that control of telecommunications and postal training be immediately transferred from the Finance and Administration Division to the Telecommunications and Postal Divisions. He commenced action to have ten positions of Senior Telecommunications Officer (five telephone, five radio) created in his Division, to be responsible for the supervision of the on-the-job segments of technician training courses.

Gordon Austin had by this time, 1978, come to much the same conclusion as Peckover. He told me in 1981:

> The Canute system was turning into a nightmare. We were spending too much effort in propping up a system that simply could not work. Open-ended courses were a great concept, but they were not practical given the standard of trainees we had to work with. We had the situation where our small number of bright students took their first course units in three months, while others took nine or ten months to cover the same ground. Too many of the recruits were poor material. We couldn't keep bright students waiting for six or seven months while the poor ones caught up. And this pattern was repeated over the five levels of training, all of which had to be completed before a student could graduate. We had gotten ourselves into a hopeless mess.

Austin, too, proposed that a number of 'Field Training Officer' positions be created, to supervise the on-the-job aspects of training courses. Up to this time, a single officer — at first Tom Ivins, then Peter O'Malley and finally Tom Bartlett — was attempting the impossible task of supervising this work, throughout Papua New Guinea.

Staff and student morale took a heavy pounding. A graphic illustration of the depressed state of the training situation was provided by a letter written and signed by eleven teletechnician trainees at the Lae Centre. Addressed to Les Canute with copies to instructors, the letter amply demonstrated the concern of trainees caught in the system:

> We were told in 1975 when we first commenced training that the course would take no more than five years to complete, but in this fifth year, 1979, we have not even completed half of the teletechnician courses . . . we therefore conclude that under the present scheme we will complete the course in nine years . . . If this present system of training, which we now have no confidence in, cannot cater for an acceleration of courses, we would like to suggest that other means of teaching should be sought in order to rectify the situation.

Deeply disturbed by the trend of events, Israel Edoni called a three-day Departmental conference into all aspects of the training situation. It was attended by Deputy Secretary Dale Kamara and the three First Assistant Secretaries, among other senior officers. Following the conference, Edoni decided to create a new Training Division, responsible directly to either himself or Dale Kamara. Unfortunately, the Public Service Commission did not grant approval for the formation of the Division.

Determined to find a solution to P and T's training problems, Israel Edoni approached Alan Kilby, an expert in training methods employed at the Administrative College. Edoni wanted a review conducted by someone outside the Department who had no axe to grind. Kilby agreed to assist, and Edoni was able to arrange for his transfer to the Department of Public Utilities.

Alan Kilby was given a brief to conduct 'an investigation into staff development and training within the Department to help formulate future staff development and training policy and guidelines, and to determine whether available staff development and training resources were being used to their maximum advantage'. Kilby worked rapidly and effectively, and in November 1978, produced a comprehensive report containing recommendations that caused some heartburn within P and T training ranks, but which were to become the basis for the programme being followed today. Edoni gave Kilby the task of getting the revised system under way.

The new philosophy of P and T training was jointly developed by Alan Kilby and Gordon Austin. The Canute system of self-paced learning using programmed teaching machines was abandoned, and defined-time teaching was reintroduced. A three-year course was developed, with the aim of producing base grade teletechnicians able to cope effectively with specific low-level tasks. A further analysis was made of the fieldwork situation, to ensure the courses were closely tailored to meet P and T needs at the basic levels. Training was simplified to some degree, but the level of instruction was retained; only the volume was reduced. Instead of learning many skills, trainees would now learn only what was strictly required for the job to be done.

The most significant departure from all past practice was in the area of trainee recruitment and standards, the bane of P and T telecommunications training since Geoff Hutton, Peter Cottell, Jim Lappin and Frank Mollinger began it in the early days of the Department. Basic to the new procedures developed by Kilby and Austin was strict insistence on a relatively high standard of education for trainee recruits.

Luckily, the entire education scene in PNG was changing. By the mid-1970s, high school graduates were becoming available in ever-increasing numbers, and many were now attracted to P and T. The dramatic advances of the World Bank Telecommunication Loan project years had made P and T a Department for ambitious young men and women to aspire to. Although education in PNG still had a very long way to go, the educational standard of trainees now available to P and T was far higher than previously, and in 1980, the first complete year of the new system, there were only three failures (two for non-academic reasons) from the fifty-two who began the three-year technicians course (roughly half telephones and half lines). There were sixty positions available for the course that began in 1981, for which there were one thousand applicants! Six women were included in both the 1980 and 1981 trainee intakes, and they have since tended to outperform the men.

The new training system could thus be set for success, although it is too soon to be absolutely certain. Past failures in themselves are indicators that success will not be easily won. Gordon Austin, who took over as Principal of the Lae Centre, as well as continuing as Manager of the ITU team, is optimistic, as is Alan Kilby. Some old hands, however, are less sanguine. Certainly, the marked improvement in the quality of education in PNG in recent years must automatically result in a higher standard of recruits for telecommunications training. In a recent letter to me, Bill Carter made the point that it was unquestionably the poor standard of basic education in PNG in earlier years that made it so difficult for P and T to produce high quality national tele-technicians during the colonial era:

> We could train nationals to be efficient in repetitive, manipulative and tradesman-type work — we produced competent welders, carpenters, telephone installers, cable jointers, telephonists, base level clerical assistants and so on — but we could not train sufficient professional and sub-professional officers. The basic standard of education of recruits was far too low, and we had also to overcome that enormous cultural barrier, that made it so hard for a trainee from a simple village background to successfully tackle advanced technical training. This problem still remains, it seems to me, despite the improvement in overall educational standards in PNG.

The fact is that many young Papua New Guinean males (there are notable exceptions, of course) still find it very difficult to accept the Western work ethic, essential to success in any highly technical field. It is of absorbing interest to note that women, on the other hand, in traditional PNG societies, the workers, appear to be coping with advanced training with considerable success. Traditional PNG societies were almost invariably male-dominated, and it will be many years before this situation changes. Women who succeed will doubtless face opposition from men who fail, for a long time to come. But at this point it does seem probable that women will play an increasingly important role in the technical field in the P and T of the future.

Thus far, the Lae Centre has concentrated on base level training, but it is recognized that P and T requires national middle and top range teletechnicians as well as base grade, and it is planned to considerably expand the number of available courses designed to upgrade the skills of serving national officers. Eventually, multi-skilled, and specialist, national teletechnicians will be trained at the Lae Centre, but only to meet specific P and T needs.

Degree and Diploma courses of a superior standard are continuing to be provided at the University of Technology. These 5½-year courses in Communications Engineering are producing engineer graduates not only for P and T, but also for the Electricity Commission and the National Broadcasting Commission. Since P and T can expect only four, and up to six, graduates per year from the University of Technology under current arrangements, it is obvious that a number of years must pass before the last expatriate engineers are replaced with nationals. Of some sixty engineers employed in the Telecommunications Division in mid-1981, only eighteen were nationals.

The Boroko Training College has experienced a new lease of life since the change of direction at Lae. The College came near to closure in 1978, but it has been revived as a centre for non-technical training (finance, administration, stores and so on) and postal training continues there pending a final decision on the ultimate development of the P and T training facilities at Lae. A new Principal, Paul Varma, was appointed in mid-1981.

On 1 July 1980, P and T celebrated its Silver Anniversary of service to the nation of Papua New Guinea. By that time, several of the remaining key expatriate officers mentioned in this account had departed. Doug MacGowan went, finally, this time, and his place was taken in June 1979, by R.J. Magin. Bob Magin had an extensive background of experience with the Corrective Institutions service, the Treasury Department and in private enterprise, and brought to the position of First Assistant Secretary, Finance and Administration, professional ability and sympathy with the overall aims of P and T. Bill Peckover handed over the position of First Assistant Secretary, Telecommunications, to R.D. Johnston, an engineer with 27 years tele-communications experience, in September 1979. Ron Johnston had previously worked in Indonesia and in Southern Queensland. With many years of experience in external plant and planning engineering, he, too, was a valuable acquisition for the Department.

With total P and T assets valued at around K100 million in mid-1981, mostly in telecommunications, continued sound management of telecommunications is certainly essential for the economic and technical welfare of the Department of Public Utilities.

Silver Anniversary celebrations were held throughout PNG. Officers who had served with P and T for the full twenty-five years of its existence were awarded silver medals. Those with fifteen years or more service received certificates. Among those honoured were Israel Edoni, Dale Kamara, Patrick Tomausi, Bill Carter, Bill Peckover, Gwaibo Mairi, Michael Dawadawareta, George Tokiene, Lawson Morove, Bert Hendry, Jim Whittaker, George Panao, Cosmos Hannett, and many others.

On 9 October 1980, soon after the Silver Jubilee celebrations, Israel Edoni, who had done so much to guide the Department during the difficult years following Independence, was appointed to the high office of Chairman of the Public Service Commission. Dale Kamara became the head of the Department of Public Utilities.

In November 1980, the Minister for Finance, John Kaputin, presented his 1981 budget speech to the national Parliament. Tucked away in the body of this long speech was a paragraph of great interest to P and T-watchers:

> With Posts and Telegraphs already conducting large scale commercial transactions, it is well past the time that they be made into a commercial entity rather than simply remain a government department. The National Executive Council has instructed that the most appropriate form of commercial structure be sought.

It looked as though Public Service financial and manpower controls, appropriate for non-revenue-earning government departments but stifling to a commercial enterprise, were at last — so many years after Bill Carter first began to fight for this objective — to be removed.

On 9 September 1981, the Prime Minister, Sir Julius Chan, announced that approval had finally been given to the changing of the status of Postal and Tele-communication Services to that of a legal commercial entity. In presenting the P and T submission to Cabinet, the Minister for Public Utilities, Angmai Bilas (who had replaced Wiwa Korowi in this post in 1981), noted that Postal and Telecommuni-cations Services 'was one of the Government's biggest enterprises. Consequently, it is appropriate that these services be treated like other commercial businesses and be given the flexibility to make normal commercial decisions'.

Given the galloping pace of technological change in the modern world, it would be a bold man who made confident predictions for the future of postal and telecommuni-cations services in Papua New Guinea. But some things may be asserted. Without doubt, telecommunications to the most remote rural districts will gradually be provided throughout the country. There will be increasing reliance on computer-controlled technology. Already the Ela Beach Telephone Exchange has been success-fully upgraded from pure electro-mechanical switching to electronic-controlled switching. In 1981, the American Honeywell Company won a contract to supply the computer hardware and software to support a state-of-the-art telephone call charge recording system. These two moves are the first stage in the planned updating of the PNG telephone exchanges. The second stage will be the supply of an integrated automatic telephone order, records and customer billing system. Satellite communi-cations will figure, too, in PNG's telecommunications future.

Opinion has always been sharply divided in PNG on the subject of television. As early as August 1965, a Commission of Inquiry into Television was appointed by the then Administrator, Sir Donald Cleland. The Commission was chaired by Professor Derek Broadbent, Co-Ordinator of Postgraduate and Extension Studies at the Univer-sity of New South Wales. The other member was Douglas Brooke, Senior Engineer in charge of Radio Maintenance Services for the PMG's Department. Their report, submitted in January 1966, concluded that the enormous expense of television in a country with the formidable geography of PNG could only be justified for educational purposes. They recommended the establishment of a pilot television project to cover the Highlands districts at an establishment cost of $2.4 million, with annual recurring expenditure of half a million. The recommendation was not accepted, and television was not introduced.

Most senior telecommunications officers in P and T today agree that it is only a matter of time before satellite technology makes the introduction of television inevitable. Shortly before leaving the Ministry, Wiwa Korowi stated in *Inside Line* that television would surely come. But he went on to say that the first obligation of the national government was to ensure that the people's basic needs for food, water, shelter, clothing, education and health were met:

> We would be failing drastically in meeting the people's mandate if we allowed the introduction of television whilst a very large percentage of our people do not even have access to one or more of these basic needs. I believe it is morally wrong, not only to consider television now but to even think television today.

Whatever the future holds for Papua New Guinea, it is safe to say that postal and tele-communication services will continue to serve the nation by uniting the people through communications, as they have done in the past.

APPENDIX A:

POST OFFICES IN PAPUA NEW GUINEA, JANUARY 1981

OFFICIAL POST OFFICES

1 Alotau	18 Kundiawa
2 Arawa	19 Lae
3 Boroko	20 Lorengau
4 Buin	21 Madang
5 Buka	22 Maprik
6 Bulolo	23 Mendi
7 Daru	24 Mount Hagen
8 Goroka	25 Panguna
9 Hohola	26 Popondetta
10 Jomba	27 Port Moresby
11 Kainantu	28 Rabaul
12 Kavieng	29 Samarai
13 Kerema	30 University
14 Kieta	31 Vanimo
15 Kimbe	32 Wabag
16 Kokopo	33 Wau
17 Konedobu	34 Wewak

AGENCY POST OFFICES

1 Abau	27 Gumine	53 Magarida
2 Afore	28 Hoskins	54 Malalaua
3 Aitape	29 Hula	55 Minj
4 Alexishafen	30 Ialibu	56 Moem Barracks
5 Ambunti	31 Igam Barracks	57 Mumeng
6 Angoram	32 Ihu	58 Namatanai
7 Asaro	33 Kabwum	59 Nuku
8 Baimuru	34 Kagua	60 Pangia
9 Baiyer River	35 Kaiapit	61 Pomio
10 Balimo	36 Kairuku	62 Rabaraba
11 Banz	37 Kandrian	63 Rouna
12 Bereina	38 Karkar	64 Saidor
13 Bogia	39 Kerevat	65 Salamo
14 Bolubolu	40 Kerowagi	66 Talasea
15 Bundi	41 Kikori	67 Tapini
16 Bwagaoia	42 Kiunga	68 Tari
17 Cape Rodney	43 Kokoda	69 Taurama Barracks
18 Chuave	44 Koroba	70 Tinputz
19 Dogura	45 Kukipi	71 Toboi
20 Erave	46 Kupiano	72 Tufi
21 Esa'ala	47 Kwikila	73 Ukarumpa
22 Ewasse	48 Laiagam	74 Unitech
23 Finschhafen	49 Lese	75 Wakunai
24 Garaina	50 Lombrum	76 Wapenamanda
25 Gembogl	51 Losuia	77 Wards Strip
26 Goldie River	52 Lumi	78 Woitape

T A B L E S

TABLE A
P&T FIXED ASSETS
(Kina)

	30 June 1969	30 June 1973	30 June 1977	31 December 1980
Administration	65,832	316,008	717,639	1,368,000
Telecommunications	6,969,059	30,403,343	57,555,942	86,300,000
Postal	504,529	1,500,737	1,766,244	2,162,000
Training	168,774	279,729	722,688	5,064,000
Work-In-Progress	166,052	1,095,297	3,848,558	3,784,000
TOTAL	**7,874,246**	**33,595,114**	**64,611,071**	**98,678,000**
Provn. for Depreciation	-	3,391,806	10,625,054	33,566,000
Net Value	**7,874,246**	**30,203,308**	**53,986,017**	**65,112,000**

Note: During negotiations for the 1968 Telecommunications Loan from the World Bank (Loan No.546) it was agreed that to put P&T Accounts on a true 'commercial' basis the Departments Fixed Assets would be re-valued as at 30th June, 1969 by independent valuers under the direction of the Valuer General and taking into account the estimated remaining operating life of each type of asset. The values shown in the above Table for 30 June 1969 are those of that independent valuation. Values at 30 June or (31 Dec.) in subsequent years are new assets added at cost, plus the 30th June 1969 valuation of the earlier assets still remaining in service.

TABLE B
P & T EARNINGS
(Kina)

	1960/61	1964/65	1968/69	1972/73	1976/77	1980
TELECOMMUNICATIONS						
Telephone Calls	257,592	402,114	993,204	6,281,055	16,126,365	26,870,800
Telephone Rental	127,204	239,572	764,743	1,537,305	1,567,567	2,435,000
Telex Calls	-	-	10,494	282,959	1,851,384	4,206,600
Telex Connection Fees	-	-	-	-	3,745	-
Telex & Teleprinter Rentals	-	11,170	55,857	128,677	321,366	654,700
Telegrams	168,008	253,828	586,484	945,385	1,139,287	979,300
Outstation Rentals	-	40,324	121,342	194,051	208,038	73,000
Coastal Radio	-	-	-	-	80,841	58,000
Leased Lines & Equipment	-	-	-	-	310,273	543,700
Directory Advertising	n.a	n.a	11,228	n.a	n.a	978,400
Other	21,990	64,968	127,645	427,696	664,819	146,700
Total Telecommunications Earnings	574,794	1,011,976	2,671,097	9,797,128	22,273,685	36,946,200
POSTAL						
Postages	386,846	712,914	1,231,091	2,239,325	2,440,995	2,175,673
Postal Order & Money Order Commissions	5,436	7,062	12,179	26,506	5,779	4,389
Other Post Office Charges	20,068	20,560	117,644	109,958	82,039	91,608
Terminal Credits Philatelic	-	-	-	-	-	367,830
Philatelic	43,118	312,490	617,395	432,854	815,379	744,600
Total Postal Earnings	455,468	1,053,026	1,978,309	2,808,643	3,344,192	3,384,100
NON-OPERATING EARNINGS	-	26,828	221,082	359,125	1,334,568	1,182,000
TOTAL P&T EARNINGS	1,030,262	2,091,830	4,870,488	12,964,896	26,952,445	41,512,300

274

TABLE C
P & T NON - CAPITAL EXPENDITURES
(Kina)

	1960/61	1964/65	1968/69	1972/73	1976/77	1980
TELECOMMUNICATIONS						
Operating Maintenance and General	1,201,942	1,602,948	2,152,634	6,132,706	13,966,314	25,362,000
Depreciation			287,162	1,089,593	2,547,340	6,952,000
Superannuation			99,863	58,117	114,459	n.a.
Interest (*)	145,816	242,118	–			
Total	1,347,758	1,845,066	2,539,659	7,280,416	16,628,113	32,314,000
POSTAL						
Operating, Maintenance and General	591,416	964,684	1,727,379	2,398,398	2,979,215	2,858,000
Depreciation			16,690	44,134	75,312	101,000
Superannuation			61,848	47,150	60,420	n.a.
Interest (*)	3,740	7,752	–			
Total	595,156	972,436	1,805,917	2,489,682	3,114,947	2,959,000
GENERAL						
Non – operating		53,902		299,547	785,754	13,000
Interest (*)		620				
Total		54,522		299,547	785,754	13,000
Total of P&T Expenses	1,942,914	2,872,024	4,345,576	10,069,645	20,528,814	35,286,000

Note: * P&T's early "commercial" accounts (up to 1966/67) included notional interest charges.

TABLE D
POSTAL SERVICES - MAIL HANDLED
(OOO's)

	1964/65	1966/67	1968/69	1970/71	1972/73	1974/75	1976/77	1978	1980
POSTED:									
LETTERS	8,194	12,531	15,056	18,523	18,037	14,790	13,397	14,133	14,486
PACKETS	1,333	2,168	2,927	2,830	3,081	2,942	2,740	2,450	2,266
PARCELS	128	140	169	293	246	139	117	98	127
REGISTERED ARTICLES	125	174	223	313	418	369	384	350	358
REGISTERED & INSURED PARCELS,	6	10	15	21	25	18	9	11	15
C.O.D.	-	-	1	1	1	-	-	-	-
TOTAL	**9,786**	**15,023**	**18,391**	**21,981**	**21,778**	**18,258**	**16,647**	**17,042**	**17,252**
DELIVERED:									
LETTERS	7,912	12,057	13,663	16,874	18,250	16,063	14,220	12,960	13,470
PACKETS	2,577	3,448	4,229	5,948	5,215	4,228	3,450	3,039	2,879
PARCELS	169	283	274	400	364	221	173	177	182
REGISTERED ARTICLES	131	191	251	347	397	368	378	353	367
REGISTERED & INSURED PARCELS	12	18	32	48	41	25	16	16	23
C.O.D.	8	15	11	1	-	-	-	-	-
DUTIABLE ARTICLES	19	33	39	48	36	27	17	20	22
TOTAL	**10,828**	**16,045**	**18,499**	**23,666**	**24,303**	**20,937**	**18,254**	**16,565**	**16,943**

TABLE E
TELEPHONE SERVICE – MANUAL EXCHANGES

Exchange	31 Dec. 1950		31 Dec. 1955		31 Dec. 1960		31 Dec. 1965		31 Dec. 1970		30 June 1975		31 Dec. 1980	
	Lines	Phones	Lines	Phones	Lines	Phones	Lines	Phones	Lines	Phones	Lines	Phones	Lines	Phones
Alotau	-	-	-	-	-	-	-	-	93	127	-	-	-	Auto from 30 Jun 1971
Boram	-	n.a	-	-	-	-	n.a	n.a	-	-	-	-	-	Auto from 14 May 1967
Boroko	52	-	339	n.a	-	-	-	-	-	-	-	-	-	Auto from 11 Mar 1956
Buka/Sohano	-	-	-	-	-	-	30	32	49	52	63	70	-	Auto from 15 Aug 1979
Bulolo	-	-	-	-	3	4	20	36	-	-	-	-	-	Auto from 21 Mar 1968
Daru	-	-	-	-	-	-	45	45	86	93	119	140	-	Auto from 11 Nov 1977
Finschhafen	-	-	7	n.a	6	28	13	33	18	34	-	-	-	Auto from 7 Feb 1972
Goroka	-	-	70	n.a	111	161	217	348	445	902	-	-	-	Auto from 18 Mar 1972
Kainantu	-	-	-	-	-	-	-	-	58	75	-	-	-	Auto from 18 Mar 1972
Kavieng	43	n.a	64	n.a	78	88	102	123	-	-	-	-	-	Auto from 12 Oct 1969
Kerema	-	-	-	-	-	-	-	-	64	75	-	-	-	Auto from 8 Jun 1972
Keita	-	-	-	-	-	-	-	-	134	532	-	-	-	Auto from 15 Jan 1972
Kimbe	-	-	-	-	-	-	-	-	-	-	Manual from 1 Apr 1971		-	Auto from 3 Jul 1974
Kokopo	133	n.a	35	n.a	-	-	-	-	-	-	-	-	-	Auto from 20 Dec 1960
Konedobu	-	-	257	n.a	-	-	-	-	-	-	-	-	-	Auto from 11 Mar 1956
Kundiawa	-	-	-	-	-	-	-	-	75	131	-	-	-	Auto from 18 Mar 1972
Lae	194	n.a	320	n.a	-	-	-	-	-	-	-	-	-	Auto from 13 Apr 1957
Lorengau	-	-	-	-	19	20	27	30	38	46	81	90	-	Auto from 6 Oct 1977
Madang	109	n.a	184	n.a	217	337	334	581	-	-	-	-	-	Auto from 30 Jul 1967
Maprik	-	-	-	-	-	-	-	-	-	-	Manual from 17 Mar 1973		-	Auto from 4 Jul 1973
Mendi	-	-	-	-	-	-	-	-	56	85	-	-	-	Auto from 18 Jun 1972
Mt. Hagen	-	-	-	-	46	56	130	224	356	719	-	-	-	Auto from 18 Jun 1972
Namatanai	-	-	-	-	16	18	58	77	20	23	32	38	-	Auto from 18 Jun 1972
Popondetta	-	-	-	-	-	-	-	-	-	-	-	-	45	60
Port Moresby Central	394	-	485	n.a	-	-	-	-	104	122	-	-	-	Auto from 6 May 1972
Rabaul	224	n.a	352	n.a	71	86	77	111	-	-	-	-	-	Auto from 11 Mar 1956
Samarai	-	-	60	n.a	19	36	-	-	-	-	-	-	-	Auto from 11 May 1957
Sogeri	21	n.a	25	n.a	-	-	-	-	-	-	-	-	-	Auto from 16 Oct 1970
Tapini	-	-	12	n.a	16	19	-	-	15	19	17	20	-	Auto from 11 Jun 1962
Toleap	7	n.a	-	-	-	-	-	-	-	-	-	-	9	12 — Rabaul from 1 Apr 1963
Vanimo	-	-	-	-	-	-	23	27	-	-	-	-	-	Auto from 14 Nov 1972
Wau	-	-	112	n.a	132	146	131	149	62	95	-	-	-	Auto from 10 Mar 1968
Wewak	-	-	65	-	100	152	167	377	245	545	-	-	-	Auto from 12 Aug 1972
Total	**1177**	**n.a**	**2387**	**n.a**	**834**	**1151**	**1374**	**2193**	**1918**	**3675**	**312**	**358**	**54**	**72**

TELEPHONE SERVICE – AUTOMATIC EXCHANGES

Exchange	31 Dec. 1956		31 Dec. 1960		31 Dec. 1965		31 Dec. 1970		30 June 1975		31 Dec. 1980	
	Lines	Phones	Lines	Phones	Lines	Phones	Lines	Phones	Lines	Phones	Lines	Phones
Alotau	-	-	-	-	-	-	-	-	141	277	207	362
Angoram	-	-	-	-	-	-	-	-	-	-	54	74
Arawa	-	-	-	-	-	-	-	-	458	570	1,600	2,092
Banz	-	-	-	-	-	-	-	-	52	84	93	107
Bereina	-	-	-	-	-	-	19	21	-	-	30	48
Bomana	16	20	19	31	29	64	63	233	102	139	163	329
Boram	-	-	-	-	-	-	101	134	148	366	-	-
Boroko	331	520	489	680	1,093	2,143	3,186	5,883	6,253	12,907	6,912	14,674
Buin	-	-	-	-	-	-	-	-	-	-	58	60
Buka	-	-	-	-	-	-	-	-	-	-	78	102
Bulolo	-	-	-	-	-	-	36	66	58	100	111	209
Daru	-	-	-	-	-	-	-	-	-	-	148	214
Ela Beach	-	-	-	-	-	-	-	-	-	-	2,587	6,118
Finschhafen	-	-	-	-	-	-	-	-	-	-	60	118
Gerehu	-	-	-	-	-	-	-	-	51	92	702	725
Goroka	-	-	-	-	-	-	-	-	213	266	1,028	2,117
Ialibu (Line Conc.)	-	-	-	-	-	-	-	-	668	1,255	18	18
Kagamuga	-	-	-	-	-	-	36	59	73	122	150	189
Kainantu	-	-	-	-	-	-	-	-	103	273	165	389
Kavieng	-	-	-	-	-	-	158	215	197	296	293	494
Kerema	-	-	-	-	-	-	-	-	71	75	151	197
Kerevat	-	-	-	-	-	-	-	-	21	60	36	84
Kieta	-	-	-	-	-	-	-	-	188	362	334	657
Kimbe	-	-	-	-	-	-	-	-	167	307	368	640
Kokopo	-	-	36	48	42	57	60	80	78	101	113	146
Konedobu	285	548	457	902	581	1,705	671	2,694	-	-	-	-
Kundiawa	-	-	-	-	-	-	-	-	141	273	206	409
Kupiano	-	-	-	-	-	-	-	-	-	-	56	69
Kwikila	-	-	-	-	-	-	-	-	-	-	32	32
Lae	-	-	525	781	922	1,384	1,554	2,818	2,301	4,811	3,325	7,162
Lorengau	-	-	-	-	-	-	-	-	-	-	217	389
Madang	-	-	-	-	-	-	630	1,141	788	1,416	1,088	2,186
Maprik	-	-	-	-	-	-	-	-	47	63	70	129
Mendi	-	-	-	-	-	-	-	-	108	181	277	340
Minj	-	-	-	-	-	-	20	25	31	35	41	51
Mount Hagen	-	-	-	-	-	-	-	-	534	1,044	769	1,487
Nairovi	-	-	-	-	-	-	-	-	24	38	37	60
Panguna	-	-	-	-	-	-	-	-	108	122	334	351
Popondetta	-	-	-	-	-	-	-	-	152	206	314	583
Port Moresby Central	507	789	580	1,060	614	1,421	1,061	2,677	1,257	3,053	1,773	3,636
Rabaul	-	-	614	1,033	954	1,606	1,292	2,475	1,431	2,723	-	-
Samarai	-	-	-	-	-	-	84	131	70	87	57	75
Sogeri	-	-	-	-	-	-	45	81	50	59	41	41
Toleap	-	-	-	-	28	41	64	94	82	168	121	248
Vanimo	-	-	-	-	-	-	-	-	93	124	140	218
Wabag	-	-	-	-	-	-	-	-	-	-	164	274
Wapenamanda	-	-	-	-	-	-	-	-	-	-	46	63
Wau	-	-	-	-	-	-	134	157	130	163	157	203
Wewak	-	-	-	-	-	-	-	-	248	419	652	1,271
Total	1,139	1,877	2,720	4,535	4,263	8,421	9,214	18,984	16,637	32,637	25,376	49,440

TABLE   G
METER PULSES*

Year	National	to Australia		Total
1959/60	5,310,209	Nil		5,310,209
1960/61	5,432,100	Nil		5,432,100
1961/62	5,635,260	Nil		5,635,260
1962/63	6,024,960	Nil		6,024,960
1963/64	6,719,340	Nil		6,719,340
1964/65	7,549,860	Nil		7,549,860
1965/66	8,600,480	Nil		8,600,480
1966/67	9,302,200	Nil		9,302,200
1967/68	10,431,500	Nil		10,431,500
1968/69	10,735,000	Nil		10,735,000
1969/70	14,102,100	Nil		14,102,000
1970/71	16,300,000	Nil		16,300,000
1971/72	18,010,000	490,000	(a)	18,500,000
1972/73	36,835,000	5,985,000	(b)	42,820,000
1973/74	59,281,000	53,425,000		112,706,000
1974/75	82,123,000	78,017,000		160,140,000
1975/76	76,639,000	83,476,000		160,115,000
1976/77	101,283,000	77,084,000	(c)	178,367,000
$\frac{1}{2}$ 1977	69,924,000	47,446,000		117,370,000
1978	129,455,000	87,839,000		217,294,000
1979	164,372,000	93,607,000		257,979,000
1980	170,588,000	100,406,000		270,994,000

*METER PULSES: All dialled telephone calls in Papua New Guinea
are metered for charging purposes.   Local (or Unit Fee) calls
advance a telephone subscriber's meter one unit when the
telephone number dialled answers, this is called one 'meter
pulse'.   Trunk line calls (i.e. long distance calls) advance the
subscribers' meter one pulse every 72,36,24,18,or 12 seconds on
National calls depending upon the time the call is made and the
charging   areas   in   which   the   two   telephone   services   are
located;   on calls to Australia the meter pulse rate is one
every four seconds.

Notes:
(a) International direct dialling to Australia was introduced on
    3rd December, 1972.   Initially it was available to
    Subscribers connected to twelve exchanges in the Goroka,
    Madang, Mount Hagen and Wewak areas.

(b) International direct dialling to Australia was extended to
    Subscribers connected to exchanges in the Port Moresby area
    on 28th May, 1973.   This accounts for most of the
    substantial increase in the 1973/74 year.

(c) International direct dialling from some telephones in
    Australia to Papua New Guinea was introduced on 1st July,
    1976.

TABLE   H
TELEX SERVICES

Year (1)	Number of Services	
	Manual	Automatic

1965/66	18	Nil
1966/67	18	Nil
1967/68	27	Nil
1968/69	41	Nil
1969/70	46	Nil
1970/71	83	Nil
1971/72	123	Nil
1972/73	131	Nil
1973/74 (2)	Nil	168
1974/75	Nil	249
1975/76	Nil	317
1976/77	Nil	430
$^1/_2$ 1977	Nil	501
1978	Nil	544
1979	Nil	735
1980	Nil	948

Notes: 1.   As at 30 June from 1965/66 to 1976/77 and at 31 December for subsequent years.

2.   Automatic telex service commenced on 5 May 1974 when a new processor controlled "ELTEX" Exchange was brought into operations.

TABLE I
TELEGRAMS

Year	Originating in Papua New Guinea			Originating Overseas	Grand Total
	National	International	Total		
1954/55	118,082	see note below	118,082	see note below	118,082
1955/56	104,282	see note below	104,282	see note below	104,282
1956/57	144,454	see note below	144,454	see note below	144,454
1957/58	170,759	see note below	170,059	see note below	170,759
1958/59	211,085	see note below	211,085	see note below	211,085
1959/60	230,372	see note below	230,372	see note below	230,372
1960/61	268,702	see note below	268,702	see note below	268,702
1961/62	256,721	see note below	256,721	see note below	256,721
1962/63	271,905	see note below	271,905	see note below	271,905
1963/64	324,777	see note below	324,777	see note below	324,777
1964/65	370,054	see note below	370,054	see note below	370,054
1965/66	401,251	see note below	401,251	see note below	401,251
1966/67	543,120	see note below	543,120	see note below	543,120
1967/68	620,956	see note below	620,956	see note below	620,956
1968/69	680,014	see note below	680,014	see note below	680,104
1969/70	784,803	see note below	784,803	see note below	784,803
1970/71	856,844	see note below	856,844	see note below	856,844
1971/72	889,000	see note below	889,000	see note below	889,000
1972/73	612,000	see note below	612,000	see note below	612,000
1973/74	311,000	209,000	520,000	not available	n.a.
1974/75	184,000	266,000	450,000	not available	n.a.
1975/76	181,000	139,000	320,000	not available	n.a.
1976/77	148,000	104,000	252,000	111,000	363,000
1977	142,000	88,000	230,000	98,000	328,000
1978	121,000	71,000	192,000	82,000	274,000
1979	96,000	57,000	153,000	68,000	221,000
1980	76,000	52,000	128,000	59,000	187,000

Note: Until 1 December 1973 when responsibility for international telecommunication services were transferred from the Overseas Telecommunications Commission (O.T.C.) to P&T the Commission maintained separate Telegraph Offices at Port Moresby, Lae and Rabaul for the acceptance and delivery of overseas telegrams. Business to and from other centres was handled by P&T and passed to (or from) O.T.C. through the P&T Telegraph Offices at Port Moresby, Lae and Rabaul. Any such traffic is included in the figures shown in this Table. However, the Table does not include the telegrams accepted or delivered by the O.T.C. offices.

BIBLIOGRAPHY

1 OFFICIAL SOURCES
(National Archives and current files, Port Moresby)

Files, reports and papers of the Department of Posts and Telegraphs, 1955-73
Files of the Posts and Telegraphs Branch, Department of the Treasury, 1945-54
Files of the Department of Public Utilities, 1973-80
Posts and Telegraphs files, Territory of Papua
Records of the British New Guinea Administration
Records of the Territory of Papua

Annual Reports

British New Guinea 1886-1906
Papua 1906-71
Territory of New Guinea 1914-71
Papua New Guinea 1971-3
German New Guinea (Neu Guinea Compagnie and Imperial government) 1886-1913, Peter
    Sack and Dymphna Clark, translators, ANU Press, Canberra, 1979
Department of Posts and Telegraphs, Queensland, 1882-93
Black Book of P and T, 1955-73, compiled by W.S. Peckover

Government Gazettes

British New Guinea
Papua
Territory of New Guinea (including British Administration, German New Guinea)
Papua New Guinea
The Rabaul Record, March 1916-June 1918

Hansard

Legislative Council debates, 1951-63
First, Second and Third House of Assembly Debates, 1964-75
Various parliamentary papers and reports

Other documents

District Annual Reports, Department of District Services and Native Affairs,
   1946-7—1956-7, all districts
Patrol Reports, Territory of Papua, Mandated Territory of New Guinea, Territory of Papua
   New Guinea
ANGAU Reports on Activities December 1943-June 1946
Various patrol reports and conference reports
United Nations Reports on the Visiting Missions to the Trust Territory of New Guinea
   1950-71

2 NEWSPAPERS, JOURNALS, HANDBOOKS

Papuan Courier, weekly, all issues
Papuan Times, weekly, various issues
Rabaul Times, weekly, all issues
South Pacific Post, daily, various issues
Papua New Guinea Post-Courier, daily, various issues
Australian Stamp Monthly, various issues
Australian Territories
Contact (OTC)
Inside Line (Department of Public Utilities)
Journal of the Morobe District Historical Society
New Guinea and Australia, the Pacific and Far East Asia
New Guinea Research Bulletins
Pacific Islands Monthly
Philatelic Magazine
Public Service Journal
The Journal of Pacific History
The Journal of the Papua New Guinea Society
The Radiogram (AWA)
Transit (OTC)
Handbook of the Territory of Papua, 1907-38
Pacific Islands Year Book, 1932-78
Papua New Guinea Handbook, 1954-80
The New Guinea Handbook, 1943

3 BOOKS, ARTICLES, UNPUBLISHED PAPERS, SELECTED DEPARTMENTAL REPORTS

Aplin, Douglas (ed.), *Rabaul 1942*, Melbourne, 1980
Attman, Artur; Kuuse, Jan and Olsson, Ulf, *L.M. Ericsson: 100 Years* (3 vols.), undated
Australian Encyclopaedia, *articles on the Overland Telegraph Line and Post and Telecommunications*
Australian Post Office, *A Documented National Telephone Plan for Papua and New Guinea*, Melbourne, 1964
Australian Post Office, *O and M Review of the Department of Posts and Telegraphs, Territory of Papua and New Guinea*, undated
AWA, *AWA and the War*, undated
— *Annual Reports*, 1936, 1937, 1938
Article on AWA wireless stations in the Mandated Territory of New Guinea, AWA Radio Guide, 1928
Australian Wireless Achievements, AWA, undated
— *Wireless Today*
— *Marine Wireless Services*, September 1933
'A War Time Episode', The Radiogram, July 1934
Barry, J.V., *Report of Commission of Inquiry into Circumstances Relating to the Suspension of the Civil Administration of the Territory of Papua in February, 1942*, 1945
Bassett, Marnie, *Letters from New Guinea, 1921*, Hawthorn, Melbourne, 1969
Beckett, Charles C., 'Bulolo, The Land of Gold and Gibbers', The Radiogram
Bishton, E.F., 'Memoirs of Service with AWA in the Mandated Territory of New Guinea 1920-41
Boyce, Ben S., *Dear Dad: Letters From New Guinea*, W.D. Boyce Co., Chicago, 1928
Bradley, F.R., 'History of the Electric Telegraph in Australia', Royal Australian Historical Society Journal, 20 (1934)
Broadcasting Services Committee, *Report*, February 1962
Brown, E.C.A., *Posts and Telegraphs Branch Annual Report 1946-7*, 29 August 1947
— *Report on the Re-Establishment of Postal and Telecommunication Facilities in Papua New Guinea*, Port Moresby, 1948
Cheesman, Evelyn, *Who Stands Alone*, Geoffrey Bles, London, 1965
— *Six-Legged Snakes in New Guinea*, Harrap, London, 1949
Cherry, Colin, *World Communication: Threat or Promise?*, Wiley-Interscience, London, 1971
Chignell, A.K., *An Outpost in Papua*, Smith, Elder & Co., London, 1915
Coates, F.A., 'The Papua New Guinea Telecommunication Network', Telecommunication Journal of Australia, Z, 2, 1978
Croaker, Hamilton, *Lakatoi 1: British New Guinea and De La Rue*, The Philatelic Society of NSW, July 1977
Downs, Ian, *The Australian Trusteeship: Papua New Guinea 1945-75*, Australian Government Publishing Service, Canberra, 1980

Dupeyrat, André, *Mitsinari*, Staples Press, London, 1955

Economics of Telecommunications in PNG, paper, April, 1975

Encyclopaedia Brittanica (1974), *articles on Postal Systems; Guglielmo Marconi; Telegraph; Telephone; Telecommunications Systems*

Evans, David A and Bryan, Elizabeth B., *'Access to Calls: A Perspective on the Economics of Telecommunications in Papua New Guinea'*, The Implementation and Management Group Pty. Ltd., Sydney, December, 1977

—— *'The Evolution of the Papua New Guinea Telecommunication System'*, undated

Feldt, E.A., *The Coastwatchers*, Oxford University Press, Melbourne, 1946

Fisk, E.K. (ed.), *New Guinea on the Threshhold*, University of Pittsburgh Press, 1968

Franklin, Mark, *Franklin's Guide to the Stamps of Papua and New Guinea*, Reed, Sydney, 1970

Garnaut, Ross, *'Public Finance for Equity and Efficiency in an Open, Dual Economy'*, New Guinea Research Unit paper, June 1973

Geeves, Philip, *'Marconi and Australia'*, AWA Technical Review, 4 (1974)

Gore, R.T., *Justice versus Sorcery*, Jacaranda, Brisbane, 1965

Griffin, H.L., *An Official in British New Guinea*, Cecil Palmer, London, undated

Harrison, J.H. and Rutherford, V.A., *The Postal History of Papua and New Guinea 1945-70: Post Offices and Post Marks* (vol. 1), The Papuan Philatelic Society and the Society of Australian Specialists, 1971

Hasluck, Paul, *A Time For Building: Australian Administration in Papua and New Guinea 1951-63*, Melbourne University Press, 1976

Hastings, Peter, *Papua New Guinea: Prospero's Other Island*, Angus and Robertson, Sydney, 1971

Hempenstall, Peter J., *Pacific Islanders under German Rule: A Study in the Meaning of Colonial Resistance*, ANU Press, Canberra, 1978

Hilder, Brett, *Navigator in the South Seas*, Percival Marshall, London, 1961

Hooke, Sir Lionel, *'Historical Notes on the AWA in Papua New Guinea'*, address at World Radio Convention, Sydney, April 1938

Hope, Penelope, *Long Ago is Far Away*, ANU Press, Canberra, 1979

Hudon, Heather E., Goldschmidt, Douglas, Parkes, Edwin B. and Hardy, Andrew, *The Role of Telecommunications in Socio-Economic Development*, Keewatin Communications, May 1979

Hurst, H.L., *Papuan Journey*, Angus & Robertson, Sydney, 1938

Instant World: A Report on Telecommunications in Canada, Ottawa, 1973

International Bank for Reconstruction and Development, *Project Performance Audit Report on PNG First Telecommunication Project (Loan 546-PNG)*, July 1975

International Telecommunication Union, *Report on Seminar on Rural Telecommunications*, New Delhi, September 1978

Jennings, J.A., *The Anglican Church in Papua 1942-5*, McClellan Printing, Gorleston, 1978

Jinks, B., Biskup, P. and Nelson, H., *Readings in New Guinea History*, Angus and Robertson, Sydney, 1973

Joyce, R.B., *Sir William MacGregor*, Oxford University Press, Melbourne, 1971

Keelan, Alice J., *In The Land of Dohori*, Angus & Robertson, Sydney, 1929

Kelly, R.J., *'A Brief Review of the Postal History of Papua and New Guinea 1885-1956'*, August 1956

Kilby, A.W., *'Postal and Telecommunication Services Staff Development and Training'*, Port Moresby, 1978

Lambert, S.M., *A Doctor in Paradise*, Dent, London, 1941

Legge, J.D., *Australian Colonial Policy: A Survey of Native Administration and European Development in Papua*, Angus & Robertson, Sydney, 1956

Lett, Lewis, *Sir Hubert Murray of Papua*, Collins, Sydney, 1949

Lingard, Rex, *PNG Stamps 1971-6*, Robert Brown & Associates, Port Moresby, 1977

Lyng, James, *Island Films*, Cornstalk, Sydney, 1925

MacKay, Ian K., *Broadcasting in Papua New Guinea*, Melbourne University Press, 1976

McCarthy, J.K., *Patrol Into Yesterday*, Cheshire, Melbourne, 1963

Mair, L.P., *Australia in New Guinea*, 2nd edition, Melbourne University Press, 1970

Marshall, A.J., *The Men and Birds of Paradise: Journeys through Equatorial New Guinea*, Heinemann, London, 1938

Matches, Margaret, *Savage Paradise*, Century, New York, 1930

Menzel, R.W., *Survey of Postal Training Needs, Papua New Guinea*, Australian Development Assistance Bureau, undated

Merriman, J.H.H., *'Engineering Innovation in a Service Industry: Post Office Telecommunications'*, inaugural address, Proceedings of Institution of Electrical Engineers, January 1975

Monckton, C.A.W., *Last Days in New Guinea*, Bodley Head, London, 1922

—— *Some Experiences of a New Guinea Resident Magistrate*, Bodley Head, London, 1921

Moses, John A. and Kennedy, Paul M., *Germany in the Pacific and Far East 1870-1914*, University of Queensland Press, 1977

Murray, J.H.P., *Diaries, papers* deposited in the Mitchell Library

Murray, J.K., *'In Retrospect: Papua New Guinea and Territory of Papua and New Guinea 1945-72'*, in *The History of Melanesia*, Second Waigani Seminar, Port Moresby, 1968

Mytinger, Caroline, *New Guinea Headhunt*, Macmillan, New York, 1947

Nicklason, Neal, *'History of Steamships Trading Co. Ltd.'*, in *The History of Melanesia*, 1968

Nelson, Hank, *Black, White and Gold*, ANU Press, Canberra, 1976

O'Brien, B.J. and Brown, E.C.A., *A Report Relating to the Postal and Telecommunication Branch of the Administration of the Territory of Papua New Guinea and the Proposed Transfer of its Functions to the Commonwealth Postmaster General's Department*, PMG's Department, Melbourne, December 1951

Oram, N.D., *Colonial Town to Melanesian City: Port Moresby 1884-1974*, ANU Press, Canberra, 1976

Overell, Lilian, *A Woman's Impression of German New Guinea*, Bodley Head, London, 1923

PA Management Consultants (PNG) Pty. Ltd., *'Marketing of Philatelic Products: Proposal for Consulting Assistance'*, Port Moresby, July 1973

Parsons, Ronald, *'The Ships of Burns Philp & Co.'*, December 1978

Peckover, W.S., *'Evolution of the Papua New Guinea Telecommunications System 1955-64'*, appendix to Evans and Bryan, *Access to Calls*, 1977

—— *'The Marketing of PNG Postage Stamps in Australia and in other Overseas Countries'*, June 1973

Peckover, W.S. and Evans, David A., *'Telecom 2000: A View from Outside'*, Port Moresby, November 1976

PNG Institute of Technology, *Report on Proposed Sub-Professional Course in Communications*, undated

Pompey, Sherman Lee, *The Post Offices of Papua and New Guinea 1885-1967*, The Society of Australian Specialists, 1967

Powell, John H., *The Postal History of the Territory of New Guinea, from 1888 to 1942*, Hawthorn, Melbourne, 1964

Preece, Cardew and Rider, *Report on the Maintenance Aspects of the PNG Telecommunications Network for the Department of Posts and Telegraphs*, Brighton, November 1971

Priest, M.J. and Chapman, S.A., *'Financial Aid for Telecommunication Projects in Developing Countries'*, Telecommunication Journal of Australia, 29, 2 1979

Posts and Telegraphs, Department of, *An Implementation Plan for the Development of the Telecommunications Network*, Port Moresby, 1968

Public Utilities Department, Public Utilities Notes, *'Brief on Bank Group Lending for Telecommunications'*, May 1975

Public Utilities Department, Guidelines Series; International Bank for Reconstruction and Development, various papers

Preece, Cardew and Rider, *Report on the Maintenance Aspects of the PNG Telecommunications Network for the Department of Posts and Telegraphs*, Brighton, November 1971

Rider, Richard L., *'The Rider Report'*, June 1973

Robinson, Neville K., *Villagers at War: Some Papua New Guinean Experiences in World War II*, ANU Press, Canberra, 1979

Romilly, Hugh Hastings, *From My Verandah in New Guinea*, David Nutt, London, 1889

Rosenblum, A.A., *Stamps of Papua*, Horticultural Press, undated

—— *'The Stamps of Papua'*, Australian Stamp Monthly, Feb.-Dec. 1966

Rowley, C.D., *The Australians in German New Guinea 1914-21*, Melbourne University Press, 1958

Russell, W.H., *The Atlantic Telegraph*, Daws and Charles Reprints, 1972

Rutherford, V.A., *The Relief Postmarks of Papua and New Guinea*, The Society of Australian Specialists, 1969

Ryan, John, *The Hot Land: Focus on New Guinea*, Macmillan, Melbourne, 1970

Searle, C.E., *'Mountains, Mist and Mud'*, The Radiogram, December 1936

Shiers, George (ed.), *The Development of Wireless to 1920*, Arno Press, New York, 1977

—— *The Electric Telegraph: An Historical Anthology*, Arno Press, New York, 1977

—— *The Telephone: An Historical Anthology*, Arno Press, New York, 1977

Sister Minnie's [Billing] Life and Work in Papua, Epworth Printing and Publishing House, Sydney, 1930

Souter, Gavin, *New Guinea: The Last Unknown*, Angus and Robertson, Sydney, 1963

Southwood, W.A., *'Who's Got the Phone On?: Telecommunications' Place in a Changing Papua New Guinea'*, Port Moresby, April 1977

Stuart, Ian, *Port Moresby: Yesterday and Today*, Pacific Publications, Sydney, 1970

Sturgeon, Charles H., *'Aitape Radio Station: A Pre-War Memory'*, The Radiogram, October 1931

Suarez, A.M. and McGuin, Carien, *'Solar-Powered Microwave for Papua New Guinea'*, Telephony, 196, 19, 1979

Telecom Australia, *Telecom 2000: An Exploration of the Long-Term Development of Telecommunications in Australia*, Melbourne, 1975

Telettra Review No. 29: *'3000 km Backbone Radio Link Based On IR-20 Repeaters in Papua New Guinea'*

The Asian and Oceanic Postal Training School, *Information Booklet*

The First 25 Years: P&T's Silver Jubilee of Service to the Nation Papua New Guinea 1980, Port Moresby, 1980

The History of Posts and Telegraphs in Papua New Guinea, Port Moresby, 1975. Booklet issued to mark Independence Day, 16 September, 1975

Tomausi, P., *'International Postal Affairs Division,' Papua New Guinea Postal Services: Proposal'*, Postal Services, Port Moresby, 1979

Townsend, G.W.L., *District Officer*, Pacific Publications, Sydney, 1968

Vandercook, John W., *Dark Islands*, Heinemann, London, 1938

'VJZ: A Page of Its History' *Radio*, January 1925

West, Francis (ed.), *J.H.P. Murray: Selected Letters*, Oxford University Press, Melbourne, 1970

—— *Hubert Murray: The Australian Pro-Consul*, Oxford University Press, Melbourne, 1968

White, V., *Report on Technical Training in Papua and New Guinea*, PMG's Department, Melbourne, 1965

Williams, W.H., *'A Survey of the Development of Communications in Papua New Guinea'*, Port Moresby, 1962

Wilson, Richard S., *A Bibliography of the Philatelic Literature of Papua and New Guinea*, New York, (limited edition) November 1968

'W.T. Bicycle Sets: Success in Pacific Islands', The Radiogram, December 1934

Woolford, Don, *Papua New Guinea: Initiation and Independence*, University of Queensland Press, 1976

World Bank, *Papua New Guinea Telecommunications*, Sector Memorandum, November 1976

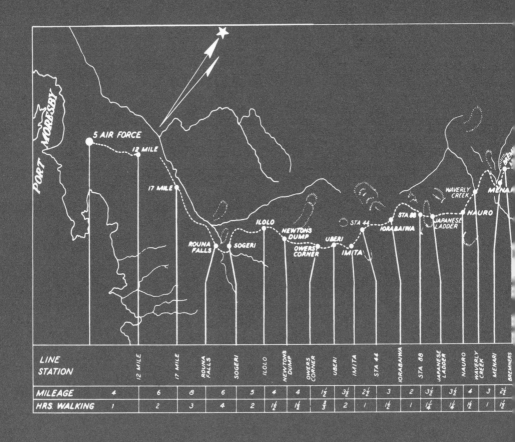

LINE STATION		12 MILE	17 MILE	ROUNA FALLS	SOGERI	ILOLO	NEWTONS DUMP	OWERS CORNER	UBERI	IMITA	STA 44	IORABAIWA	STA 88	JAPANESE LADDER	NAURO	WAVERLY CREEK	MENARI	BREMNERS
MILEAGE	4	6	8	6	5	4	4	1½	3½	2½	3	2	3½	3¼	4	3	2¼
HRS. WALKING	1	2	3	4	2	1½	1½	⅔	2	1	1½	1	1¼	1¼	1½	1	1⅛